DISCARDED

TYPES OF MEN

THE PSYCHOLOGY AND ETHICS OF PERSONALITY

BY

EDUARD SPRANGER

PROFESSOR OF PHILOSOPHY AND PEDAGOGICS
IN THE UNIVERSITY OF BERLIN

AUTHORIZED TRANSLATION OF THE FIFTH GERMAN EDITION

BY

PAUL J. W. PIGORS Ph.D.

MAX NIEMEYER VERLAG
HALLE (SAALE)
1928

HAFNER PUBLISHING COMPANY
NEW YORK

All rights reserved
Copyright by Max Niemeyer Verlag, Halle (Saale), 1928
Printed in Germany

Printed by Karras, Kröber & Nietschmann, Halle (Saale)

DEDICATED TO

ALOIS AND SOFIE RIEHL

WITH LOVE EVERLASTING

TABLE OF CONTENTS

	Page
Author's Preface	VII

Part I: *Philosophical Basis.*

Chapter 1. Two Kinds of Psychology	3
„ 2. Methods of Geisteswissenschaft: Analytical and Synthetical	21
„ 3. Individual Mental Acts	33
„ 4. Mental Acts of Solidarity	55
„ 5. The Elementary Mental Laws	64
„ 6. Subjective Spheres of Interests and Objective Levels	84
„ 7. Summary and Outline	104

Part II: *The Ideally Basic Types of Individuality.*

Chapter 1. The Theoretic Attitude	109
„ 2. The Economic Attitude	130
„ 3. The Aesthetic Attitude	147
„ 4. The Social Attitude	172
„ 5. The Political Attitude	188
„ 6. The Religious Attitude	210

Part III: *Consequences for Ethics.*

Chapter 1. The Ethical Problem	249
„ 2. The One-sided Systems of Ethics	257
„ 3. Collective and Individual Morality	267
„ 4. The Hierarchy of Values	278
„ 5. The Personal Ideal	304

Part IV: *The Understanding of Mental Structures.*

Chapter 1. Complex Types	319
„ 2. Historically determined Types	348
„ 3. On Understanding	366
„ 4. The Rhythm of Life	391

AUTHOR'S PREFACE

Perhaps the study of man is more worthy of consideration than any other science. And it is curious that though for centuries we have classified the numerous species of plants and animals in a well-ordered system, and have scientific names for the rarest mosses and each minute insect, we still regard man, whose classification should be more important to us, as if he were all of one species: *homo*. At any rate, we classify the species: man, only according to race, nationality and clan; that is by relations of descent. But this is only genealogy not morphology. Noah's Ark contains an infinite variety of human differences and if there were a Linnaeus of anthropology he would need many more than twenty-four classes to cover the most important forms of the human body, even disregarding the human soul.

This book attempts to carry out a new method of differentiating human types, especially types of the soul. There have been many attempts to solve this problem, and the old theory of Temperaments has endured for thousands of years. The '*Characters*' of Theophrastus ranks with the most important literature of the world. Classification of man according to his dominant emotions also dates back to ancient times. The more a biological and genetic study of the organic world is carried over into the world of man the more frequent are the attempts to utilize the instincts or original tendencies of man as a basis for classifying the individual. And the more the differences of intelligence and general endowment are emphasized, the finer are the methods developed for determining them on a qualitative and quantitative basis. In these psychological efforts America is undoubtedly the leader.

Everyone must admit that man can be entirely understood only by interpreting him as a multiform phenomenon among the psychic organisms of the earth, and as a biologically determined being having great possibilities of variation. As such a being man is dependent on the conditions of his natural environment like any other animal, regardless of whether one considers his psychic differentiations only as the result of environmental differences or as the outcome of different mental directives. But man lives not only in a natural but also in a cultural environment. And at the level which he has achieved today the formation and preservation of his life depend as much on cultural forces as on the powers and energies of nature which his mind has learned largely to control. The differentiations which he represents today are therefore not only biological but also mental (cultural) categories. In this book I consider the problem primarily from the latter viewpoint. I do so not because I think that the biological foundations of life are unimportant but because scientists have minutely studied the biological region and have hitherto neglected these superbiological levels in which meaning-contents become significant beyond mere adaptation to conditions which barely preserve life.

American, English, and to a large extent French scientists also, usually consider these psychic attitudes of behavior as sociological problems. In Germany another line of thought has been developed, called the 'Philosophy of Culture' (*Kulturphilosophie*). This school starts with the conception that there are determinants of higher developmental levels other than the mere fact of social relations. These factors are unique objective contents of experiencing and creating that can, of course, appear only in social forms but nevertheless obey laws which cannot be deduced from the mere fact that people live and act in common.

Thus there is a marked difference between the sociology of Western nations and German '*Geistesphilosophie* or *Kulturphilosophie*'. For this reason many points of view set forth here may seem foreign to the American reader. I ask therefore that he may give these chapters a friendly consideration and at least attempt to follow the general trend of the argument before condemning it as misleading. For, the facts considered by both American and German psychologists are to a large extent the same. And these facts which we try to understand scientifically will appear most clearly if the reader begins with the summary of the first part (pp. 104—106) and then reads Part II. The first part might give the impression that this is another instance of what Claparède (at the recent International Congress of Psychology in Groningen,

1926) complained of as the German passion for writing systematic treatises. But we are not dealing here with abstract questions. On the contrary, as indicated by the German title '*Lebensformen*', these are genuine life-forms. It is my belief that we cannot solve these questions by such simple psychological concepts as 'Idea', 'Feeling', 'Striving', 'Instinct', 'Adaptation' and 'Inheritance and Variation', but that we need more complex tools of analysis. Modern German psychologists usually speak of the investigation of total forms (*Ganzheitsforschung*). We no longer believe that the higher psychic achievements can be understood through the summation or elaboration of simple psychological elements. We regard these elements as dependent phenomena in a *meaningful life-totality* the whole of which must be known if one wants to understand the part played in the psychic whole by each individual psychic function. In a word, which also becomes the fundamental concept of this new psychology: the *structure, life-context,* or *meaningful total context* is of primary importance for psychology, and the elementary functions receive their significance only from this total. Even a physical organism is more than a mere summation or aggregation of cells each one of which could exist alone. It is a life-unity in which the function of each cell or group of cells is determined by its relation or contribution to the whole. Besides that, the total organism is also placed in an environment for whose conditions it is internally organized and from which, by means of its sense organs and vegetative functions, it chooses just those factors that are of 'vital importance' for it, that is, of biological significance.

The same relation is more apparent on a mental level. No one can deny that ideas, feelings, instincts and volitional acts belong just as much to *scientific* investigation as to *artistic* creation, *economic* activity or *religious* contemplation. But for the very reason that these elements appear in *all* these connections, the importance lies not so much in the elements themselves as in their peculiar kind of interaction. And this interaction to form a total achievement of unique significance I call a *structure*.

The concept structure or law of construction (*Aufbaugesetz*) is familiar to biologists, and this concept of totality appears in the theory of organisms. But it is always difficult for science to grasp the whole both in its totality and individuality. For this reason we follow a procedure that is divided into four steps, each step of which is as artificial as all mental analysis of an organism must be. (1) First we *isolate* a psychic value-tendency from the totality of the soul. (2) Then we think of this value-tendency in its pure form; that is, we *idealize* it. In this way we construct ideal types which we use as regular though artificial outlines. This abstraction is counteracted by our third step; (3) the relation of the one-sided type to the whole (the method of *totalization*). (4) The fourth step also counterbalances the initial artificiality of our method by the process of *individualization* which emphasizes special historical, geographical and wholly personal circumstances. Thus we develop a scientific method similar to Galileo's. First we think of the abstract pure case and then we add more and more concrete conditions.

In this way the psychology of higher psychic phenomena can be made into a science suitable for the foundation of the various social sciences *insofar* as the overindividual cultural forms can be understood at all through their reactions on individual mental life. Even though this whole method may seem too abstract, nevertheless abstraction is an essential preliminary for science. Even analytical geometry does not begin at once with curves of the second order but rather with regular figures such as the straight line, the circle or the sphere, and then proceeds to the most complex forms, provided that such forms still illustrate a law by means of which they were evolved.

Our aim is to cognize psychologically the context of our real contemporaneous life as it goes on in the frame of a civilized society. In Germany we are convinced that this life not only can be understood psychologically but that it also represents an overindividual context of unique laws of meaning. Here, however, we only venture to deal with what can be experienced in individual mental life. It would be wholly erroneous to believe that any one of these types really exists as described by our wholly one-sided method. They exist as little as we may expect to find a perfect cube, or a rigid body or a body falling in a vacuum. The construction of these ideal basic types of human nature serves only to clarify and bring order to the confusion of complex real forms. There must be some way for our thought to approach these realities more and more closely.

Therefore it is most important to question whether our types suffice to understand the most significant forms of personality.

Perhaps the reader misses a basic type that has been more definitely expressed in America. The translator asked why I did not consider the '*Pioneer*' (the adventurer, explorer and inventor) as an independent type. I grant that it represents a unique and very important phenomenon. But I consider it as an expression of the political type. For the centre of this attitude lies in the feeling of power, in the conquest of human and material obstacles. Usually the pioneer busies himself with the urgent problems of colonisation, the struggle for existence and the conquest of the elements. He needs, therefore, great vitality; that is, well trained energies, decisive volitional powers and self-control. To this extent his roots, like those of *all* mental impulses, are biological. When the feeling of power is enjoyed only in the preliminary exercise (as it were, formally, with no immediately utilitarian aim) it has a leaning to the aesthetic side. Thus man in the consciousness of his own achievements is filled with a joyous pride, even if he is only participating in the peaceful competition of sport. And if he breaks a record he glows with the feeling of superiority in which he experiences the apotheosis of his vital energies. Sport becomes a substitute for military training for the modern man whose combative instincts tend to atrophy in peaceful society; all the more insofar as it includes real dangers and serious obstacles. Indeed sport has now become almost a separate region of culture which might have its own typical attitude. Nevertheless I have not developed it as such because this sphere lies on the borderline where the region of power and the aesthetic sphere of play partly touch and partly overlap. Sport is a divergence from the political instinct into an imaginatively determined form of play as demanded by a peaceful, industrialized and democratic community.

Some people have objected that this book abandons the concrete ground of experience and reduces psychology to mere speculation. I cannot admit this objection and beg indulgence finally to indicate the reasons for my stand. Psychological experience is not gained only in the laboratory or the clinic or merely from contemporary human beings but also from the vast number of men of the past of whom we know only through literary documents. We need this broadening of our experience all the more since otherwise we should learn only psychological phenomena which correspond to our cultural determinants. What is the value of the most comprehensive mass-statistics compared to the enormous material of different psychic structures which history transmits to us? My psychology aims at an understanding of these historical structures and their transformation even though I can give little space to this aspect. The supplement to this type psychology would be a developmental psychology emphasizing on one hand structural transformations in the different ages of individuals and on the other, structural changes in the human soul itself during its thousand-year-old history. So far I have only attacked the first part of this problem in my '*Psychologie des Jugendalters*' 10th ed. Leipzig 1928. It is also necessary to study the mental structure of primitive people or earlier cultural epochs, and a few attempts have been made in this direction. To Stanley Hall's well-known book '*Adolescence*' I owe many suggestions. And Spengler and the explorer Frobenius in Germany have shown an especially fine psychological sense in this direction.

To summarize: this book only takes a first step, but in a direction which I am convinced must be pursued further if psychology is to go beyond elementary phenomena to the understanding of higher mental life. The more differentiated modern men and cultures become, the greater will be our need of these insights for our practical life. We must bridge the gap between soul and soul, and if possible in the same way between group and group. This is, as it were, the conscious re-establishment of the divine total context of life from which our modern culture has drifted away but without which a higher culture in the long run cannot last. —

I want to thank the translator for the great pains he has taken in preparing this book for the English-reading public. I am also much indebted to Dr. Japha in Halle (Saale) for the reading of the English text and careful revision of the proof. She has thus aided greatly in the success of a difficult undertaking. And finally I wish to thank my friend and pupil Dr. Wenke in Berlin for his help.

Berlin, February 25. 1928.

Eduard Spranger.

PART I
PHILOSOPHICAL BASIS

1
TWO KINDS OF PSYCHOLOGY

One might begin a study of character and its possible types with the question: Is there such a thing as character from a scientific point of view? Empiricists maintain that we must limit character study strictly to actual psychological processes and their variations. They also believe that there is no ground for assuming a carrier of these experiences and reactions, either constant or developing according to definite laws. For, even though empiricists admit that there is an individual connected with psychological states, many of them regard this individual as a flux or an event (*Aktus*) and so declare that it is unwarranted to conceive it as a substance.

If by substance we necessarily mean 'material substance' this attitude is only too well justified. Kant too limited the concept of substance to the permanent substratum which we think of apriori as underlying all temporally changing natural phenomena. This, however, is only the transcendental conception of substance, that is, the concept of permanence in a theory of cognition. But the scientist means by substance not only what is absolutely permanent and unchanging but also a unifying law or a sum total of laws by means of which we think of a subject relatively permanent in time. Thus the scientist divides substance into a complex of 'legal' relations which are valid for a mental subject localised in space and time.

I cannot conceive how the *Geisteswissenschaften* could get along without such a concept of substance; namely the assumption that the behavior of a subject which is identical in time may be scientifically investigated. Only by means of this conception is the mental subject determined as having 'being' and the manifoldness of its behavior reduced to essential correlations (*Wesensverknuepfungen*).

The problem however, is further complicated by the fact that we cannot regard the individual as stable, but must think of it as undergoing some sort of development in which its 'being' is preserved according to certain laws in spite of organic deformation, i. e. certain changes of condition which necessarily follow one from another. But we do not intend to elaborate here a developmental psychology. We shall, rather, take a cross-section of the subject at the stage of maturity and view it as the carrier of constant attitudes of mental behavior. That we are here dealing with definite laws is shown by the fact that we assume in the individual, over and above temporal experience and 'acts', enduring dispositions to experiences and acts. These dispositions are then, for science, not mysterious qualities but precipitations of cognized laws and the mental grasp of identity in temporal changes. A subject can only become an object of knowledge if we presuppose lawful behavior. If the individual were a chaos devoid of laws, that is, if it could not be reduced to general ideal entities (and interdependent relations of ideal entities), we should have to abandon a scientific characterology. But we should follow Kant when he maintains that the very attempt to formulate a science involves certain assumptions which afterward become the foundation of the science itself. —

All this discussion however, has as yet given us no specific information about the kind of law peculiar to the mental realm. But let us not be detained by questions pertaining solely to a theory of cognition. We want rather to present characterology itself and our preliminary question is meant to bring out the principle of differentiating the basic types in mental attitudes. We want to reduce each to a special law by means of which its internal construction may be understood. Let us now, therefore, consider in more detail whether such an investigation would come within the field of psychology.

Some psychologists confine their study to the subject, that is, to processes and conditions belonging to an individual which another consciousness can only reconstruct indirectly through the aid of its own subjective processes. For such a science even to approach the subjectivity of another being would be a riddle.

As a matter of fact, subjectivity is always related to objective creations. By 'objective' I mean (a) only what is independent of the single individual, that which confronts and influences it and may mean the sectional area of sensory phenomena with which socalled Nature presents each individual; (b) Secondly we have too the mental objects which are naturally attached to matter and derive therefrom their enduring form (i. e. tools, language, writing, works of art, rites etc.) These latter however, represent at the same time psychologically determined effectual relations by which the individual is constantly surrounded. A third and very important distinction remains to be made. We must differentiate (c) the over-individual meaning contained in the material points of contact of these objects from the psychic reciprocal interrelation by which they are built up socio-historically. When I consider a book (primarily a part of matter) as a saleable object I give it an economic significance; again looking upon it as an intellectual achievement I classify it theoretically; or once more from the point of view of its appearance, I may view it aesthetically. These three distinctions clearly give us a systematic division of the objective mind which is based in each case on an ideal relation to a unique system of values. This division is reflected in consciousness by the giving and experiencing of meaning which always has a corresponding objective system of values. Each of these fundamental attitudes must be based on a unique law. Thus the laws of cognition are different from those underlying economic behavior, or those upon which artistic creation and enjoyment are based.

By considering the subject with its experiences and creations as interwoven with the configurations of the historical and social world, we free it from the isolation of purely subjective states and relate it to objective realities. They are objective for three reasons: (1) because they are attached to physical forms -whether these function as direct carriers of value, as signs or symbols, or as means of artistic expression- (2) because they have been developed from the reciprocal relations of many single subjects -in this context I call them collectively determined forms- and (3) because they are based on definite laws of meaning which have an over-individual validity. This last point needs elucidation.

The whole of nature is never present to our senses at any one time, and in the same way the historico-mental world is never given to us in its totality. Rather both must be 'actualized' again and again in individual experience. And as the context of nature which exists 'for us' is infinitely greater than our limited sensory field, so also is the mental world only partially present in the individual's immediate experience or achievement. And just as an ordered whole can be built up in our minds by means of cognitive laws (in whose interlacing structure the outline of objective nature is assumed *a priori*) in the same way our knowledge of and participation in the intellectual world must be based on laws of mental behavior. These laws are embodied in the individual as ideal directive constants which control the acts of its productive imagination as well as the acts of its mental activity. By means of this living systematic structure within the individual we can understand intellectual creations even if they have been developed under different historical conditions and in historically divergent souls. We must constantly keep in mind however that this *a priori* data only gives us the basis of mental structure. It is just as hard for the comprehending subject to evolve manifold historical differentiations and developmental phases as it is to disclose special natural laws. But if these differentiations were wholly chaotic and arbitrary noone could understand them. They would be as incomprehensible to us as pathological degenerations.

Here the objectivity of the intellect appears in a third sense. It is based solely neither on the fact that the individual finds these laws there, starting from the Self (transsubjectivity); nor upon the psychic reciprocal interrelation of many people (collectivity); but upon mental laws of creation and reproduction (normativity). I shall in future refer to this third meaning of the objective as the critical objective, while mentality as we find it before it is referred to structural laws, may be designated transsubjective and collective.

Let us return to the psychological aspect of our problem. Psychology is the science of the individual. But no subject can be separated from its objective counterpart, since subject and object can only be understood in terms of their mutual relations. *Geisteswissenschaft* puts the emphasis on the objective side. This science is occupied (1) with transsubjective and collective creations which concern individuals in overindividual effectual relations. Secondly (2) it deals with ideal mental laws, the norms according to whose measure the individual creates some mental fact in the critical-objective sense, or assimilates it by adequate comprehension. Psychology however places the emphasis on the subject and investigates (1) the experiences which arise from the interrelations of the individual with the trans-subjective and the collective; and (2) the acts and experiences which correspond to or deviate from the critical-objective laws.

We see now, that psychology in this sense, can only be carried on in the closest relation with the objective sciences; the historically descriptive and the normative sciences. Just as the psychology of cognition always presupposes some degree of finished knowledge and a theory of cognition so psychology as a whole presupposes at least the attitude of philosophy. The subjective must always be reflected, on a background of objectivity. When I speak of psychology therefore I always mean *geisteswissenschaftliche* psychology. —

That the problem of psychology is viewed today in a wholly different light[1]) hardly needs to be proved at length. It is generally regarded as dependent on the point of view and method of natural science in three ways. The body and mind problem, here of great importance, characterizes the first dependence. The question is not so much the mental relation to which the psychic process is subordinated as its relations to bodily processes, especially those of the nervous system. This association of the physical and the psychical, or more correctly, of nervous and psychic processes results in ignoring the context of meaning in which an experience is found and attending solely to material determinations. From this point of view, the feeling of satisfaction while eating and the pleasure accompanying aesthetic enjoyment are classed together and their objective counterparts (objective only in the sense for instance that the rhythm of physiological processes can be charted) are to be explored. This could only be possible if we presuppose physiological knowledge, a part of natural science.

The second kind of dependence of modern psychology on natural science is found in the relation of psychic phenomena to a specific form of the objective world, namely external nature which is determined purely by cognition. The psychologist then

---

[1]) *Today* refers to the situation in 1920. I allow this sentence to remain as it indicates the historical connections from which this book developed.

seeks to find which psychic processes correspond to the objectively determined and accurately determinable natural phenomena from which they deviate. Here he presupposes the data of physics. He also seeks to determine the scale of impressions corresponding to the mathematically measureable and graded stimuli. *Reizschwellen* (thresholds) are looked for, sense illusions are discovered and the relation of objective mathematical space to optical or tactual space is experimented with etc. — (Both forms of psychology are thus called physiological psychology or psycho-physics.) They have a direct subject-object relation to given data. But the object to which the soul is related is only the cognitive content of the material world. The acts of cognating nature itself, and their results in mathematics, physics, chemistry and physiology are not investigated but are assumed by every psychology based upon natural science.

The third dependence upon physics is shown in the way psychological concepts are formed. In common with the physicist who tries to build up all physical events from single elements in their constant relations, the allied psychologist tries to understand the complex of mental processes by a study of elements. He attempts for instance to build up the psychical world from simple sensations or from sharply defined and supposedly independent ideas.

On account of this methodological ideal I call psychology based on natural science a *psychology of elements*. Let us consider for the time being some of its peculiarities in order later to contrast it with a *structural psychology* as representing the form of psychology which clearly has a philosophical approach.

The psychology of elements attempts to analyze the processes of individual consciousness into their last differentiable components. It must be emphasized at this point that a psychology conscious of its purpose can only deal with elements discoverable in experience. Physiological psychology, of course, investigates the relation of psychic contents to material (physical or physiological) elements, as for instance of sense stimuli that can be varied and composed according to some fixed plan. But as Felix Krueger accurately points out, these must be regarded as determinants but not as the content of psychological experience. A pure psychology should only investigate differences which can be experienced regardless of whether or not there are phenomena on the physical side which could themselves be further analyzed. We must emphasize furthermore that the term 'elements' must never be taken to mean spatially separated parts; for, the psychical is not spatial, not even when it refers to space as its object, as in visual impressions.[1]) Elements here are rather to be conceived as conscious contents which differentiate themselves qualitatively and can be introspectively analyzed as independent phenomena, if need be through artificial isolation. Those qualities of the elements which can no longer appear independently in consciousness are aptly designated 'attributes', that is, dependent simple contents. Thus, for instance, many psychologists classify single sound impressions as independent conscious elements, but differentiate nevertheless the attributes of pitch, volume and timbre.

This psychology usually considers only so many classes of conscious elements as are necessary and sufficient to build up the total process of individual consciousness. This is an imitation of the method successfully used in all natural sciences. The illustration of psychic atoms (i. e. conscious particles) has in fact been used to make clear the intention of this synthetic process. The actual development of the method differs widely with individual psychologists. Some start with a primary class of psychological elements and deduce others from them, conceiving the latter in some way as attributes. Herbart attempts to build up conscious life as a mechanism of ideas in which feeling and desire are only accompaniments of the one class of primary ideas. Muensterberg, in his physiological psychology treats the simple sensation as a psychic atom. This conception receives a slightly different emphasis if we agree with Wundt that the soul is not a substantial being, but a process. In this case however, simple processes merely replace the simplest elements.

Psychologists do not always go so far as to postulate only one class of primary elements or processes. Some of them retain a limited number of basic classes. The outstanding example is the tripartite division into ideas, feelings and desires (corresponding to cognition, feeling and conation). Usually these classes are then further subdivided.

---

[1]) The external object, for instance, and not the idea is two inches long.

We are not interested in giving a detailed account of the attempts in this direction and in subjecting each to criticism. One can certainly find no fault with the attempt to give similar and fundamental phenomena in experience general names and to utilize these in a more specific description first of the simpler and then of the more complex psychological states. But we must question whether the province of psychology is thus exhausted. And in asking this we find that the above method fails to accomplish the most important results for the understanding of psychological processes. Noone denies that the poet, the historian, the minister and the educator must be good psychologists in the accepted sense of the word. But it is a striking fact that those who have made notable achievements in this field often knew nothing whatever about a psychology of elements. The psychology in Gottfried Keller's *Romeo und Julia auf dem Dorfe,* for instance, has nothing in common with such a form of analysis. And yet who would deny that this is a profound psychological study? Or take the psychology of politics, can this study be mastered by means of these elementary concepts?

It always makes an essential difference whether one dissects a psychological process or whether one treats it as a whole in broader contexts of meaning. Moses, angry with the Jewish people, was certainly in a state of emotion. One might analyze his condition according to its feeling states and ideas, according to the course and rhythm of these feelings and their tension and relaxation. But the historian takes all this for granted and is satisfied to indicate only the complex state. If one wants to explain psychologically the decision of a historical figure, one does not begin by analyzing this judgment into ideas, feelings and desires, but classifies only the motive which ultimately prevailed in a historical meaning- and value complex. The rest is self-explanatory unless some abnormal conditions have intervened. As a rule, the *Geisteswissenschaften* do not go back to the last distinguishable elements. They remain on a higher conceptual level, and immediately consider the inner process as a significant whole which has importance because it is a part of a total mental situation. Noone thinks that a poet merely mixes ideas, feelings and desires in order to create the psychological world of his heroes. They are, on the contrary, immediately present to his imagination as significant wholes.

To destroy the soul's meaningful total is the scientific limit of the psychology of elements. One might compare its procedure with the vivisection of a frog. Anyone who eviscerates a frog may learn its inner construction and also, by reflection, the physiological functions of its organs. He must not, however, expect to be able to put the parts together again and so to recreate the living frog. Similarly, the mere synthesis of psychic elements can never create the totality of a soul whose meaningful complex is related to the entire mental world. On the contrary, the significant whole is primary. Analysis, however, merely differentiates its elements which do not in the least give the fundamental reason for the insight of the whole. Wundt, in the methodological principles of his psychology acknowledged this in the socalled principles of 'creative synthesis' and 'relative analysis'. His psychology, too, is a psychology of elements. This is shown in the construction of his classic outline of psychology which begins with the elements of the soul and advances by way of mental formations to the more complex configurations and finally to psychic development. But Wundt strongly emphasizes the fact that forms composed of elements contain qualities which could not be deduced from the qualities of the elements themselves. What Mill called 'mental chemistry', Wundt designates 'creative synthesis'. Complex forms contain characteristics which could not be predicted from the original elements. But this does not really formulate a *law* of creative synthesis, for that would have to be a law which enunciated an irrational complex of relations that could not be grasped scientifically. I rather think that this principle designates the constant error of Wundt's method. It is absolutely impossible to build up a mental world from elements as one does a mechanism out of material parts. Rather, in this case the total is the fundamental thing and analysis is only significant and valid if one thinks of the elements and moments in relation to the whole. I should, therefore, reverse the point of view and replace the principle of creative synthesis by that of destructive analysis.

The above simile has already indicated that the attitude which we have described is not without analogy in the natural sciences. Noone has yet realized the hope of understanding an organism by means of purely physico-chemical principles. True, partial physical and chemical processes are perceptible everywhere in the organic realm. But they are never sufficient to explain the organism as a total function. The problem of the organic evidently lies on a higher conceptual level than the scientific concepts of chemistry and physics. But I shall not pursue this problem any further and shall instead develop the philosophical question. This is easier because the fact that we do find an influence of mental forces on material processes is regarded by *Geisteswissenschaft* as sufficient proof that such a relation is possible. Therefore in the following we shall leave aside the psycho-physical problem and deal exclusively with the more general region of meaning relations.

We said above that it was a peculiarity of the mental totality to represent a meaning relation. What does that signify? Meaning always has reference to value. Any functional relation is significant if all its partial processes can be understood through a reference to valuable total achievements. It does not at present concern us for whom these achievements are of value; whether the relation takes place in an individual who can experience the values himself or in another consciousness, or if one may even speak of a thing as valuable *per se*. A machine, for instance, may be said to be meaningful because all its partial achievements work together for a total effect which somehow has value. An organism is meaningful insofar as its functions tend toward the preservation of its existence under given environmental conditions, since its preservation may be considered valuable for itself. But most significant of all is the psychic life of an individual because an individual experiences within itself the valuable or valueless significance of its total actions and the relations of its partial functions. Dilthey, for this reason, called the soul a purpose complex, or teleological structure. Through the inner teleology he ascribed to the psychological total a structure such that it registered the valuable and harmful by means of some sort of feeling regulator.

But the problem is not so simple as Dilthey implies by this concept of structure.

If the soul were really nothing more than such an immanent teleology one could conceive it purely biologically; that is all its acts and experiences would be regulated by the desired goal of self preservation, to which one might add a reference to the preservation of the species. Many people do conceive the soul as such a structure tending only toward the preservation of self and species. The human soul, however (the abbreviation 'soul' will be used throughout for the inclusive concept of an individual's actions, reactions and experiences), is interwoven with a far larger system of value contexts than that of pure satisfaction of self. On a lower level, perhaps, the soul is purely biologically[1]) determined. On a higher level, the historical for instance, the soul participates in objective values which cannot be deduced from the simple value of self preservation. We mean by mind, mental life or objective culture, those realized values which were formed in the process of history and which have an overindividual meaning and validity.

That the individual soul is more than a teleological structure concerned solely for self-preservation and physical enjoyment is determined by its interrelation with this mental context. This is illustrated in two ways: (1) an individual experiences as valuable objects and achievements which have no immediate relation to the preservation of life. Thus the isolated achievement of pure cognition which satisfies no vital needs can be experienced as an actual value. While aesthetic enjoyment cannot, in all its forms, be regarded as a result of biological expediency. An intellectual human being is different from the fictitious primitive man because the former has higher and more far-reaching needs for satisfaction than mere existence and animal pleasure. His achievements and experiences reach to higher levels of value and his internal makeup is differentiated accordingly. (2) The teleological structure of the soul deviates to a still more noticeable extent from the simple biological regulative system. It is a well known fact that no individual experiences as valuable all that is valuable. And conversely, much is experienced as valuable that is *per se* valueless. To express this in psychological terms: the subjective values (with their individual peculiarities) by no means coincide with the objective values. This brings up the very difficult problem of the critical-objective or genuine values. Some tend to regard as valuable only what is actually valued. This view, however, is no better than the opinion that nothing is real unless it is the object of actual sense perception. Nor can this

---

[1]) I mean by biological any structure which seeks solely to preserve self or species.

extreme empiricism and relativism be saved by the fiction that the collective evaluations of all people (correspondingly the sense perceptions of all human beings) are the subjective correlative for the objectively valuable (the objectively real). For the question is: do all these people value correctly? By the critical-objective value we do not conceive anything susceptible of purely intellectual demonstration. But we do intend to imply that evaluation is subject to definite laws, and that only those values are 'genuine' or 'valid' which coincide with these laws of evaluation. The accidental factual consciousness of any individual is not the measure of the objectively valuable, but merely of what he subjectively values. Just as we have added the idea of an overindividual cognitive consciousness, within the empirical self, to the genuine cognition of being, so we need to construct an overindividual consciousness for genuine evaluation. It would be totally erroneous, however, to believe that this overindividual 'normative consciousness' could be understood as a collective (social) consciousness. For society is just as liable as an individual to err in value judgments, that is, they may be just as purely subjective. We must instead construct a normative consciousness i. e. a consciousness guided by objective laws, which shall be arbiter of collective as well as individual judgments.

This construction of a normative consciousness is only a metaphysical shortcut for an exceedingly complex conception of laws. In contrast with Rickert, we shall proceed to investigate minutely the special laws of evaluation and their interrelations. And in the third section of this book we shall consider their synthesis into a normative ideal of culture. Here we only wish to indicate how objective value from a critical point of view transcends subjectivity in *geisteswissenschaftliche* philosophy.

An intellectual life as it represents itself in history, a culture, not only means the actualisation of genuine values, but also contains apparent values (such as erroneous values based on theoretically false judgments, or subjective values which arise from purely momentary and disparate evaluations, or unsolved value conflicts). Whatever is objectively valuable in a culture must be thought of as the fulfillment of norms of evaluation, as the results of laws of evaluation which confront the individual as demands unless he obeys them of his own accord.

Let us now look back to the concept of the objective mind upon whose threefold significance we have already touched. It has been projected into the field of objects as something trans-subjective which can be understood only through the historical interrelation and summation of the behavior of an infinite number of subjects. The acts which created this mental world were not always lawful. A mass of pure subjectivity and obscured norms of vague interrelations, of chance and failure helped to make up this objective mind. This mind now confronts the individual and is objective at least in this sense that it is, to a very high degree, independent of the self, and that it is a not-I which exercises a reflex action on the individual. Furthermore one might include in objective mentality the very complex concept of mental norms which found the valid, objective and genuine values by excluding perverted values and errors. This objective mind does not yet exist. It is, instead, the ideal complex of norms which either in its totality or in sections confronts society, as well as the individual, as a real demand of how one should evaluate. It is then 'objective' not only in the sense that it exists outside of the individual, but also in the sense that it is normative, genuine and valid; 'subjective' then would mean not only the isolated individual as opposed to the overindividual historico-mental sphere, but everything which deviates from the norm. For the sake of greater clarity we shall in future call the first form '*objektiver Geist*' and the second '*normativer Geist*' (corresponding for instance to Hegel's *absolutem Geist*).

The individual, insofar as it is mental, must be thought of as belonging to both though in different senses. The objective mind with its content of genuine and false values signifies the socially determined milieu, the intellectual environment which has become history. The normative mind, however, means the cultural ethical directive which aims beyond every given condition, that is only of relative value, toward that which has genuine and true value. The first then represents reality, the second that which should become so.

Geisteswissenschaftliche psychology therefore draws the following conclusions. The individual soul must be thought of as a meaningful content of functions in which different value tendencies are correlated in the unity of consciousness. These value attitudes are determined by specific normative laws of value which correspond to the various classes of value. The empirical self finds itself already surrounded by overindividual mental configurations of value which in their realization have become detached from the experiencing selves. In them the constructive laws of value have already created an overindividual meaning which transcends the individual. Insofar then as we seek the structure of the overindividual resultant connections we find ourselves in the field of general (descriptive) *Geisteswissenschaft*. And insofar as we direct our interest to normative laws of value and to the mental value formations which follow these laws, we study the ethics of culture. Should we, however, place the meaningful experiences and acts of the individual in the foreground (regardless of whether these coincide with or deviate from the ideal norms) our study is *geisteswissenschaftliche* psychology. For psychology is a descriptive and understanding but not a normative science, though one must not think that psychology is possible without knowledge of the normative or the critical objective. On the contrary we regarded it as the unique problem of psychology to outline the subjective against the background of objectivity in all its significations. The psychology of elements constantly presupposes physical and physiological knowledge. In like manner *geisteswissenschaftliche* psychology presupposes the knowledge of mental objectivities in general.

Mental life accordingly is a complex of significant contexts in which attitudes can be differentiated and in which the objective and subjective senses often conflict. The cognitive is one of such attitudes. This is dominated by a definite law though the individual does not always experience and behave in accordance with it. The aesthetic is another attitude. A work of art is based upon an objective law of construction even if it cannot be formulated; but the subject does not always realize in himself the complete objective sense of the artistic object. A third attitude is one of economic evaluation and creation. But even though the subject is usually inclined to behave according to these objective laws of value, subjective deviations are found. And these can only be understood psychologically.

In concluding let us compare the two psychologies. *Geisteswissenschaftliche* psychology begins with the totality of the mental structure. (By structure we mean a context of achievements, and by achievement we mean the realization of objective value). There are partial structures which derive their meaning from the total mental structure of which they are a part; such partial structures are for instance the cognitive, that of technical work and the specifically religious consciousness. The collective mind develops whenever the achievements of these total or partial structures of various subjects co-operate and result in an objective (trans-subjective) precipitation. And if these achievements are based upon definite laws, that is, if they are according to norms, then they found the objective mind in the critical normative sense: that is, as the inclusive concept of overindividual configurations whose mental 'content' is accessible to any consciousness that can place itself in the concrete situation upon which this content is founded. Consequently, above the limited and fortuitous individuals there develops a mental world of overindividual sense, which in the historical process grows, changes and under certain conditions disintegrates.

The psychology of elements on the contrary, can only be methodologically justified if it investigates, in every case, the last distinguishable content in relation to the partial structures (single achievements), and beyond these the total structure. This psychology is thus dependent upon structural psychology and must come after it. Ideas, feelings and desires take part in acts of pure cognition as well as in technical creation or in aesthetic behavior; but in each case in a unique organic combination. This may be expressed as follows: ideas, feelings and desires are in themselves senseless material. Therefore the psychology of elements, taken alone and if it consistently followed its own method, would be a science of meaningless parts, and would be as futile as the natural sciences which build up nature from material elements but can never find the significance of natural phenomena. The psychic elements only have a meaning if embedded in a structural context, just as the parts of an organism have a meaning through their correlation. Then ideas and their connections become a cognitive order of objective significance in contrast to the elementary purely subjective play of association. Or, on the other hand, they receive an aesthetic meaning if they appear in the lawful structure which corresponds to the aesthetic attitude.

Our comparison of the two kinds of psychology consciously emphasizes the points of extreme difference. To the question of whether there is any possible agreement or mediate steps between them we must answer that the different points of view which are determined by the different intended objects cannot be abolished; but that we can adjust the difference in the formation of concepts and methods. Physiological psychology which expressly investigates the relation of the psychical to the anatomical and physiological facts can never coincide with a psychology which investigates the psychical in its relation to the mind. But the method which is based upon an analogy of atomic and mechanical theory can be improved upon. Indeed this was attempted long ago even by psychologists who started from the point of view of natural science. The very adoption of biological terms and the point of view of developmental theory signifies a reconciliation of the different psychologies. The discussions of the concepts: 'psychic development', 'structure', 'totality' and *Gestalt* (i. e. *Gegliedertheit*) are in too great a state of flux to allow a summary at this point. A reference to William Stern, E. R. Jaensch, Felix Krueger, Koehler-Wertheimer-Koffka, must suffice, since they are, despite their differences, all exponents of the movement which has as its goal the unification of psychological method.

Meanwhile no one of the above mentioned concepts suffices to designate the peculiarity of *geisteswissenschaftliche* psychology. The ultimate distinction lies in the fact that the latter deals with meaningfully related acts and experiences of the subject. This subjective meaning, however, could never be understood by another individual if it did not present itself as a special case, no matter how unique, of objectively valid meaning contexts; because objective laws of construction play a role in the structures, even if not wholly unqualifiedly. There is thus created, over and above the individual, a meaning which is comprehensible to others.[1] I should call a mental achievement the interweaving of subjective mental functions by means of which an overindividual meaning-complex, an objective mental configuration is created. Insofar as the soul is not merely a self-preservative system but a mental structure

---

[1] There is, however, also a purely subjective meaning such as for instance, is found in a wholly private set of symbols or certain pathological mental states. If however we still call this meaningful we have already made a reference to the fact that indirectly, through objective meaning tendencies, their final individual specification is generally obvious.

complex it is capable of achievements, of creating overindividual meaning constellations. The psychical elements on the contrary, are and remain bound to the individual. They are always purely subjective and isolated. Another individual can never share with me *his* ideas, *his* feelings and *his* desires. For essentially they are purely individual states or functions. I have my own states and they also are inseparable from my experience of self. Accordingly the psychology of elements deals with phenomena which can be directly experienced only by the introspecting individual. It is possible, however, for another individual to communicate to me the meaning of his experiences. He first creates something objective, either a cognitive achievement fixed in language or a work of art, or a technical product. Then by empathic relation with this object I may develop a corresponding mental act. The structure of this act may again be an interweaving of ideas, feelings and desires. But then they are *my* ideas etc. which of course do not correspond with his ideas in kind and content. The meaning is all we have in common. As creating and experiencing meaning then the individual soul reaches into overindividual mentality.

It is greatly to the credit of E. R. Jaensch to have worked in this connection too toward a reunion of both psychologies (i. e. the psychology of elements and *geisteswissenschaftliche* psychology). He says quite rightly: 'It should set us thinking, that the distinction of two kinds of psychology implies a resurrection of the doctrine of the dual nature of truth. It is an indubitable fact, however, that no matter how deeply we explore sensations and perceptions we find that never, even in these regions is there a consciousness of reality which is wholly devoid of meaning value. The illusion that two independent psychologies are possible was fostered by the stratified structure of consciousness which we have elucidated in our work. Our investigations of these conscious strata showed that the intentions which referred to meaning and value are those which are most completely realized in the higher level of consciousness. And therefore it is impossible to miss them here, though in the lower levels they are only brought to light by a very searching investigation. But this difference is one of degree and not of essence.'[1])

---

[1]) E. R. Jaensch, *Ueber den Aufbau der Wahrnehmungswelt.* Leipzig 1923. p. 413.

The individual soul participates in the mental world by means of its lawful structure in which there is intellectual experience and creation and evaluation for the total soul.[1]) The individual soul cannot always wholly grasp the objective sense of this region, at other times it transcends it with its activity which follows certain norms. There is thus a tension between the soul and the mind. There is also a continual tension between the historical mind and the eternal laws which are in themselves only tendencies of the creation of meaning. The discovery of these laws and their branching relations will be our next problem. We have previously called their inclusive concept the normative mind. This *geisteswissenschaftliche* problem immediately becomes one of psychology because we shall attempt to investigate the manifold subjects with a view to discovering which of the mental laws is dominant in each one and typically determines its structure. For, these divergences from the idea of a normal structure of man deal with the historical and individual peculiarities, the description of which is specifically in the domain of psychology.

The presentation of the human soul structure as such in relation to the total structure of the objective and normative mind would be the subject matter of general *geisteswissenschaftliche* psychology. The region of differential *geisteswissenschaftliche* psychology is the study of types of individualized structures in which some aspect of the objective and normative mind is predominantly expressed.

---

[1]) How far this mental objectivity must be affixed to the materially objective in order to attain an enduring temporal existence we cannot here investigate. Cf. my essay in the Festschrift fuer Volkelt 1918 *Zur Theorie des Verstehens und zur geisteswissenschaftlichen Psychologie*.

2
METHODS OF GEISTESWISSENSCHAFT: ANALYTICAL AND SYNTHETICAL

The unity of the soul is founded in the relation of all its single acts and experiences to the individual. This self cannot be defined but only experienced. We shall see later that experience of self is by no means unequivocal but has different meanings in different mental achievements. What is ordinarily called 'ego' is the experiencing center which in some mysterious way, is bound to the body and therefore definitely localized in space and time. Insofar as all acts and experiences are processes in a coherent individuality they belong to a closed structure. They must, therefore, culminate in a unitary meaning. But this structure is differentiated in its achievements. The total structure is composed of a number of partial structures each of which has its unique function and so also its specific value. An illustration of this is found in any division of labor on the basis of a coherent plan.

For the sake of clarity I shall now define a few necessary expressions. By 'mental act' I mean the activity of an individual (i. e. the structural interweaving of many different psychic functions,) to create a mental achievement of overindividual sense. Thus, for instance, a judgment is a mental act; while the participating ideas, associations, reproductions, feelings and conative processes are only psychic functions. If I should give a meaning to a few notes that I hum to myself and thus make them a sort of objective carrier this would also represent a mental act. The love which unites me to another person is a mental act, and likewise the claim by which I define my right against his.

Corresponding to the act as spontaneous or meaning-giving behavior (*sinngebendes Verhalten*) there is the receptive or meaning-given behavior, (*sinnerfüllendes Verhalten*) the 'experience'. In experience I actualize the overindividual meaning which is attached to mental creations. I translate the meaning into the actual psychic states of my soul. When I understand what another person says, when I 'enjoy' a work of art, when I recognize the hand of God in my destiny and when I feel myself beloved by another human being I may be said to experience.

Acts and experiences cannot be sharply distinguished. For, in all acts there is an experiential factor which has a reflex action on the individual; and in all experiences there is a resisting act character. In the following we shall, therefore, generally use the word 'act' even when the mental relation is more an experience than a creation, more a reception of meaning than a giving of significance.

A special class of mental acts, then, creates its own meaning. This sense is grasped and interpreted by a corresponding class of experiences. Thus, for instance, cognition has a peculiar meaning which must not be mistaken for that of art or of religion. The visual experience involved in seeing a star may be interpreted in various ways, according as to whether my mood inclines toward astronomy, or whether it is lyric or religious. Therefore each class of acts and its associated class of experiences has a specific region of meaning. When one thinks both of the possible varieties of its appearance in history and of the human achievements contained in it one refers to a sphere of culture. Every cultural realm has its ideal independence because it subserves a definite significance.

We have already defined meaning as something associated with value. Overindividual meaning is thus related to overindividual value. 'Overindividual' here signifies not the collective (which in the critical sense might still be subjective) but only critical objective, that which follows certain norms. A definite class of objective values is thus intended and realized by the mental acts. And correspondingly a value of the associated class is apprehended in the particular experience. It should follow, therefore, that it is possible to derive classes of acts from classes of value.

Now however, we must guard against a misunderstanding. The structure of the individual mind is, so to speak, articulated in the value acts and experiences. But the mental acts and experiences themselves are not necessarily evaluations. More accurately, when mental acts are carried out according to their specific laws, evaluations and value experiences are founded upon them because the specific mental tendency has been objectively satisfied by means of the mental acts. But the acts themselves are not evaluations, or at least not necessarily so. It would be wholly erroneous, for instance, to regard the acts of cognition as evaluating acts, as has been done now and then. Affirmations and negations are not predicates of positive or negative value which must be ascribed to propositions. On the contrary, cognitive acts have their own structure which must be derived through examination of the pure cognitive attitude itself. And cognitive acts are indifferent to value as far as the feeling of individual increase or decrease of life does not play any determining role. The categories by which we cognize reality are purely mental attitudes with a reference to objects which cannot be derived from any evaluation of the same. It is true, however that to any lawfully carried out act of cognition there is affixed, for the active subject, a specific experience of value and this belongs to the class of pure cognitive values. Or again, aesthetic behavior as a definite class of acts and experiences has in it no element of evaluation. Whenever I empathically appreciate or re-live the tonal sequence of a symphony, and find a certain mood portrayed, it is the mood and not the tones or tonal sequence which I evaluate. But another specific value experience is added to the previous series of acts and experiences, namely the purely aesthetic one. And finally, the complex of technical acts involved in the actual energy which a farmer expends in tilling his field is not evaluation. But in the successful completion of his work there is contained a third kind of value experience, the economic. To express this in a general formula: every field of mental activity, insofar as it becomes the object of actual endeavor, is dominated by a specific attitude of evaluation. In its temporal appearance it becomes a constellation of purpose. And from the realization of this purpose, the specific value experience, as in any teleology, is reflected on the means and tools. These 'have' value, but are not of course evaluations. In a machine too the technical value of any part is proportional to its contribution to the achievement of the whole But one cannot understand the parts solely from the total value. They are rather, the objects of chemical and physical consideration. They are subject not only to laws of value, but primarily to laws of mathematics, statics and dynamics. In applying this consideration to our problem, we find that theories of cognition, aesthetics and economics are not theories of value, though it is possible to consider cognitive achievements, aesthetic experience and economic production from the standpoint of their specific classes of value.

If, finally, one may correlate each class of mental acts to a corresponding system of values; if one may speak of cognitive, aesthetic and economic values which are, nevertheless, all formed to a mental unity in the individual, then it is obvious that each system of values must somehow shade off into the others and that each experience of a definite class of values must be related to the whole value experience of the mental subject. Otherwise the mental subject would have no structure, i. e. no closed constellation of achievements. It would be instead a bundle of achievements conjoined at random. This center, in which the value of every mental achievement is experienced as related to the mental totality of life, we shall later call the religious realm. Therefore a character of finality is peculiar to the religious acts, and every mental experience is religious insofar as it is of ultimate importance for the individual's total value experience. But we are getting too far ahead of our subject.

It must suffice for the introductory definition of concepts to emphasize here that we consider different value directions as indicative of the division of the mental realm. We shall, however, see that its every region has its unique laws of construction, requiring a special analysis. Our method, then, shall be to view each specific value as a goal which the total act and experience structure of the specific region subserves. Pure cognitive value is achieved whenever the pure law of cognition is realized in specific acts. When the law of economics is actualized in a specific group of acts or experiences, the purely economic value is attached to it. But unless experience follows the laws of its specific region it has no value.

In conclusion: acts and experiences are, as the names indicate, temporal processes; that is, they occur as real events in time. But this does not imply that their content is merely temporal. We have said that mental acts realize value, and here we must make two distinctions: first, their eternal tendency and the mental law which suffuses them, and secondly, the historic reality which is created by them, or rather, which they endow with meaning. Above economic goods there is the 'Economic', superior to cognition there is 'Truth' and higher than works of art is 'Beauty'. These eternal objects or laws, for instance Truth, Beauty and Justice, become temporal in a double sense; first in respect to the real world of space and time they are actualized in a peculiar manner, at least are achieved in a struggle with the world, for instance, they are given a material representation; and secondly as actualized in the factual experience of some soul. It is obvious however, that the mental content of acts is timeless since it can be understood regardless of intervening space and time. This is only possible because the acts contain a law or validity which is independent of their actualisation in the world, or their realization in individual experience. We understand the significance of mental acts by putting ourselves in an actual historical situation, in which meaning was created according to certain norms. The mental realm participates in the timeless by means of its laws, just as nature can be conceived from a timeless point of view as configuration following definite laws, even though the manifoldness of its phenomena is always temporally determined and can never be wholly understood *a priori*. Mental phenomena are determined or enclosed temporally but their mental content, their lawful structure is eternal. Mental comprehension, then, means reducing a temporal mental phenomenon to its eternal system of meaning.

The main problem of a psychology of acts is to find the fundamental directions in which the objective mind is built; or in other words, to determine the lines of contact which exist between the overindividual mental life and the individual act center. For it cannot be doubted that the objective mind, with its positive and negative value content, has its roots in the experiences and creations of finite individuals. Through these individuals it was developed and in them it must always be awakened to new life. We may assume therefore that the mental structure of a subjective soul coincides, in its fundamental lines with the structure of the objective mind. The meaning directions in which the acts and experiences of the individual move, reflect the cultural regions of value, but only in regard to the fundamental tendencies and not the historical content. For, the normative mind operates in both as the formative principle.[1])

---

[1]) It is absolutely futile to try to understand simply by the category of 'expression' the relation to the historically unique individual of the

There is also a reciprocal relation. The meaning of an individual life is determined by the meaning of historically given objective culture, and culture is always re-created and transformed by the living souls which sustain it and are sustained by it. Above both, however, there is a guiding star; the all-inclusive concept of norms which are valid for the individual soul, the idea of humanity. The application of this concept to the objective mind leads to the idea of a genuine culture.

Thus, in order to determine the fundamental directions of mental life we might avail ourselves of either of two methods. We might start from the historically given objective culture and deduce from its organisation the attitudes which must always be contained in an individual soul structure. Or we may try to build up an articulated culture synthetically from the eternal attitudes of the soul. Let us take up both methods in greater detail.

I

A culture or historically given mental life, on the higher developmental levels, is composed of a number of cultural spheres which are kept separate in the consciousness and language of the subjects. (This is done apparently regardless of time and space.) Culture is divided into a number of regions of activity or achievement. In each of these regions a specific kind of value is realized. We may also call each sphere of value, as seen from the point of view of real purposes, a purpose constellation insofar as it determines the goal. In every purpose constellation there is immanent, one may be allowed to surmise, a definite law[1]) which regulates the system of structural means which satisfy its dominant purpose. Let us enumerate, for the present, regardless of system, the regions which may be considered independent: pure and applied science, economics, art, morality, religion, society, politics, law and education. Of course these regions are not spatially conjoined like parts of the body. They are rather interlaced to form a structure, i. e. a

---

objective mind, in any definite historical form. The objective mind embraces far more than the mere expression of the individual soul structure which is historically connected with it.

[1]) The abbreviated expression 'law' of course always indicates a complex of laws which is often greatly differentiated.

constellation of achievements. Thus modern theoretical science has aspects which are political, economic, moral and pedagogical. And in economics we find judicial, scientific, technical, moral and even religious factors. The differentiation of each region is thus not a real division, but rather a theoretical isolation according to the value which is intended in each case. But the motives for this division must have been very obvious. For, the general boundaries are realized *instinctively* even by the uneducated classes. But they do not grasp more than the general boundaries, because finer differentiation is not easy. The modern discussion of the question 'belief or knowledge' for instance, shows how difficult it is to separate science and religion. And the problem of distinguishing politics, law, society and the field of morals leads us into the most complicated questions. If we want to find a corresponding purposive region of the individual soul for each cultural region, as for instance a scientific, economic, technical or aesthetic urge, a moral and religious heredity, and a political, judicial and social nature, we are faced with the same riddle which demanded a solution in our previous consideration of various cultural spheres. What constitutes the religious yearning of the soul? How is it distinguished from the scientific and aesthetic motives? Where does the social nature end and the political begin? etc. It is, of course, possible to use the objective cultural systems as principles of discovering the basic mental attitudes, as I did in the first edition of this volume (1914). But it is not sufficient merely to reduce the overindividual context to individual tendencies. For we cannot in this way satisfactorily explain the significance of these acts.

There is a further difficulty. Every historical region of culture has peculiarities which belong solely to that particular epoch. Economy may be of money and of credit, science may be positivistic, society a class system, religion interwoven with philosophy to the point of confusion, and law perhaps be any positivistic individual law. If we were to construct types of behavior which correspond to the above spheres we should arrive not at eternal types, valid for all differentiated cultures, but rather at historically determined types. Thus Woelfflin in his magnificent work *Kunstgeschichtliche Grundbegriffe* has set side by side historical and eternal types which are derived from the eternal being of plastic art. We must therefore, carefully direct our inquiry so that we reach the eternal laws of economics, art and religion themselves. This can scarcely be done by a reductive method. How difficult it would be for instance, to reduce the historical chance data of an epoch to eternal and separable laws of economics and jurisprudence. What a difference there would be in the final concept of religion if we started with Spinoza's world view or the neo-protestant Christianity of Ritschl. It is obvious that one can only achieve a relatively correct picture in this way after a preliminary comparison of cultural systems in different cultural levels and cultural individualities. But such a comparison is admittedly futile if we merely collect material empirically. Our study must be based on deductive principles so that we only compare those forms in which one can assume *a priori,* an identical law of structure. Otherwise we might classify as science something that is essentially more nearly related to religion or aesthetic intuition. Or we might take as moral what is really of a legal nature.

As a second alternative one might think of utilising as principles for the systematic division of mental regions the single cultural levels which have been found by reflecting upon mental life. Science, fine arts, religion, economics, politics, sociology, jurisprudence, ethics and pedagogy would then point toward specific mental motives. But even if the situation were more clearly defined than it is, who would be able to make a systematic division of the social sciences?[1]

We must insist that it would not do to arrive at philosophical conclusions from the actual situation of the individual sciences which as a rule have been so developed for practical reasons. Thus pure economics is really different from economics as it is customarily taught. So this alternative is also fruitless.

No matter how difficult it is and how insufficiently at first we may satisfy our ambition, we must accept the synthetic instead of the analytic, the deductive rather than the reductive method. Thus we must try to deduce from the eternal attitudes of human nature the fundamental directions which each culture embodies in unique arrangement and irrational interrelation.

---

[1] Cf. Georg v. Mayr: *Begriff und Gliederung der Staatswissenschaften.* Tübingen 1910 (3).

II

It follows from the conclusions in the first chapter that the synthetic method must not be thought of as if concerned with the last differentiable elements out of which the mental life or the soul is built up. For, the psychic elements which have been partially deduced from their correlation to external and internal material elements are no longer constellations of meaning. And it is impossible to understand significant matter by means of material devoid of meaning. In the realm of psychology of structure we may consider as building material only what has an independent meaning or a significant attitude. Our problem then is to build up the total structure of the soul from qualitatively different, yet always significantly interrelated mental attitudes. To this end it is necessary to completely determine the various attitudes. Completely, meaning all classes of acts which are clearly distinct from each other because of their different immanent meanings i. e. which are necessary and sufficient to explain the manifoldness of the mental phenomena. The qualification 'necessary' indicates that no independent attitude should be excluded; 'sufficient' means that no complex act which might be deduced from the combination of simpler acts which endow with meaning should be included.

Since both the deductive and inductive methods are essential to every genuine science, so the final test of the validity of *a priori* principles is there also the fact that by means of these principles one really can understand the manifoldness of empirical phenomena. But this historical verification is a second step. The central point of our method lies rather in the fact that all mental attitudes and their intended meanings can be understood *a priori*.[1]) The filling in of these tendencies with material which may be taken from nature or historical life can never be reasoned out beforehand, for, this necessitates a knowledge of facts, just as individual natural

---

[1]) *A priori*, of course, does not mean previous to all experience, but with all experience. It is not our intention to spin out the mental world from *a priori* concepts, but to understand its fundamental laws of meaning which are already assumed when we classify in any particular region any single phenomenon. The encroaching of what is evidently *a priori* into psychological factual contexts has been treated more in detail by Theodor Erismann: *Die Eigenart des Geistigen, Inductive und einsichtige Psychologie.* Leipzig 1924.

laws can only be derived through observation of real natural occurrences. But the formative principles, (in this case fundamental directions of meaning, in the case of natural science the general law of causality) are conditions necessary to the understanding of mind and nature. If every human being were a chaos of changing tendencies there would be no possibility of interpreting the historical and social world. But the mental nucleus of man always has the same structure. Even though the degrees of differentiation change with the developmental processes of the mind (as well in the latent form as in the most developed) there are eternal tendencies, eternal directions of acts and experiences, without which it would be impossible to 'understand' the inner context of a foreign and distant soul. We carry in our own being the scaffolding of the mind. And for this reason it may be presented *a priori* without consideration of historical and geographical differences. Yes, it must even be possible to predict that wherever we find human culture we shall find the same fundamental attitudes. And that with the special emphasis of one attitude there are necessary displacements of all the others in the total value of life. The fundamental laws of these attitudes can be understood *a priori*. The examples only explain, affirm and make vivid.

I must confess, however, that I have found this methodological principle only after years of study. This was because it is necessary to free one's vision from the great complexity which is involved in every historical representation of mind before one can single out the fundamental mental attitudes. I shall try to illustrate this by a metaphor which seems to me illuminating. It takes practice to hear the limited number of leitmotifs which interweave to form the sounding symphony of life. Certain motifs force themselves on our attention and cannot be overlooked, but others have been so elaborated and varied by the composer that we can only grasp them after hearing them once in their simple form.

Life is always for us a complex process and the simple components of meaning hardly ever appear in an isolation such that we might express them immediately in abstract thought. Quite suddenly, however, in 1920, I perceived that it was precisely this interweaving which should be the starting point for our new method. Perhaps unconsciously influenced by a neo-Platonic point of view I became convinced that everything is a part of everything else.

In each section of mental life, though in different proportions, all mental attitudes are present. Each total mental act displays to the analyzing observer all the aspects into which the mind could possibly be differentiated.

One must certainly be prepared to alter all one's concepts in order to understand this line of thought. No complicated theory is proposed, on the contrary it is extraordinarily simple. All fruitful and far-reaching scientific principles are simple and clear. But the alteration of one's thought is necessitated by the fact that we are here analyzing not a single mental region but rather all of them in relation to each other. For apparently this complexity has not been previously considered and consequently the simple and limited essence of each attitude has not been understood. This mental transformation will not be easy for everyone. But one can only learn to see structure if one recognizes the necessity of first isolating and idealizing in order later to understand the interrelations of life as a complication of originally very simple threads.

A bias which is a necessary consequence of every determined methodological procedure is caused by the fact that we must start from the single mental subject. But we find this starting point only in the objective mental medium which is created by many generations and carried on by entire groups. We must not, however, forget that the accompanying social reciprocal interrelation and summation is really only the form in which the mental life expands and complicates itself. Mental life itself must previously exist in the individual as a tendency. For unless some germ of it could be found in him we should go on indefinitely adding zero to zero. True, the single acts in this or that individual first find visible extension in society. And in the historical development of society they grow into an ever increasing stream which surrounds the individual and bears him away. But analysis must begin with the individual consciousness, ignoring as far as possible its historical peculiarities. We shall, therefore, speak first of the individual mental acts, meaning those which a single individual, no matter how primitive, must carry out. Even Robinson Crusoe must cognize, have economic and aesthetic relations and reverently appreciate the meaning of the course of life. But he could neither love nor rule. Here we come to the turning point where we must postulate social mental acts. By individual mental acts then, we mean those to whose significant completion a second ego is not necessary. By social mental acts we mean those which expressly imply, or have as their object the experiential context of another person. The mere fact that a mental act is occasioned by social correlations or appears in social interrelation is not sufficient to characterize it as social; for here society is merely the carrier of the mental content. Those mental acts, however, which intend another person or a group as such, constitute a special class for themselves.

3
INDIVIDUAL MENTAL ACTS

When we are in a reverie we find, in and about us, a mass of impressions which really mean nothing. This condition cannot be adequately portrayed in words, since verbal definitions immediately include intellectual and other associated meanings which are excluded when we are semi-conscious. We are drowned in a sea of light and color without form or limit. There is a wealth of undifferentiated sounds and dull bodily pressures which are not clearly localized. There is a scarcely apperceived general feeling state which merges vaguely into other states. Such a chaos is characteristic of mind antecedent to its creation. Subject and object are not separated nor is the object recognized and given meaning.

It has been asserted that in waking consciousness only do we confront 'reality', and that we then separate our ego from the objective order around us and build up a conceptual world which is the same for all observers. This is a wholly mistaken idea. Even the scientist does not for a moment think of translating the sense impressions of his daily experience into a scientific and strictly theoretic form. He is satisfied to let the sun rise and set, he sees colors and hears tones even though he 'knows' that these are qualities of his own soul and not immediately of the things themselves. He continues to speak of the sun's hiding behind clouds, of its looking down upon the earth and of 'nature' as arranged in a certain manner and as having either a beneficent or a maleficient attitude toward man. He chooses to be interested in a certain object rather than others, finds his mood reflected in the universe so that the coming of autumn gives him a premonition of his own approaching death. In a word: the conscious attitude is not by any means synonymous with the scientific or purely theoretic attitude. The naive consciousness of reality is not absolutely determinable for all times and all people. Secondly, this naive apprehension of reality is not merely a preliminary step in cognizing behavior, but contains in a curious jumble a totality of relations to life. Added to this is the fact that our present attitude to the world is intermingled with a wealth of historical occurrences and not only theoretic but also value judgments. We think we see in the nature of a plant that it is 'poisonous', and attach this judgment as a stigma. And on the other hand we feel a natural sympathy with certain people for which the reasons are no longer clearly conscious. And there are also individual differences. What to one person is a sacred object is to another merely a stone. One sees a landscape suffused with the colorful memories of his youth, while another sees nothing but a meaningless desert. All this shows how impossible it would be to develop anything like a primary or pre-scientific consciousness. For, the view of the world of the naive observer as well as of the scientist combines the most divergent points of view. We find it quite impossible to present an unequivocal primary consciousness, so that one might be tempted to say: every human being has an absolutely individual picture of the world. Even though the general outlines coincide, the relief is different in every case.

Where then can we find a support, a principle of order or a guide line?

There is nothing for it but to introduce a hypothesis, the meaning of which I want to illustrate by means of the following picture. White sunlight contains all the primary colors of the spectrum. Whenever this white light is present, red, green and blue etc. are there also, though these colors are not visible. But it is possible to sort them out by sending the ray through a refracting medium. It is also conceiveable, (for instance by means of a color top or a color wheel) so to increase the proportion of a single color that it predominates in the total mixture. But all the other colors are still there.

Let us apply this to our problem. The manifold and apparently infinitely varied attitudes toward the socalled 'given' world, which is itself only a methodological fiction, can be reduced to a number of basic attitudes. These are not spatially conjoined so that we cognize one part, evaluate another economically and appreciate a third aesthetically or religiously. Rather all conceivable attitudes are contained in every mental glance, but in different degrees, emphasized now more now less and present in complicated acts in manifold relations of founding or being founded.

The methodological hypothesis which we postulate may be stated in the following sentence. In every total act which gives meaning, all basic forms of such acts are simultaneously present; the totality of mind is present in every mental act. The systematic division of the *Geisteswissenschaften* has been unsuccessful because it has always overlooked this principle. It has sought among disparate elements what is really to be found only in a total. The fact has been neglected that in all scientific behavior, aesthetic, economic, religious factors, and so on in the three further combinations, are simultaneously present.

Assume that something is given to my sense perception. Before I cognize it, I, as a psycho-physical subject, experience an impression of it which confronts me as an external force. Its pressure may be so strong and its chemical influence so intense that my physical system is unable to cope with it. But it may also influence my organs in a satisfying manner favorable to life. In any case it is related to my psycho-physical constitution in a manner which is unconsciously felt in the qualitative terms of feeling: 'pleasant or unpleasant', and which with continued experience and reflection develops into the specific value experience of the favorable or harmful. Whatever is evaluated in such a manner has an economic significance, no matter how primitive. In every real act of apprehension the fact that I must attend in an optimal manner if I wish to enter into relation with the object, is in itself an economic factor. The economy of the eye demands, for instance, that I bring the given object into the place of clearest vision, the fovea. This necessitates an expenditure of energy on my part, and purely psychologically, attention is part of the psychic economy.

At the same time an act of another kind takes place: the 'objectively given' (really only a condition of the sense organ) is changed into an object. This object is mentally separated from its environment, emphasized like a relief and intended for its own sake. And in this act of mental attention the object becomes an identical being which in every future act of the same significance may be again intended. The object, even if it existed but once, has thus been lifted into the sphere of generality, the realm of things which can be recognized or re-intended, or as we usually say the sphere of identification.[1]) In this we have the germ of the determining acts which we call cognitive. These acts are related not only to identical beings but also to identical essential correlations (*Wesensverknuepfungen*).

This sort of mental construction, however, cannot completely exhaust the socalled object. The absolute sensuousness and concreteness of its appearance is intended, but not completely fathomed, by cognition. For, its unique outline, color, tonality or touch impression influence me in still another manner. This impression has nothing of material weight and my behavior nothing of desirous interest. I 'feel' myself into the object, i. e. I move around its outlines with a certain attitude of visual appreciation, a certain psychic rhythm. I sense in its color or tones immediate psychic moods which are related in my psychic structure to the same colors and sensual nuances. In this we find a unique process of unification with the object. Or to put it more generally: the sensible concrete impression arouses in my affective powers such impulses that the impression may also be called an expression. Something related to my soul seems to lie in the sensuous character of the object (as in fact all sense qualities have been shown to be finally psychic qualities). Every sensible concrete phenomenon is to me both impression and expression. (*Eindruck - Ausdruck*). That is, I find in the phenomenon a psychic impulse, which however is only called forth by the object and is then unconsciously attributed by me to it. The resulting feeling of empathy is so spontaneously fused with the object that a certain psychic quality seems to lie within the thing itself. This is the germ of aesthetic acts.[2])

---

[1]) Cf. Volkelt, *Gewissheit und Wahrheit* Muenchen 1918 p. 499 Identity has the character of generality.

[2]) By 'impression' I mean here the sensuous experiencing of an object plus the resulting mood or affective impulse which I immediately connect with the act of vision and ascribe to the influence of the object. This excludes any desirous or interested relation to the object. By 'expression' I mean on the contrary the conscious or unconscious ascription of psychic impulse to a sensibly apprehensible configuration. Whatever is impression in the object I ascribe to its characteristic form. Its expression is referred to my present mood. The fusion of both into one experience (impression-expression) creates a kind of neutral psychic state which belongs exclusively neither to me nor to the object but seems to lie for the observer in the object as something essentially psychic (*Seelisches Ueberhaupt*), comparable

One last remark: obviously a single experience presents itself as a mere segment objectively and subjectively. Objectively it seems to have been carved out of infinity. Subjectively it is only a wave in the meaningful flow of my inner life. Insofar as this isolated experience is meaningfully related to my whole life, even in the vague mood which we call reverence, it has a religious emphasis. There is nothing, not even the smallest stimulus which is without significance for the total meaning and value of my life. Without being able to express my mood in words I can quietly contemplate a dew drop on a blade of grass, and after I have cognized and aesthetically appreciated it, experience a mood in which there is a vague premonition of sadness on the mutability of life and the awe of eternity.

It has been our endeavor to present the attitudes which might be contained in a single mental glance so that all later mediations by means of association and reflection, shall be excluded as far as possible. In every attitude we have considered only the primary aspects. To formulate the result briefly:

Economic significance lies in the experience of psycho-physical relations of energy between the subject and the object. (Measurement of energy, *Kraftmass*).

Theoretic significance is founded in the general identity of the intended object. (Essence, *Wesen*).

Aesthetic significance consists in the impression-expression character of a sensible concrete phenomenon. (The imaginative, *Bild*).

Religious significance comes with the relating of a single experience to the total meaning of the individual life. (Total meaning, *Totalsinn*).

In reality we rarely find such simple acts, because for one reason acts are not temporally isolated. The summated results of cognition enter into all acts and form a foundation upon which are built other reflected experiences of economic, aesthetic or religious significance. If I contemplate an autumn landscape my aesthetic experience is not only of the riotous coloring of the leaves and the undulating line of the hills, but also a knowledge of fruits

---

to a phenomenon of contact and penetration. It is clear however that there are different degrees of participation of expression and impression between the aesthetic object and the subject.

and their ripeness, of coming winter, of sleeping and waking, of death and languor (feelings of interpretation). The turbulent ocean seems to be mysterious for one reason because it is dangerous. I feel in the warmth of the sun a vitalising power, in the grape I anticipate the coming wine. In the sound of a word there seems to lie for me the total meaning for life, of what it designates theoretically. Thus everything is interwoven by acquired knowledge, by meaning contexts which found and are being founded. The mental acts interweave in their meaning again and again, so that all experience is finally full of significance and infinitely rich in meaning. But should we disentangle these interwoven structures, we should find everywhere the same simple motifs but interrelated, varied and enhanced; just as the finale of the *Meistersinger* brings out in full meaning all the past experience.

We must sharpen our vision to apprehend the interweaving factors in a total mental act. I shall therefore give one illustrative example, and for the present leave it undecided which one of the many attitudes is emphasized. Later, in part II. we shall investigate all classes of acts, bearing in mind the question of how they are formed as dominant attitudes in themselves, and how they contrast with other attitudes.

I

For the purpose of illustration let us assume that there is present to my apprehending consciousness what is called in the language of cognition a mountain range. At first it is only experienced as 'something'. And this experience may contain the following aspects.

a) I, as a cognizing subject, attend to it. I advance mentally beyond the optic stimulation in my sense organ and see the picture in a definite place in space which is thought of as three dimensional. And only then does the retinal affection become an object. To this object I direct my attention, and exclude the environmental surrounding, the sky and the foothills, (a kind of abstraction) I intend only the mountain range. And in attending to it in thought and determination, or even only in labeling it 'this' I posit it as an object having identity. It is not entirely new to me. I know objects which have the same essential identity. And the cognitive attitude is directed only to this 'essence'. Perhaps I am content with the most general essence which is designated by the name 'mountain range'. Or perhaps other sources of knowledge enrich my cognition. Then I may label this 'special essence' the Presidential Range. But even this noun lies in the sphere of generality. For the name is only a command to view this, no matter how concrete, as identical in all the mental acts related to it. The constituent factors of cognition are then: (1) to posit the object; (2) to intend this and to abstract all irrelevant data; (3) to view as identical in essence. The last factor means that the cognizing act in all circumstances is directed to the general, that is an act which is directed toward the identical essence. Thus from the experienced impression we derive the cognized identical object.

b) In this experienced something there remains a factor, however, which cannot be included in the general aspect; namely the sensible concrete phenomenon of exactly this mountain range from exactly this point of vantage. The sensible concrete consists in the individuality of its present form (which cannot wholly be grasped by any general concept of geometry) and in the unique combination of exactly this distribution of light, shade, color and mass. True, I can cognitively determine this unique configuration by means of still more general essences. But the individuality, the sensibly concrete phenomenon is apprehended differently. This creates in me, even while all directly desirous interest is still quiescent a totally unique psychic impulse. As observer I am influenced not only intellectually but also affectively. In future I shall refer to this sensibly concrete individuality (which according to circumstances may be a symphony, a phenomenon affecting taste, smell or touch organs,) as a sensible phenomenon. (*das Bildhafte.*) In the shape of the whole there is for me a psychic *Gestaltqualitaet* which coincides with my perceptive apprehension. In every separate color and in the total color effect there is a wave of psychic feeling quality. In other words, the picture's impression on me is also an expression i. e. a reflexion of psychic qualities in the object. And this substantiates the scientific conclusion that the sensory qualities have a subjective (i. e. psychical) nature. We say that this sensible phenomenon reflects what one might call the soul of the object (its moods). But we know very well that in this way we only 'lend' the object in an act *sui generis* our own psychic impulse. The problem of the essence of aesthetic empathy has not been solved even today. It must suffice here to observe that it is not, or at least not necessarily, my actual psychic condition which is empathically experienced. In the same way it must not be supposed that the object necessarily has a soul or that the empathic relation is a personification. The subject of empathy is, rather, a kind of enlarged imaginative soul. In the contemplative condition this soul is united with the aesthetic object in such a way that it seems to reside in the object and no longer in me. Thus while my empathically expanded ego fuses in experience with the uniqueness of the object, the experienced concrete impression also becomes for me an expression of the excited psychic impulse. For, the object forces me into a definite psychic mood. This interrelation of impression and expression is the germ of the aesthetic experience. It fills in the individual dimension which is left free by the cognitive acts directed toward the general. Thus there are, belonging to the foundational being of the aesthetic acts; (1) the purely contemplative, disinterested state of consciousness; (2) the directing of intention to the sensibly concrete picture of the object; (3) the empathic relation with a mentally significant content of the object, based upon the coincidence of impression and expression.[1])

c) Cognitive and aesthetic acts are both of a purely contemplative nature. (*beschaulich*). But there is nothing in reality which has significance only for contemplation. We are a part of nature as physiologically determined beings having definite needs. Everything physical about us makes demands upon our psycho-physical system. The mere question of whether we are able to grasp the field of vision in one act or whether we need continuous optic attention indicates a relation to the energy of the subject. In the above illustration we have, at least as an associated thought, the idea that this mountain range hinders our progress like a wall. The extension which would leave us indifferent if it were in the form of a level plane, for, what is the distance of one kilometre, taken as a dimension of height has a tremendous effect. We 'know' by experience how much physical energy is needed to surmount such an obstacle. And this association mingles to a great extent with the aesthetic experience. There is something overwhelming in such a mass. It does not harm us in reality but nevertheless affects

---

[1]) By object I mean not the cognitively determined object but that which is independent of the self and adheres to the aesthetically significant form.

us like some resistance, as a narrowing pressure of our environment. The sport of mountain-climbing consists in the test of this experiential aspect, which is closely related to the economic attitude. It is not, however, useful but stands in the category of play. Its attraction lies in the overcoming of an obstacle. Everyone who has climbed a high mountain remembers how the mountain is related to him as a real obstacle. The equilibrium of the purely aesthetic relation is only restored again when we have reached the summit. Previous to this moment there is a measuring of energy by which the mountain must be technically overcome and subordinated to the service of our purpose. This aspect of the situation is much more comprehensible when the mountain is regarded from the outset with the eyes of an engineer who wishes to survey the ground for a railroad. In this case the mountain, as an aesthetic object wholly disappears from view and is looked upon only from the standpoint of its resistance and its relation to our needs. But even without this explanation it is clear that from the beginning there is, in the total act, a factor of interested opposition, the experience of an object which has resistance and challenges my will to live. This relation of the object in experience to my economy of strength I call its economic aspect. Economic acts are thus; (1) acts of actual desire or rejection; (2) acts in which the relation of energies to the psycho-physical subject is experienced; (3) acts which are directed toward the maintainance of life and the actualisation of real purposes in physical nature.

d) We have considered the process from the purely objective disinterested attitude of cognition to the fusion of aesthetic feeling and hence to the direct utilitarian evaluation. One might say roughly: the first attitude is dominated by the pure object freed from the ego, in the second attitude we have the imaginative fusion of ego and object and in the third the purely 'material' desirous interest of self. But each one has a value for the individual, in the first case the cognitive value, in the second the aesthetic and in the third the economic. The illustration may also be considered in such a way that in every case a positive value is replaced by a negative one, as in the third relation. If these three experiences are to meet in the same ego they must be related to a total significance or total value. And not only to the total significance of this moment in life, for the mental ego is not of the moment. We must therefore relate the experience with its whole content to the total significance (for the time being) of individual life. And as a matter of fact there is such a factor present in every segment of experience. There is an indication of its significance for the total value of life. And this even without any reflection in purely formless veneration (*Andacht*).[1]) Thus while I cognize the mountain range, allow its form to influence me and measure my system of energy, there also develops in me a transcendent value experience which is more or less closely related to the total value of my life. The meaning of religious experience is this value relation which is necessarily a total experience, since an isolated value cannot be experienced in its relative position. But there are many intellectual mediations and half noticeable experiential accompaniments which take part. A tension develops between the aesthetic and the interested behavior, that is, there is a mixture in the empathic relation of fear and shrinking. Former experiences and cognitions cling to the aesthetic impression and also clarify the aspect of the economy of energy. We know that these mountains existed thousands of years before us and that they will exist thousands of years after we are gone. We think of the change from summer to winter. We remember that these mountains were the background of the former experience of whole epochs in us. Our individual life is conceived mentally as a context of manifold occurrences, and the single experience is subordinated in theoretic reflection. Thus there develops finally, the complexly interwoven total experience, with its hard realism and deep symbolism, an experience of the grandeur of the object and my own insignificance, of my mental struggle against its overwhelming greatness and of its peace and eternity, its isolation and significance of life and goodness which are somehow related to me. All this is religious. In the relation of the experienced value to the total significance of my life there is manifested the religious meaning as contrasted with the theoretic, aesthetic and economic. In the religious acts there are thus; (1) the surrender to the purely mental content of the individual; (2) the comprehension of the individual experience in relation to the total experience; (3) the awareness of the individual value measured according to

---

[1]) Cf. Schleiermacher's definition of religious experience in his *Reden über die Religion*.

its position and significance in the totality of the individual value experience.

The above example dealt with a complex of acts which had reference to a segment of the real world. Otherwise, it was an example chosen at random. We may therefore say once more in general: the surrender to the objectively general creates theoretic significance; the inclination to the character of impression—expression of the sensible phenomenon creates the aesthetic meaning; its measurement with respect to my psycho-physical system of energy and my real purposes in life, the economic significance; and finally the relation of all these single value experiences to the mental total value of the individual life determines the religious content.

In our example we purposely omitted to state which aspect of the total act was emphasized. In the following we shall consider the nature of each class of acts by itself and explain briefly in what sense the others may be said to be included or subordinated. It will be found that every species of act is limited by the others. Each one has its independent function which cannot be replaced by the other. But it can achieve only what is in accordance with its special meaning and cannot replace any of the other acts.

II

1. Cognitive acts.

These acts are directed to the general identical essence of the objects, or more accurately, they intend what reappears as the general essences in concrete phenomena, what logically follows from them and can be reduced to general ideational principles. The keynote everywhere is the translation of the concrete into the ideational, the establishment of mental identical essences and the creation of a context of general essential correlations. It is because of this tendency to the general that cognitive acts are limited by the sensibly concrete, which can be grasped only aesthetically. Their being directed to the purely objective differentiates them from economic acts in which there is always a specific qualitative relation of the object to the subject which is really experienced even though this relation is subsequently formulated in a general law. Cognitive acts are further distinguished from religious acts because they refer to definite things, disregarding everything not identical, and thus cut a definite and limited part out of the infinite data even though this part is then elevated to the realm of eternal Truth. Furthermore, the cognitive acts work out a purely objective order regardless of their biological harm or value to the individual. They are 'free of value' insofar as the part of the subject is reduced to a minimum, namely to the pure cognitive interest and the value of the immanent theoretic law.

This degree of separation of the object from the evaluating experience context is, of course, different in the individual sciences. Wherever science makes value acts and value contexts the subject of objective comprehension there naturally develops a conflict between the inner reproduction of the mental act and the problem of coolly objectifying it. The world of facts makes it easy for us to become what Nietzsche calls a 'cold demon of cognition.'

The most instructive examples of this are found in geometry: which as a science is concerned, for instance, with the general essence of a sphere, and so deduces a wealth of general laws all of which are valid for the sphere as such. This cognition cannot of course be accomplished without contemplation. The concrete picture of the sphere, especially in a definite size and color, has always something aesthetic and pleasing about it. Thus an aesthetic empathic factor re-echoes in the cognitive act. And there also vibrates a delicate religious significance: the socalled completeness of the sphere makes it a natural symbol of the inclusive, the unitary and the harmonious. Thus the sphere has often been used to represent the form of the angels, or as the symbol of God. Finally we cannot wholly exclude the factor of utility and technical significance in such a limited geometrical body, I refer to Froebel who has carried out this line of thought in his individual manner. For, the geometric forms which he develops in his games, he also evaluates as cognitive, aesthetic and 'use' forms. Finally he considers the whole in the same religio-mythical context which we find with the Pythagoreans, with Dionysius Areopagita, Nicolaus Cusanus, Jakob Boehme etc. up to Schelling and Fechner.

There are sciences which closely approach the border of aesthetics. These are the descriptive sciences. Their scientific character is derived from the fact that they aim to comprehend objectivity in general identical essences. But they combine these essences uniquely until they reach a point where they are obliged to use formative artistic imagination. This is true of the descriptive natural sciences which cannot get along without illustrations and collections as well as of history which needs for its representation definite aesthetic imagery.

Furthermore, men have attempted, not without justification, to find an economic tendency in the cognitive acts insofar as they attempt to comprehend the infinite manifoldness of the objects in accordance with the principle of least action (*Prinzip des kleinsten Kraftmasses.*) Thought may be considered as a purposive instrument. One must be careful, however, not to look upon these heterogeneous relations (the economy of thought) as the original essence of cognitive acts themselves.

Finally, we need a more accurate determination of how cognition relates to values and value experiences. Evaluations are a primary function of the mind. They are not created by cognitive acts. Any valuation may be founded upon theoretical cognition, in fact there hardly exists any evaluation wholly without this foundation. On the other hand, the significance of the evaluation may subsequently be uttered in a form of value judgment (as can everything that has a general essence). Only by means of this form is the valuation differentiated from merely blind and transitory affective states. But in neither case is the act of evaluation itself intellectual. In the first case it is intellectually founded, in the second case it is intellectually formulated, i. e. elevated into the realm of thought. But it is a new and unique mental function. It is so too in a third different case, when over and above cognition as such we have a qualitatively unique value which we call the pure cognitive value and which must be distinguished from both the economic and aesthetic evaluations.

It follows from all this that cognition for itself and by its own methods cannot give us a religious conclusion. It is possible of course to think of a science which is concerned with the whole of the purely objective order and attempts to round out the general essences and essential correlations into a total system which we call the world. But this does not tell us anything about the value of this total science for the total experience of the mental individuality. The valuating relation of the cognized object to the experiencing subject enters into this as a new act of giving meaning. This act then is of course theoretically founded. Now if this unique (religious) experience is again theoretically formulated we have a reflected religiosity. But reflection has not created the religious act. It has grasped only a general essence and moulded it into the form of a judgment. Therefore the cognitive acts find their limit in the religious acts. They may help to found them or formulate them but they cannot create religious meaning. This, on the contrary, has an entirely independent meaning compared to cognition. To summarize: cognition finds its limits in the aesthetic, the economic and the religious. Beyond this limit there takes place a $\mu\varepsilon\tau\acute{\alpha}\beta\alpha\sigma\iota\varsigma$ $\varepsilon\grave{\iota}\varsigma$ $\ddot{\alpha}\lambda\lambda o$ $\gamma\acute{\varepsilon}\nu o\varsigma$.

2. Aesthetic acts.

They are primarily directed to that which cannot be completely grasped intellectually, namely the sensible concrete, the form of things. Neither in nature nor in art is there anything of aesthetic importance which is solely composed of general essences. There must, on the contrary, be present in each case a single phenomenon either real or created in imagination with which we can mentally fuse ourselves, so that its impression on us becomes our expression. This means that from the simplest rhythm to the highest feelings of significance our psychic impulses fuse with the data[1]) and seem to radiate through them.

This, however, does not mean that other acts which endow with meaning might not possibly stay in a subservient relation to the primary act. Cognitive acts are usually present and sometimes in such a way that they vibrate like inaudible overtones. In every painting there is a mathematical factor even if it is only the symmetry of the frame. Every sculpture, besides mathematical symmetry, partially embodies laws of statics and dynamics. In many cases a work of art must first be intellectually interpreted before it can affect us. The spatial interpretation of patches of color and the cognition of what is intended belong in this category. The main thing is always the sensible phenomenon; but the work of art as a whole is then a secondary and often a tertiary aesthetic form. I might refer to Piglhein's painting of the blind lady walking through a field of red poppy flowers. Without the general judgment

---

[1]) I avoid the expression 'object' because we grasp the pure object only in the theoretic attitude. In the aesthetic attitude there are two fused factors of which the objective one is often not accurately interpreted theoretically.

that blind people have no experience of color vision, the concatenation of colors and forms remains meaningless. But this general judgment plays here only a subservient role for a totally different final relation to the objective data. If it comes explicitly into consciousness it destroys the specifically aesthetic. For this reason, too many intellectual preliminary conditions are dangerous for a purely aesthetic attitude. Instead of allowing the picture to influence them, many do not get beyond the material, that is, questions of cognition. It is for this reason that music approaches more closely than any other art the pure artistic ideal. But even here a solely theoretic factor is present. For even the making of tones in music is based on rational principles, and Leibniz quite justifiably called music an unconscious mathematical activity. At least there is in all music a rational division of time which is based on the principles of identity and equality. And the recognition of identical tonal sequences also plays a role in the enjoyment of music. As soon as one begins to pay attention to this one studies music instead of experiencing it. In poetry the rhythm and sound of words is an incentive to the hearer to create optic imagery and in order to do this he must first have understanding and insight. Non-imaginative people find thus in poetry only description and instruction or at the most verbal representation, especially if they are more ear-minded than eye-minded and so miss the specifically poetical element. But aesthetics only begin after the theoretic attitude is subordinated so that we no longer aim at the general concept as an end in itself but that it appears only in the particular.

The economic factor participates in the aesthetic acts in a similar manner as in the theoretic acts. Whatever tires or even puts a strain on the psycho-physical organism of the subject can no longer have any aesthetic importance for him. All aesthetic impressions are therefore partially determined by psycho-physical laws. On the other hand that which is aesthetically significant must not be considered synonymous with the useful or the harmful; nor can it enter into direct relation with our physical desires, otherwise the disinterested condition of contemplation, which is alone aesthetic cannot develop. Therefore one best reaches the purely aesthetic (in contrast to practical beauty which is partly included in the region of economics) if the aesthetic picture is isolated from the context of real forces and translated into an imaginative objectivity. This is the real reason for 'imitation' which, for the aesthetics of antiquity was the main factor of art. The joy of imitating (for we do not imitate the rough object but the impression) is not the motive of art. Rather, a kind of relative separation from the material takes place so that the object is withdrawn from the sphere of desire. Among the materials which are needed to produce purely aesthetic creations we prefer those which have the highest aesthetic value (marble, gold, fullness of sound, rhythm.) Even man, the greatest form of beauty, is only beautiful when he is no longer physically desired. (Marble statues can of course only give a faint reflection of the beauty of a soul). Even the experience of utility may become aesthetically significant in this withdrawal from reality, namely as mere re-echoing and harmoniously vibrating experience. It has been lifted from the material realm into the zone of purely spiritual enjoyment. Still-lifes, scenes of work, and studies of tools belong in this context.

If one says that all artistic creation is rooted in experience, one must add for the sake of accuracy that it is rooted only in aesthetic experience. A rose may influence my soul so strongly that I reproduce its impression transformed into other material as expression. In this artistic form then there lies only the joy of just this single colored form. But in the soul's structure aesthetic experience is never isolated. It might adhere to pictures and occurrences of the most vital significance so that the individual picture gives a flash of the total meaning of life. Then the aesthetic experience becomes also religious. And the creation which is born out of this circumstance, no matter how limited is the object to which it refers, is suffused with a universal impulse. It approaches the *Weltanschauungskunst*. But insofar as it claims to be art the religious factor must be subordinated. It cannot and must not reproduce this pregnant meaning otherwise than in a sensible concrete form. Cognitions and total relations of values finally meet in psychic fusion by means of which the impression of this form is capable of expressing our final meaning. If we remain in pure reverence or dogmatic description of the pious state of mind, we are no longer in the realm of the specifically aesthetic meaning. On the other hand, the shortest poem may fix for us something of religious infinity. And it does not need lofty pictures or logical argument. All can be expressed in a very few words:

„Der du von dem Himmel bist,
Alles Leid und Schmerzen stillest....."[1])

To summarize: the independence of the aesthetic realm is manifested by the fact that it is limited by the theoretic, the economic and the religious. All these attitudes have their part in it but the aesthetic cannot be replaced by them, they cannot express its unique essence. Rather, the other meaning contexts are translated into the aesthetic by the fact that they are transferred to the sphere of creative imagination, of pure contemplation and the relation of impression—expression. This fact is at the basis of specific aesthetic experience which must not be confused with religious experience. As soon as a socalled work of art is principally intended as a theoretic object lesson, a religious confession or a useful object it has lost its unique significance.

3. Economic acts.

In economic mental acts we acknowledge or found a relation of usefulness between object and subject. The useful, as whatever serves to maintain and increase life is always related to the psychophysical structure of the subject. Now, since the objects of economic behavior are always of a physical nature, namely masses and forces which belong to the socalled world of nature, and since they are related to the physical side of a subject, (which science also comprehends physically, chemically and physiologically) we might infer that we are not dealing here with a mental region at all but with the natural aspect of life. It is true that the substrata of economic evaluation are always physical and that the effects of these goods are also physical. And yet, insofar as they can be evaluated, they are placed in a context of meaning. Under certain conditions, natural objects and forces have the qualitatively unique value called economic value. And so, under the organising influence of this value there develops a purpose system of unique structure: economics. Everything that is systematically related to a value context has meaning. Therefore economic behavior has a mental aspect, even though its means, methods and objects of value are physical. We shall not at present mention the ethical rank of this value region.

---

[1]) Thou, who in the heaven art
Every pain and sorrow stillest ..
Longfellow's translation of Goethe.

If now we reduce this region to its primary structure we find, in every case, a comparison of energy between subject and object. Even prior to scientific reflection we feel, by virtue of our psychophysical organisation that material objects are either pleasant or unpleasant. These experiential qualities are mediated by the various sense organs: from the most diffuse external pressure which contains the original experience of our limit of energy to the biologically important smell and taste processes, we find these new relations between the subject and the objective data. We carry part of them as inherited pre-formations of our psycho-physical system in the form of instincts. There is no need of intellectual mediation because the agreeableness of the object is immediately given through our feeling regulator, not to be confused with our aesthetic feelings. Thus the economic is fundamentally rooted in the biological. Later we shall have occasion to expand the concept of the economic beyond the region of self preservation and physical adaptation.

But the other meaning contexts may be subordinated to this dominant meaning: the achievements of cognition partially serve the apparatus of self-preservation, and the result is far-seeing provision, scientific investigation of useful qualities as well as of the physiological conditions of life and the rationalisation of the whole process of self-preservation. The useful is differentiated from the merely pleasant, the harmful from the unpleasant. But needs and desires and finally satisfaction of drives remain to the end the outstanding factors of this subject-object relation. For science as such neither creates needs nor makes anything useful (equal to means of satisfying needs) except what was correlated with a need from the outset. Here, as in the religious field, science does not create value but rather occasionally founds values or subsequently formulates them (see above). The relations of utility are inexhaustible intellectually. Insight only acquaints us with the systematic context of the world of goods by means of which new utilities might appear to the subject. One can also formulate the relations of utility as general insights. But the relation of utility (satisfaction of need) as such is not insight but an experience *sui generis*.

In economic experiences aesthetic factors are interwoven. It would appear that even on the biological level there is present an inner connection. Some fruits are aesthetically pleasant and the sexual characteristics also are often aesthetically emphasized.

And yet the significance of the aesthetic is only a subservient one, a preliminary lure as it were. For, in real sensual enjoyment and use the aesthetic is immediately destroyed. The beauty of a strawberry which adheres to it concretely in form, color and aroma, is destroyed the moment I eat it. In this sense also the difference of the two regions is shown. Beauty may be unreal and be created purely by the imagination for the imagination, while the useful is necessarily real, and as we saw must be included in the physical context.

The experience of utility (satisfaction of need) may also have a religious side. When its specific and limited value content is related to the total value of life the economic appears in that religious light which is indicated by the expression „Give us this day our daily bread". Whatever serves the mere preservation of life is the more closely related to the religious significance the more life is endangered. Indicative of this is the formless feeling of gratitude that we have when we really enjoy. But religion can never be wholly exhausted in the economic context, because the latter adheres to the physical and is distributed over temporally disparate and constantly repeated individual experiences. From this alone we cannot derive the meaning of life. Even though the economic is an important preliminary condition for the mere fact of life, it does not fully exhaust life's content. But it does give the freedom from environmental pressure which is a necessary condition of all higher intellectual achievements.

4. Religious acts.

Their essence is found in the relation of the value of any isolated experience to the total value of the individual life. Whatever is for us the total value of life may also be called the highest value. For that only is finally valuable which endows all of life with value.[1]) Whatever possesses this force is at the same time my highest value or conversely: let us assume that an experience (whether unique or capable of repetition) signifies for the experiencer the 'highest moment' then the content of this moment would radiate over the whole of the rest of his life and everything else would only be finally significant for his life in proportion as it approaches

---

[1]) Our highest moments will put us under greatest obligation. (Nietzsche.)

or contributes to this ultimate source of happiness. Characters perhaps are differentiated by the fact that to some this highest content of life comes like a momentary flash, while others possess it in a uniform attitude toward life and gradually increase it. The final meaning of life is, of course, never wholly attainable since man, because of the changing content of time and the rising tide of fate, is constantly immersed in new value experiences. What is commonly called happiness is often only the affection of the moment or the onesided satisfaction of life. Superior to this there is a blessedness which warrants the highest, most comprehensive and eternal satisfaction of the soul. The road to this goal is the object of religious striving. The partly meaningful and partly foreign structure confronting us we call 'world', whenever it as a total opposes the structure of our soul. And the final content, or the last meaning endowing principle of the world which *reveals* to us the highest value experience we call in religious language, God. With this religious factor as a subject we can therefore best study the essence of religious acts.

For the highest experiential value may be found in the negation of all other values as partial, finite or subordinate. Then religious behavior rejects cognition since God, as a mere theoretical concept is not sufficient. It also rejects the aesthetic attitude since a picture in its concrete limitation can never be the expression of the last experiential content. And finally, it rejects economic evaluation since earthly goods cannot even be preliminary steps to spiritual values. Religious acts of this world-rejecting attitude lead to transcendental (formless) mysticism. But there is also a religious attitude of a totally different nature. The highest knowledge, the highest pictorial expression, the greatest finite enjoyment of life and its pleasures found, in their interrelated and combined effort, the religious attitude and behavior. This is immanent (formgiving) mysticism. The symbols: all cognisance, all beauty and omniscience of God indicate these sources of religious experience. The mysticism which renounces this world seeks a special path to the revelation of the highest value. The latter seeks only to fulfill the valuable paths of the other meaning attitudes to the final goal. As a matter of fact no religious act can wholly dispense with the subordinate meaningful acts and moreover there is a double relation between them and the religious acts.

The other acts formerly created meaningful structures of a limited nature which are now part of the total meaning form as all partial structures group themselves into the total structure of the individual mind. Whatever we have cognized of this world is (regardless of its pure cognitive value) also placed in a relation to the religious value. Whatever we have received from the world in the form of goods which further the preservation of life seems to point from the religious standpoint to a higher teleological context, perhaps to a sort of providence. And whatever we have grasped of the beauty and grandeur of this world becomes an occasion for us to view the whole colorful, sounding and formed world as a veil, a 'mantle of God' who shines through everything.

Secondly these significations are invoked when we endeavor subsequently to form objectively whatever is contained in the pious reverent condition of the soul in such a manner that we can communicate it. Under no condition must this function be confused with the first. The latter symbolises, the former founds the religious experience. The symbolising function of cognition is made up of the effort to pronounce the sacred experiences in general laws. But these laws are no longer cosmologically but psychologically interpretive. They deal with a religiously affected soul, not with a purely objective world context. The symbolising function of the aesthetic is found in the 'expression' of the religious experience. It is put in a picture, sound or word so that others may empathize it. Finally there is a sort of economy of religious experience, a technique and conduct of life in order to produce the religious blessedness. In connection with the aesthetic factor there develops a cult just as from the theoretic factor (insofar as it formulates the religious experience) there is created that dogma which does not pretend to be knowledge of the world but only a mythical symbolisation of a religious evaluation of life.

Even transcendental mysticism cannot do without such forms of expression since the religious experience as an inner essence has no objective form of its own. No matter then whether one looks upon the subordinated meaning context in a positive, negative or a combined point of view, they are always the starting point and source of religious excitation which collects its rays in a final and highest point called in religious language simply 'the soul.' And we may say then: everything is of a religious importance whether or not in actual experience it closely approaches the religious center. Everything relates to this religious center, even the stone at my feet. The unity of value experience is reflected in the all embracing religious value emphasis (*Wertbetonung*). Finally everything deserves respect or condemnation because it is a part of the total value context of life.

But this is the place to call attention to the fact that the same is true of the other meaning contexts. Every form is aesthetically significant whether it be in the real or the imaginative zone. The grey of a ruined wall is as much an aesthetic experience as the red of a full blown rose. For both have the character of impression-expression. Likewise everything may become the object of general identification, differentiation and essential correlations. The theoretic acts may also grasp any conscious content. As for instance this study, which is directed to the total of the meaning contexts seeks only to grasp in them identities, differences and identical contexts of plastic life. In the last analysis, everything, even the non-physical may be significant for the immediate economic value context. For, everything is for the psycho-physical state of my materially determined self either advantageous or harmful, furthering or hindering. Nothing is of economic indifference, just as nothing is of theoretic or aesthetic indifference or of indifference to value at all. If, however, in these partial values and in the partial significance of life, everything can have its place, then even more in the final meaning everything must harmonize together just as melodies and phrases interweave to make a symphony. And the great leitmotif of life's symphony is the experience: πάντα θεῖα.

# 4
MENTAL ACTS OF SOLIDARITY

The acts which we have so far studied may have all their essential characteristics without social reciprocity of any sort. They merely add, to the subjective experiential context, objective configurations which in themselves experience nothing and are the subjects neither of acts nor experiences. It is possible, however, for the cognitive, aesthetic, economic and religious attitudes to have reference to objects which are in themselves the subjects of acts (i. e. persons). The change which then occurs in the regions of meaning is that the interpretation of foreign experiential contexts becomes a fundamental factor. The life of a second subject can only be understood through the significant interpretation of the mental acts which he accomplishes in his individual situation. Only after one has entered into an empathic relation with his mental process (a relation which need not necessarily be cognitive) can one enjoy him as a psycho-aesthetical phenomenon. If his economic acts, his 'work', is favorable to our system of economic purposes he is experienced as useful. And finally if his mental and bodily life is related to the ultimate meaning of our life he becomes the object of religious experience.

Whether these interpretative acts are to be classed only in the cognitive region, or whether they also belong in each case to the mental world to whose meaning they are empathically related is a question which requires further investigation. But however we answer it the problem is very closely related to that of value judgments in the *Geisteswissenschaften*. At any rate we have here nothing new, and are instead still concerned with the four meaning giving acts which we have previously considered.

Omitting for the moment the peculiarities of the interpretative acts which are required when persons become the object of theoretic, aesthetic, economic and religious acts, we might say: even

Robinson Crusoe could develop in these directions. There is nothing posited which requires for its meaningful completion a second experiential subject. True, these acts would be very primitive if they had no socio-reciprocal action or historical summation. But their essence and fundamental content is the same. There are however, without doubt some mental acts and experiences which are possible only in a social context. Robinson Crusoe, especially if we separate him from his animals, could not have political, juristic, social or pedagogical experiences. Let us investigate more closely the social phenomena of mental life. The first question which confronts us is whether there are independent mental acts which are essentially different from the four basic mental attitudes and which correspond to the phenomenon of society.

The methodological difficulty which is found in all investigations of society is that society is an overindividual context of effects into which the individual is born. Without this context we cannot imagine any individual. It determines from the very beginning every individual's whole mental structure. And through it he shares in the unique level of mind which in each case is the result of the historical developmental process. In contrast with this, however, we must emphasize that the experiential context of the individual who is a part of any society can be the only place in which society can be experienced or its meaning actualized. It is true that one may consider the social groups as overindividual entities which act in space and time as vitalized masses, but even then one understands them in the cognitive scheme of mental individualities. The individual mental structure is our only cognitive means of understanding mental configurations, and for this reason the complexly interwoven inner structure of sociological formations is for ever beyond our cognition and understanding.

This limitation of our cognitive means, which is as a rule not sufficiently observed, is however of no importance for the psychology of individuality. On the contrary, our interest in this investigation is directed to those bonds which unite one individual soul to another and thus to the truly experiential foundations of the social relations. The new and unique reflexes which the latter, as overindividual formations, are capable of eliciting in the individual experience will not be considered in this study.

If we wished to answer the above question in a purely analytical manner we should have to assume for every objective (overindividual) form of society a corresponding individual form of experience. Individualized family experiences would correspond to the family, experiences of friendship to friendship, experiences of a shareholder to the stockcompany etc. One might perhaps start off with the main classes of objective social forms, but that would not solve the question of the point of view from which one should classify these experiences. The psychological point of view, the basic forms of social experience are exactly what we are looking for and thus cannot serve as the starting point. Another difficulty with this procedure is that we might thus take into account historical peculiarities rather than really foundational phenomena. Assuming for instance, that one reduces the historically given cultural system of the state to political basic acts, the legal system to law and the many extra-state and extra-legal forms of society to specifically „social" acts one cannot derive in this way the borderline between state and society. Some people consider the objective state only as a special form of society; and think that the forces at work in it are the same as in any other kind of „socialisation" (*Vergesellschaftung*). Others, influenced by the fact that the state wields the highest social power within a sectional region (sovereignty) and that the state alone fixes the laws (as it also moulds itself in these forms), separate the state from the totality of the other associations and oppose it to society in a narrower sense.

Obviously we are dealing in such cases with complicated historical levels, the peculiarities of which are easily taken over into an analytical procedure. If we wish to grasp the fundamental social acts we should instead proceed synthetically and ask which simple attitudes of association are possible within a group of human beings, whether of two or of thousands. Thus we do not attempt a classification of empirical forms of society but a differentiation on the basis of social psychology. And temporarily disregarding any purpose of society we wish to emphasize those unique meaningful acts in which the consciousness of union builds itself up.

Every form of society (we repeat here the method used in the foregoing chapter) rests, in the consciousness of its members, on two interwoven mental acts, either of which may be dominant.

Human beings are united by means of acts of power or sympathy, by subordination or coordination. They confront each other on an equal basis or are gradated. Every one knows that we are dealing with two dimensions when we mention the two corresponding act directions of the subjects: the first limited by the extremes of domination and dependency, the second by love and hate. One act direction, if isolated, would result in a social power system (which would not at all correspond to the state), the other in a system of community. I may be united with others by relations of power or by bonds of sympathy. Acts of dominance and sympathy seem then to designate the fundamental meaning tendencies in the social realm. Corresponding receptive sets are the experiences of subjection and of sympathy.[1])

According to our fundamental hypothesis both components are present in every social act: the consciousness of union by means of value community or contrast, and through superiority of one's own value direction, or through its dependence upon another person's value direction. Relations of domination cannot be thought of without simultaneous relations of community and in these there are again present factors both of superordination and subordination, regardless of whether these meaning relations are permanently or only temporarily actualized in the consciousness of the participants. Soon, however, the act of domination may become predominant,

---

[1]) By acts of sympathy I mean here mental acts which are directed to the essential value or the mentally dominant value direction of another being; they thus determine, at least on one side, a consciousness of identical intention and of unity. We do not refer here to the sphere of passing association through emotion (feeling of equality, compassion, suggestion). The truly mental acts of sympathy are differentiated from each other by the depth, extent and duration of the intention toward the other. And this differentiation depends again upon the depth and content of the value 'for the sake of which' one sympathizes with the other. A love founded on religion according to depth, extent and duration would be the highest, on the other hand sympathy in regard to external economic purposes would be comparitively low, no matter whether it appears in the form of solidarity, of mutualism or the more valuable form of altruism. As a midpoint we might choose the aesthetic-erotic empathy which Scheler in his important and learned *Wesen und Formen der Sympathie* Bonn 1923 (2) designates as the vital feeling of oneness (*vitale Einsfuehlung*). But a comprehensive comparison with Scheler's presentation at this point would go beyond the limits of this study.

then the 'social' act[1]) becomes subservient; or if the 'social' act is decisive then the superiority of the one subserves the still deeper sympathetic relationship and vice versa. In a social context one may feel oneself either as leader or follower; but in leadership there is an unescapable factor of comradeship, and comradeship has many subtle gradations.

The problem, however, is more complicated than has as yet appeared. We said above that we judge the independence of mental acts by the question of whether there is a corresponding specific region of value in the structural context of the soul. Do power and sympathy actually found unique classes of value? One might object that we are here dealing only with sociological forms of alternate relation or cooperation (*Wechselwirkungs- oder Zusammenwirkungsformen*) in which the previously disclosed value tendencies are actualized. And indeed power and sympathy cannot be thought of as independent of definite value contents. One might say that power signifies the superiority of the personal value content and value striving over a foreign value system, so that the influence of superiority initiates in others definite and lasting motives of behavior. This result, however, is possible only insofar as the other person affirms, even if only indirectly, the superior value direction. Thus finally the factor of community is here present also. But the unique side of this relation of superordination lies in the fact that the superior person has realized for and in himself a group of values which places the other in a relation of inner dependency. Power is therefore always an actual superiority which can be understood only by means of the value content of the powerful subject and is consequently based throughout upon this content. Power can only be thought of as superiority of actual knowledge, or of technical means (hence derives the relation of property) or of capacity to express oneself aesthetically and thus influence people strongly (power of oratory for instance) or of religious conviction (enthusiasm i. e. charismatic power).

And similarly with sympathy: sympathy, one might say, is a turning toward the other due to a community of interests and a striving for the same values. We love another person as a carrier of value or because he posits or searches for value. This factor

---
[1] I use the expression 'social' in what follows in a different sense rom the popular usage as meaning 'based upon sympathy'.

also presupposes something empirical for we cannot deduce *a priori* whether the other actualizes a value direction in himself or at least strives to do so. The abstract kinds of sympathy necessarily coincide with the value regions which were previously deduced. If we are dealing with a community of cognitive values then the bond is one of equality of convictions, of theoretic investigation. If we look upon another person as the subject of technico-economical values then the act of sympathy is founded in an economic community. We call the aesthetic form of this psychic harmony, eroticism. All the constituent factors of the aesthetic process recur in it, primarily directed to the sensible concrete impression of the other and are comprehended as the expression of a psychic content. Aesthetic empathy here forms the basis of and gives color to the sympathetic act. And finally we have the religious love which is totally independent of external appearance. It is directed to the other simply as the carrier of religious values i. e. the values upon which the total significance of life is founded. Here all varieties of form are possible, from the love which is directed to the developed divinity of the other (his revelational character) to the love which turns to the other's wholly hidden divinity. This last attitude is merely the feeling for the sanctity of life itself which may, in certain cases, include all animal and plant life.

This survey must be completed by two further forms. On the side of power we have also a power of love; i. e. to the personal value form which may determine the value system of the other individual there belongs also the spirit of love. And conversely, on the side of love we have a love for power i. e. an upward looking toward the mental power and spiritual greatness of another. Both powers, the power of love and the love for power are the supporting arches of the patriarchal form of society.

On the other hand it is just this sympathetic interest in others which is peculiar to all 'social' mental acts that is an independent factor. It is of course true that power and love appear at first to be only forms in which the above mentioned individual mental acts are realized between human beings. But it is also possible to experience these forms as mental (secondary) values. The inner power, the heroic quality, the mental force quite regardless in which of the five regions it is actually expressed, indicates a characteristic feature which may be experienced as a value both by the carrier himself and by others. The field of power in its formal expression also belongs to the mental value region. And on the other hand: the mental set to act sympathetically, regardless in which of the value regions it is actually expressed, is, as a purely formal tendency, valuable for whoever possesses or experiences it. The organising power which controls values and the socialising value-uniting inclination are secondary value regions. For these we shall coin two technical expressions derived from their forms of actualisation: *political and 'social' values. It is important, however, constantly to keep in mind the inclusive significance of these expressions.* We shall see in the second part that these values may also dominate the soul's structure. We shall find natures political to such a degree that their classification in the class of the theoretic or aesthetic, the economic or religious types is really only secondary. In the same manner we shall find 'social' natures which are so wholly without specific reference to the beauty or wisdom, the efficiency or holiness of the other person. We must not forget, however, that the two sociological types always tend toward one of the four primary value directions and so to speak carry their color. We shall see furthermore that through the predominance of either one of the 'social' acts the adjustment to the other value directions will undergo a peculiar transformation.

This classification is capable of still finer analysis. And in this situation we find expressed the fact that life itself, even previous to any differentiation into particular value regions, has value. The mere feeling of power regardless of which end it subserves contains an affirmation of individuation. And in this fact we find, from a purely biological standpoint, the germ of political acts: one wants to affirm one's own set of values as opposed to the evaluations of another, one feels the energy of one's own value life. Ethically this attitude toward life can work for evil as well as for good, but with this we are not concerned here. It must suffice that to affirm one's own value system as opposed to any other has a meaning. Our sympathy, similarly, is directed merely to life itself if we disregard for a moment the peculiar value content which one finds in the other life or which one wants to assist. It is a turning of one's own life toward the soul of another as a unique mental life. One feels an obligation to the other life because it is the germ of life itself. Here also the ethical point of view is at first wholly neglected. To further the life of another merely from regard for the genuine latent value possibilities which it contains also has its proper significance. Whether love always 'knows' just where these genuine values lie is another question.

Because power and love are closely bound up together previous to any value set whatever, it appears that these metaphysical primary forces must already exist in the sphere of the isolated soul. If we regard the manifold and partially opposing value tendencies as a sort of society we may speak even here of love and power. The self, as the unitary center of experience, strives then to bring the central value direction into a dominant position over the others, and the one which embodies the true life is sympathetically regarded. We assume that the genuine and objectively highest value is preferred to all others in the alternative experience of our inner life, even though the normative (ethical) point of view will not be considered until later. I first experience this genuine value as something foreign which has power over me, as if it were a demand. And if I affirm this value and this idea I love it and, so to speak, commune with it. Thus sympathy is primarily directed to value and only indirectly to man insofar as he is a carrier of value, posits values or contains any value possibilities whatever. Furthermore: there is a constant conflict in my consciousness between different value tendencies. An expenditure of energy is necessary to maintain the value direction which (for my ethical consciousness) is highest. With this value I control the rest of my being. If I succeed in keeping myself free from the demands of other values which I cannot affirm in my innermost heart, I have inner or moral freedom. In other words, the germ of the political experience lies within me and self control is an absolute condition of all genuine power over others. Inner freedom is the prototype of all liberty from external and heteronomous influences. In the mental sense, I do not become free by rejecting the higher evaluations of others, but by making them the dominant value forces of my own being. All energy must first be energy of one's own value life before it can become the energy of external deeds. This explains the frequently mistaken dialectic of politics. In the next chapter we shall again refer to this when we see that to all exercise of power (self control and the control of others) the lawfulness or consistency of the will is essential. Anything which is only temporarily willed is contrary to the law of genuine political influence. Not arbitrariness but only consistently directed willing, in which one value direction as opposed to all others is constantly affirmed, constitutes true power.

But in spite of this it is very important for the theory of mental life to realize that the values dealt with in this chapter are social values; that is, the acts of domination and of sympathy receive for our discussion their distinguishing characteristic by the fact that they are directed to the experiential context of others (meaning those who intend values). The energetic man and the man who surrenders himself to value have their significance as special types only when their energy expresses itself in a sociological context, and when their devotion is dedicated to another life or a social whole. Only where this is the case are all primary mental acts so transformed that two new types develop though they may depend, to a very great degree upon the four first mental types. Political acts and acts of sympathy in the objective mental context are attitudes directed toward *others,* quite regardless of the medium by which one rules or for what reason one loves.

5
THE ELEMENTARY MENTAL LAWS

The forms of meaning-giving acts of which we have spoken up to this point are fundamentally nothing more than relations to life or subject-object relations. It is of course true that in every one of these different forms the terms subject and object have different meanings, and it is unfortunate that science must subject all other forms to the theoretic division between the center of experience and the pure objectivity, as a sort of normal form. In every one of these relations toward life there is an immanent tendency which subserves a specific achievement. But this meaning is not always completely realized. So far our analysis has been directed to the actual structure of the soul and its differentiations. We have disclosed the meaning which is found in the individual acts and is often only vaguely experienced and quickly forgotten. If, however, in every mental attitude a definite class of values is actualized, our study may take a normative turn and attempt to disclose from each particular value the law which it prescribes for the formation of its own mental region. Mental laws are never mere laws of process (*Ablaufsgesetze*) but since the mind has a teleological structure, they are also normative. Mental achievements are not merely described but measured in relation to objective values or ideas. Such normative laws are present even in the naive unconscious and unrelated form of experience. But they become more pronounced as soon as the specific mental direction is consciously and actively sought by the subject and is formed into a coherent configuration with a unitary meaning. Then the previously complexly interwoven mental acts are so finely differentiated that the peculiar law of every specific mental achievement appears clearly and can be formulated.[1]

---

[1] In this and the following section we shall deal principally with the normativity of partial structures. The normativity of the total structure is the subject matter of the third part.

Each one of the spheres of interest which we have previously treated has such a normative law. Only when the sphere is developed in accordance with this law does it satisfy its idea and have inner coherence. Of course, there are more frequent deviations from these differentiated laws as long as the mind acts as an indissoluble totality. Nor can one understand the total significance of the mind until one has brought clearly into one's consciousness the onesided tendencies into which it is differentiated. We shall see that the normative law of economics is based on the principle of least action (*Prinzip des kleinsten Kraftmasses*), that of the aesthetic region on the principle of form, and that of science on the principle of adequate reason. The law of the political sphere lies in the will to law or consistency, and the social law in the idea of loyalty. Finally the normative law of religious behavior is found in the total norm of life which we usually call morality. In all these mental laws especially if they are formulated there is of course a theoretical factor. But the rational guiding rules are no more clearly in consciousness than are the individual mental regions. On the contrary it is their peculiarity that they also are unconsciously present in the mind, as it were, instinctive. To this kind of lawfulness which need not necessarily become conscious as a guide to behavior but is active as a sort of immanent driving force I shall give the name of instinctive rationality (*eingehüllte Rationalität*).

We shall derive the individual mental norms by isolating the meaning of the temporarily dominant value and regarding it as being developed to its ultimate consequence and the maximum of its realization.

1. The economic sphere has its origin in the instinctive forms of self-preservation found in primitive man who takes his food when and where he finds it, who changes his shelter as chance directs and owns nothing but what his physical strength can master. Even on this level we have experiences of utility or harmfulness and simple experiences of technical purposiveness. But the real meaning of the economic sphere appears only when the active will to acquire food, shelter and clothing transforms the chance conditions of economic goods. Beside the arbitrary consumption, the transformation and manufacture of goods and tools for production now enters in. There is then, perhaps wholly unconscious, in all

of this economic work an immanent law in operation which founds the unique sphere of meaning of economics as a part of culture over and above the purely biological play of impulses and instincts, needs and their satisfaction. Insofar as this law emphasizes the meaning of economics and the genuine economic values it is not merely a simple law of actual mental behavior but a normative law which, even though it is not explicit in consciousness or definitely formulated, regulates the tendency of economic occurrences under an ultimate and general economic point of view. It acts, then, in the economic behavior of individuals as a norm.

We must expressly emphasize here, with regard also to the other mental regions, that such normative laws of meaning do not achieve their effect because the agent consciously formulates them as general theoretic rules. To the contrary, just as nature does not follow its laws as conscious precepts, so also these normative laws of mental life are not always present in consciousness as theoretically formulated laws. The formulated law is only deduced from the reality of the purely abstractly considered region and brought to consciousness afterwards. Such laws are always the result of an isolating and idealising mental process. The procedure is isolating in so far as all determinating factors which come from other mental regions are excluded, and idealising insofar as the specific value-character of the sphere in question is regarded as the single organising principle in every individual process.

The economic region is the simplest illustration of our theory. And our procedure has been repeatedly applied, notably in the brilliant and logical treatise of Freiherr von Wieser *The Theory of Social Economics*.[1]) The essence of economic values is found in the fact that they subserve the preservation of life, its comfortable maintainance and all necessary adaptations which depend upon natural means, physical forces and goods. These values are present, as an elementary world of goods, even for biological instinctive behavior. But only through the regulation of acquisition and use do they become expressly economic goods. We ascribe to them a specific value of utility since we designate as 'useful' whatever subserves the maintainance of life. Later we shall develop a more inclusive meaning of the term. In the total economic behavior of each individual (which for the sake of greater simplicity

---

[1]) Grundriss der Sozialoekonomik, Abt. 1. Tuebingen 1914.

we shall take as a starting point) many heterogeneous factors play a part, such as his intelligence, the accepted positive laws of property, his aesthetic leanings and religious and general moral evaluations. But all of this cannot make up the specific economic law, which can only be determined if one isolates the economic acts and works out their specific significance. If this procedure has been carried out as far as is possible in a 'mental experiment', then there is no doubt but that the idea which controls all the economic behavior of the individual as well as of society is that of the maximum of utility. We must exclude all ethical standards regarding the rank of this idea, this current value. It must suffice that we have here a normative law of pure economics. One can expand this conception a little more by starting from the idea of economic work. This is always connected with a waste of physical power and also of economic goods, such as raw materials, tools etc., which are necessarily used up in the manufacturing process. Thus the dominant principle in economic activity is that of the relative maximum of utility or the norm: to achieve the greatest amount of utility with the least expenditure of energy. Liefmann has formulated the economic principle too rationally when he says: 'Economics means a comparison of utility and costs.'[1]) For, the principle of least action is also found, unformulated and unreflected, in the 'immanent logic' of economic behavior itself. If I approach a goal in a straight line (or at least in the most direct line possible) I unconsciously behave economically. I save time and energy as goods of great importance to life. This unformulated logic of any mental sphere we called its instinctive rationality.

    Thus we have emphasized the dominant and normative law of economics. As soon as it is thought of as the formative law of the entire region all other basic economic laws may be formulated as laws of actual psychical behavior. An example of this is Gossen's *law of the satisfaction of need*, the *law of final utility* and the *law of the formation of price*. But one must not forget that they are valid only if the principle of pure economics (the maximum of general utility) is pre-supposed. They only hold true for pure economics just as the laws of gravity are intended for a vacuum which does not exist anywhere. In the case of medical

---

[1]) Robert Liefmann, *Grundsätze der Volkswirtschaftslehre*, Vol. I. (Grundlegung), Stuttgart 1917, p. 288 and elsewhere.

advice to increase weight for physical reasons, the law of *the satisfaction of need* is invalid. The *law of final utility* is invalid unless we pre-suppose, as the highest single aim of conduct, the will to preserve physical existence. In the same manner the law of the formation of price is invalid if a collector finds himself in the uneconomic frame of mind, 'at any price'.

In an analogous manner we must now formulate the laws of the other cultural spheres.

2. Aesthetic behavior, just like the striving for self-preservation, has its place in the primitive attitudes of life which are forcing themselves on consciousness. We have seen that every simple form, every color, every note, every rhythm has its primarily aesthetic value insofar as it occasions a psychic impulse which one empathically sees into the given object. Imagination, in the widest sense of the word, is the term which we shall give to this kind of perception which, contrary to the theoretical attitude finds immediate psychic qualities, such as feelings, moods and impulses in the data themselves. Imagination may be active even in real objects, that is, objects which are independent of ideational production. We always endow reality unconsciously with an aesthetic meaning, whatsoever other meanings we may attribute to it. But this kind of immediate experience is intermingled with heterogeneous attitudes. Reality awakens my desire, urges me to study, and is often overpowering, formless, oppressive and far too meaningless. Thus from the aesthetic experience there develops the desire to purely elaborate its content in productive creation.[1]) The aesthetically significant experience of reality is thus the first unconscious impulse to every intentional art. Art, as free and productive aesthetic activity has the possibility of emphasizing the isolated and idealised law of aesthetic experience in all its purity. Here all theory of cognition, utility and religious elements are subordinated to the main aesthetic purpose. But what is this purpose? It is that of psychic significance. By means of the sensibly concrete, the form, a psychic impulse with all its experiences of significance is to be made visible, audible or in short presented

---

[1]) The old classical idea that art is based upon a $\mu\iota\mu\eta\sigma\iota\varsigma$ is a great mistake. Art does not imitate the simple object but always the aesthetically perceived object. One might say paradoxically: art is not imitation of things but imitation (that is conscious creation) of aesthetic experiences.

to the mind through the senses. To this end the full reality of the object is not always necessary. The surface character of things, that which appeals to the senses, is, so to speak sufficient. For this reason aesthetic creation may be nothing but the stimulation of a concrete sequence of ideas, as in poetry, or of the purely external outline as in sculpture.

We might say thus that the law of art or of the imaginative region is the law of the complete fusion of impression and expression. But the object which I perceive and psychic content and not only the raw object and my passing state of mind must fuse. One must abolish the limits between the object and the subject by creating a configuration the psychic unity of which transcends both the object and the observer. The structure of the aesthetically important form is consequently dependent upon two kinds of law which must be completely balanced in the work of art: the law of the object and the law of the mind. The object under artistic treatment has its unique laws. It is for this reason that the art student learns anatomy, the poet observes life and its chain of motives and the musician studies counterpoint. Here we must also include the laws of physical material by means of which expression is realized, such as: stones, colors, words, and sound. These laws of course are not explicitly in consciousness as theoretic insights but become aesthetic only because they are worked out in each specific case and seen into the concrete form. The psychic element, however, that is to appear in the object also has its own laws. These laws progress from very primitive psycho-physical determinants such as tension, relaxation and fatigue to the entire subjective structure and inner development. The accomplished aesthetic object must be woven into this subjective process so that it appears as a part of an animistic world.

In this mysterious woof the object, with its psychic effects, may be predominant. In this case we speak of impressionism in the widest sense of the word. But, on the other hand, the subjective part may be dominant. And this is the essence of expressionism. Both styles are aesthetic forms. For I mean by '*form*' the fusion of impression and expression, the union of the soul and of the objective configuration in imaginative experience.[1])

---

[1]) The expression 'form' has many different meanings in aesthetics and is often limited, as for instance in fine arts, to the mere outline of

We shall use the word form only when the fusion has the highest degree of immanent lawfulness. Even a single note of feeling, a very pronounced impression may be called aesthetically significant. Art, in the highest degree and in a normative sense is achieved only when the unitary principle of the soul has organised the whole aesthetic object. We must remember that even the laws of the object are only a kind of perception in which the mental subject regulates the phenomena. Mathematical symmetry, mechanical equilibration, and psychological association are forms of apprehension which are determined theoretically. If another mysterious law (which organises the soul itself as a total and which one might call the radiations of its entelechy) combines with this law, then we have the highest form which is nothing but the *total form of the soul mirrored in a sensible concrete formation* which is either embedded in reality or belongs to the realm of creative imagination. When the total psychic law (by which all kinds of experiencing and apprehending of the object are united in a mental organism) influences the creative imagination then it achieves form in the highest sense. Form, then, is nothing but the reflection of the contemplating soul in a concrete object. The human body, in which (from the aesthetical point of view) the soul seems to be objectified, is the best example of this. From a scientific point of view, therefore, Aristotle regarded the soul as the entelechy. That is, as the formative principle of the body. We see in the conception of entelechy an originally aesthetic concept (without which we cannot apparently get along in science). Just as the soul gives the body a visible form for aesthetic apprehension, so also does it choose other sensual foundations in order to develop on them its peculiar formative power. It is of no use to try to describe the essence of this form intellectually for it is more than intellect. One might find paraphrases for it such as: harmony of the rhythm of feeling, unity in manifoldness (but nevertheless sensibly perceptible unity of a manifoldness of conceived feelings of significance) equilibrium, moderation and ideality in form. But all this is futile. For, since art is sensibly concrete the mystery of form may appear

---

the aesthetic creation. It cannot be emphasized too strongly that even this outline must first be created or at least imitated in aesthetic experience. I mean by 'form' what Schiller has called 'living form' or 'freedom' (that is the mental) in the phenomenal.

in the individual work of art but cannot be put into words and calculated beforehand. And finally there is only one criterion of perfect art: the purely aesthetic effect.

The content of the soul which art attempts to express is determined historio-geographically in the individual as is the soul which it influences. For this reason epochs with a new structure of experience oscillate between onesided impressionism and expressionism since they have not yet found a definite inner psychic structure. Even in art they radiate more excitement than expressed mental life. Such an art lacks 'general validity' in the aesthetic sense. The only sort of art which is eternal is the socalled classic art which emphasizes the most general outlines of the psychic laws and so is capable of adequate experience without any variation in historical attitude. It is, however, rational to a very high degree, it is theoretically definite. And in it the eternal formative principles of the soul and of the objective world are so fused that they appear purified in the concrete creation. There is always a mathematical element in art of this kind, something simple, regular and according to type. It is, in short, inner and outer world-legality exhibited in a concrete instance. It is as has been well said; the presentation of the general in the particular.

This is true of the classic art $\varkappa\alpha\tau'$ $\dot{\varepsilon}\xi o\chi\acute{\eta}\nu$, because it allows the law to become clearly visible. At bottom, however, it is true of all forms of art, only that the general element, the subjective-objective mental law is more and more differentiated into more and more daring individual instances. To surmise this law in the apparently chaotic experience is the secret of every aesthetic effect. It often seems, as for instance in modern music, that there is nothing but chaos. But if the work of art is designed to be not only an expression of feeling states, but also expression according to law, real form, then the legal psychical context must be felt through all the tensions and relaxations in aesthetic experience.

Nothing more can be said of the normative law of art or form since it is preeminently instinctive rationality. And this rationality is not only the lawfulness of the objective order but is also the lawfulness of the soul since both are fused in art just as, for a higher comprehension, they originate even in reality from the same fountain of life. This is expressed in Bacon's simple law: art is *homo additus rebus,* animation of things. Form is then the presentation of sensibly concrete objects in creations through the totality of contemplative psychical forces whose laws are interwoven with the apprehended or surmised laws of the object.[1])

3. In the cognitive sphere also the primitive level of cognition exhibits the quality of instinctive behavior. The identity of events which are either similar or resemble each other in certain characteristics, forces itself on one's attention. Thus we may regard the recognition of certain situations and occurrences, with their complex qualities, as the basic level of cognition. And as a matter of fact this level may be assumed in animals. Everybody even without a theoretic set carries out simple cognitive functions which, of course, remain in the sphere of biological purposive behavior as long as tradition and education do not supplement them.

But as in the former mental regions so in cognition also there develops, out of the instinctive reactive behavior, a productive behavior. The will to cognize awakens, a will which is regulated by a definite meaning and on the mythological level is still wholly fused with aesthetic and religious tendencies. Gradually the pure law of cognition is developed and appears first of all in the concept of unitary existence which may be grasped through mental concepts. Science has learned very slowly to work out its own immanent law and grasp it in an isolating idealising method. Logics and the theory of cognition are the framework of the whole conceptual and real world, since the cognizeable must necessarily appear in forms which realize the specific sense of cognition. Laws of being are in reality laws of cognition applied to the manifoldness of reality, that is, the data in the sensible complex. We know that these data are susceptible of other mental formations. But cognition wants to work out the intrinsic qualities and purely objective order without the least regard to the subjective interrelations in which

---

[1]) The 'artistic man' whose inner senses are fully awakened, whether he wants to or not, whether he knows it or not, sees harmony into the object. The form under which he sees things as complete entities is his own, the observer's inner harmony. Whatever such an individual looks at he sees in its cosmic inevitability; everything is perfect for him in every moment. And if he is an 'active' artist he gladdens everybody who has 'eyes to see and ears to hear' with the experience of complete harmony by making it easy to understand that everything as it is, is perfect, necessary, just and beautiful. Georg Fuchs, *Deutsche Form*. Mit einer Einleitung: 'Von den letzten Dingen in der Kunst.' Muenchen 1907. p. 45.

it appears or the peculiarities of any experiencing self. All additions of empathy, desirous interest, of religious interpretation, of fear, hope and passion are to be excluded. As far as possible we must remove the subjective perspective in which the cognizing individuality, because of its temporal and spatial limitations sees objects mentally.

This is possible only because cognition perceives identical essences and identical essential correlations (laws) in the manifold data by a very complicated process of finding the similarities and differences of things, of separating and uniting them. While this is being done the data, quite regardless of whether they have been seen previously as socalled real objects (that is, as influencing me and as being experienced as independent by me) or as mere pictures of my imagination with objective relations, or as purely psychical states (as for instance feelings), are projected upon a new plane: namely the plane of thought or ideational plane. Cognition translates all temporally and spatially individualized phenomena into the realm of thought. To popularize this: all cognition is carried on in terms of concepts and judgments. These are, however, of an ideational nature, according to their content, that is, if one regards them not purely psychologically as temporal processes generated by the soul, but in the light of their meaning. They appear as realities but they intend and contain idealities.[1] They have an eternal validity and an eternal meaning, insofar as they are really formed after the pure law of cognition. This does not come explicitly into consciousness in all cognitive acts. It operates as instinctive rationality which is typical of pure rationality. Now what is this law?

The essence of cognition is not realized if it only emphasizes and perceives some given object purely objectively. It must instead consistently unite all single objects of knowledge in overindividual validity. This union is ideational. It is nothing but the application of the principle of identity to the cognized whole. Thoughts are related to each other through logical proof. Adequate reason refers us to the particular essential relation to which a judgment must be reduced in order to recognize as valid its synthetic con-

---

[1] Leibnitz's distinction of eternal and factual truths refers to the differences of the objects of conceptual knowledge of which some are eternal and others transitory. Every truth however, as truth, that is, as a valid datum of knowledge, is eternal. This applies equally to factual truths.

junction. We might therefore interpret with Riehl the law of adequate reason as the synthetic principle of identity, that is, as an expansion of mental identity to the identity which is not immediately recognizeable.

Therefore the law which dominates the field of cognition is the principle of adequate reason in all its forms. Formulated as a norm with regard to a cognizing consciousness we might state it as follows: give reasons for your judgment and bring them into mental relations which are consistent and correspond to the objective context.[1])

The ideal of cognition would be a thorough system of concepts and judgments founded on sufficient reasons by means of which the changing objective order which is given to experience might be 'thought'. Finally, we ought to be able to deduce the entire objective order from one highest concept or law. The world of fact limits this ideal because the factual (as sensible experience) cannot wholly be deduced from general essences and essential correlations. Our cognition is always, figuratively speaking, a network of thoughts which we throw over reality. But we cannot in this way include all of concrete reality. So that we can only say that our concepts and laws refer to reality and are partially founded in experience. But experienced reality cannot be exhausted by this means, and the surplus may, as we saw, be immediately (aesthetically) experienced.

This conception, that cognition translates reality into an ideational context of reasons, may be made clear by the illustration of causal relations. Cause and effect are not, as is commonly thought, realities but rather mental distinctions by which we cognitively perceive sensible data. These latter are at most made up of complex impressions which are immediately conjoined. When, however, we place them in objective time and determine one as the cause of the other, we have changed the sensible into the ideational. For if we call one thing the cause of something else, we really view its essence as a cognitive reason for another process whose essence is also perceived in purely conceptual terms: the effect. Kant is therefore right when he maintains that the principle

---

[1]) Compare Riehl, *Philosophischer Kritizismus II.* 1 (1879) p. 240 ff. and Volkelt, *Gewissheit und Wahrheit* p. 393.

of causality is merely the conceptual relation of reason and consequence applied to temporal phenomena.[1]) We do not grasp the entire complex process of sensory phenomena but always the relation of one general essence to another, and in such a manner that on the basis of our conception of the essential context of one the other can, in a purely mental operation be deduced.

What occurs in reality is thus transformed by cognition into an ideational context of reason. And to this end it is necessary that the 'essence' designated as the cause should somehow be identically retained in the item designated as effect. On the lower level cognition is satisfied with a mythological hypostatization of forces. For instance, it puts into the essence of the sun which warms the rock, a 'warming power'. On a higher level one demands conceptual or special quantitative identities (for instance identities which can be grasped in functional equations).

But these details do not concern us here. It must suffice that a valid cognition is obtained only when the phenomena, no matter how individual are somehow reduced to a general (categorical, mental) context of reasons, which are finally rooted in the one objective context of a given whole. The immanent law of cognition is the logical principle of sufficient or adequate reason in the differentiated manifoldness of its applications. And this again is nothing but the principle of identity applied to the continued acts of cognition.[2]) The goal of these acts is a closed system of thought in which every single principle is based on reason and can be consistently related to the others.

4. Before considering the immanent law of the religious sphere we shall take up the two 'social' regions whose corresponding acts have a specific lawfulness. This appears more clearly when social life rises from the instinctive level to the consciously willed and desired form. Or, in the words of Toennies, when the will to do makes itself felt instead of the will to be. But this lawfulness is of course influential previous to this change and here too in the form of instinctive rationality.

---

[1]) Riehl op. cit. p. 240 'Causality is the application of the principle of adequate reason to temporal changes of phenomena, or in short, the principle of adequate reason in time.'

[2]) Identity must be understood here in the sense of synthetical not analytical identity.

The will to power, or the attempt to force one's own value direction upon the valuation of another person, would have to be dominated as in the other regions, by the law of the development of the highest power. Just as the greatest utility, the highest 'form' and the supreme systematic objective order determined the laws of economics, art and science, so here the greatest freedom and the maximum of power over others should give the norm. And such is indeed the case. Since the highest power over others is not gained in merely momentary mental superiority over others so here too permanence and consistency are required. A genuine will to power cannot be conceived in the form of changing moods and whims and must itself be based on general laws. The content of these laws cannot, as we know, be determined from the power system itself. Only the general form of autonomous lawfulness belongs to the will to power.[1]) Even extreme despotism must exhibit constant effort of will if it is to be effective over more than a mere moment and a limited space. That is, a system of power must be founded. And this is the injunction which is necessary to liberty: not whim but will to law. The will is constant if it is determined by enduringly valuable purposes. The will to power is constant if it binds the action of others through general commands to these purposes, even if they are only indirectly of value to them. Such a regulated will to power is lawful at least to the extent of having the form of a general maxim of conduct; the content itself need not be social. Within the compass of the mere power system the content is nothing but the aim of regulating power to the mind of the commanding subject.

5. It seems to be more difficult to find a law for the region of sympathy and the community which is founded upon it and which goes beyond instinctive attraction to regulate the union of men in regard to values. It must be in the nature of a regulative power which is immanently active in social behavior, but need not necessarily come to consciousness as a formulated guide of conduct. Such an instinctive rationality in social acts might be called loyalty. Loyalty is the will to community and not to a temporary but a permanent and lasting community, guaranteed

---

[1]) We find this factor also and not only the theoretic one of consistency in itself in the ethics of Kant: namely the formal freedom to will what one really desires.

through a constancy of value directions. Insofar now as loyalty refers to another, namely a carrier of the same value or a soul that is capable of value, it is eager to help the other and to further their common values. Loyalty is, therefore, the lasting inclination towards another soul to realize in it or in community with it constantly willed life values. Loyalty appears in a lower form in a union for the sake of mutual ends, that is, the realization of external real valuable ends. Here loyalty is merely the maintainance of a limited and temporarily existing end of mutual willing, which is also called solidarity.[1]) If, however, love is directed to the essence of another being that is, to his personal value structure, then loyalty becomes the loyalty of essence. And here we must differentiate the love which gives, that is, which helps the other in his value existence, and the love which takes, that is, which feels itself furthered in some direction of value and the unfolding community of value in which human beings know themselves united through the mutual developed love of some value (as of some kind or direction of value). To each of these forms of love there is a corresponding form of loyalty which is nothing more than constancy in the community of essence and evaluation.[2])

We might mention at this point that the two social norms which we have just derived, the autonomous will to law and loyalty represent two important factors in our judicial system. For in this system there is on one hand the community in law, that is, the obligation that comes because the members feel themselves comrades in the cause of law and accordingly carry out the obligation to contract. On the other hand there is the will to law which — seen from the point of view of every member — brings the claims to power and restrictions (rights and duties) under general norms of conduct. Since we cannot assume an agreement of these individual wills to law (as is deduced by rational natural law from the stoical concept of reason) we must assume as a third factor of law that it arises from an overindividual will which satisfies the following conditions: 1. it must contain the factor of loyalty, that is, the

---

[1]) Compare the footnote on page 67.
[2]) From what has been said before (p. 73) it follows that one may speak of loyalty to one's self. And furthermore that one may love the essence of another even if one cannot approve of what he actually is for the time being.

consciousness of union; 2. it must bring about a distribution of spheres of power (spheres of liberty) from an overindividual point of view by permitting or prohibiting, by granting or by restricting freedom; and 3. it must achieve this in the form of general rules which do not refer to any one person or object, but rather to persons or objects in general (*volonté générale* is not summated collective will but a normative will, directed toward the general and issuing from what is overindividually valid). Through this last point of view law is influenced by the fundamental character of the theoretic sphere. This, however, is a detail which does not concern us here and we shall return to it in section four.

6. Let us now take up the discussion of the immanent law of the religious sphere, and with this we naturally reach the climax of the mental structure. In chapter three we purposely considered religious behavior only in its most instinctive forms. We said that the meaning of religious acts is the relating of all experiences of value to the highest total value of individual life. But there are many difficulties to this conception. If we speak only of the 'highest total value of the individual life' then we refer primarily to the highest value of individual experience (of the actual capacity to experience). This, however, may be wholly subjective and very low in the ethical scale. We have already emphasized in the first chapter that individual value experiences need not at all coincide with the objective value of mental things. This is also true of the value of life. The striving of a human being to harmonise his total existence with the highest yearning for value (ideal) in his individual consciousness is his striving for happiness. Thus the relating of all individual values to the total value is nothing but the striving for some happiness which shall embrace all of life.

And actually, there is present in much religious behavior nothing more than this yearning for happiness. The religious attitudes are as diverse as the individual forms of happiness. And the conceptions of God are just as varied and are often nothing more than the theoretic-aesthetic-social symbol for the giver of happiness. This God is then also the highest value object of which the experiencing subject is capable. We find, as the core of primitive religions, certain magic ceremonies which are designed by the individual who strives for happiness to propitiate the gods or demons.

This is, of course, connected with the complete lack of theoretic clearness about the course of world history and the sources of genuine happiness. As a rule, they imagine human social relations into the relation between god and men which imitate sometimes trade and barter relations, and sometimes those of law or the family.

The progress of religion depends on the development of the other mental spheres which one might designate as the individual regions which found religion. Now, if the normative laws of the economic, theoretic, aesthetic, political and social spheres are more clearly realized then genuine values develop for individual consciousness and naturally enter into relation with the total value of life. But these norms are inherently always partial norms. If the subject of the mental acts and values represents a unitary structure then these onesided norms must coincide in his consciousness. They will be interwoven but may, under certain circumstances, conflict with one another. In section three we shall take up in greater detail these phenomena of moral consciousness and differentiate two kinds of norm: the expanding and the restricting (commanding and forbidding). Here we shall be content to ascertain that the interrelation of all onesided norms or mental laws in the individual consciousness represents a complex experience which we shall call the total norm. It does not prescribe how man shall behave in any one direction, but rather how he, as a unitary subject, shall think and act. Furthermore, it contains decisions concerning the difference in rank of the manifold norms and norm syntheses, or to express this in another way: it indicates which highest norm of his evaluation endows himself as a person with the highest objective and unitary value. It prescribes in this sense a definite inner value configuration in a normative manner. Either it appears as an expectation and as a demand which other mental beings direct to me as a subject who is not yet normative in their sense of the word. In this heteronomy there is then an element of the type of social power over me which we have described above. Or, on the other hand, the total norm rises as my highest mental achievement, as my own genuine will to value, out of the depths of my individual consciousness. Then we have autonomy. It does not always act as a formulated general law nor is it always in unfolded rational consciousness. It is often only instinctive rationality, a feeling of our ultimate mental destination. It is conscience.

It does not necessitate a lengthy proof to demonstrate that this total norm, as heteronomy and as autonomy is the same as morality. The moral norm determines where my highest normative (genuine) value lies, or which values I shall accept and follow in my thoughts as well as in my behavior in order to give me the highest value. We have genuine religion only when this normative total experience (which, of course branches out in extraordinarily varied individual norms) enters into the basic religious behavior. Then life and its value are perceived not only from the point of view of what I should like but also of what I ought to do. And in this sense morality is the real core of genuine religion and also the source of the happiness which comes from the fullfilment of our true destiny.

But in order wholly to understand the relation between religion and morality we must make finer distinctions. On the side of religion we must separate religious consciousness, as a subjective mental attitude from religion as objective historical phenomena and religious objects, that is, these facts in higher mental life which appear in the specifically religious attitude of the subject and which are the intended meaning in objective religions. Now, the essence of the religious object must not be defined as a mysteriously active power (this leads to the belief in demons) nor as the Absolute Beyond, the acosmic which is opposed to the world (this only leads to a purely negative theology). The history of religion teaches us that many different things can become the objects of religious veneration. But we are not here concerned with what might be, but rather with what must be experienced. So we shall only deal with the normative law to which the religious consciousness must be subject to be in harmony with the genuine religious meaning. And this meaning must be final and absolute. Everything else is only the preliminary step to a religious content, but not the content itself.

And this is the only element in religion which is timeless. The way in which this meaning is discovered depends on the structure of epochs as well as of individual souls. Here two decisive basic forms are possible which we shall find again later under the life forms. The absolute significance, and with this the highest value of the world order, can be interpreted only from the object; then religion is primarily a feeling of passive reception, a final surrender and blessedness. Or one may be convinced that this absolute and highest experience can only occur in the solitary soul so that its light radiates above the turbulent course of the world. (The religions of dependence and of freedom: Schleiermacher and Kant.)

Let us return from here to the relation of religion and morality. They are different if only for the reason that the law of morality is a norm directed to personal thought and behavior, while religion aims at the perception of the highest value content in or above the world, or in any event, at objective contexts. But both share the tendency to the highest value in which it is the destiny of persons as well as of objective contexts to rest and to live. Insofar now as religious consciousness intends this Absolute we maintain that only when it develops in accordance with the highest value, (that is, when it is dominated by the ethical norm), can it fully receive the Absolute. This is the only mental attitude which makes the soul fit for the highest power which lives above us.

Certain mental structures show especially clearly the correlation of the religious and the moral. Here the absolute or highest value is not taken into the soul in the form of an overpowering experience of being, and consequently the force of the absolute and total 'ought', that is, the moral revelation of the inner self, can also confront the present world order as an 'ought'. This religious consciousness does not surrender itself quietly to the higher meaning which it guesses, but develops it in an internal struggle; so to speak creates it on the apex of its own being and is not satisfied with a God or a world principle which it cannot respect in the highest ethical sense. Such a postulating ethos is more than moral because it enters actively, over and above mere thought and behavior, in the total world structure. And because of its objective influence it is religious.

And even where this postulating structure of the inner world does not come in, it is structurally clear that noone would pray to a religious object which is not *a priori* equal to or even higher than his highest value-demands.[1] It is for this reason that there is an acosmic element in all Divinity. But we could not find it if the moral law in our own breast did not make us ripe and receptive for the Highest.

---

[1] Whoever does not believe in a highest value over and above the mere self knows nothing either holy or religious. It is this which is called sin against the Holy Ghost.

In every case, even in those which are less clear, the laws of moral consciousness in the restricted sense and those which found religious consciousness are related like two hemispheres which together form the whole. The religious object (as world content or over-world content) is perceived only by a person who submits himself to the norm of the highest value. This object may therefore be thought of as that which gives us the absolute norm and brings our personal destiny into harmony with the highest meaning of the world. The moral subject, on the other hand, must determine itself in accordance with the law of the highest value, whether it is to be capable of mercy or to carry and radiate a spark of the Divine.

Let us consider the relation between religion and morality from the mental structure of the latter type. This will show us particularly clearly the specific law of religious consciousness and thus also the law of the development of religion (which is, of course, not the creation of the religious object itself). Here too the normative positing of moral value is directed at first only to me, to my thoughts and the behavior which grows out of them On the other hand, the religious conception of life regards the value of the world (fate, the world order) also from the point of view of a moral determinism.[1]) It is therefore moral judgment not only of self but also of the world. It confronts the present world picture (whether its emphasis is theoretic, aesthetic or social etc.) with the demand to harmonize with the highest ethical value. Wherever the given world order fails to satisfy this highest norm it has the courage to surmount it with another world order which is higher and more in accordance with the normative. Thus mental life finally brings out of itself a higher consciousness than can be satisfied by the real context of individual life if the world order grasped merely theoretically. The categories of value transcend is that of existence (thus for instance in Kant's *Primat der praktischen Vernunft*). And this normative value consciousness is world-creative insofar as it creates for itself the outline of another world order which satisfies the highest value (in a peculiar combination of theoretical formulations and aesthetic symbols). It is at first immaterial whether this world order (supported by the

---

[1]) Cf. Simmel, *Hauptprobleme der Philosophie*, Sammlung Goeschen p. 167 ff.

evidence of the highest value) is opposed to the present world order as a second and transcendent one, or whether in the specific religious attitude it is interpreted as the deepest meaning of the present reality. When we consider the religious type we shall see that each of these two conceptions corresponds to different mental structures. Here we are only concerned with the normative law which acts in a religious attitude as a sort of instinctive rationality. The normative significance of life thus born postulates a highest world meaning. It confronts all separated and unformed mental life as a final and uplifting power for unity. And we shall now go even further than at the close of the third chapter when we said that everything was susceptible of religious interpretation, and say: everything is included in the law of the religious norm which interprets from the disparate meanings the one highest meaning. This we call God, and the life which strives toward it and contains God as instinctive law, we call *Morality.*

6
SUBJECTIVE SPHERES OF INTERESTS AND OBJECTIVE LEVELS

The essence of mental acts is that they issue from a unitary individual consciousness, a self, and are directed to a not-self. In order to make clear the peculiarity of this way of thinking one might construct in imagination a superior mind which could grasp the overindividual configurations of the historico-mental life *uno intuitu*. We can do this only by actualizing the content of objective configurations in a series of temporal achievements of meaning. When we attempt to describe the x which confronts the self, to which mental acts are directed and which is only represented 'somehow' in our experience, we observe that we only know it in very definite objective orders, which because of their value-significance we call contexts of meaning for a center of experience. We can no more approach the unformed, single and raw material than the neo-platonist could designate his concept of matter by means of positive predicates, since it meant for him something wholly indeterminate or the mere possibility of assuming determination. We might still ask, however, whether there is not a sort of original formation which serves as a foundation for all others, so that they seem to be derived from or founded on it. In philosophy there is a tendency to regard the theoretic forms of determination (thought alone or expanded to cognition) as original form. This is comprehensible since philosophy itself is a science and consequently places the theoretic attitude above all others. It is, however, a great mistake, I might say the hereditary sin of philosophy that it secretly transforms the peculiarity of an instrument into a quality of the material. Philosophy must always be cognition. The object of cognition is always more than and different from a merely theoretic context. Philosophy can no more include all the meaning of life in mere theory than aesthetics can transform art into science. But instead, both philosophy and aesthetics merely illuminate present pictures of life with their own light, that of theoretic analysis. But the atheoretic content must always be preserved in the theoretic form.

Previous to the present discussion we allowed for this fact by asserting that in every meaningful experience all other directions of meaning are contained, even if under the domination of one which colors the whole experience. This was at first a methodological start. We can now illustrate it by the following example.

When we speak of Nature we obviously imply more than an 'experience'. For, nature as a whole cannot be experienced. We can refer to the whole only in thought, or in brief: nature is a thought. The connotations of this thought may be wholly different, and it is not necessarily itself mainly a theoretic act. This would be the case only if we conceived the meaning of nature to be a closed system, an inclusive concept of identically recurring essences which behaved according to identical laws. This is what nature means for the scientist who throws the network of thought-forms and categories over nature, and where it is a matter of indifference whether he finally reduces everything to quantitative mathematical equations or whether he stops at the explanatory principle of substantial forms. It is, however, also possible to confront this 'totality of nature' in another attitude. One can empathically feel oneself into its life, its color, its light, its smell, its rhythm, its play of form and harmony. This is the aesthetic interpretation of nature. Or again the selection of values might be regarded from the utilitarian standpoint for the preservation or comfortable maintainance of human life. Or finally, nature (which only the theorist believes to be always identical) can enter into a religious context of meaning and intend, according to its emphasis, that totality of life in which every individual has his being, or the sinful level of the physical and the material, or even an inferior illusion beyond which the real meaning of life may be found. Indeed, some will perhaps incline to call all these meaning interpretations metaphysical-religious, because they are related to that totality of nature which is never given. But the different act-colorations remain, even if in every case only a section of socalled nature (for instance a plant) is grasped and classified in the corresponding regions of meaning.

Of course these differentiations of meaning regions are again only abstractions arrived at by theoretic reflection. In the performance of acts there is undivided life and in every total act we shall find all directions of meaning, as we have explained above. But that was only a preliminary rough determination. The real problem of analysis is to determine in the meaningful total act the act structure which is unique in every case and which builds up exactly this complex. For the meanings interrelate not once only but again and again so that, as in the Volta column, the same strata may be found several times. Later when we consider types we shall treat only the primary complications but we must say here that this too is just a methodological shortcut. I shall cite only two relatively simple examples of stratified forms.

The aesthetic effect of a mediaeval cathedral is based on a great many heterogeneous acts. First there is the very primitive act of cognition in which we determine as a part of the real world the outline of the cathedral's external shape, see regularities of form, relations of distance and repetitions of parts of figures etc. Elementary aesthetic impressions are in this experience too. So also the knowledge of its purpose. We cannot, without a harmonic of religious veneration comprehend it in its fullest sense, so we add the silent judgment: it is the house of God. Over and above this is the latent historical knowledge that it has a past of seven hundred years. When we appreciate its size we realize the enormous insignificance of the individual in the effort involved. Perhaps we form on the basis of this a new theoretic, though scarcely conscious judgment: 'that is a tremendous achievement of human coöperation which would have been impossible without the harmonious relation of all their souls.' Much more may be woven together in such an experience, and the whole could, and does with many people, have a religious significance. But there may also be nothing more than an aesthetic act; an empathic experience of formed grandeur.

Or take a simpler example: 'This ring shines' (primitive aesthetic experience). 'The ring is gold' (theoretic evaluation). 'Gold is rare' (economic valuation). 'My mother gave it to me' (the significance of this relation of love enters in). 'I prize it as my life' (comparison of economic and religious values). 'I give it to you.' The full significance of this act which finally becomes a condensed single act is, therefore, mentally founded through a complex of other mental acts and can be adequately understood by empathy.

Here is an enormous field for individual analysis of *Geisteswissenschaften*. The problem is to study the many different kinds of foundations of value acts, experiences and constant dispositions. In order to draw a few simple lines through this field of enormous possibilities we must make use of a simplifying construction, as follows. For every one of the main spheres of meaning we posit on the one hand its subjective attitude and on the other its characteristic form of objective existence. Even though the outlines which we give here can only be crude it seems to me that we thus open up a new world of questions which philosophy has hardly considered.

The one-sided influence of the natural sciences upon previous psychology shows itself in the narrow conception of the ego. Many believe that its connection with the physical is the most essential part of the self. It is, therefore, for them a psychical fact which is connected with nature (nature being interpreted solely in physical and physiological terms) and in its spatial and temporal localisation must itself be interpreted as a product of nature. From this view, which is wholly under the influence of a ready-made physical picture of the world, another differs by at least starting from an immanent psychological consideration. According to this latter, the self is merely the content (or its unique form of union with a total experience) which happens to be in the individual consciousness but which is of no importance beyond this transitory structure. Against theories of this kind K. Oesterreich[1] has recently successfully defended the point of view that the self is the independent unitary prius of all the acts, contents, functions and conditions which are found in it. It cannot be denied that for a psychology which disregards trans-subjective meaning relations the soul is nothing but a bundle of individual functions (sensations, ideas and feelings) and of contents of these functions which are accidentally brought together by the external senses and the associative structure of reproduction. The ego is then nothing but the indifferent running-off (*Ablauf*) of these contents. But if one relates these positivistically interpreted elements of the merely psychic to the acts in which an object is grasped, then one finds just as many

---
[1] *Die Phaenomenologie des Ich.* Vol. I. Leipzig 1910.

different interpretations of the self as there are objective regions of significance into which the individual process of acts and experiences is interwoven. These acts and experiences are, of course, themselves temporal processes which are psychologically built up from a limited number of elementary functions and contents. But in every case there is perceived in these acts and experiences a specific sense which also gives their subject a unique color. To every objective content of meaning there is correlated a specifically subjective content of meaning, or in other words: in every sphere of meaning there is opened up a unique subject-object relation which can be illuminated from either side, the subjective or the objective. We might elucidate this alternate significance by the following diagram in which the changing meaning of the self is symbolized by concentric circles. For, the self in the different sense attitudes seems to be bigger or smaller. To each one of

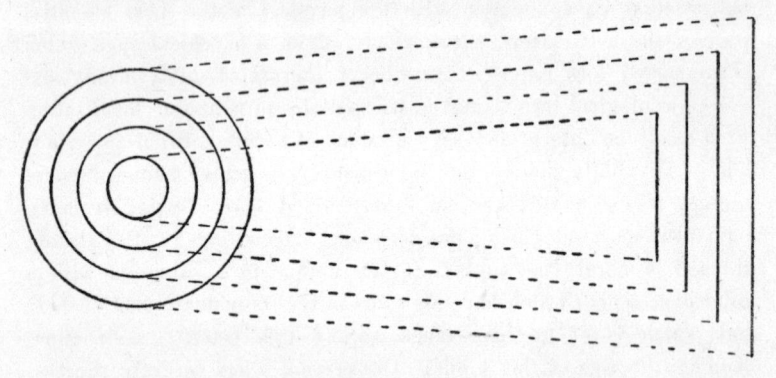

these circles there is correlated a specific level of objects. In every basic class of meaningful experiences a peculiar phase of existence is comprehended. Or vice versa; every level of objects corresponds to a specific class of values. This fact too has been overlooked by the philosophy of the past. 'Reality', for instance, has been conceived as something capable of only one interpretation, even though it is an interfusion in relief of many objective levels. And to such a degree is reality dependent upon the current historical and individual state of consciousness that one might write a history of the consciousness of reality. But we shall omit here (as well as in regard to the self) the interfusions of life, and attempt to reconstruct in an abstract manner the most important basic forms of objectivity. The differences may be seen most clearly in the changing conceptions of space and time. For each level of objects has its unique form of space and time.

1. The smallest circle is formed by the self of needs and desires, the pure ego which must be thought of as the subject of the instinct of self preservation and of all physical urges and instincts. I refer to the biological self (see page 13 footnote). Its functions are most closely related to those of the body and it may therefore be called the physical self. One can only reconstruct it with any degree of success by eliminating from the practical orientation of life of the subject all reflection and thought. One must consider the self as a structure regulated by stimuli and sensual urges to which, however, the objective purposes of these drives are not represented by the ideas of aims but only by the feelings which accompany the acts. There are many people who experience the strongest feeling of self in this zone of satisfaction of physical needs and are inclined to think that the self is only what is under the skin. For them the bodily feelings are the real feelings which build up the ego. Some trace of this biological self is to be found, in reflective consciousness, as scarcely noticed sensations of pressure, as needs without any clear idea of the result at which the instinct aims, as pain or as well being, in short as a diffuse psychic background. There are also primitive experiences the presence and absence of which guide the self on this level, namely the feelings of pleasant and unpleasant which are always very important guides of behavior even in the most highly developed minds. For such minds too there is an automatic selection between pleasant and unpleasant positions of the body. They also must satisfy their physical needs in order to live. Even though later complicated mental regulators enter in, the basic system could not be preserved for one hour without the biological relation of the material stimuli and physical reactions of the psycho-physical self. Breathing, eating, the beating of the heart and reproduction are fortunately not dependent upon reason but upon a symbolic system of experiential forms, which functions, as it were, intelligently though our intelligence does not have anything to do with it.

A specific level of objects corresponds of course to this unique center of experience. Nothing exists for this self except what is transmitted through the medium of physical organs and thus acts upon it. In the pressure of the outer world and the simultaneously given experience of the resistance of the self lies the real core of the experience of reality which no later theoretic conception can replace. The objects of this self are transmitted through sense organs which have their original form in the mechanical touch sense but are capable of developing into a mechanism whose activity has been disclosed by subsequent scientific research as a very complicated chemical process. From the point of view of this later and superior science the relation between objects and subject can be clearly comprehended as being a relation which is relatively purposive for the life activity of the individual and the species. The sense organs of living beings are selective organs which transmit only impressions of biological importance, just as the motor organs are proportionate to the necessary functions of life. It is exceedingly difficult, perhaps even impossible, to picture the psychic processes of a wholly differently organised soul (of an animal or perhaps even a plant). J. von Uexkuell has rightly directed our attention to the objectively measureable relations between stimuli and reactions. He says: 'Every animal has a unique world, which is made up of the characteristic impressions which he receives of the outer world.'[1]) To this specific 'world' a specific world of effects is added as an active correlative. The same thing of course applies to the human world. The reality, which science builds up according to the testimony of the senses with the aid of categories and schematic outlines, is based on a biological reality which reveals itself in primitive sense experiences; but indubitably has immanent purposive relations to our practical adjustments and satisfactions of needs. This biological reality needs to be described and the relative purposiveness of its system of symbols followed.

The spatial and temporal relations within biological reality are, of course, represented wholly differently in consciousness than by the theoretic construction of mathematical space and time. Space appears biologically perhaps in qualitatively unique experiences of movement which are connected with experiences of exertion (processes of fatigue). Time perhaps appears in the qualitative interfusion of experiences which Bergson describes, and which are also complicated by feelings of exertion. All this can be reconstructed

[1]) J. v. Uexkuell, *Bausteine zu einer biologischen Weltanschauung.* Muenchen 1913. p. 67 ff.

only with the utmost difficulty since thinking man no longer exists only in this biological reality but builds up, out of his objective experiences a reality into which thought and cognition have already woven many threads, not to mention the fact that aesthetic and religious strands also enter in.

2. The economic self is closely related to the biological because its central value relation grows immediately out of the biological one. For this self also the real regulator of behavior is the satisfaction of needs. But in this case it is transmitted through theoretic reflection or rationalized in an economic sense. In place of the pleasant and the unpleasant we have the evaluation as useful or harmful; greater intervals of space and time and more numerous and more diverse goods are taken into consideration. But the satisfaction of needs is still the decisive factor in experience. The economic evaluation depends in each case on the two variables, (the degree of satisfaction and the amount of goods available) as formulated in the greatest abstraction by the law of diminishing utility. Calculation, however, (a theoretical factor) is not the decisive factor here but need (an economic element). And so one might say: the economic self is the biological self plus thought and insight. Its fundamental instinct is found in desire which is directed to purely temporal things, to real possession and use. And this fact also explains its peculiar fatality. For, this ego taken by itself is incapable of permanent satisfaction. It demands more and more and must always go on demanding more. Only in productive economic work is there, perhaps, a trace of self forgetfulness, since it is a primitive way of transcending time, a first domination of matter and perhaps a partial giving of oneself to others.

Just as the reality of the biological self forms the enduring nucleus of the material world so the economic self is for the time being confronted by a material objective order, the world of goods. Whatever is economically important is either matter itself or else it dwells in material forces. Matter, however, is spatially distributed over the world. To procure and work it necessitates time. And in this sense space and time are related to the economic point of view. They must be transcended or conquered. But not by means of a mental conquest or by imagination but through a saving of energy. For, space and time appear to the subject from the economic point of view as factors in the expenditure of energy. To minimize these as far as possible is the aim of all means of transportation and methods of work which are designed to shorten the period of production. 'Time is money.' The purely economic world perspective reduces the entire world to the point of view of matter and energy. Everything non-material must somehow be translated into this plane if it is to be a part of the economy of matter and energy; for instance, by means of reducing mental creations to the period of work required and the mere use of matter and energy. This seems out of proportion. But the world view of the purely economically orientated self is based on a constant conflict with matter. If the interest of enjoyment and consumption conquers the productive technical aspect we have therefore necessarily, practical materialism. And this again must not be mistaken for theoretic materialism, for the latter is an ideology and is rooted in the fanatic desire of the theoretic mind for unity.

3. The aesthetic self is obviously much larger and much more independent of matter. For, the imaginative self enters into the most varied objects even those which are created in imagination. It does not live only in its own body but creates for itself a much greater space in physical forms of expression and a more extensive resonator. But one must not think of this empathic process as if it were always a personification. That is only a special case which may serve the purpose of purely theoretic interpretation as well. The expression used by Lipps, that empathy is objectivated enjoyment of self, is liable to be misunderstood. For, one might think that this ego is the real ego in the sense of the really desiring, suffering and acting ego. But this putting oneself in another's place and empathic action is obviously something wholly different from the aesthetic attitude.[1]) In aesthetic contemplation we do not find in the particular object our real self but only 'something psychical'. The liveliness of a red is not our vivacity, but there is, in the specific object (for instance in the perceived or imagined red) 'something vivacious' and it is this which radiates back and gives our self the corresponding quality. One must not call these cognized feelings but, more accurately, feelings of empathy. Our soul, in the aesthetic state, apprehends in the object (besides the qualities

---

[1]) Volkelt takes up in great detail the coloring of the ego-feeling (*Ichgefühl*) in aesthetic behavior. See his *Das Ästhetische Bewusstsein*, Muenchen 1920, p. 48 ff.

which can be conceptually determined) psychical accompanying qualities, and when we live in these concretely our soul expands above the real sphere of its struggle with the external world to a free and floating imaginative self. Foreign selves too can be absorbed aesthetically. Then, however, the emphasis does not lie on the understanding or affirming of their individual existence and behavior, but on a psychic empathy of our subjectivity which is expanded by the object and into it.

This aesthetic expansion is throughout a process *sui generis*. Empathy is something wholly different, and obviously more inclusive than the psychological interpretation (understanding) of another soul. It is the expansion of our soul into the life of the observed objectivity. We feel subjectively broadened when we see the vast ocean, we are wafted upward with the gothic arch, are oppressed by the heavy load of a cliff, and variously affected by the smiling green, the somber darkness, the dead gray. All this is, in the words of Schleiermacher: an affection of our self consciousness, but nevertheless entirely a condition of an expanded self which is liberated from the body and the pressure of material reality. Now we can explain the peculiar antinomy that though one forgets oneself in aesthetic appreciation one yet feels oneself enhanced. We do not mean the same self. One forgets one's self, that is, one's limited, struggling and desiring self, when the self roams as in a dream and is so to speak outside of itself. But in a different sense one gains another higher and freer self which has surmounted bodily and material dependence. Herein is also a preliminary stage of salvation, namely a liberation from space and time and the restrictions of energy and matter. But the aesthetic liberation is not the ultimate and highest salvation, which can only be attained in the religious condition, if only because this liberated imagination may occupy itself with the smallest and most whimsical bits of reality without searching for or even guessing the relation to the whole meaning of the world. Only religious art, that is art in which the ultimate meaning of life colors the play of rich phantastic figures, can really become an art of salvation; just as the enjoyment of nature only becomes religious when it attains the metaphysical level. (See below).

These remarks have already characterized the peculiarity of the aesthetic level of objects. A further description however is necessary to delimit it from the reality which influences our psycho-physical system of energy in the biological or economic sense. The aesthetic can indubitably be immediately seen in any real thing. A plant, a landscape, a human body may be beautiful even though it confront me as a part of reality. But obviously what I apprehend as beautiful is seen by me in totally different acts than its material reality. And if these acts predominate, the objects are withdrawn from the context of material reality into a zone which one might be inclined to think of as having a lesser reality if one compared it with the relation of pressure and resistance, of desire and consumption, which predominates in the material world. (cf. Volkelt op. cit. p. 188.) Here we find ourselves already in the imaginative sphere, in the domain of imagination.

What is true of the aesthetic in nature appears even more clearly in the sphere of art. For, art rests primarily on the will to create a world of objects which are, as far as possible, liberated from the weight of material reality. As a productive aesthetic behavior it attempts to free the aesthetically important from reality and build it up as a world in its own right. This is not achieved, as has been thought through mere imitation of things but through the singling out of their aesthetic content. The contexts of reality serve as material which can be treated with relative freedom. From this we must differentiate the means of expression which are always physical and serve here only as the vehicle of imaginative activity. The same artistic object (for instance the human body) may be fashioned in clay, marble or bronze. This is only the substratum for our empathy. The real aesthetic object is not the stone or the metal but the picture which is thus stimulated in the imagination and the psychic impulse which is objectivated. Thus the language of poetry builds up a second world beside the world of reality. In certain lineaments it imitates the latter but really obeys its own laws. Other arts stay closer to their material but whatever is aesthetically effective never lies in the same plane with pure reality. From a material point of view the cathedral of Cologne is a mass of stone, but for our empathy it is something imaginative, free and soaring. If during a concert we should for one moment break the charm of the flowing tones on which we seem to be wafted along, we should find ourselves in the presence of a number of men who are scraping, blowing and drumming, men who are struggling with material. But we do not notice this.

The uniqueness of the imaginative zone of objects is brought out most clearly in its different comprehension of space and time. Aesthetic space and time are not part of the one space or the one time in which scientifically constructed reality is found but they are from the beginning, on an entirely different plane. Who could say in what time *Wallenstein* is played? It is not played in the seventeenth century, nor this evening from seven to ten o'clock, but in the real period of the performance involves a wholly different sort of time which we should have to call the poetic time. A painting likewise has real length, breadth and thickness. But the pictured space is not identical with the colored space of the canvas but is, on the contrary, for our empathy a space of the imagination. This level of objects is therefore the imaginative one and is determined for each art by special peculiarities which we cannot here pursue in greater detail.

4. The theoretic self has been most studied previously. It has an important place in all philosophy, with Kant as '*transszendentale Apperception*' and '*Bewusstsein überhaupt*', with Rickert as '*erkenntnistheoretisches Bewusstsein*', with Husserl as '*reines Ich*' and also with others. According to the idea, the subject, which carries out objectively valid judgments, is identical in all empirical individuals. One might question therefore whether one should still give the name of self to the subject which has been lifted above individuation or whether it would not be more accurate simply to call it 'logos'. But one must remember that this pure self is only an attitude and that actually cognitive acts also only appear in an individual consciousness with whose other acts it is closely interrelated. The cognizer and the thinker are always *hic et nunc* in every definite historico-geographic situation. Something is reflected back to the individual from the significance of the truth which he grasps and it gives him a generally valid content and an aspect of eternity. This ego, however, is never identical with truth itself but is only directed to it and partially grasps it with the help of acts whose peculiarity it is to found a purely objective order. The more purely these forms appear the more purely the theoretic content of experience is worked out. There is indubitably something in this attitude of the self which prepares the way for the individual's liberation from individuation. But this rise above mere chance and singleness into the general and the systematic is bought at

the price of the concrete plastic content of life. The pure cognitive attitude has about it something two-dimensional. In it one achieves extensive domination even over the most distant element, but the complete absorption of the concrete immediate content of life is possible only in aesthetic empathy, which must itself purchase its intensity at the price of extensity. Thus both avenues to salvation must always be incomplete.

The objective order which confronts the thinking and cognising self is under all circumstances ideational, (mental). We are accustomed of course to differentiate cognition, which is directed to objects of experience, from thought, which refers only to concepts. And it might seem that cognition itself contains material reality. But it does not. Because before these experiences of the effective, or this material of the senses can be at all determined, it must first be translated from the sensible into the ideational form. In other words: cognition does not grasp reality itself but a theorem, a thought structure whose unique relation to socalled reality cannot here be described. Scientific reality is itself a theorem and does not correspond to the reality of the biological self or of prescientific thought. Theoretic physics is, for instance, a thought complex which is supposed to be valid for nature but is not a copy of nature itself. Historical science is very different from the historical (even if past) reality. The minute we begin to theorize we translate reality into ideality. I think this is what Meinong means to say when he maintains that ideas present objects but that judgments always present objectivities and that these objectivities which are grasped in judgments are already objects of thought. (*Über Annahmen,* ed. 2, p. 74.)

It is nevertheless true that cognition builds upon biological experiences of reality. But just as the imaginative self grasps an aesthetic side of the material objects, so the cognizing self comprehends a theoretical one. And just as in art the productive aesthetic function is more detached from the material foundation than is the aesthetic comprehension of the physical data, so the productive theoretic function in purely conceptual thought separates itself even further from the given than the cognition which clings to the object. The classification of ideal objects has in itself many levels, from cognition (categorical determination) of the objects given *hic et nunc* to speculative thought which progresses in pure concepts, laws and theorems without wholly freeing itself from its foundation in the material of experience.

This stratification of theoretic objects cannot be followed in detail. We shall now explain what we have just rapidly sketched with reference to the significance of space and time as ideal objects. We do not refer to the fact that the meaning grasped in theoretic acts is eternally valid. Of course, even the most confined judgment of fact, insofar as it is true, is also eternally valid and not only the socalled eternal truths which transcend time because their objects belong not to the temporal but to the purely logical sphere. The significance which is, however, grasped in an aesthetic act is also eternal, as is all objective meaning content. But we are talking here of space and time as objects of cognition. They also are lifted by cognition out of the zone of biological experience into the level of thought. The space and time to which science refers are mental space and time. The general achievement of cognition to grasp identical elements in the phenomena expresses itself here in the mathematisation of space and time. And thus it is possible to think of spaces and times, even in terms of measurement and comparison, which reach far beyond the zone of individual experience. And the liberating effect of cognition is precisely that it comprehends through thought any space which cannot be really measured, and that through thought it stops time, which as experienced always goes on and only offers us in full actuality the one moment of present experience. Reality which expands in mathematical space and time is no longer material but is instead a conceptual objective order which is built up with the help of thought beyond experiences of effects (experiences of reality). It may even be possible finally to regard this theory which refers to reality merely as a special case of theoretic order just as Euclidean geometry is the immediate special case of all possible geometries (mathematical speculation).

5. The ultimate content of the self's meaning can only lie in that expansion of the soul which, as nearly as possible, abolishes individuation and leads to the highest blessedness, to *salvation*. Neither the aesthetic nor the theoretic attitude can effect this. Even if the single rays of values focus, with some natures, very closely in the zone of the self of imagination, and with others in the realm of the theoretic self, the center of the finally decisive experiences of meaning will be something other than the source

of aesthetic forms of expression or theoretic forms of thought. It seems as if the uniqueness of this highest point could only be determined either through the negation or the most extreme enhancement of all other classes of experience. The religious self is either enhancement to boundless fulness of life or negation of existence and a retreat to the value sources of formless subjectivity. But in any case it is, even when it negates, the real meaning-giver of life by means of which the partial meaning of the individual mental acts is placed and measured. One glance at the philosophies which make the metaphysical or the intelligible self or the *Âtman* their point of departure, verifies this statement.

This final self, however, is the focal point not only of value experiences but also of norm experiences. Indeed this is just the mental productivity of the deepest subjectivity, that it grants a hearing to the genuine value demands instead of merely measuring the actual value experiences with regard to their content of happiness. In a word, this self is conscience. It experiences in itself a normativity which demands the accomplishment of the highest value and the highest determination. It not only strives for ultimate blessedness, but founds this blessedness upon its ethical worth. If one follows these thoughts to their ultimate conclusion one meets with a curious antinomy which cannot be wholly solved by any theoretical metaphysics. Namely, if the self carried out all its acts according to norms without conflicting, in any side of its value life, with finality, then it would be completely unified with God, (as the highest value object). It would be blotted out and become wholly one with what Hegel called the 'Absolute Mind'. But this complete absorption in God is already limited by the fact that this religious process necessarily takes place in a self, that is, a limited field of experience. As a subject of the highest value demands (norms) the self is godlike. But the very fact that it is a self differentiates it from God, since it is limited, in need of mercy and incapable of grasping the final meaning of the world except as refracted through an individuality, like a shadow or parable. Between the two most extreme forms in which the significance of the individual self can be experienced (the most complete ecstasy and utter self denial) lies the most common form of experience. It is the significance of the religio-moral process to assert the higher self as opposed to the lower and at least approach in this way the ideal of sanctity and of likeness to God. And in this form the religious self is the most inclusive that a human being can achieve. But a tension continues in the subject-object fissure which is expressed in the religious formula: God and the soul. Therein lies both the ultimate suffering of and the final refuge from individuation. Religious yearning usually makes for a complete surrender to God: the feeling of dependence predominates and the individual soul appears as a creature of God, as a mere blossom on His stem or as one wave in the ocean of infinity. It is, however, also conceivable that religious energy should transfer itself to the side of finality, whether in the consciousness of moral freedom or the mere impossibility of abolishing individuation. Thus the mystic says:

'I know that without me God cannot live a moment.'[1])

At this point the carrying capacity of all cognitive determinations, and indeed even that of the aesthetic forms of expression, fail and there remains only the content of religious life which lies beyond all theoretic limitation and in whose real nucleus there opens up a sphere of meaning in its own right.

The fundamental question of religious philosophy is well known to be the question of whether it can be proved that there is a specific object of religious experience besides 'other' experiences. In my opinion this question is badly put since it assumes that the scientific order of objects is the normal one, so that there remain only the lacunae of science as the field of endeavor for religion. I should state the problem wholly differently as follows:

Indubitably religious experiences are possible in all the spheres of meaning which we have discussed, if only the partial meaning of these spheres is somehow raised from within to a total meaning which radiates over all of life. In other words: biologic, economic, theoretic, aesthetic, social and political formations can also be grasped in religious experiences if they enter into the decisive center of life valuation. And the socalled given reality (a very complex mental form of data) especially can easily be made the point of departure for religious impulses. But since we can call religious only that which builds up the final meaning of life, the decisive factor will always originate in the inner structure of the soul

---

[1]) Another significant citation of this kind is taken from Rainer Maria Rilke by Heinrich Scholz, *Religionsphilosophie* ed. 1, p. 182.

which not only finds classes of value but also demands their actualisation. Accordingly there are already two possible forms of contact, either in the positive form where the value of the individual region is thought of as enhanced into infinity (plus ultra) or in the negative form. In the latter the conviction that the world is without any value follows the insight that compared with the infinite longing for values all actually given values are insufficient. Both of these contrasting objective orders may be called transcendent: the first since the present data are thought of as infinitely enhanced by subjectivity and the second because it contrasts the present data with something else. This 'something else' can originate in a longing for the abolition of the world (then it is like Nirvana) or it can be based upon a postulating contrasting creation of the mind, when it signifies 'another and a better world'. In their meaning content the two religious worlds, Nirvana and the Beyond (analogously negation of self and ecstasy), are not so very different as might at first appear.

In all three forms of religious objectivity (the pantheistic, the acosmic[1]) and the supernatural) space and time receive a transformation which borders on extinction. The first conception infinitely enlarges them to the All, that is, until they correspond to infinity and eternity. The remaining two devaluate space and time as the sources of all finity and relativity and replace them by their valuable contrast, the spaceless and the timeless. One can see how both conceptions meet here. The tendency to abolish any form of space and time brings the religious object into a transcendent order. And only in complete surrender to them can the self be eternal in the midst of the temporal and the finite.

But all these conceptions could only be wish-worlds which are contrasted to or built above the socalled world. The world pictures which are created from the longing for happiness of the soul which is attuned to religious contemplation may easily be mistaken for the dreamlike worlds designed by poetic phantasy. It is quite another thing if such mental creations arise from genuine norm experiences in which the highest value determination of the soul is expressed. The ideal world picture which is opposed to the present world is then based on the power, the seriousness and

[1]) The word is here taken in the popular sense and not as Heinrich Scholz uses it in his philosophy of religion. (Berlin 1921, ed. 1.)

the validity of this value system. The experience of obligation to the highest value is thus the real foundation of the religious order of objects. This does not contain any elements whatever which are not found in other spheres of meaning. But the productive arrangement of these elements takes place from the focal point of total and absolute value positing. Just as art and science must always work with primitive conceptual material which finally originates in the biological zone so religion also is tied to these elements. The formations of theoretic and aesthetic acts partly are fundaments of religious impulses, but partly it makes use of these acts in order to formulate and to symbolize its own unique arrangement of the given. Out of this develop, for objective religions, the most complicated structural relations which cannot possibly be understood if they are investigated from the viewpoint of their theoretic context of meaning.

The most important point of origin of 'genuine' religion must always be the tension between the normatively demanded values and values as they are really found, indeed in the limits of value realization as such. The more vividly this tension is experienced in the innermost soul, the more clearly the transcendency of the religious objects appears. The pronounced theorists may avow a panlogism, the aesthetes an aesthetic pantheism and already these monisms go far beyond the biological data. The outspoken lovers of freedom however, who wish to assert ethical values as opposed to the humdrum world, usually experience it as a harsh (theistic or atheistic) dualism.

Since every other meaning order in this field is rejected as insufficient or is at least devaluated, and since we lack every specific means of expression of religiosity, what is really final remains everywhere unexpressible. The confessions of the mystics contain in themselves nothing that can be taken hold of or communicated in itself. They only paraphrase again and again, either in the form of enhancement or of the negation of the 'earthly' the subjective vision of the highest value. 'God lives in a light which noone can approach.' The fact that the religious attitude lacks any adequate means of expression, and speaks now the language of aesthetics and now that of cognition without really meaning either, is a new reason for calling the religious object transcendent. At bottom everything is found only in the depths of the lonely soul. Whatever one projects from this silent Âtman always has the unique metaphysical character of an 'other world'. This seems to be the source of 'revelation' even though it really only flows internally; and in a place which is figuratively either before all the formation of the other value regions (immanent mysticism — *gestaltlose Mystik*) or beyond all special forms in the infinitely distant focal point of these separated values (*gestaltgebende Mystik*).

The contour of life results from the fusion and interfusion of the aforementioned layers in the process of mental existence. But in regard to the ego we have a further complication in the fact that the meaning content of the self is also determined by the social basic acts. In the political self there is a pronounced ego emphasis since its significance consists entirely in the affirmation of its own value positings. The social self on the other hand, contains a subjective expansion (which must not be confused with that of aesthetic empathy) since it signifies surrender to foreign values and value positings, most of all when it appears in its highest form as a person who loves. On one hand we have a decisive emphasis of individuation, on the other its conquest whether in the form of giving, receiving or the unfolding community of values.

Every total or partial value community founds a new level of self consciousness, which we shall call the collective self. The individual is doubly a member of the community to which he feels, or knows through reflection, that he belongs as a part and as a sample. He is a part because he receives from and gives to the community mental effects, with which may be mingled political acts, and is thus in effectual reciprocal relation with it. On this is built already a consciousness of union which becomes stronger if the correlation of effects originates in a summating likeness of essential characteristics or results in an inner adaptation of the individual members. The individual is a sample because he may be regarded in his entire mental makeup, or at least in one of its sides, as a special case of the species which recurs typically in the members of the community. He will usually have as a member of the community these identical traits as a definite direction of value consciousness. If both join; consciousness of union and consciousness of identical value direction, then there develops in the self a kind of overindividual mind. The group as such has no soul, but it gives to every one of its members, insofar as it affects them as a mental reality, an overindividual psychic content, a kind of collective self.

This form of overindividual consciousness must by no means be confused with the overindividuality of the theoretic self. For, the significance of the latter is the ideal general validity. That of the collective self, however, is only a socially founded common direction of value attitude. The idea is that the subject of the theory of cognition is identical in all cognizing individuals: it can only be thought of as one. There are on the contrary (as overindividual meaning attitudes) as many collective selves in the individual self as the latter has voluntary relations in social groups. I can feel myself simultaneously a member and representative of a people, a member of a profession, a member of a club and a member of a family. The many collective attitudes in the single self can conflict not only with the ego but with each other. Over and above all this we must consider the value content of the different groups of community; and according as to whether this is economic, aesthetic, theoretic or religious the content of the collective self in question undergoes an expansion or restriction. All these points of view would have to be dealt with in a theory of overindividual subjects. But this new problem far exceeds the limit of this book as I have planned it. And in the consideration of individual types we shall not deal with it, excepting for a few chance side views in regard to the social and political types which very seldom appear on the level of the individual self but have instead an overindividual collective content.

SUMMARY AND OUTLINE

The studies which we have made so far, are of the general nature of a philosophy of culture or *Geisteswissenschaft*. We shall now apply them to the problem of mental individuality, where it is our intention to found a *geisteswissenschaftliche* psychology of individuality, an ethology or characterology. This limitation of the problem is an artifice since it allows us to study mental phenomena on a level of relatively low complexity. It must be borne in mind that the basic types which we develop are not photographs of real life but are based upon an isolating and idealising method. In this way eternal and ideal types are developed which are to be used as constructions or normal structures in connection with the phenomena of historical and social reality.

We find them by considering in each case one definite meaning and value direction as the dominant one in the individual structure.[1] And in view of our principle that in every mental phenomenon the totality of mind is somehow immanent, the other mental acts cannot be absent. But their achievements are transformed in every case in such a way that they seem to be subordinated to the dominant value direction in a way which will be explained in greater detail. They carry its color, or if this is not possible, are repressed to utter meaninglessness. We may symbolize this in the figure of a gambler's die, of which in every instance one side with its figures must lie uppermost. The others are not,

---

[1] I have never maintained that characterology cannot orient itself by other elements than the dominant value direction of the individual. I do, however, insist that the mental character of man is principally determined through the value organ by means of which he lives and shapes his own life. When I wrote this book I did not know that Max Scheler in his very important work *der Formalismus in der Ethik und die materiale Wertethik* Halle 1916, 2. ed. 1921, p. 607, also brings forward the idea of definite personal value types.

however, absent but are instead in a definite relation to the figures on top. The isolating and idealising method is thus reenforced by the totalising (*totalisierende*) method. Here we remain. If we wanted to describe the manifoldness of the historically determined types we should have to add an individualising (*individualisierende*) procedure. But this point of view of historical peculiarities does not enter in here. We want only to work out the few most general forms of personality.

In the following we shall start with each type from the central region and relate the five others to it. The direction of relation must appear to us *a priori* from the meaning of the basic sphere. For, the directions of mental acts and their interrelation to a total structure are within us *a priori* (even though not in every single detail). This is not the merely intellectual *a priori* but the plastic basic structure of life by means of which we are able with a variation of our individual attitude to anticipate or to follow intelligently situations which we have not experienced. Besides these five points of view we shall present a section on the type of motivation which belongs to each life form. For, it will be clearly seen that the reasonable choice of one or more value emphasized purposes and the causal-theoretical calculation of the means necessary to their attainment, is only a special kind of motivation which originates in a blend of the theoretic and economic types and which we might call the type of technical motivation. This type is characteristic of our time, but not of all time nor indeed of all beings of our time. With the consideration of motivation we already touch upon the specific ethics of this region, but we must remember that this section is purely psychological. In other words, no value judgments are made in regard to the types except those which refer to what follows of their inner construction. Even where we speak of an ethical tendency we refer only to the psychology of these ethics. For, we can grasp psychologically the psychic mental attitude which belongs to every ethical attitude of an individual. Normative experiences always have a psychological slant even though the norms themselves and their validity cannot be the object of purely psychological consideration. Besides the question of the type of motivation and the type of ethics we shall make a survey of the most important forms into which the types can be differentiated. The standpoint of such differentiation will be drawn from the unique structure of each region and thus differ for every type. Many examples will be given, but these of course have a historically determined factor and are never clear cases. It will, furthermore, be difficult for us to avoid taking most of the examples from our own and classic culture. For, this study can only be applied without mediating interpretations to cultures whose meaning directions are already clearly differentiated. This is often so pronounced on the modern (*neuzeitlichen*) level of development (in the classic period as well as our own time) that the unitary structure of the mind seems to have been broken up. The great onesided types are forms of heroic proportion. There are however, onesided structures which represent malformations and border on an incapacity to cope with life. Development and decay are phases of the same process, and thus for a long time objective dissolution appears subjectively as progress. The historico-philosophical considerations which press themselves upon us are only touched upon at the end of this book even though I have very decided opinions on this subject. — And finally we add to the differentiated forms which belong to these types a few remarks about the counterparts of each which, if one likes the ambiguous expression, may be called a *Ressentimenterscheinung*. Often, however, it originates in other and much deeper roots than is indicated by this name of a decaying epoch.

The second section is purposely limited to the basic types. All questions of normativity and mixed types, and specially all collective subjects are temporarily omitted. The third section considers the ethical problem. The surprising fact that we do not advance a specifically moral sphere and moral type must be accepted until then without any further reason being given. The fourth section offers remarks on types of mixed and historically determined characters and adds supplementary data by means of which the application of the developed *geisteswissenschaftliche* psychology in research and life will be made a little clearer.

In carrying out this plan we shall refer throughout to the basic discussion in this first section. We do not, however, have to give any further proof that the problem which we have set is justified, even though others should reach conclusions which differ in some details from those we have drawn.

PART II

THE IDEALLY BASIC TYPES OF INDIVIDUALITY

1
THE THEORETIC ATTITUDE

I

On higher developmental levels, cognition is such an integral part of all other mental acts that it almost seems to be the essential achievement of mental life.[1] This impression is strengthened by the fact that science intends to draw a picture of the world and the soul as they are in themselves. Furthermore, all other attitudes are necessarily viewed in this scientific light if one subsequently makes them the object of introspection or historical representation. But merely because a thing can become an object of scientific reflection it need not for that reason be a purely intellectual phenomenon. Cognition is thus one, but not the only function of mental life. It has its unique act-structure which is most clearly seen when the will to cognize appears; that is when the value of purely objective behavior in conscious mental activity (which usually only carries on a work already begun by history) becomes dominant. Logic attempts to discover the purely immanent structure of thought; the theory of cognition investigates the application of

---

[1] It has been said in controversion to the delineation which I have here given of the theoretic man, that it did not coincide with many historically given forms of science; for instance with philology and the history of mental life. It could not have been more highly praised. For, I particularly wish to call the reader's attention to the fact that the $\vartheta\varepsilon\omega\varrho\iota\alpha$ of Plato and Aristotle for instance, is not identical with the pure scientific spirit but contains aesthetic and religious factors. In the same way there is no writing of history, no understanding interpretation of Mind without some admixture of aesthetic empathy, artistic imagery, ethical normativity or ultimate world view characteristics. It is all the more necessary, therefore, to show how inseparably pure theoretic Mind is interwoven in every complex structure of reality. Cf. my essay *Der gegenwaertige Stand der Geisteswissenschaften und die Schule*. 2. ed. Leipzig 1925, especially footnote 8.

this structure to the world of space and time or other objects. Insofar as such a science aims only at the inner validity of cognition in its widest sense (i. e. its objective validity), the psychological interweaving of cognitive acts with those of other attitudes, indeed even the psychic functions and contents which play a role in cognition, are only of secondary interest. Cognition, however, is never given in its unique act structure, but is constantly interwoven with aesthestic, religious or economic motives. This is clearly seen on the mythological level and it would be a great mistake to think that mythology has been wholly banished from our present scientific cognition. The theoretic attitude is in fact only a tendency, which, like all other tendencies, never appears in human beings either in complete isolation or in perfect harmony with value (ideality). It is only a fiction and never found in reality, though its inner consequence may be approximately attained by a man in whom the cognitive attitude dominates.

What is such a cognitive set? Our aim is not to develop a complete logic and theory of cognition. This would only involve us in an endless discussion. Our problem is to delimit this attitude from all others and determine the general meaning which must be realized in cognition.

The meaning of cognition, in contrast with all other mental activity is objectivity. Entities which appear in consciousness with a specific not-I character are so treated that their content is freed from everything which appertains to individual peculiarities or immediate states of mind of the experiencing subject. The result is the 'pure object'. According to the idea of cognition it has to prove its objective character by giving the same picture to every observer. The general validity of pure cognition then lies in the fact that it is valid for every cognitive consciousness. Modern theories of cognition have shown, however, that objectivity cannot be achieved as 'pure' experience but is always mingled with other active achievements of the conscious subject. It depends upon certain acts whose unique significance is to grasp or constitute objective reality. The general character of these acts is centered in the fact (1) that they mean or intend something (this is the basis of the transsubjective achievement of all thought); (2) that they posit this intended something as an identical factor in all similar acts and so distinguish its essence from all other objects.

This view of identity and non-identity may be applied in two ways: (a) it may be directed to the general essence which then comprises a wealth of special phenomena which may even be in different levels of generality; (this is the second form of generality — the objective) and (b) it may consist in a conjunction or separation of entities which are thus emphasized.[1]) In the former we find an activity which transforms or builds up an essential context. This activity is always dependent on the law of adequate reason. The unitary achievement of cognition consists in the assigning of reasons. There develops thus a complex of laws which follow one from another according to strict cognitive legality. In its highest development such a body of laws is called a system.

Whenever this attitude aiming at objectivity, the attitude which identifies and differentiates, generalizes and individualizes, conjoins and separates, reasons and systematizes, whenever this attitude becomes dominant, it is self-evident that all subjective relations such as: feeling and desiring, attraction and repulsion, fearing and hoping must sink into the background. For, this method of apprehending belongs only to the subject, whether the subjectivity is rooted in the species: man, an individual, or in his temporary state of mind. Pure science (unless it makes value-qualities the object of cognition) recognizes nothing as beautiful or ugly, useful or useless, holy or impious but only as true or false. Only the objective essence of the phenomenon must be realized. The state of mind of the cognising scientist is characterized by the absence of affectivity. General objective validity is his only aim. To give him an old psychological name, he is necessarily an 'intellectualist'. He can have only one passion, that for objective knowledge; only one kind of longing, to solve a problem, explain a question or formulate a theory. He despairs when ignorant and rejoices over a purely theoretic discovery even if it should be an insight which would mean his death. He exhausts himself as a physical being to give birth to a purely intellectual world based on reason. He has a feeling for the purity of the cognitive process, a feeling which cares for nothing but truth. His world becomes a network of general entities and a system of

---

[1]) General validity then, comprehends: (1) validity for all subjects (universality of the subject). (2) Validity of all objects which have been included in this general concept or law (universality of the object).

interrelations. And by means of this he transcends the moment. He lives in an eternal world, his eyes gazing into the distant future and sometimes comprehending whole epochs of the world's history. And in this reflection he intertwines past and present in an ordered whole which his mind can master. He partakes of the immortality which radiates from the eternal validity of his truths. Even his practical behavior is systematized to a degree which is impossible for the instinctive creature of the moment. He has become, so to speak, all objectivity, necessity, general validity and applied logic. We can find this attitude most easily among scholars who follow chosen careers in their lives' work. But elementary forms of this type may be found independent of vocational life. Here the structural aspect appears perhaps even more clearly than in the more complex natures of great men.

II

To attempt to comprehend the whole experiential content objectively is like projecting a plastic object upon a plane. When the cognitive value is placed first the others must necessarily suffer. At least they undergo a structurally determined transformation which can only be understood if we constantly remind ourselves of their relation to the theoretic man's life center.

No complete life is possible without economic acts. External pressure, physical needs and all the material bases of intellectual achievement make themselves felt even though one wishes to dedicate oneself to purely objective study. But no other side of existence is to him so unimportant subjectively, as these immediate needs. For, utilitarian interests necessitate such a strong subjective emphasis that they injure all pure cognition. And this disinterested cognitive attitude is just what has led to objective systems which would never have been developed if observation had been restricted to the directly useful and 'applied'. For this reason any purely scientific training consciously repudiates all immediately practical application and utilitarian interest. (I might cite here the idealism of our classical period which followed the utilitarian rationalism of the eighteenth century.) The necessary consequence is that in the face of the practical problems of life the pure theorist is helpless. He has not learned to relate his reflections to specific practical situations and the necessary purpose-means considerations.

He is ill fitted for a struggle for existence, not because he lacks understanding, but because such an attitude is foreign to his nature. His consequent helplessness is often carried over to the simplest technical problems. 'Kant, the great theorist, and Lampe, the small mechanic, the first all head, the second all hands, were often nonplussed by insignificant things.'[1]) *Philosophari necesse est, vivere non est necesse!* A scholar may surround himself with a mass of books and instruments and yet have no bed to sleep in, as Hermann Reich reports of Paul von Winterfeldt. — Plato depreciates the economic type of man. Spinoza carries on a modest trade which does not satisfy him. — In seeming contradiction to all this we find that scholars sometimes develop a pathological miserliness or even an astonishing passion to accumulate wealth. 'Where your treasure is, there will your heart be also': perhaps these are not born theorists and, like many of the old (and new) sophists, really are utilitarians. We can understand however, that the pure theorist might exhibit such traits. They come from the feeling that the practical side of life presents almost insuperable difficulties. For this reason their deficiency expresses itself in haphazard accumulation, not so much for the love of possession as in the desire for freedom from such material worries. The theorist loathes the economic attitude with its very specific law. Where we find the earnest conviction that economic possessions make for independence, there we no longer have the pure theoretic type but instead a mixed attitude. Schopenhauer was not a pure theorist; his limits were set by the will.

This contrast between the theoretic and economic attitudes has been most strongly expressed by the Greek thinkers who looked scornfully upon any form of earning one's living. They felt that the business interest of the sophists was definitely opposed to the purely philosophic state of mind. And since the $\vartheta\varepsilon\omega\varrho\iota\alpha$ which also stood for the aesthetic set was their highest value, the word $\beta\acute{\alpha}\nu\alpha\upsilon\sigma\varsigma$ acquired the same deprecatory meaning which they gave to the word $\beta\acute{\alpha}\varrho\beta\alpha\varrho\varsigma$. And when today we are offended by the mixing of the commercial attitude with research, quest for truth and philosophic reflection, this is not only an aftereffect of the ancient Greek point of view but is expressive of an

---
[1]) Wasianski, Immanuel Kant in seinen letzten Lebensjahren, Deutsche Bibliothek. p. 239.

eternal psychology. The economic and the theoretic attitudes cannot both have a place in the same soul, at least not in equal proportions.

The economic attitude nevertheless enters cognitive behavior as a subordinated factor. For, even cognitive acts demand a certain economy; they are without injuring their immanent lawfulness psycho-physiological achievements which must obey the economy of energy. A physical formula, perhaps a yard long, may be accurate, but it cannot thus be used as a means of cognition. A certain technique underlies all scientific research (the historical as well as the physical) which often necessitates very precise instruments and consequently presupposes a certain mechanical aptitude. But all this must be subordinated. Where economy of thought becomes the ruling principle, as in certain forms of pragmatism, pure cognitive laws are abolished and cognition once more becomes a means to biological ends which perhaps it once was upon an undifferentiated level. The same may be said of certain perversions of experimental psychology where the chief requirement is no longer thought, but rather technical ability.

The aesthetic attitude is also necessarily devaluated by the theoretic type because of his dominant set. His goal is truth and this can be achieved only by critically purging cognition of all subjective additions. Aesthetic imagination, on the other hand, is distinctly subjective; it is empathy, sometimes even productive of imaginative combinations and artistic inventions. The theorist's passionate objection to all such dreamers and Romanticists, who want to enter into the object with all their emotional powers, is thus quite easily understood. 'Intuition' may become a method now and then but fundamentally it is devoid of method and purely impulsive (whim). Hegel used to say that one could do nothing with people who were entirely guided by emotion. In addition, the aesthetic type ultimately clings with his whole soul to form while the scientist strives to master it intellectually and analyze it into general essences. Only that is scientific which has been grasped in a generally valid sense, and therefore the aim of science is conceptual description but not the stimulation of an emotional attitude. Plato, himself a poet, banished poets from his philosophic state in which the theoretic ideal was placed above everything else because poets did not desire primarily truth but rather to excite feelings and to stimulate emotions which were often ethically dangerous.[1]) He also saw in them beings twice removed from reality because they copied single objects which were in themselves copies, instead of going back to the original, eternal and generally valid Idea. The stoics believed imagination to be the greatest danger of the wise man who strove to regulate his life by general laws, because the *imaginatio* chained man to single objects and external things. This devaluation of the pictorial imagination, the *imaginatio*, can be traced up to modern rationalism, and Spinoza's position in this regard is well known. In the Leibnitzean school the *imaginatio* rises from the level of a confused cognition to an independent aesthetic importance. The theorist, however, does not lack conceptual imagination, but he subjects it to strict relation and discipline. It is *Vorbildungskraft* which is dominated throughout by objective laws.[2])

When the theorist views artistic objects he judges them with his own peculiar bias. He traces their influences from a purely scientific standpoint and tries to formulate his conclusions in aesthetics, not content until he has based the concrete artistic object upon a formulated general idea which satisfies his rational needs. Kant's objection to music is probably not due only to a natural defect in his ear but also to his psychological structure. To him music was the most unintellectual art since he never understood or discovered the general laws upon which it is based (*die Thematik*).[3]) The pure theorist is primarily interested in the object, in rational technique or pure concepts in a manner directly opposed to the aesthetic attitude.

And yet even the purest theorist cannot quite exclude the aesthetic factor but must recognize this attitude at least as a

---

[1]) A similar fanatical adherence to truth as an enemy of art is found in Rousseau, based here, however, on ascetic rather than theoretic motives. Here we must also class the objection which is felt by some philosophers with a decided logical trend to the socalled philosophy of life. They scent in this an aesthetic or mystical element which they cannot understand.

[2]) Cf. Gladstone, Faraday (p. 47 of the German translation). On the function of imagination in science see my essay: *Phantasie und Weltanschauung* in the collected volume *Weltanschauung* Berlin 1911 p. 142 ff; and also Heinrich Maier *Psychologie des emotionalen Denkens*. Tuebingen 1908 ch. 5: Kognitive Phantasietaetigkeit und Phantasieurteile.

[3]) The mathematician's question on hearing a Beethoven symphony is famous: 'Beautiful, but what is thus proved by it?'

8*

subordinate act. All thought finally borders on the individual, the pictorial. Even the most abstract logical process seems to have a substratum, no matter how inadequate, which is imaginative. No thought is wholly possible without illustrative and representative ideas. It has often been demonstrated that the fruitfulness of empirical thought ultimately depends upon the wealth and plasticity of such ideas. An empirical thinker (botanist, geographer etc.) for this reason is most closely related to the aesthetic type: though Kant's abstract intellect too seems to have achieved a great deal in this aesthetic direction. Geometry exhibits an aesthetic character because its concepts also have form, even though it is only empathic (rational) form of the theoretic 'soul'.

Similar aesthetic claims are perhaps even more valid in those sciences which make the single instance not the starting point but rather the aim of their endeavor; that is, the descriptive sciences and fine art. In them the general (namely concept und lawful context) are means. The problem itself, however, consists in drawing a picture (representation) which all art uses in order to suggest a concrete imaginative picture. No matter how closely history seems to be bound up with factual material and mental laws which are embodied in the understanding, it ultimately approaches art. The various reasons for this cannot be developed in detail here.[1]) Especially today when the conceptual outfit of the historian is still so imperfectly developed, the aesthetic acts are very much in the foreground and it is in the nature of things that this attitude cannot be completely abolished. For, historical reconstruction is directed to isolated occurrences which are only accessible to the imagination. Besides this, history must enter into empathic relations with past eras and their unique states of mind. This empathic relation is not indicative of aesthetic enjoyment, but is a necessary foundation for the specific *geisteswissenschaftliche*

---

[1]) Cf. W. v. Humboldt's famous comparison of the poet and the historian in his *Rede ueber die Aufgabe des Geschichtschreibers* and Novalis *Ofterdingen* I. 5.; also my essay *W. v. H.'s Rede ueber die Aufgabe des Geschichtschreibers und die Schellingsche Philosophie*. Historische Zeitschrift vol. 100. Indicative of the aesthetic attitude is the interweaving of the particular with the general, so that the seemingly individual cases of history illustrate a general law. This attitude is expressed again and again in Ranke's solemn phrase: 'And here I believe I see a general law of life.'

cognitive acts which we call concrete understanding. The historian is, however, more subjective in these achievements than if he were only trying to understand triangles and circles. A student of *Geisteswissenschaft* is, therefore, always less theoretic than the investigator of cognate objects which cannot be value subjects in themselves. The pure theorist appears more clearly when special methods which have been developed to explain natural objects are artificially applied to *geisteswissenschaftliche* objects.

Let us now turn to the social field where we at once observe one striking fact; namely, that the theorist is a complete individualist. Despite the ideational general validity of all knowledge, the critical will, the will to the autonomous rethinking of naive convictions, is something so distinctly personal, that every intellectualism is therefore perforce an individualism. This explains why the pure theorist cannot be a social nature. His coolly objective mental attitude is antithetical to sympathetic or empathic relations with others, with their broad or narrow but always strongly subjective minds. He cares neither for his ancestors nor his neighbors, nor is he interested in public meetings as Plato illustrates in the beautiful interlude on the wise man in Theaetet.[1] The wise man lives in the eternal no matter how distant. In contemplating eternity, the occasional and haphazard in his immediate environment may escape his observation. Family ties seem to him unimportant. For, neither blood relation nor an altruistic desire to help ties him to mankind. Not aesthetic enjoyment of the human soul, but the brotherhood of research, truth, and knowledge unites him to others. The only kind of community which is in accordance with his nature is that of convictions held in common. Wherever his attitude is understood he feels at home. When science was not so differentiated as now an invisible academy of thought united even thinkers of different nations. This form of social relation also is not plastic. It is based upon a onesided knowledge of mankind. No matter how carefully the theorist studies men, his powers of understanding are limited by his dominant attitude. Everywhere he finds intellectual motives and abilities and tends to generalize his observations. The individuality and irrationality of any single occurrence which can only be grasped by intuition are beyond him. Approach the theorist for advice in a practical

---

[1] Theaitetos. p. 175.

situation and he inclines to look upon the issue from the standpoint of all human experience or definite laws and to overlook the subtle and individualizing points. The consolation which he offers will probably be based on some such generality as: 'This often happens in life.' In regard to single instances of everyday life he has more wisdom than shrewdness. This explains perhaps why we have no satisfactory psychologies or moral philosophies which deal adequately with life. In these fields the eye of the artist is more keen than that of the scholar.

The same phenomena are repeated in the political sphere. It cannot be denied that the theorist has a decided feeling of superiority because of his mental achievements. But he cannot make use of it because he lacks the interest in the concrete which comprehends the individual peculiarities of any given case. The dictum: knowledge is power, should thus be qualified: insofar as one knows how to use it. But executive ability is lacking in the specifically theoretic type. The consciousness of power is here expressed instead in the vague feeling: I could if I would. But he has no desire to do so since in that very moment he would deny the central interest of his life. Ranke, who cried in his old age: 'But I cannot die yet; I know so much that noone else knows!'; and Hegel, who comprehended his tumultuous period from an almost eschatological point of view that the world not only was as it was, but must be so and signified a mental apex; are very similar natures. Fichte is a totally different character. For him all science points to a formative art of reason (*gestaltende Vernunftkunst.*) The theorist's will to act usually spends itself in criticism and polemics. These are his weapons. Once he has shown that a current opinion is false he does not know what remains to be done. His entire ambition can be centered in the solution of a limited problem. Erasmus could not understand how anyone found Luther's German translation of the New Testament more important than his own Latin translation. The ambition of the scholar is proverbial. Perhaps his need for concrete and immediate recognition is due to the fact that minor scholars who engage in isolating research, want at least to be recompensed for the sacrifice of their immediate nearness to life, by having the eyes of others upon them. But anyone who investigates truly great problems and is seized by the passion for knowledge needs no other blessedness than he finds in quiet activity, and his unremarked existence is solaced by the conviction that the truth will make its own way after his death. Nevertheless it is striking that so few scholars love the anonymity into which all really general truth must finally sink. Apparently everybody likes to be compensated for his expenditure of energy.

Wherever the theorist, misapprehending his own nature, does actively enter politics, his limitations are immediately seen. He is inclined to think that education is the only road to progress. All positivists from Condorcet to Buckle and those of today represent this intellectualistic dogma. They forget that knowledge is of positive value only when it has been brought into organic relation with the other mental powers of its possessor. Human beings are not mere creatures of reason. And even though we may pardon the theorist's error in looking upon all human intelligence as equal because the results of correct thinking are equally valid, we must insist that the nonintellectual structure of man is an eternal obstacle to their equality. This passion for equality is often nothing but an offshoot of the purely theoretic attitude. But in the following we shall relate it to other states of mind also. The average intellectualist has a political affinity for radicalism because he bases manysided reality upon conceptual generalities. So he is also a cosmopolitan; for, racial differences lie not so much in intellectual structure (though here too) as in imagination, sociological viewpoints and religion.

The more advanced theorist, however, tends to be aristocratic and is very sceptical as to the educability of the masses. He even doubts whether such education if possible would be a blessing. Plato only planned for a few rulers and those were philosophers. But the development of his rational state is nevertheless radical since the historico-psychological attitude was far from his mind in those days and also because he not only knew but made demands. A democracy executed Socrates. Perhaps Protagoras had already seen the truth which Seneca[1]) and Fichte later developed; that it is not a matter of indifference on what background of character knowledge is developed. Or to express this in ethical terms: character is essential to real knowledge. *The knower in the highest sense is however never the doer.* For, action necessitates something

---
[1]) Epist. 114.

like Cassandra's veil. Otherwise who would dare to oppose the hand of fate?

In order to evaluate the theorist's religious behavior one must make it clear that pure cognition does not create values; i. e. no values can be proved or disproved in a purely intellectual manner. (See above p. 45). Or to put it more simply: valuations are neither true nor false. They can only be based upon true or false judgments. Scientific progress necessitates a structural transformation of value attitudes.[1]) In like manner it may be possible for science to make value-contexts its object. Pure knowledge does not create values. The valuing attitude is innate. With increasing insight into objective occurrences valuations are changed. Even the reflection on values (finally developed to Theory of value or Ethics) may bring about structural changes. But science cannot reach the heart of valuation. And consequently the relating of a partial value experience to the total value of life is not an intellectual achievement. The theorist nevertheless hopes that he has included the total value of the universe in a comprehensive cognition of existence. He can maintain this by virtue of his own nature because the value which is associated with the highest cognition actually is his highest value.

We find, however, two theoretic religious attitudes. On one hand the theorist clings so strongly to pure objective cognition that every other longing is banished from his mind, and he has no other passion than for the critically purified knowledge which is directed only to facts and their functional relations. This is the positivistic type who rejects religion because it seems to him only an antiquated form of cognition. Others may accept the fundamental tendency of religion, i. e. its attitude toward totality and the highest value in life. They believe, however that even this ultimate might be satisfied by cognitive means, and accordingly explain cognition as a comprehension of the absolute and the socalled transcendental. This is the eternal type of metaphysician. He embodies the undying longing for knowledge which strives to reach the Absolute. For him the world is nothing but a context of thought. This idea, born out of logical principles and a religious attitude toward life, can be traced back to the Stoic *ratio*, whose influence could still be found in the natural

---

[2]) Cf. *Der gegenwaertige Stand der Geisteswissenschaften* p. 55 ff.

system of the *Geisteswissenschaften* of the 16th., 17th., and 18th. centuries, and played a role even in the speculative systems of Fichte, Schelling and Hegel. Its essence was thought to be the source of eternal, immutable and generally valid principles. Since these can only be seen in logic we can understand that in this way all mental spheres were made logical and rational. The concept of the *ratio* could not, therefore, survive when the historical attitude, the experience of the will and individualisation came to the fore in modern thought. To subject even reason to the process of historical development and individualisation was the grandiose attempt Hegel made in his system of philosophy.[1]) This rationalism appears today as the modernised formal rationalism of the Marburg and Rickert schools. But all these are based on the theoretic type, a kind of deification of logical and cognitive acts. Aristotle's god already reflected the attitude of this philosopher because he was the highest personification of the βίος θεωρητικός. Spinoza of course knew that he did not comprehend God the universal by the *ratio* only and that he must necessarily postulate a sort of super-cognition, the *intuitio*. Nevertheless his love for God remains an *amor intellectualis*. Kant made the moral 'ought' the basis of religion. But rational deism shows itself here also, insofar as he too strives for a 'religion within the boundaries of pure reason', even though it is only practical reason. Hegel saw all partial knowledge, even purely imaginative, i. e. mythological religion completed in the conceptual self-apprehension of the Absolute Mind. Afterwards a reaction took place with Feuerbach and A. Ritschl. Desire and evaluation were looked upon as sources of religiosity. But even upon this irrational ground a less pure theoretic type can settle, namely the theorist who wants to reduce the content of religious consciousness (the state of piety) to general laws which are to be understood of course in a psychological sense. His scientific goal is the descriptive understanding of the religious mood and the conceptual determination of its basic phenomena. This is the type of the religious dogmatist. As a rule such men only advance the content of a historical tradition. But to them also religion is essentially a 'dogma'.

All theoretic types share in their religious attitude a repugnance for mysticism, that is, for pure feeling and whatever cannot be

---

[1]) Cf. W. Dilthey, *Die Jugendgeschichte Hegels*. — E. Cassirer, *Idee und Gestalt*. Berlin 1921. p. 142. 145.

put into strict categories. Cognition must either conquer God or lead to him and it is only a natural reflection of their behavior that God appears to them as the greatest thinker whose original intellect (*intellectus archetypus*) has impressed the forms of the universe upon matter. The irrationality of a creation out of nothing is usually avoided. It is easy, however, to picture God as the first thinker of this ideational cosmos if the universe has been reduced to a pure context of thought. The most specific theoretic form of religion is a rational metaphysics.

III

The theoretic type has a special form of motivation which corresponds to the subordination of what they regard as secondary values to the dominant value of cognition. It is clear that this attitude is no longer dependent on feeling. But even such an independence of any practical aim offered by the environment does not satisfy the theorist's love for rational completeness and systematisation. For, every individual purpose would necessitate a new evaluation of its value character and the causal means which are at hand. The theorist, however, wants to raise even his practical behavior to the sphere of general legality. He is, therefore, guided by principles. It is his ideal to be consistent in his willing and to make his personality approach the strictness and unequivocality of a logical system. Or, to reduce it to its basic value factor: out of a multitude of value classes his highest class is that of ordinating values which are based upon the general and generally valid legality of occurrences. The theorist does not wish to be an inconsistent entity in a world of order; he does not want to be the means of bringing something chaotic into the world. For this reason he is motivated by general validity of behavior, by maxims. And in this way he is at one with himself and inwardly consistent. He himself becomes the fountain head -if we may use this expression- of practical logic. The contemplative Stoic is the best illustration of this behavior and tries to act according to the laws of his own nature, i. e. according to the principle of inner consistency. He frees himself from the allurements of his worldly imagination and excludes as far as possible the factor of receptivity. Kant really only modernised this type with the addition of a slight political tinge. In the class of motives which he deems ethically valuable neither love, utility, inner harmony nor striving for mental happiness is included. There is instead only the form of legality which, a second nature, is built into the kingdom of ends. This does not represent the only true form of ethics, even though methodologically, as we shall see later, Kant has found the decisive factor of morality, but rather a perfect reflection of his noble and yet biassed attitude. 'Kant's outstanding characteristic (according to all who knew him) was a constant endeavor to act according to carefully thought out principles which, at least as far as he knew, were wellfounded. He was always eager to establish maxims from which one must start and to which one must return, no matter how small or great, how important or trivial was the issue.'[1]) One must admit that such an attitude, if carried over to trivial relations, must necessarily become pedantic, and in very important cases, impossible. Nevertheless this represents not only the peculiar motivation of the theoretic type but also its Ethos. Consistency of behavior, purely as form, is of course an ethics without flesh and blood. It fits the theoretic type all the better since in his equitempered contemplative life there is seldom any call for action. As a social virtue he has of course, truth. This virtue is so important to the theorist that he will set it above everything else in his human relations, provided of course that he has the courage. The theorist can as little understand the individualizing love which, in certain circumstances, will hide a truth as the shrewd calculation which will see only truths which are convenient. Self-control, consistency of behavior and passionate truth-telling characterize the Ethos of the theorist. And we must expressly remind ourselves that this attitude is not confined to the scholar. It may appear, as everyone knows from personal experience, in simple walks of life.

IV

When we examine the differentiated forms in which the theoretic attitude can be found, we also disclose the degrees in which this type is realized. Since, however, the scholarly profession -a social calling which is partially determined by external influences- does not entirely coincide with these deeper essential traits, we shall, in the following utilize the basic directions which may

[1]) Borowski, *Immanuel Kant*, Deutsche Buecherei p. 51. Cf. there also Jachmann p. 150.

appear in the scientific attitude only as symptoms of a psychic structure which may dominate the entire course of life. The theorist in this widest sense always views life with the eyes of a reflective observer and is therefore not born to act. But if he acts he does so as a result of cool cognition and reflection. For him all of life is colored by theory, but the theory itself is susceptible of as many variations as there are kinds of cognition.

The division according to cognitive factors must be given the first place since they make the most important differences. All cognition is based upon two factors: the empirical and the *a priori*, no matter where the line between them is drawn. The empiricist is dependent upon his material and must possess faithful powers of observation. This necessitates a certain acoustic, optic, motor etc. ability which is investigated by the differential psychology of elements.[1] A certain incapacity for intellectual mastery is often characteristic of the empiricist. He is easily lost in the wealth of material whether made up of historical or natural facts. The *a priori* thinker, on the contrary, starts with the immanent lawfulness of thought. He develops concepts out of his inner constructive activity. He regards intensely the *denominationes intrinsicae*, the inner criteria of truth. Thus he is in danger of arriving at conceptual structures which are unrelated to the world of facts. Hegel, when confronted with the incongruence between his speculations and reality, answered: 'All the worse for reality'. This form of speculative theorist is a specially interesting type. He is, as it were immured in his conceptual world and is incapable of a simple relation with concrete phenomena. Our investigation is itself in danger of becoming a mere schematic outline and only a constant observation of life can help us to avoid this. The most fruitful cognitive set is found in a combination of the empirical and conceptual attitudes. In agreement with Kant we might call this the critical type. For it is the problem of criticism to evolve the decisive categories in which the application of thought to experiential data is bound up, or better: upon which the intellectual determinability of the imaginative rests. One may differentiate thinkers of substance, functions, numbers and geometry.[2] The types increase in number but become indistinguishable if we add the reflexive categories to

[1] Cf. William Stern, *Differentielle Psychologie*. Leipzig 1921. 3rd ed.
[2] Cf. Eleatics, Heraclitus, Pythagoreans, Plato.

the constitutive categories. Obviously the latter belong to natural sciences; we must add the *geisteswissenschaftlichen*. Thus the capacity for delicate *geisteswissenschaftlichen* understanding depends upon the mental attitude which is secondary in the judging theorist. The above analyzed psychological acts are also categories of *geisteswissenschaftliche* judgment, as I have indicated in the introduction to the first edition of this work in 1914. The psychology of elements can go back further to more elementary psychological functions which take part in a special theoretic type. The direction of concrete imagination (spatial or psychological) and the corresponding reproductive type are always of a special importance. Here the work of the elementary intelligence tests begins. The first problem is to discover how many individual functions are included in the popular concept of 'intelligence'.

The above named three points of view: empiricism, rationalism, criticism, may dominate the entire basis of life far beyond a man's scientific applications. Some people confront existence, so to speak, as interested receptive observers. They live inductively and yet they often lack the power to synthesize their individual impressions. To use an expression of Goethe's, they do not achieve any '*Resultate des Lebens*'. Every new experience forces them into a new direction. — Differing from them are the people who experience on the basis of fixed categories and notice nothing that does not fit into this scheme. And it is wholly immaterial whether these categories are actually based on facts or whether they are 'prejudices' and 'idols of the marketplace.' There is a well known type of person who, especially in old age, is so hedged in by theories and maxims that he is incapable of new experiences, or unable to experience the unusual as such. For such people everything confirms their own point of view. Travel descriptions furnish us with abundant material on this point. Thus there are people who have become (and not only in their scientific opinions either) all psychoanalytic theory. But all of us carry within us, as an endowment of our period and environment such a fixed theory of life. If we could free ourselves of this how different the world would be in many details! — The road which leads to the golden mean, the compromise between the given and new experiences, is here too the healthiest one. This is the normal human structure. The onesided theoretic type develops only when a person lives merely to discover general results and maxims. The stoic literature offers the best illustration of this. Some stoics are nothing but reflection. They do not live in everyday life but observe themselves and ask: 'What is going on now within me?' This urge to intense introspection and self-analysis may become a dominant part of religious life too. The γνῶθι σεαυτόν of Socrates includes the far-reaching belief that theoretic insight into the Good makes us good and leads to good action. But in the majority of people, who do not belong to the theoretic type, many complicated structures are found in between.

A second essential point of view in classification starts not from the structure of cognitive acts but from the differences between its objects. This, of course, also posits differences in the cognitive procedure. But Rickert went too far in thinking that the distinction between natural sciences and the *Geisteswissenschaften* could be replaced by a mere logical point of view. It is true that nature is not cognized only by means of mathematical physics and quantitative chemistry. And it cannot be denied that man and his intellect are closely interrelated with socalled natural contexts. The boundary must therefore be very carefully drawn, but this is not our task. It is obvious without further investigation that the feeling for psychic life and mental contexts presupposes a wholly different structure than is necessitated by observation and collection by arrangement and interpretation of material objects. Whether one speaks here of an 'inner and outer imagination' or of 'understanding and explaining' the fact remains that these are two types which are differently organized. The 'vision' is different in the two cases and the difference reaches so far back into the total mental structure that for instance, human beings and epochs appear again and again who interpret the external by means of psychic meaning contexts, or vice versa, who treat mental achievements according to the scheme of mere external causal explanations. There results therefore, as an insight into the plasticity of total life, the far-reaching difference between the type who apprehends mankind as a region of mechanical legal necessity and the other type who deduces everything from meaningful value motives and spontaneous purpose striving.

The distinction between analytic and synthetic direction belongs more to the formal side of cognition. The importance for science of these predominating tendencies is well known. There are some minds which are principally directed to the differences of phenomena. Others chiefly notice the identities. Correspondingly, some people unravel life in continuous reflection and others, because they realize its constantly recurring traits, elevate life into the sphere of generally valid contexts.

For the classical logician there existed a characteristic equalisation between generality (i. e. that which is according to species and law) and totality. For them species or law was so to speak the unity out of which the special differentiated itself or emanated. And indeed logically both are related. For, anyone who has grasped the general law also includes an entire region of phenomena; but only a region and not the whole cosmos of that which can be cognized and thought. There is, therefore, another difference between specialising and universalising thinkers. There are some people who, like Robert Mayer devote their whole lives to the intensive investigation of one special problem. To others, however, the cognitive problem appears as a systematic whole which one must master in order really to understand the particular. Therefore the essence of real science includes a tendency not only to the general but also to the whole. Where this tendency is lacking or only partially developed we are at the border of real science. The mere aphorist for instance, like Nietzsche voices aesthetic impressions rather than theoretically founded and identical contexts. The metaphysician on the other hand has a comprehensive vision in which the individual phenomenon is no longer strictly differentiated or thought through and which is born from the religious drive to the Absolute or from the aesthetic urge to form. When Hegel speaks reverently of the 'general', that which is according to species and that which is according to totality (the General and the Total) flows together to form an undifferentiated unity. If one applies the distinction of partial and comprehensive thinkers to the theoretical type in the widest sense, one finds, beside the specialists who again see and think through one side of life, the universal theorists for whom existence is essentially *one* tremendous problem and who are not satisfied until they have erected a monistic structure of thought on the totality of life. They live their lives in one dominating thought or one comprehensive Logos whose manysidedness issues from an Absolute Unity.

Let us make a final point in regard to classification, the differentiation of the theoretically productive and the receptive. This antithesis, however, is not mutually exclusive. For, even the appreciation of other peoples' thoughts is creative. Noone can understand by merely adopting. On the contrary all real thinking and reasoning is an inner activity, a productive achievement. Nevertheless there is a difference between the theorist who breaks open, often with enormous difficulty, new roads in understanding and conquers new land; and the other who 'thinks himself into' an accepted line of thought and cannot go beyond. Fichte is a really creative thinker though he accomplished nothing which could be termed a mental discovery. But noone had a stronger feeling than he for the activity of thought, and he would certainly have translated the phrase: $\dot{\epsilon}\nu\ \dot{\alpha}\varrho\chi\tilde{\eta}\ \tilde{\eta}\nu\ \dot{o}\ \lambda\acute{o}\gamma o\varsigma$ 'In the beginning there was the deed'.

V

Finally, we are only justified in discussing here the type which is antithetical to the theorist if the contrast is based upon a hidden inner affinity. The theoretical sceptic is the only such contrast. This scepticism presupposes the experience of the theoretic ideal. Scepticism is only meaningful if the thing which it renounces is opposed to it as a scientific thought. In this way the sceptic is related to the scientific fanatic. He has buried an ideal and lives in the quiet tears which he weeps for it even if his outward demeanor is one of harsh pride. One can be a sceptic for different reasons, from religious veneration, wealth of aesthetic imagination, desire for action in society, politics or industry. None of these attitudes concern us here. But one can also be a theoretical sceptic. That is, scepticism may be based upon scientific critical reasons. When the cognitive theorist constantly objects to this point of view that it was inconsequential because it denied the possibility of every theory by means of a new theory which it held generally valid, he only proves that he himself belongs to the theoretic type without having understood its psychologic limits. The negation of science because of certain scientific experiences may seem illogical, but as an attitude it is a very interesting and possible structure which may be subjectively understood. Although scepticism rarely appears in this form it is characteristic of the theoretic type since it represents this type with the wildest expectations and keenest self-criticism. Perhaps Hume was such a man. His honesty and truthfulness, however, finally made even his scepticism productive. It sounds paradoxical when we declare that a certain atheistic type is the most religious. But there is some foundation of truth for this statement, because the pure atheist is so only because of a disappointed religious impulse. In the same way we might say that the systematic sceptic is in a certain sense the purest form of theorist because he transcends himself.

2
THE ECONOMIC ATTITUDE

I

Man and nature are closely interwoven. The preservation of life depends upon natural products and forces which are apt to satisfy man's needs. These needs are not constant but increase with his development. Even after the most urgent needs have been satisfied his wants grow until he is finally satiated. But this point is seldom or never reached. The capacity of natural products to satisfy needs (by maintaining and developing physical life) is called their utility. The useful is thus always a physical means to satisfy needs. We shall accept without further discussion the fact that the maintainance of life by means of appropriate adjustments to given conditions is the aim of this process. The value quality of this aim is represented in experience not only by the feeling of 'pleasant' and 'unpleasant', but on the higher mental levels by the terms 'useful' or 'harmful'. But whatever is useful or harmful is measured first of all in regard to the value of the mere preservation of biological life and the instincts which regulate the satisfaction of needs.

Utilities are then, in general, goods in the form of physical products and forces. Even purely intellectual achievements are only mediated by the aid of physical means of objectivation. A painting, for instance, cannot be created without canvas, color and wood. A certain technical skill in line and color plays a part in its production. Many physical processes are involved in the publication of a book. A speech fatigues the speaker and his hearers unless a certain economy of energy and time is observed. In a word, the physical and physiological forces enter even the intellectual realm, because it is based upon a certain technique and with this material aspect it is connected with economic values and exchangeable goods. Thus the useful can also serve the realization of the non-physical world of objects which we have mentioned above: the ideational, imaginative and transcendental world. And in this respect mental work can be economically evaluated. Physical energy, time and material are used. But the inner value of cognition, of a work of art or a religious manifestation is incommensurable economically. Such value cannot be expressed in terms of self-preservative units. They are luxuries from the economic point of view, which in a favorable economic period are highly valued and in times of dearth may sink to the zero point. This explains the constant difficulty of all cultural epochs in measuring the value of intellectual products in a narrow economic sense.

In the following pages our discussion will be confined to that economy which takes place in the region of life-preserving physical goods and natural forces. Such utilities are not unlimited, nor are there even enough for minimum satisfaction. Rational activity (i. e. purposive behavior) is necessary to bring goods from different places and to transform them by the application of known natural laws. This expenditure of energy is work and is economic only when the gain in power overbalances the expenditure of energy. This is true even if the economic process extends over generations.

We see therefore that the economic man might appear in two very different forms: as producer or as consumer. This is, of course, only a designation *a potiori*. For, every man is necessarily and simultaneously both. His economic environment and his needs determine which of these natures shall predominate. (The influence of his inner structure will only be mentioned when we begin to differentiate the economic type). A man with few wants or with an abundant subsistence and goods suited to his individual needs, may limit his economic activity almost solely to consumption. He is then an enjoyer even though he must feed himself and thus accomplish a minimum of productive work. The economic phenomenon is more clearly expressed, however, by the individual who is productive in a certain line in order to be able to consume these or other goods. In him the balance between utility and disutility can be clearly seen. But even he, in the background of his activity, strives to free himself from the pressure of immediate wants. It is to misunderstand the entire psychology of economics not to recognize this longing for freedom of action as its fundamental impulse. One must remember that human wants, if the individual is unrestrained in his economic drive, do not cease at a definite average but grow beyond the given point of satisfaction. All economic striving even if confined to the compass of nature, has an infinite constantly self re-creating power. On one hand this might appear as a hopeless circle of ever unsatisfied endeavor, on the other, however, it might be considered as the powerful impulse by means of which economic and technical behavior grow beyond the isolated individual and become objective meaningful phenomena.

Our isolating and idealising method must solve two difficulties. We must, at present, disregard the special economic forms which correspond to changing cultural epochs. We cannot dwell onesidedly on agriculture or trade and industry, natural, money, or credit economy but only on the eternal economic motive as a constant function between the subject and utilities despite the variability of both. Furthermore: we must disregard the special historical forms of society in which production, exchange and consumption are carried on. We must carry our method of isolation to the point where a single man could subsist, even though in reality people only work in definite social and legal relations. My opinion is that the purely economic type shows only one mental attitude no matter whether he carries on independent or city, national or world economy. And it is only the type that interests us.

We did not find the theoretic type limited to scholars. It developed as a unique structure of the soul which might appear apart from pure science. The same is true here. The economic structure need not necessarily be confined to men who earn their daily bread. On the contrary, the basic motive of utility appears in many phases of personality, dominates regions in which we should really expect to find different attitudes and even becomes the decisive ethics of existence. Conversely, people who constantly emphasize the economic factor as their last word need not necessarily be born utilitarians. The Marxists for instance are predominantly theorists or politicians. Their theory does not correspond to their practice. This fact might be utilized in a critique of the economic interpretation of history if the latter did not apply a psychology of unconscious determination which is pure constructive metaphysics and no longer description.

The economic man is, in general, he who in all the relations of life prefers utility to all other values. He sees everything as a means for self-preservation, an aid in the natural struggle for existence and a possibility to render life pleasant. He economizes goods and forces, time and space in order to gain the maximum of useful effect for himself. As moderns we might call this the 'practical type', partly because (as we shall later see) the entire technical field is included in the economic point of view. But the value of practical activity lies not in the depths of a value determining disposition but in the wholly external useful result. The Greeks would call this type the maker ($\pi o i o \tilde{v} \nu \tau a$) but never the doer ($\pi \varrho \acute{a} \tau \tau o \nu \tau a$).[1])

II

Thus the economic type sees cognition from his purposive viewpoint. The theorist seeks truth for itself but the economic type asks: 'How can this fact be used?' He interprets Goethe's expression: 'Anything that is not useful is a burden',[2]) in a narrow utilitarian sense. Unapplied knowledge is for him merely unnecessary ballast. The economic type seeks only wisdom that can be utilized and, disregarding its pure objective context combines knowledge according to its application. Thus we have the type embodying technical knowledge, who organizes everything by its practical use. This attitude gave birth to pragmatism which does not allow any special law of cognition but calls whatever is biologically useful or harmful, true or false. Truth is to them nothing but proved worth reflected back upon the theoretical act. Spencer's pedagogy is indicative of this evaluation of science. He attempts to summarize all knowledge according to the degree in which it contributes to the self-preservation of the knower, (or maybe to the preservation of the species).

---

[1]) Herbert Schack in *Der rationale Begriff des Wirtschaftsmenschen,* Jahrbuecher fuer Nationaloekonomie und Statistik, vol. 122 (1924) p. 439 gives a valuable and strictly methodological survey of the different forms in which the doctrine of the 'homo oeconomicus' appears in the history of economics. In another essay *Der irrationale Begriff des Wirtschaftsmenschen* op. cit. p. 192 he discusses the historical actualisations of the general type which arise by its being crossed with other motives. An excellently worked out special illustration is developed by Alfred Ruehl *Die Wirtschaftspsychologie des Spaniers,* Zeitschrift der Gesellschaft fuer Erdkunde zu Berlin. 1922.

[2]) 'Was man nicht nützt, ist eine schwere Last.' Goethe's Faust.

Even though it seems that the value of theory is dependent on that of utility it may nevertheless often be interwoven with economic behavior as a subordinate act. Civilized man lives upon a level where self-preservation is no longer regulated purely by instinct. He is aided in his struggle for existence by the knowledge of the quality of objects and their causal relations. Utilitarian knowledge more and more outbalances pure wisdom. With increasing complexity of economic methods greater intellectual capacity is demanded of man. He no longer needs to know merely the economic value of things but also the economic essence of man.[1] Such onesided study of man reaches its climax in Taylorism which considers only economic usefulness. Of course according to our general formula nothing is economically insignificant. No span of time or space, or object, no intellectual product or characterological trait is economically unimportant. The economic man must therefore have a 'business head'. It is no longer possible on higher levels to get along with nothing but that common sense which is sufficient on lower levels. The ideal goal of the economic type is an economic rationalism, the transformation of the whole process of life into a comprehensive calculation in which no factor is unknown.[2] The limits of cognition always set also the limits of economics. On the other hand the irrationality of natural phenomena cannot wholly be abolished by any 'forwardlooking attitude', partly because unique future circumstances cannot be predicted. Intellectual ability finds its natural limits at this point and calculation and rationalisation end. Consequently another quality is needed which is not purely intellectual but is rather a matter of imaginative intuition or belief: the willingness to take a chance. However well economic behavior may have calculated, some factors are always lacking. And here the element of chance enters in either supported by imagination or based upon a belief in 'luck'. And thus the economic type touches the region of aesthetics and religion.

---

[1] This is carried so far that the art of stimulating new needs is practiced, instead of satisfying existing ones. The psychology of advertising has recently been developed into a separate branch of science.

[2] Cf. Werner Sombart, *Der Bourgeois*, Muenchen 1920 on the calculation of capitalism. And further Max Weber, *Die Wirtschaft und die gesellschaftlichen Ordnungen und Maechte* (Grundriss der Sozialoekonomik III, 1. p. 35) § 4 on the typical measures of rational economics.

The aesthetic component is characterized by the fact, that it has a psychic-experiental but not a utilitarian value.[1] *The two regions are mutually exclusive.* The useful is as a rule inimical to the beautiful. Splendid landscapes are destroyed from economic motives, works of art demolished and happy moods spoiled. Earth seems to have no room for both side by side; neither does the soul. Noone who strives for inner beauty and harmony can afford to enter the struggle for existence which develops his power along certain onesided lines. But if the aesthetically important is viewed from an economic point of view it is regarded as luxury.[2] Luxuries may of course gradually become economically necessary goods through a refinement of wants. Cultured people have a certain need for artistic surroundings. Their imagination demands stimulation and satisfaction especially if by vocation they are put under the pressure of some division of labor. Thus the aesthetic cannot be wholly separated from the economic. The aesthetic makeup of possessions becomes in social relations a factor which increases prestige. It signifies that narrow needs have been outdistanced and luxuries can be afforded. This explains the desire in many economic natures to be patrons of art. They utilize art as a means of social elevation but fail to appreciate its inner significances. Another point of contact between the aesthetic and the economic seems to lie in the fact that scarcity goods (gold and silver) have an aesthetic significance. Then again articles which can never be replaced (the work of a great master for instance) have a very high exchange value. This is of course also included in the class of luxuries. A gold standard is always a sign of luxury.

Let us now turn to the social region. The purely economic type is egotistical since he regards it as his first duty to preserve his own life. Everybody else is consequently of lesser importance. It is highly atypical in the economic man to renounce anything of his own free will for the sake of others. Only egoism and

---

[1] This statement is not intended to deny that the aesthetic and the biologically useful have some developmental factors in common.

[2] Luxury has here a double meaning: It is (1) the preparation and consumption of a surplus of goods beyond purely economic needs; and (2) everything which is not immediately useful but belonging to the other regions of value, especially the aesthetic, may be designated as luxury. In both cases we are dealing with a unique category of economic value determination.

mutualism are primarily economic forms of the social attitude. Wherever altruism, as the principle of renunciation of goods in favor of someone else, appears, it must be born from some motive other than economic ones. A consistent economic system has no place for charity. The economic man's interest in other human beings is only utilitarian. He sees man purely from the point of view of economy, that is, as a producer, consumer or a buyer. He accepts help but even this mutual relation is included in the economic point of view. There must always be a positive balance in his favor. Such an attitude can be carried as far as pure economic exploitation which from the strict point of view of economic rentability would be perfectly logical.[1]) Economic calculation must also consider moral qualities, but only insofar as they are economically important, such as: thrift, industry, efficiency, order, reliability, in short the vocational-economic abilities. Any man possessing such qualities deserves credit. That credit is only a moral emphasis of economic qualities is testified by the current business expression: 'The man is good.' One should observe the way in which business men create social relations. All forms of honorary demonstration, of good will or sympathy enter into the economic relation. They make for good business. But with the pure economic type such relations do not go beyond business interests. From the purely economic point of view man is necessarily only a means to an end and can be evaluated according to his ability to work, his capital or his purchasing power.[2]) The fact that there are real business friendships and mutual interests is not a contradiction of what has just been said. For, the economic subject is not necessarily a

---

[1]) Rudolf Goldscheid has lately introduced into sociology the principle of human economy (*Menschenoekonomie*) as an ethico-political point of view. There are of course such considerations in politics. One should, however, avoid such a term where really 'social' purposes are in question. For, in economic relations man can only be considered as an economic means or as the subject of economic values. This principle does not lead us into higher value contexts.

[2]) 'Man is regarded only as a unit of work and nature only as a means of production. All life is one huge business relation.' Sombart; *Der kapitalistische Unternehmer*, Archiv fuer Sozialwissenschaft. vol. 29. p. 711. This is true not only of the capitalist but of every purely economic man. Conversely, capitalism too, as an economic phenomenon in history, is often dominated by other motives.

single individual but often a collective subject: a family, two or more partners, a corporation, a nation or a group of nations. But of each collective subject the same can be said as of the individual in regard to economic egoism. The unit has merely been enlarged. The specific associations in themselves have of course another structure than the purely economic. As collective entities however their activities make themselves felt in an economic-egoistic sense.

Wealth is power. The economic man has power over nature; its forces, material, extension and the technical means necessary to its control. This also implies power over people. But this power again has a pronounced economic character if the type is pure. The dominant attitude is always a desire to own more than other people. Thus economic striving for power appears in the form of *competition*. This attitude dominates even the lowest level and can be extirpated only with the economic motive itself. The power of money is based upon its motivating influence, which again presupposes economic natures. And as if to emphasize this point, money today gives prestige even if it has not been earned by the owner and is connected neither with his industry nor his shrewdness.

But all this is based upon an assumption which is no longer purely economical; namely the validity of the legal order which guarantees the rights of private property. The principle of the natural right that private property must be the result of one's own exertion, could only be strictly carried out if there were no law of inheritance in the economic system in question. But even here it could not be enforced on account of economico-technical reasons. The principle itself is incomplete, for savings become 'possession' only if an overindividual social will recognizes this claim (as correctly seen by Fichte) by excluding all other competitors. It is right however that the economic man should have a special interest in such a legal status. Private property is the result of economic motives and is only the legal recognition of that attitude which makes itself felt in isolated economic egoism. Thus wherever the economic type legislates all economic claims are given preference. Law appears then as the social normative form in which economics is taken as the material of social life. Such a conception is of course very narrow and as abstract as the type of which we speak. A purely economic conception of the state would correspond to this type and indeed the state appears to many people as nothing more than the superindividual organisation of economic life, as a sort of higher productive community, a corporation or a stock company. We have no right here to take up a position against such a conception from the normative point of view and must satisfy ourselves with the observation that it is again the pure economic type which gives rise to this relation to questions of power. This same type would judge all social vocations according to their earning capacity. Vocation and earning-power are in fact for him absolutely identical concepts.

It cannot surprise us therefore that the evaluation not only of human beings but also of the entire world is seen from this point of view. The economic value is for this type the highest value. In a religious sense it is, therefore, no longer necessary to relate it to a higher meaning, but it must only be posited in its totality i. e. as world-embracing value.[1]) God appears then as the owner of all wealth, as the giver of all useful gifts. Every religion which tries to interpret the meaning of life of course contains such a factor; for, without daily bread life would be impossible. The deepest mysteries of the world seem to begin with bread and its life giving power. One can imagine a religion born from purely economic motives, when the economic religious views and cults naturally reflect the special system of economics. The god of the herdsman is different from that of the agriculturalist, that of the trader again different from that of the miner. If nothing remains but a passion for wealth without consideration of the way in which it is acquired, *Mammon* is the highest god. The religio-superstitious concepts of the stockbrokers and speculators are dominated by curious beliefs in fate and chance. They secretly worship a power which they imagine to be in control of the great world-lottery. This relation between economics and religion has been historically investigated by Max Weber and Troeltsch. One should, as far as possible try to differentiate between religious concepts which are definitely determined by economic motives; and conversely, those economic forms of behavior which are determined by religio-ethical views which existed independently of the economic region.[2]) The

---

[1]) Cf. Werner Sombart, *Der Bourgeois*, p. 137 ff. 'sacred economics.'
[2]) Max Weber in the introduction to his treatises on *Die Wirtschafts-ethik der Weltreligionen* (Gesammelte Aufsaetze zur Religionssoziologie.

two factors could however hardly be separated in such a narrow reciprocal mental relation. To look upon economic prosperity as a gift from God, or to strive for economic success in order visibly to justify such grace does not wholly belong to the economic point of view. For, here the desire to obtain the grace of God seems to supercede the economic motive. We are only concerned with the deification of utility as such, the birth of deities out of economic interests -God as giver, as protector of the fields, as increaser of the sheep, as safe guide on the sea, as giver of the sun and rain etc- in short of all useful gifts which enrich the physical-desiring rather than the spiritual part of man. We have not the slightest doubt that an analysis of religions (especially of primitive ones) would lead to a wealth of such symbols which originated in fear or hope, in the desire and will to live, and in the psychology of work and enjoyment.

III

Economic motives can be distinguished from theoretic ones because their deciding values are not the logical ones of ordination but those of utility. The useful is not identical with the pleasant. The latter is a mere momentary feeling-effect which is enjoyable even though it may be dangerous in the long run. The useful always presupposes a certain degree of theoretic insight into the practical and psychological conditions of life. Therefore all judgments of useful or useless are built on a rational foundation. Also the economic principle which we developed in the first part of this volume, the principle of least action, is as we said instinctive rationality. But nevertheless theoretic factors are not decisive in the motivation of the economic man. On the contrary, this is rooted in the specific form in which he experiences utilitarian values, as wants and their satisfaction. Economic behavior is thus motivated by the satisfying of needs. This determination may take place in two ways which differ externally: there are useful goods or habits which play a definite role in a whole life and there are, on the other hand, purposive endeavors which are only called forth by a specific and sometimes entirely transitory situation.

Vol. I. Tuebingen 1922. p. 240. 265 ff.) also emphasizes this necessity. He primarily investigated the functional relations between the structures of society and religion. This context leads to historic types and thus touches more complicated phenomena than we have here in mind.

Biologically speaking, we might differentiate between constant conditions of life which must be met with a permanent adaptation, and momentary needs to which one must react specifically. If the first situation is the motivating power we have the *foresighted* type of man and in the second case we have the type who is readily adaptable to *emergencies*.

The motive of foresight is the constant motive of work. There is no special demand for an unusual versatility to suit customary satisfactions to customary needs. But it does necessitate constancy of purpose, strength of will, order and thrift. Therefore this group of virtues is built up from the motive of foresight. The motives of emergency necessitated by the need to choose a means suitable to carry out an unexpected purpose demand a practical ability. We call resourcefulness that form of individual adaptability which quickly finds the most suitable causal means for any purpose. If this resourcefulness is based on the imaginative grasp of single instances then it resembles aesthetic intuition. If, however, general and practical causal means (technical rules) and their application are considered then we have the reflective and rational resourcefulness. Keen judgment, presence of mind, inventiveness, ability to make quick decisions and versatility are the virtues which belong to this type of motivation. To act according to general maxims, which one has developed in contemplative wisdom into a system of life, is obviously entirely different from simply facing every particular instance with practical resourcefulness and suitable means. This distinction of motives is, in the first case, an intellectual one. But in the second case the primary directive factor is the economic motive which guides the intelligent choice of means to aim in each case for the useful. This may become the central force of a person's makeup. We shall not here discuss the ethical value of this type. In any case we are certain that we are dealing here with a value region that is not wholly unimportant for ethics. For, the aim of self-preservation and external adaptation is itself a specific kind of value which colors all the utilitarian values which subserve it. Because they belong to a specific value we subsume them under the head of utilitarian values in a narrow sense, i. e. the primarily economic values. And noone will deny that at least in the ethics of economic work there is a specifically moral factor.

The man guided by economic motives is obviously more closely related to reality than the theorist. He also must reflect but in the end he takes an active part in the development of actuality. 'The painless conception of a thought does not result in an economic act. The unique side of business which is unknown to intellectualists is the knitting up of thought with reality and through this connection letting thought crystallize into reality.'[1] But it is not necessary that the motives should always be fully conscious. This is seldom the case in practical life and perhaps least of all in active natures. Every decided attitude has elemental power and can become a form of genius if one stresses its unconscious creativity. Even the economic man of exceptional ability acts in his individual way because he 'must'. Sombart emphasizes this: 'In regard to the problem of motivation we must investigate in this case as well as in any other the extent to which conscious reasons are the real driving forces of economic activity' (op. cit. p. 699). Sombart has in mind the capitalistic entrepreneur but this sentence also applies to the economic type as such. On the primitive level the utilitarian tendency acts with the certainty of an instinct. On higher levels it often becomes such a passion that it must have unlimited scope. Quite regardless of the fact that big capitalists often act not from purely economic motives but from social and political ones, the abstract economic tendency rises in many instances above mere striving for personal advantage. It is, so to speak, the idea of the useful and of the productive which becomes a daemonic passion. But the net return, the rentability and profit are the decisive factors even in undertakings of superindividual dimensions and thus determine the limit of the economic type. Anyone who can stand constantly working with a deficit may have special reasons for doing so but he is no longer a purely economic type. The converse is also true: sometimes an undertaking is supposed to be only in the interest of the public, yet there is nothing behind it but a hidden desire for purely personal gain.[2] I add here an excerpt from the Hamburg prospectus of the re-creation of the German

---

[1] W. Rathenau cited by Werner Sombart, Archiv fuer Sozialwissenschaft. vol. 29. p. 728.
[2] Werner Sombart, 'As if a capitalistic Shoe Factory were an institution to manufacture shoes (instead of profit)'. In connection with this topic cf. also R. Ehrenberg, *Grosse Vermoegen*, I. Jena 1925. ed. 2.

Foreign Service (Hamburg, April 1918, p. 4) which expresses with incisive clearness what, in many cases, acts only as a half conscious motive. 'As far as the general attitude of foreign trade is concerned everything is ruled by motives of utility. Our foreign trade does not wish to force anything on its customers but rather to satisfy them. For this reason trade is adapted to the desires and needs of other nations. This is not done in order to please or to make moral conquests but to achieve utility and to acquire a steady customer.

IV

A striking contrast between differentiated forms of the economic type has already attracted our attention in the beginning of this chapter. It makes a great difference whether a man produces goods himself (even if only by increasing their value through some additional work) or whether he merely consumes them. The first type has the superiority which comes with effective activity. The other faces the economic world with some embarrassment. The terms worker and enjoyer themselves embody an ethical value judgment whose purely external emphasis is however apparent since most people consider that only physical labor or direct employment is productive and do not fully appreciate the utilization of physical and mental power for intellectual productivity.[1] In a strict economic sense even the consumer may occupy various positions. If he commands a wealth of goods which can be used without any productive return on his part he scarcely belongs any more to the economic type. On a higher plane he approaches the aesthetic attitude and in a lower form he no longer lives in a spiritual context but leads instead a brutish existence; according to Luther 'Ir Bauch, ir Gott.' Should the consumer, however, be limited to a small amount of goods then the economic principle shows itself onesidedly as a cutting down of consumption. Thus we have the saver, whose constant endeavor is to limit the goods which he uses to the smallest possible amount. Many educated spinsters (and bachelors also at the present time) spend their lives in such a painful, because really negative, existence. Though the productive

---

[1] W. Eliasberg in the Archiv fuer Sozialwissenschaft, vol. 50 (1922) p. 87 treats in general of *Psychology and Work* from the point of view of a psychology of meaning contexts.

saver is forced to live a sad ascetic life unless he ennobles his existence by aims which are rooted in some other value context.

Different employments give rise to other special forms of the economic type. Perhaps no power in adult life moulds a man so strongly as his vocation. The whole mentality of the agriculturalist is entirely different from that of the stock raiser; the artisan differs from the clerk and the fisherman from the miner. Nature seems to stamp the soul with the special conditions under which he wrests his livelihood from her. The trader finds a unique place in economic life partly through his manysided activities and partly because of the unproductive trait which clings to him even though he fills an essential place in the economic system. The publisher, who unites art and science with economic endeavor, presents a curious combination of mental motives which nevertheless center in the economic region. These economically determined vocational types have long been utilized by writers in psychological studies. Gustav Freytag has drawn the different forms of the merchant in his *Soll und Haben;* peasants have been made literary subjects by Pestalozzi, Gotthelf, G. Keller and the recent *Heimatdichter* like Rosegger, Hansjakob, Frenssen and Ganghofer.[1]) Not until the artisan became a social problem, however, did he find his poets. Of late, sociology which grew out of national economy, has made psychological studies of vocational types. The *geisteswissenschaftliche* work is at present unrelated to vocational psychology which is a branch of the psychology of elements and has not yet fully developed its methods. I here remind the reader of the masterful treatment of peasant types by Pestalozzi in his *Schweizerblatt of* 1782 (published at present by Seyffart 1901. Vol. 6. pp. 30—54).

The methods employed in economics differ according to the subjects of economic endeavor. It makes a radical difference whether the economic type appears in a natural, money or credit economy. In the second case we have to deal also with the psychology of money and a beginning of an extensive pathology of the economic type which I cannot develop in this outline. The proper appreciation of money is often beyond the character and understanding even of highly developed people. In the third case we have the psychology of the banker and the speculator. The basic outline of the economic

---

[1]) Compare with this attitude the depreciatory treatment of the working man in Plato's Republic. II. 372 etc.

type remains, but in favorable cases we find economic reflection take the place of actually productive work. This reflection, happily named 'speculation' because it is not founded on a safe experiential basis, is an essential achievement in national and world economy. The main reason for the failure of the projected economic revolution in Germany 1918 is to be sought in the worker's inability to speculate. On this level, however, unhealthy symptoms of economics rapidly increase. The wild speculator on the exchange, the unproductive gambler etc. create economic types in which the productive side of labor has completely disappeared. As human beings they are at the border of what may be called mental types. But unfortunately such types are even essential to the mechanism of our complicated modern economic system. And this exhibits the 'soullessness' to which the historical development of economics and its constant separation from individual will and power has led.

The problem becomes even more complex when we add to the subject of our discussion (the object and method of economics) the extent of economic operations. We are interested of course only in the reflex action upon the soul. It makes a great difference psychologically whether one owns one cow or two hundred, whether one tills one acre or employs laborers to cultivate hundreds, whether one retails soap or supplies the world with machinery, whether one works on a handloom or simply tends the lever of an automatic loom. A *geisteswissenschaftliche* psychology must trace all the psychic influences which correspond to these economic forms. There have been some attempts in the psychology of the artisan as contrasted with a factory worker. This includes of course not only the isolated economic motive but also social, political and religious contexts. We must be content here with an observation which is taken from the midpoint of the discussion. Whether a man works in a meaningful whole or only mechanically creates parts which are in themselves absolutely meaningless, establishes a wholly different sort of relationship between a man and his work. In this comparison we have a repetition of the antithesis between structural psychology and the psychology of elements on the economic level. A psychology which neglected the meaningful relations of life could have only been developed in a period where the division of labor had split up the meaningful whole to such an extent that the single worker no longer comprehended it (at least economically). For, the factory workers on one hand no longer grasp the significance of the system in which they are engaged while the directors of such mass production transcend the finer individual relations to economic goods. Even in the days of Rousseau the farmer seemed the only complete man; for he is closely in touch with the meaning of economics, a very essential side of life. For him, as for the artisan, there is some meaning in his work because he deals directly with the consumer. The others are mere cogs in a machine which although it masters nature to an extent never dreamed of in former times has as a totality developed a domination over the mass of mankind almost more terrible than the power of nature.

This already touches upon the final point of view, which has some importance for the differentiation of the economic type even though it is not in itself of a purely economic nature. This is the social form of economy. If we emphasize only the most well known and visible differences it is clear that the man of house economy is nearest to the total economic problem of life. He is much nearer and perhaps more powerful than the individual of a greatly differentiated territorial economy. And if finally the national economy becomes so complicated as to be utterly dependent on world economy, man might well feel in regard to this very complex system like the magician's apprentice over whom the spirits, who had formerly been his servants, had gained a fateful power. With increasing social interrelation there is a more complex division of labor. And this introduces into the soul structure of the individual an overindividual factor which mechanizes rather than organizes him. Economically we are a more dependent people than those of any previous epoch. We can no longer control needs which have been stimulated from earliest infancy. The means for their satisfaction make us dependent upon people whom we have never seen and who are as indifferent to us as human beings as we are to them. Thus economy is more and more interwoven into the present legal and political system until we reach a point where its individual nature is completely blotted out. Enormously complicated objective structures have come between the living man and the economic process so that the simple personal economic structure has almost become unrecognizeable. As an organized humanity we are to an incredible degree masters of nature, but have become so interdependent that noone of us can now stand on his own feet. And yet economic self-sufficiency is perhaps more necessary to a complete man than all the wealth which a world-wide organisation can offer as long as it functions properly.[1])

V

In some people the economic sense seems to have died, not because a different motive (social or aesthetic) has become predominant, but because the single motive of economic behavior is carried to a ridiculous extreme. If the economic is originally rooted in the balance of energy between the individual and the objective world of goods and their purposive utilisation, then this meaning cannot be achieved if the expenditure of energy exceeds any utilitarian result, or if energy is stored up beyond the point where it can be used. In the first instance we have the waster, i. e. the unproductive consumer; aud in the other the miser, the uneconomic acquirer and saver.[2]) Both types are perversions of the economic type. Their decisive value experience is economic. But in their endeavor fully to enjoy the value of this region they lose the real meaning of economy which can only be found in the golden mean. Both types are thus structurally not only perversions but also extreme exaggerations of the economic type. By trying to grasp everything they lose the real meaning of life. But they have their own blissful moments — the glorious thrill of extremes.

---

[1]) I remind the reader that all these remarks should only be interpreted psychologically. They do not however refer only to the psychology of specifically economic ethics but also to the psychology of chance which is at present very much neglected.

[2]) For the psychology of the miser cf. Scheler, *Der Formalismus in der Ethik und die materiale Wertethik.* p. 239. Herbert Schack op. cit. p. 200.

3
THE AESTHETIC ATTITUDE

I

In the first section we attempted to reduce the aesthetic factor in nature and the various forms of art to one form of mental endowment of meaning. If we wished to summarize the essence of aestheticism we should say: 'it is the formed expression of an impression'. Herein are contained three stages; (1) there is the *impression*, a sensuous concrete objective picture given in reality or created by the imagination, and which is psychically experienced in *its* emotional significance; (2) the *expression*, a sensuous-concrete presentation of *my* psychological content enlarged by imagination in a physical or imagined material; (3) this *form* as the product of the mutual interfusion of impression and expression which is achieved in its most pronounced sense if a condition of equilibrium or harmony is established between the objective and subjective factors. Since we know that theoretic acts are always present in our comprehension of the given; and since the object usually has no soul of its own, we generally deal in giving or experiencing form with a fusion of conceptual and empathic acts. Theoretic constitutive acts and those of psychic empathy participate in every aesthetic experience.

The problem of aesthetics is to investigate more accurately the border-line between the object as such and the attributes with which my soul endows it. By first defining the object from a purely theoretical standpoint the object is necessarily brought into a conceptual isolation which is unknown to the naive aesthetic enjoyer.[1])

---

[1]) Joseph Strzygowski elevates this unsafe positivistic procedure to a fundamental methodological principle whenever he wants strictly to differentiate between *Sachforschung* and *Beschauerforschung* in aesthetics. (*Die Krisis der Geisteswissenschaften*, Wien 1923.) Even science finds the bald 'fact' problematic, and as for art. . . .

The latter, on the contrary lives, as it were, in the aesthetic objects and simultaneously experiences both them and himself. If in this condition he is conscious of a manifold, free and unique psychic impulse he experiences 'form'.

We generally look for this process in an artist or an artlover. If, however, we look more closely we find that really we have before us only a derived, very limited and occasional appearance of the aesthetic type. As radiations of something deeper the aesthetic state of mind is called forth by a work of art, just as that same state of mind created the work of art. The process itself may take place wholly internally. When one says that Raphael would have been a great painter even if he had been born without hands one means that he understood things like a painter. He always looked at the world with a painter's eye even when he did not fix his impression in the roundabout technical procedure of painting. In a word, only from a soul that experiences aesthetically, works of art are born; only out of the inner vision grows the externally visible; only as a result of inner rhythm of the soul does music arise. But just as the work of art is a derived phenomenon so also is the aesthetic appreciation which it calls forth. To approach the origin of aesthetics we must describe aesthetic experience as compared with the theoretic, economic and religious attitudes.

We know that all aesthetic conduct is undesirous. It is a state of pure contemplation, a letting oneself go in the manifold nature of actual or imagined objects. Real contact with the world is always passionate and teems with the struggle for material and spiritual existence. But there is a further experience in which pain is just as welcome as joy, suffering just as blessed as happiness. This second experience is the imaginative grasp, i. e. the forming and transforming powers of emotion. We are all familiar with this peculiar transmutation which in the acts of our memory lifts the torments of the past into the plane of enjoyable contemplation. And we know that some people always shroud themselves with a veil of imagination through which they see themselves and daily experience.

The same factors take part in this all-animating form of experience which we have analyzed above in the process of artistic creation or enjoyment. Fate and environment provide the impression, the individual supplies the unique quality of feeling. When this feeling completely embraces the impressions they are transformed into expressions of psychic impulse and are assimilated as personal possessions. The aesthetic type cherishes his experiences and feelings in a very characteristic way. He lives in their concreteness and perceptual abundance with a minimum of logical reflection. An erotic tendency, for instance, immediately loses its singular attraction if it becomes mere desire, and also at the first theoretical reflection that hundreds of thousands have loved thus and that there is nothing unusual about it. Only aesthetic experience brings out the incomparability of the situation's emotional content.[1]

If there is nothing but the fanciful enjoyment of a single situation we have only a poetic mood, or an aesthetic whim. But if the whole soul acts as a forming power in every bit of life, (giving color, mood, rhythm) then we have the aesthetic type. We can briefly define its nature as one which forms all impressions to expressions. We cannot approach any more closely the mystery of these spiritual powers. An objective work of art (which can only be born from such a soul) most clearly reveals the soul's structure. The aesthetic soul shares with a work of art its wholly concrete and perceptual shape. In its accentuated form we call this individuality. For, even though all types establish it, what we generally call 'individuality', or a formed personality which arouses interest, is an aesthetic phenomenon. Bound up with aestheticism there is always a peculiar kind of self enjoyment, because these natures live as it were second hand. They do not come into immediate contact with that reality which awakens desire and action. They look on at the moving picture of life not reflecting, but empathically contemplating and enjoying it.

According as to which of the three aspects of experience is predominant, we can differentiate three aesthetic types. Some people give themselves up to external 'impressions' with intense enjoyment.[2] They are hungry for 'experience' and therefore

---

[1] Schiller's central concept of 'aesthetic determinability', used in his 21st letter on aesthetic education refers to this psychic structure and thus denotes the condition of highest formativity. According to him we must regard 'the power which is given back to man in the aesthetic mood as the highest of all gifts, as the gift of humanity (of being human)'.

[2] 'Impression' must be understood here in the aesthetic and not in the theoretic or practical utilitarian sense.

everything easily becomes an experience for them. If the inner binding and forming power is lacking we have the *Impressionists* of life who hurry from one impression to the other skimming only the surface from each.[1]) Others, however, live so intensely in their inner emotional world that they meet and color every impression with a subjective tint. These are the frankly subjective natures, the *Expressionists* of existence. They lack the possibility of an objective surrender to the visible concrete objectivity of life. Only when both aspects of existence: impression and our inner world come to a perfect balance, do we have the men of '*inner form*', the truly plastic natures, whom we might also call the classic type. In them the inner unfolding is at once an assimilation of life's impressions: *self-development*. Characteristic of them is formation in the clearly aesthetic sense, which must be differentiated from mere knowledge and technical aptitude. They make out of their lives works of art. They are themselves form, beauty, harmony and proportion. Even in their earliest tendencies they have a certain moral grace; but often enough too, they only complete themselves through conscious inner culture. 'I will keep myself pure even as the artist', says Hoelderlin in *Hyperion*.[2])

Yet here we must emphasize the difference between the virtuoso of life (Shaftesbury) and the externally creative artist. Certainly an artist's soul must be constituted so as to create from his inner rhythm outer rhythm, from his inward sense of life the external form, from his subjective harmony, the outer tone. But as compared to the inner artist he has both advantages and disadvantages. He

---

[1]) Cf. Kierkegaard, *Either-Or*. (Works, German translation Vol. I.) Διαψάλματα. — Richard Hamann, *Der Impressionismus in Leben und Kunst*, Koeln 1907 especially p. 143 ff. In this brilliant book much is classed as specifically impressionistic which is true of the aesthetic type in general.

[2]) WW. I. (Diederichs) p. 165. One compare in general Hegel, *Philosophie der Geschichte* ('the forms of beautiful individuality'); Jakob Burckhardt, *Kultur der Renaissance*; Eduard Spranger, *Wilhelm v. Humboldt und die Humanitaetsidee;* Christian Weiser, *Shaftesbury und das deutsche Geistesleben*. — Cf. the seldom remarked book of K. Borinski, *Balthasar Gracian und die Hofliteratur in Deutschland*, Halle 1894 on the history of the concept of inner form which goes back to Cicero and is best known under the term 'the beautiful soul'. See further v. Waldberg, *Studien und Quellen zur Geschichte des Romans* I: *The developmental history of the beautiful soul in Spanish mysticism*. (Literarhistorische Forschungen, Heft 41. 1910.)

has the advantage of being able to project his experiences into any form, (colors, tones, poetic pictures) i. e. the power of self-expression, which is not identical with the inner forming power. K. Ph. Moritz[1]) and Humboldt were aesthetic natures but without truly objective 'sensible' creative powers. They struggled in vain for expression, since they were at bottom only self-creators. Conversely the disadvantage of the artist who can create externally is that he is forced by this very fact to linger over some *single* creation (he creates a Zeus, or an Aphrodite, a lyric poem, a drama, a dance or a song). Thus his vital energy is so concentrated on a single point that he never quite reaches, or may even lose the *inner* form. Therefore genuine artists have an insatiable longing wholly to express themselves in a masterpiece; but only a few, who like Goethe carry a work through their whole growth succeed. Most artists do not go beyond single or limited expressions, in which now the impressionistic element (the occasion) now the expressionistic element (the inner world) predominates. In some creative artists successive works signify rather a struggle for inner form than actual creations from that form.[2])

We shall consider the aesthetic type only insofar as its mental structure rests on the inner forming power which tries to strike a balance between objective experience and its subjective penetration. Within this type we shall draw only the most decided lines so that the main outline will not be blurred by the variations. We should have to write a whole Aesthetics if we wished to describe the manifold forms of the external artistic world. We are only interested in the inner artist; he whose inward life is aesthetically organized.

II

The various regions of value into which human life is organized are, for the aesthetic type, wholly illuminated by aesthetic standards.

---

[1]) What I mean here, K. Ph. Moritz, starting from the background of an aesthetically determined metaphysics of the universal relation in creative nature, called 'the capacity which is implanted in the finer texture of the organism to develop'. This is a beginning of a structural psychology. Cf. extracts from his writings in Goethe's *Italienischer Reise*, and my lecture *Goethe und die Metamorphose des Menschen*, Goethejahrbuch 1924.

[2]) Gerhart Hauptmann in a speech on the celebration of his 50th birthday in the university of Leipzig, spoke in this sense of 'eternal beginning' and of 'the productive scepticism'.

Consequently he sees everywhere that which enlarges his own inner forming power. Knowledge can add but little since it destroys the perceptual and classifies everything according to concepts of general validity. This explains the aversion of the truly aesthetic type to the conceptual. It seems to him to have a certain paucity, a lack of plasticity and color and to be an almost lifeless husk. One of the liberating effects of art and indeed also of artistic experience, is found in its teaching us to question the conventional and traditional picture of reality and to see it again 'originally', i. e. animated (*beseelt sehen*). This factor dominates the aesthetics of Konrad Fiedler. In the impressionistic aesthetician there is usually a leaning toward relativism. Dilthey, as a historian, was so organized that although he made, in visualizing his characters, conceptual determinations of all of them, he eliminated them in the final presentation because they did not satisfy his need for pictorial individuality. He called this 'caution'. But it really was an aesthetic factor in his mind which led sometimes to a fear of generalisations and forced him to leave his figures shrouded in the veil which is ultimately characteristic of life itself. But he had been untiring in visualizing actual historical figures. This example shows that scientific reflection is for the purely aesthetic man what the study of anatomy is for the creative artist; or the philosophic analysis of art for a Schiller or a Goethe, an intermediary stage, through which he struggles to full plasticity, color and individuality of life. Thus the theoretic attitude may be found as a subordinated factor in the aesthetic man.[1]) But his goal is the presentation of life's eternal laws in his own concrete individuality, and the formation of his personality so that the general radiates through the specific.

To do this he must make a certain choice between different sciences. At first only the *Geisteswissenschaften* (language, literature

---

[1]) What Worringer called 'abstraction' in his *Abstraktion und Einfuehlung* Jena 1911 is at bottom not an independent phenomenon. A mathematically organized soul feels mathematics into and out of forms. Counterpoint is an example in music of this high degree of rationality. But it still remains audible mathematics just as the mathematics which is visible in the formative arts. It contains the fundamental factor of aesthetics, although the form is here highly rationalized. Volkelt *Das aesthetische Bewusstsein* p. 74 criticises Worringer's conception of abstraction in the same way.

and history) seemed directly to serve the creation of an inner world. Because of their eminently educational content they were called by the aesthetic Frenchmen *'belles lettres'*. Herder was the first to apply this conception to all sciences, including those of nature, since they also aid the formation of the inner life.[1]) And it is well known how much just these natural sciences meant to Goethe in his longing for form and culture.

The aesthetic man's conception of the essence of Nature is wholly different from that of the theoretic man. He has a close affinity with the mythological method of thought which feels a related life in nature.[2]) For, there is an aspect of nature which cannot be grasped except by an aesthetic sense, since in nature, too, creative form seems to play a part. Everything organic appears to be guided by an inner urge for development so immanently teleological that one might almost ascribe a soul to it. Aristotle, though no poet has nevertheless made the conception of entelechy the center of his system. He was a Greek, and the Greeks had a higher sense of form than any other nation. So inner form (the law of the purposive organic development of the inner being) became for him, and for long centuries of the socalled middle ages, the main explanatory principle of nature, even though such an individualizing law (similar to the character of a single man) can be grasped only by aesthetic intuition. Modern natural science has attempted to destroy these *formae substantiales,* but they always crop up again. It is comprehensible that a man like Goethe, who experienced himself as an organic developmental process, a lawful metamorphosis, saw in nature the same forming power; especially since the 17th century and its later offspring, Shaftesbury and Leibnitz, determined the intellectual world from which he came. He possessed the power of organic thought in the same astonishing degree as the power of organic vision.[3]) The same intellectual trend ruled the philosophy of Schelling and Froebel and was again expressed by Fechner who could not be satisfied with the 'nightview' of nature, but again called upon the soul as an explanatory

---

[1]) Herbart in a dry moralising manner has also drawn a borderline between the sciences, those which enable an aesthetic presentation of the world and those which only reproduce the necessity of fate.

[2]) Cf. Schiller: *Die Freundschaft.*

[3]) Cf. my lecture cited above.

principle. The conflict of the organic and mechanical conceptions of nature is as eternal as the human types which lie behind them. We must make it clear that we find ourselves at the limit of exact science. For, the soul of nature, and the individual souls or types living in it, can be grasped only through empathy. 'Nature is neither kernel nor shell, but everything at the same time.' The same is true of historical *Geisteswissenschaften.* The psychic individuality of a man or an epoch can only be discerned by such an empathic form sense. Here art borders on science, and it seems as if reality could only be more deeply penetrated if grasped by all the forces of the mind over and above the purely theoretical (conceptual). Insofar, therefore, the aesthetic type has its special organ for understanding the world (a sort of 'hunch'); an empathic intuition. For the pure theorist, a man with such a tendency is only an extravagant romanticist.[1]) For the theorist, nature is a system of functional equations, or a complexity of conceptually defined energies. But let us bear in mind that Plato believed moderation to be the factor which made the world, (the cosmos) and the soul beautiful. Thus vital empathy may find in mathematics, too, the source of experiences of form and beauty.

Now let us turn to the relations of the aesthetic type with economic values. The practical and aesthetic points of view are in sharp contrast. Anyone who ascribes a use to an aesthetic object be it technical or moral; a value, either for education or enjoyment, destroys its pure being. The aesthetic man is as indifferent and helpless in the face of the practical demands of life as the theorist. (Here the above mentioned points still hold even in view of the apparent contradictions.) The artist as well as he who develops himself would destroy his whole position toward life if he subscribed all his energies to utility.[2]) To comprehend life with a forming and enjoying fancy is quite different from

---

[1]) Anyone who comprehends his own life as an organic developmental process, which is dominated by a constant form — an attitude which does not seem to have existed before Goethe — understands himself aesthetically.

[2]) Even the practical everyday things are too much for the aesthetic mind. I see in my mind's eye the picture of these natures who take life hard, who are always frightened by real life because they are always looking for the formed echo and are unused to so much material. I also see, however, others who treat the heavy material of life as if it were only chimerical, as if the whole world were only an aesthetic 'phenomenon'.

'working'. Wilhelm Meister hoped to achieve completion by an empathic participation in all human life which the stage seemed to offer him. So he wanted to develop himself in the world of illusion. Even though this developmental novel ends with the praise of individual limitation, profession and useful work, it is not a contradiction of the aforesaid. But it means that he planned here a rejection of the mere cult of aesthetic illusion, the pure ideal of a contemplative self-development; though not in the sense that it is totally misguided. For, Goethe certainly would not have glorified a mere businessman. It means instead that one must have had real experiences before one can work them over into form. Wilhelm Meister erred, not in his aim but in the material. He could not become a narrow worker, in spite of his limitations because his life purpose was so comprehensive that he had to remain a complete personality.[1]) Thus Goethe thought; he, who struggled from the universal indefiniteness of the aesthetic form of life to another in order to create above them a more potent form. In a far different way, Schiller, who had to lift himself above the necessities of life, and to free himself from mere matter and its limitations, sought power of imagination, the play impulse and aesthetic cultivation.[2]) Devotion to the purely useful, when it becomes a ruling urge, destroys the aesthetic attitude. And it seems strange at first that Goethe in his old age (in agreement with the classic Kalokagathie) should designate the purely practical Susanna, at the end of his *Wanderjahre,* as 'Good and Beautiful' (die Gute-Schoene). But this strangeness disappears if we remind ourselves that even in the first part, he had called the expressions of a purely religio-erotic type the Confessions of a beautiful soul.

---

[1]) Cf. Jonas Cohn, *Der Geist der Erziehung* 1919 p. 91. I cannot agree that a desire for vocational education is particularly strongly felt by artists. Perhaps we have here instead the conquest of mere artistry. — Schiller too was impressed in this way by Meister; 'that he achieved determination without losing his beautiful flexibility, that he learned to control himself but found in this limitation the passage through form to the infinite'. (Letter to Goethe. July 8th, 1796). Schiller's conception of aesthetic determination (see above) represents what we have called the aesthetic type.

[2]) The impulse to form means for Schiller something different than for us, namely the purely rational forming capacity of Reason in the Kantian sense. Cf. my book *Wilhelm v. Humboldt und die Humanitaetsidee* p. 341 ff. and p. 281. What we call form, Schiller called living form or freedom in appearance.

His inner assimilative and formative power was so universal that it united all other types in a comprehensive form. This greatest of all self-creators had, to use a Romantic expression, such an allround 'sensorium' that his aesthetic attitude toward life included all the others. The nucleus, however, remains his striving for inner form, or better, the formation of his entelechy with the aid of everything which life brought to him in the way of material.[1])

The practical factor also necessarily appears as a subordinate item in the principles of aesthetic form. In every art we observe an economy of medium, applied not only to the magnitude but also to the intensity of the medium. Every gradation and tension is measured according to the psycho-physical energy of the enjoying subject. Similar to this is the formation of life itself. Here economy is shown by not desiring anything unattainable and by restricting the power of imagination. It appears further in the fact that for the purely aesthetic man periods of depression must necessarily follow upon those of enthusiasm. The aesthetic type differs from the severely stoic in striving for abundant and manysided experience and in not being content with a pure intellectualizing of life. But every aesthetic enthusiasm demands a subsequent quietude, every act of expansion one of limitation. And thus a stoic trait, the pathos of limitation, necessarily belongs to the aesthetic type. It is introduced by the factor of power economy which enters into every mental act.

The aesthetic man is by no means an unsocial type. But since individuality is a part of his nature, he tends in social relations toward eccentricity and self-importance. In other words, individualism and not self-denial is characteristic of the aesthetic type socially. Where this type is strongly marked the man is not ruled by a desire to help others in the practical or spiritual needs of life, but they become like all of life, objects of aesthetic enjoyment and differentiating empathy. This aesthetic factor appears very clearly in social relations. There is an easy-going, mostly superficial association of people in which neither personal needs nor professional interests but the peculiar manner of receptivity and self-expression is enjoyed. People here come in contact through the medium of expression and impression; temporarily there arises a synthesis or fusion of souls, but it carries with it no sense of obligation and reminds one of the play of butterflies. The charm of such social

---

[1]) 'From utility through truth to beauty.' (*Wanderjahre*).

activities arises from the free and easy contact of individualities that are mutually interesting, but in a pure case without any real binding of interests.

Eroticism illustrates a higher and more enduring form of this aesthetico-social relation. We mean by this the frankly aesthetically determined form of love. Eroticism is rooted primarily in the fact that the human body operates as a symbol of a pure, free, natural, forming power of the soul. It appears as an expression of something psychological, which the enjoying subject experiences as longing. The body is here considered the adequate symbol of a truly valuable soul. Eroticism may be reciprocal but that is not essential to its nature. In higher stages the bodily aspects may drop out and an act of love may turn directly to the inner form of another soul. Perhaps Plato first showed the way to this kind of eroticism.[1] Every pronounced aesthete is markedly erotic. And it seems that the eroticism of a reflecting soul is attracted by the natural and youthful,[2] while the naive on the contrary strives for the profound. Everybody seeks those form powers which he lacks. The interlacing of this eroticism with sexuality is undeniable. A hidden relation between the plastic powers of body and soul is present, but the form of its appearance in consciousness may be purely spiritual and usually is so with youthful pure natures in whom the erotic fancy is more powerful than the reproductive drive. Bound up with this is the fact that the mental phenomenon of eroticism between people of the same sex is entirely normal because only two different spiritual principles are necessary to the erotic, one of which plays the male, the other the female role. The concentrated onesided mental force is always male, the spiritual totality in which a naive form power is preformed is female. But form results from the spiritual union of both; form, that is the harmonious no longer onesided or purely vegetative man. Thus humanity, as illustrated by the aesthetic type, only completely fulfills itself in eroticism. For, every man is in his deeper nature as mental-unisexual being incomplete and incompletable.[3]

---

[1] In his *Symposion*.
[2] 'Anyone who has thought deepest, loves the most vivacious.' Hoelderlin.
[3] For further detail see my *Psychologie des Jugendalters* Leipzig 1924 4th ed. Ch. 4: Youthful eroticism.

What we called the female principle is most clearly realized in the female soul. She is the necessary complement to the male spirit who strives for inner form. He only matures through empathy with her. 'The eternal feminine leads us upward.' The spiritual relation of the two sexes is, therefore, insofar as physical sexuality does not take the upper hand, an aesthetic one. The meaning of true marriage is neither physical nor practical but a mutual spiritual completion; development, in the highest sense of the word, of inner form. For this reason only early marriage can fulfill this highest purpose. But the real meaning of such a union finally surpasses the merely aesthetic factor which is only a preliminary symbol, and leads into a total life unity which culminates in religious values.[1]

If we turn back to social relations, it is now explicable why its aesthetic character rests especially on the spiritual contact of the sexes; only that there it is a union which is temporary and stimulating to the imagination. The pure aesthetic type allows too much imagination to enter into his social relations. He has no understanding of the active loyalty which helps another person even if his soul is devoid of charm and attraction. Aesthetes have no feeling at all for the practical side of solidarity. Because they have no real comprehension of mankind they interpret socialism, for instance, in a peculiar way which, seen from the point of view of political socialism, can only be called a miscomprehension. Illustrative of this is the essay on *Socialism and the Soul of Man* by the aesthete Oscar Wilde. Socialism is for him only a means of aesthetic individualism, and is valuable only because it leads to that and to a most complete life. This most complete life however man can only find in the sphere of artistic imagination. It is the most intensive kind of individualism known. Only in voluntary associations is man beautiful, although his purpose is to be beautiful. The proper duties of the state are the useful; those of the individual, the beautiful. The aesthetic socialism of Oscar Wilde and Gustav Landauer is thus a protection against ugly impressions, a spiritual insurance against distressing experiences. The real value of life is only achieved if everyone lets his whole

---

[1] On the difference between the vital feeling of oneness which I call Eros or aesthetic love and the real understanding personal love cf. Scheler *Wesen und Formen der Sympathie*. Bonn 1923.

being well up from within and lives, a complete individual, creating and enjoying.[1]

Let us now proceed to the political sphere. Like the theorist in his knowledge, so the aesthetic man in his consciousness of individuality and personality has a feeling of power. This is of course the characteristic inner power, which even Nietzsche never transcended. The aesthetic type naturally finds outer means to power in his own sphere, that is, the effects of artistic creation.[2] This is the language by which he tries to influence people; by decorative appearance, by aesthetic beauty of clothes and house, rhetorical suggestion etc. But when ambition predominates we pass over into the political type. The aesthetic man as an aristocrat and an individualist withdraws from mankind and is self-sufficient, as soon as his position is threatened by others, '*Odi profanum vulgus et arceo.*' And here he is unconsciously influenced by the realization that he is unable to cope mentally with the world of power. If the aesthetic type does not practise this reserve but participates in politics he finds that he has no aptitude for it. He judges everything by himself. Now nothing is more fundamentally crippling to the aesthete than subordination to overindividual social forces which demand from him something definite, limited and real. He conceives even the state aesthetically.[3] Under favorable

---

[1] Oscar Wilde, *Der Sozialismus und die Seele des Menschen* usw. Translated by Hedwig Lachmann and Gustav Landauer. Berlin 1904. — Gustav Landauer, *Aufruf zum Sozialismus* Berlin ed. 2, 1919. (Page for page is evidence of the type developed above) 'We are poets; and shall do away with the scientific swindlers, the Marxists, the frigid, the hollow and mindless ones so that poetic vision, the artistically concentrated creativity, the enthusiasm and prophetic power finds a place where they may in future work, create and build, in life, with human bodies, for the achievements and social life of groups, communities and peoples.' p. 34.

[2] The feeling of power projected on aesthetic presentations creates the phenomenon of sublimity and heroism. As Kant has already shown, it is not purely aesthetic. According to our differentiation it is to be understood as the appearance of another type; namely that of moral elevation above nature which is made the object of aesthetic reflection and enjoyment.

[3] Cf. Schleiermacher in his romantic stage. *Monologen III.* 'Where are the old legends of the state told by the wise men? Where is the power which this highest stage of existence should give, to each man, where the consciousness each should have, to be part of its reason, imagination (!) and power?' — Schmitt-Dorotič, *Politische Romantik* ed. 2,

circumstances he sees in the state a form, in unfavorable conditions, a fetter. For this reason he is a liberal and limits the state to a minimum of activity; as Wilhelm v. Humboldt and Leopold v. Wiese. Or he is even an anarchist who considers the state superfluous and desires to help mankind to a life of liberty and beauty.[1]) The pure impressionists or expressionists of existence specially lack the inner self-discipline, which is necessary in subordination to a ruler and in dependent relations. Even the classic man, the complete personality, would prefer to live according to the pure law of his own nature; to have room for his own growth and unfolding, to find liberty through organic self-development. His creed is the liberalism of harmonious mankind, which is not to be confused with Kantian liberalism of duty. We find the strong contrast of the political and aesthetic points of view in Hoelderlin's Hyperion; the men near Alabanda that appear so terrible to him are only politicians and propagandists for activity. But Hyperion dreams of a theocracy of beauty.[2])

We now approach the relation of the aesthetic type to religion. The aesthetically important, — which I call the beautiful in a wider sense (in contrast to purely harmonious beauty) — has for him the highest value. His creed is a religion of beauty. For this reason, the harsh dualism between life here and in Heaven, the devaluation of the physical, seems to him intolerable; likewise the

---

Muenchen 1925 gives a masterly psychological analysis of the romantic type of mind which he too subordinates to the aesthetic type. For this reason must romanticism deform real politics: 'It gives a political romanticism as well as a political Lyric' (ed. 1. p. 115.)

[1]) Cf. Oscar Wilde's antagonism to every kind of authoritative socialism, and Gustav Landauer op. cit. p. 19 ff. 'Where there is no spirit and no inner necessity, there is external power, regulation and the state.' ... 'The state never resides in the inner individual, it has never become a quality of individuality nor of free will' etc. — W. v. Humboldt, *Ideen zu einem Versuch, die Grenzen der Wirksamkeit des Staates zu bestimmen*, especially the three first chapters. Works (Akademieausgabe) I. p. 117. 'Therefore the interesting man is interesting in all occupations and positions; therefore he flowers into rapturous beauty in a manner of life which coincides with his character.' (i. e. outside of the state in freedom). Leopold v. Wiese, *Der Liberalismus in Vergangenheit und Zukunft* Berlin 1917; above all p. 155 ff.: *Die romantischen Metapolitiker*.

[2]) Cf. my essay *Hoelderlin und das deutsche Nationalbewusstsein*, in *Kultur und Erziehung* ed. 3. Leipzig 1925.

creation of a fully formed world out of nothing instead of from chaos. Political natures think that the world was created by a voluntary act. The aesthetic man on the other hand conceives it as a forming process, a unity in manifoldness, a cosmos. A sort of aesthetic Pantheism or Panentheism finds favor with the aesthetic type. God is for him the highest ordering and form-giving Power; a soul breathing in the world itself. And the universe is a harmony and an ocean of beauty as conceived in a continuation of Platonic thought by Bruno, Leibniz and Shaftesbury, Schelling and Goethe in their youth.[1]) Religion is to them a union with this harmony. The aesthetico-religious conception of the world is Animism.[2]) It must be remembered that Schleiermacher's analysis of religion, in the first edition of his *Reden über die Religion*, shows a pronounced aesthetico-religious type. It is remarkable how little space he gives to the factor of morality, to the normative value. And the description of the bridal embrace in which we become one with the universe has throughout the form of empathy or a fusion of souls, which is very characteristic of the aesthetic process. A consciousness of distance from God, sin, a sense of disparity, of imprisonment in the dungeon of individuality and a desperate wrestling for the Lord have no place in this religion. Later on, Schleiermacher took up more historico-Christian factors in his theory of religion. But the pure aesthete has little use for this realm of experience. Men like Humboldt and Goethe in their youth have not found in themselves this consciousness of duality of which the conception of transcendency is only a reflex. Like Hoelderlin they felt borne up by the beauty of the world. 'Religion is the love of beauty.' (Hoelderlin W. I. 105). 'The most beautiful is also the most holy.' (W. I. 72). For them the aesthetic becomes the metaphysical world principle. But to all Platonists it is no longer merely appearance, veil, illusion, segment, but essentially

---

[1]) 'What other point of comparison for genuine beauty is there except in the inclusive concept of all the harmonious relations of the entirety of Nature, which cannot be grasped by any thought?' Goethe *Italienische Reise*, cited bei Moritz.

[2]) Scheler in his much quoted book on sympathy differentiates beyond aesthetic empathy the still deeper vital feeling of oneness which can grow into a feeling of unity with cosmic life. (op. cit. p. 16 ff. p. 84 ff. p. 90 ff.) I incline to classify both feelings as aesthetic insofar as they are mental. Scheler adds another sphere of vital values. Cf. section IV 1.

world structure; the final, and (from a religious point of view) most valid meaning that lies behind all crude, unformed and ugly phenomena of the world. Even suffering, death and sickness are tinged for them with a delicate poetic tint. The interpretation of Christianity peculiar to the aesthetic type is clearly illustrated in Oscar Wilde's reference to Christ as the 'Aesthete of the soul.'[1]) While the pure theorist or purely religious man then, looks upon beauty only as a preliminary element in which the final meaning of the world is concealed, it becomes for the aesthetic type the fulfilment of sense itself, and the real value of life.

There is a great difference between a man with an aesthetically organized soul who treats materials with a religious meaning and the point of view of the productive artist, or a religious type who paints or composes. The borderline between the two, however, is very difficult to find in any specific case. It presupposes a differentiation of mental life which is not always given historically. At the height of the middle ages every man's notion of the world as well as of the self was so strongly influenced by an objective religion and tradition that outside of religion there was no art, just as there was no philosophy. If a markedly aesthetic mind appears on this level it will certainly choose the available figurative language, even though in this context it wishes to express something that has been purely aesthetically experienced and visualized. Dante was a striking example of this. The very complex relation between the sensibly perceptible and the super-sensible during the middle ages was first interpreted structurally for the formative arts by Max Dvorák. The unique desire and problem of this art was to transform the spiritual which could only be grasped subjectively, into the sensibly perceptible. 'The uniqueness of the development of mediaeval art lies not only in the religious character which is familiar to everyone — (the art of the counter-reformation was equally religious and yet, despite the many points in common very different from the Gothic) — but in this omnipotence of a mental construction which lies beyond material experience and whose influence was so great that every immediate reference to sensible experience in spiritual things (comparable to our modern impulse to depreciate the same) was conceived as a meaningless and

---

[1]) Schiller in a curious letter to Goethe also designates Christianity as 'the only aesthetic religion.' (August 17th, 1795.)

damnable sin against truth and human reason.'[1]) Thus Gothic art represents the only attempt to strike a balance between the super-sensible explanation of life and the consequent reaction to the sensible.

A soul structure which is closer to the natural-sensible and is more free from religious tradition has the possibility of letting its inner aesthetic organisation develop toward the infinite relations which characterize religion in the wider sense. Regardless of whether one considers aesthetic pantheism (which is really based not upon a doctrine but rather upon an organisation of the soul) primarily as religious or aesthetic, the creations of such a mind will have, without any historico-religious symbolism, a religious significance which expresses Schleiermacher's '*Sinn und Geschmack fuers Uuiversum*'. (This is especially true, of course, if they choose nature for their object). There are innumerable examples of this in poetry. Oskar Beyer has developed this point of view for formative art very brilliantly in writing and illustration. But here we reach the point where these structures cannot be further explained and one must rely upon spiritual insight (*beseeltes Sehen*).[2])

This infinite expansion of the aesthetic organ has been consciously formulated in a description of renewed and deepened feeling of nature by Gottfried Keller:[3]) „*Es war die hingebende Liebe an alles Gewordene und Bestehende, welche das Recht und die Bedeutung jeglichen Dinges ehrt und den Zusammenhang und die Tiefe der Welt empfindet. Diese Liebe steht hoeher als das kuenstlerische Heraustehlen des einzelnen zu eigennuetzigem Zwecke, welches zuletzt immer zu Kleinlichkeit und Laune fuehrt, sie steht auch hoeher als das Geniessen und Absondern nach Stimmungen und romantischen Liebhabereien, und nur sie allein vermag eine gleichmaessige, dauernde Glut zu geben.*" And again: „*Die Welt ist innerlich ruhig und still, und so muss es auch der Mann sein, der sie verstehen und als ein wirkender Teil von ihr sie widerspiegeln will. Ruhe zieht das Leben an, Unruhe verscheucht es; Gott haelt sich maeuschenstill, darum bewegt sich die Welt um ihn.*"

---

[1]) Max Dvorak, *Kunstgeschichte als Geistesgeschichte*. Muenchen 1924. p. 60.
[2]) Oskar Beyer, *Die unendliche Landschaft. Über religioese Naturmalerei und ihre Meister*. With 34 reproductions. Furcheverlag, Berlin 1922.
[3]) *Gruener Heinrich* III. 1.

Fuer den kuenstlerischen Menschen nun waere dies so anzuwenden, dass er sich eher leidend und zusehend verhalten und die Dinge an sich vorueberziehen lassen, als ihnen nachjagen soll; denn wer in einem festlicheu Zuge mitzieht, kann denselben nicht so beschreiben, wie der, welcher am Wege steht. Dieser ist darum nicht ueberfluessig und muessig, und der Seher ist erst das ganze Leben des Gesehenen."

III

All these data show the specific form of motivation characteristic of the aesthetic type. It is determined (in the deeper affairs of life) not by general laws nor utilitarian considerations but by the will to form. This, alas, is often a misdirected impulse which does not reach its goal, but gets side-tracked in biassed subjectivity or impressionism. But even these unsuccessful attempts are motivated by a desire to develop one's imagined self. Self-realization, self-fulfilment, self-enjoyment are aesthetic aims. The final gospel of Ibsen and Oscar Wilde is 'Be yourself'. But such inner form-development results not from rational consideration but rather from unconscious inspiration. The bunglers of the type often confuse this creed with riotous living. Some, especially young people, follow enthusiasm; which, unfortunately, often reacts into stoic resignation. But the more moderate are guided by 'good taste', by tact and a sense of decorum or fitness. They reject a course of action, not because it is dangerous or inconsistent but because it lacks style. (For this reason those who talk most of this generally remain in the vestibule of the aesthetic form of life). In all actions they are led by a sense of beauty and moderation. They would avoid playing the flute because it distorts their faces. And their last wish would be to die beautifully. (Hedda Gabler). Pausanias, in Plato's *Symposion,* represents this type on a lower plane, and confuses decorum with purity. But the Socrates described here and in *Phaedra* is the discoverer of real spiritual beauty. We find this aesthetic moral code in different degrees: somewhat vague in Cicero's '*decorum et honestum*'; in the '*máze*' of conventional knighthood; in the whole Renaissance as the style of life, and finally with Baltasar Gracian, Shaftesbury, Herder, Goethe, Schiller, Humboldt, Heinse and Hoelderlin.[1]

---

[1] Cf. Herder's *Schulreden* on 'moral grace'. We have already mentioned Goethe's conception of entelechy and its higher aesthetic character. Schiller

Bound up with this individual culture is a striving for development as a conscious means of shaping one's self into inner form. The motive of self-development, the inward enrichment from life, also belongs to this aesthetic group. I have shown in earlier writings that the aesthetic humanism of Germany's classic period comprises three aspects: individuality, as a onesided expression of humanity; universality, as the wealth of experience and formation; totality, as the union of both in a living form. The aesthetic attitude toward life is radically opposed to the stoic. It is directed toward the manifoldness of existence with an infinite desire for observation and capacity for enjoyment. In spite of this it does not simply diffuse itself in every direction but, as individuality, it has a law of organic growth, an innate desire for development. Mental growth appears only as a continuation of the organic drive (*nisus formativus*). And this is not a mere cramming of knowledge, but a free, manysided and peculiarly mental drawing in of the 'world' with all the receptive and productive organs of the soul. And this fact reveals the ethical principle peculiar to the type: *inner form*, spiritual self-realization based on the rhythm, proportion and harmony of inner movement.[1])

German Romanticism, taken as a type, exhibits a unique interweaving of the aesthetic and religious forms of motivation. Schmitt-Dorotič has carefully analized just this aspect in his book entitled: *Die okkasionalistische Struktur der Romantik*. The unquenchable longing of the romanticist for an 'all' makes for an annulling of contrasts. But his aesthetically active mind, which everywhere keeps the subject in its imaginative freedom, does not allow of a onesided decision since this would make for limitation and restraint. Thus there arises an aesthetic harmonizing of contrasts as opposed to the deeper religious logic which we shall see in the religious type. The Romanticist does not reconcile contrasts but avoids them by a third alternative. Just as the Occasionalist regards all individual activity as sinful and eludes it through divine causality, so also the Romanticist escapes not through God

---

(23rd letter) 'One does more than one's duty not from a moral but from an aesthetic motive. And such behavior is noble.' Cf. the citation from W. v. Humboldt's juvenilia on page 160 footnote 1.

[1]) One might add the erotic motive to the motives of form and self-development. — This type moreover includes as a rule the development and culture of the body.

but through the liberty of his imagination: 'In Romanticism the genius takes the place of God and regards the external world as the occasion of his own activity and productivity. The most startling external occurrence, a revolution or a world war, leaves him indifferent and is significant only if it gives him a great experience or a brilliant *aperçu*. Nothing has true reality except what has been made the object of the subject's creative interest. The subject becomes, by means of a simple reversal, the creator of the world. He recognizes as world only what he himself has created. Here a strong consciousness of personality seems to concentrate itself in a great activity. And yet despite this, the Romanticist's feeling of self leaves unchanged the psychic condition which is always found in the Occasionalistic type, namely that his moods are his only activity.' (Ed. 1. p. 89) — 'The Romanticist does not want to act, he only wants to experience and to form his experience.' All these traits are not only characteristic of one definite type of aesthetic motivation, but they also illuminate its contrast to the genuinely religious: it lacks the character of finality and of decisive obligation.

IV

In treating the aesthetic type we have had in mind more the artist of himself, the man of inner aesthetic structure, than the externally creative artist. But if it is true that we must conceive external artistry as a reflex of the forming soul power, then the onesided forms in which the artist appears must be symptoms of the differentiation of aesthetic soul structure. Now the abundance of objective presentation of beauty is boundless:

> '*Sie steiget hernieder in tausend Gebilden,*
> *Sie schwebet auf Wassern, sie schreitet auf Gefilden,*
> *Nach heiligen Massen erglaenzt sie und schallt,*
> *Und einzig veredelt die Form den Gehalt,*
> *Verleiht ihm, verleiht sich die hoechste Gewalt,*
> *Mir erschien sie in Jugend-, in Frauengestalt.*'
>
> (Goethe, *Pandora*.)

For us the original type of beauty is humanity; the human body, the human soul. For man it is the 'eternal feminine', the idea of woman whose physical-spiritual mystery is bound up most of all with the context of a mentally creative nature: Madonna and child halfway between Heaven and earth. Since, however, the spiritual is the only principle which bestows beauty (because its radiance alone makes the body beautiful) so beauty of soul appears as the really original Beauty. The beauty of nature, as well as artistic beauty must be understood as derived forms which receive their power only because, in the aesthetic process, a soul or a soul spark is bestowed upon them. Consequently, in considering aesthetic types we must investigate whether they have an open mind for beauty of soul (they are nearest to the original and need little from drama and novels); or whether their inner life catches fire more from nature (they are the favored children of nature who seek their brothers in the still woods, the air or the water); or whether finally, they can feel beauty only in the expressed form with which the artist stamps his sensible concrete creations.

The difference between aesthetic creative and merely enjoying natures reappears in the sub-types. Some people surrender themselves to the impressions of life with female passivity and let them re-echo harmoniously in their souls. Opposed to these are the male active people who through energetic mental work impress the stamp of their inner form on their whole sphere of life. They are also conscious self-developers who subject the material of life to a sort of aesthetic sifting process. Usually they regard the world as material to form their personalities, and classify all mental goods according to their fruitfulness for culture.

A further difference comes with the relation of the aesthetic man to reality. We have seen that the plane of reality upon which we project the sensibly mediated experiences is by no means unequivocal. Its nucleus is perhaps made up of what we called above 'biological reality'. But even this is not free from theoretical determinations. The kind and proportion of theoretic constructions change with periods of time and scientific systems. For these reasons alone, reality as fact[1] is not entirely constant for the experiencing subject. But there is also the complicating factor of the unique imaginative standpoint of the individual. For, even in comprehending the given, apperceptive and reproductive imagination are already influential, and also fill in the gaps of experience and create an image of nature's total system.[2] Herein lies a subjective

---

[1] Reality is for science a border-line concept, an idea which must be approached by conceptual interrelations.
[2] Cf. my essay: *Phantasie und Weltanschauung* in the Symposium *Weltanschauung* 1911.

addition to the never wholly isolable objective factor. Not only the world but also the subordinated self is colored and formed by this imaginative tendency. We call *Realists*[1]) those whose attitude is objective in the sense that the inevitable external impressions are accepted as facts without any attempt at a deeper intellectual or ethical mastery. If the direct influence on feeling predominates, then we have the *Impressionists* of existence, of whom we have spoken above, the type of *Reizsamkeit* (Lamprecht). *Idealists* we call those who form the material of experience in thought and evaluate it ethically, regarding only the product of this forming process as their 'world'. If, however, the subjective world of feeling is so much over-valued that it usurps the place of objectivity, then we have the *Expressionist*. He finds in everything only an echo of his own feelings, often with astonishing disregard of objective data. The realist as the naive, the expressionist as the sentimental, form the opposite points of a sequence in which many intermediary steps can be found. These are, as we saw, determined not purely aesthetically but also theoretically through the share of perception and thought. When, however, theoretic acts are subordinated and their objects finally related to the inner formation of life, we have a clearly aesthetic attitude. The aesthetic type can thus be either realistic or idealistic: the two differ only in the amount of subjective metamorphosis the impressions of the world receive in passing through their mental structure. The phenomena of '*Anschauungsbilder*' which have lately been carefully investigated by E. R. Jaensch[2]) show how great a part subjective production of ideas even on the primitive level of the development of perception, plays in the perceived objects. If this factor is controlling for the total psychic organisation, as in the artist of eidetic organisation, from this most vivid experience an entire type can develop, that which lives in concrete pictures, the men of great formative 'powers of imagination'. Dilthey,[3]) in his psychology of the poet has attempted to formulate the laws by which ideas are freely transformed, under the influence of feeling structure,

---

[1]) These and the following terms must however not be understood in the sense of a theory of cognition.

[2]) E. R. Jaensch, *Ueber den Aufbau der Wahrnehmungswelt*, Leipzig 1923.

[3]) W. Dilthey, *Die Einbildungskraft des Dichters*. Works. Vol. VI, 2. p. 163 ff.

beyond the limits of reality. I regard as most important two types of experience which are related to this: the man of after-enjoyment for whom the content of experience is resplendent only in memory, and who therefore finds his decisive relations to life only in this distance from the immediate pressure of reality; and secondly the universal symbolist who empathically divines, behind every form and experience, deeper relations and more decisive contents. All finite things become for him a parable of hidden meaning contexts. The gift of seeing and composing things in this way is still aesthetic, although its effects are related to the religious realm. This is the position of the mystic in regard to reality, if he grants it any importance at all and if he has any imagination. Jakob Boehme, Schelling and Froebel had this rare world picture. Both tendencies, after-enjoyment and symbolism, are found in all Romanticists. For, just this factor seems to found the romantic mental type. And this too accounts for their tendency to grant mythology a higher cognitive importance than strict theoretic science because it is based upon an empathy of all sentiments. This type is becoming more and more frequent.[1])

We found these differences by considering the distance of the aesthete from reality. Other closely allied differences result from the magnitude of the aesthetic forming process, or, in other words, from the breadth of the aesthetically apprehending senses. Lyric natures pause over a very small unit and its aesthetic momentary effect; epic natures turn toward life in its total breadth, viewing and enjoying it all.[2]) Between these extremes stand the dramatic natures who follow their activity as it is interwoven with fate with an intensity that demands solution. Thus the epic re-echoes in the lyric. One might call the lyric natures men of moods. The epic and dramatic types were formerly classified as temperaments. But in their case it is not a question of a purely emotional rhythm which would belong to the psychology of elements. The question is rather how these emotional processes are filled with an objective content. And only thus do they determine a mental type.

The contrast between optimist and pessimist reaches beyond the aesthetic into the religious type. Naturally a religious evaluation of life always echoes in the aesthetic type. The combination of

---

[1]) Cf. Ernst Cassirer, *Idee und Gestalt*, Berlin 1921: *Hoelderlin*.
[2]) Cf. my book: *Wilhelm v. Humboldt und die Humanitaetsidee.* p. 369.

negative and positive evaluations of the world determines the aesthetic style of life. If the happy factor predominates we have the typical humorist, if the negative preponderates we have the satirist. Both laugh at life, one with gentle tenderness, the other with bitter superiority. Finally the tragedian looks at life as a battle between light and darkness, in which even though light is condemned to defeat it nevertheless gives out an afterglow of aesthetic splendor. Nietzsche maintains in this tragic sense that the world can only be justified as an aesthetic phenomenon. Insofar, however, as aestheticism is bound up with a belief in redemption it borders on the religious type.

V

We must look for the reverse of the aesthetic man not only among the other pure types, but above all in a man who, having the forming power of imagination, nevertheless rejects the aesthetic attitude toward life. Some natures fight the ideal glowing within them from their highest and most purely artistic motives, because they cannot see it in its highest perfection. Plato, though certainly an artist, condemns artists because they only imitate and copy but can never attain the truth, the original elements. Rousseau called novel-writing in which he was so skilled, dangerous, since it aroused passions without ethically mastering them. Goethe experienced within himself something of Tasso's fate. Tolstoy fought himself or at least one phase or one side of his nature, when he attacked the immorality of art as representing art itself. And yet they all had to speak the aesthetic language. In declaring war on the aesthetic ideal they only wanted to surpass it; like Schiller who in his idyll *Der verklaerte Herkules* tried to reach his highest poetic self.[1] The aesthetic formation of existence is only possible if one loves the human, all too human, if one also loves the 'veil of Maya' and finds in one's passions, joys. The final malediction with which man curses the artistic and emotional part of his individual life is itself an aesthetic expression. Many people fight aestheticism only because of the pain that it is denied them to say, or create in themselves, the highest. The incompleteability of aesthetic expression which must be experienced by the soul in a titanic struggle has been well empathized by Bettina von Arnim

---

[1] Cf. Schiller to Humboldt, November 30th, 1795 (Leitzmann p. 224 f.).

when she puts these words into the mouth of Beethoven: 'Even though I have in my work the feeling of success, I nevertheless feel an eternal hunger like a child to begin again what just now seemed to me finished with a last beat of the drum with which I transmitted my enjoyment and musical conviction to the listeners.'[1])

Over and above the incompleteability of the aesthetic will to form, however, there is a second tormenting limitation; the irresponsibility and imagination of the aesthetic style of life which Kierkegaard was the first to see and to scourge. Even though the aesthetic man avoids the *salto mortale* into the ethically religious realm, he nevertheless struggles with the raw material of existence which influences his inner world according to its own laws which are foreign to him. Therefore the man of inner form is always haunted by an eternal fear and a last tragic shadow which he cannot banish: *Fate.*

---

[1]) Cf. my lecture *Beethoven und die Musik als Weltanschauungsausdruck.* Leipzig, Wiegandt 1910.

4
THE SOCIAL ATTITUDE

I

One might object to the presentation of a specific social type (in the sense of the term outlined on p. 58) that such a type has no content of its own. For, all sympathy must be directed to some value content of another person and all community would have to further either economic or theoretic, aesthetic or religious values, or all of them combined. We have seen however in the first part of the book that social behavior contains a unique act, namely the value affirming interest in another being and the taking-the-place-of-another. Wherever this impulse to give oneself to another appears as a dominant drive, a special type originates which we have called social. We must, from the outset exclude all social acts which are based upon rational consideration of means. For, in them the dominant factor is not social but some other, economic or political for instance. The specific social type is founded only when the sympathetic spirit becomes the original impulse of the soul and its immediate direction of life. Interest in others is encountered even on the animal level: as love of the mate or the young, as herd instinct and feeling of community. But these instincts do not rise to the specifically mental zone. And the social attitude does not become the subject of our characterology until it operates as the organizing principle of mental life. Mere pity is not mental. As a feeling of equality and of sympathy [1] it may come and go with the moment and have a reflex character. But such superficial impulses of the soul do not determine its structure.

The social quality in its highest development is called love. And this may come from the firm conviction that all life is related

---

[1] Cf. Groethuysen, *Das Mitgefuehl* Zeitschrift fuer Psychologie, Vol. 34 and also Max Scheler *Wesen und Formen der Sympathie.* Bonn 1923.

and perhaps even essentially one. Such an all-inclusive love is religious.[1]) On the other hand this love may be directed to a single individual or to a limited group without losing the decisive character of the basic drive which dominates the entire existence of the social type. But its essence lies deeper than the mere phenomena: the man himself as a carrier of value becomes the object of love. One may love a soul because the value of the true, the beautiful or the holy appears in its being and striving, or because in the combination of all three its powers may represent an elevated humanity. It is therefore possible that an instinctive longing for the value contents of life, which are differentiated in the main directions as classified above, is part of love. Love itself, however, lies still deeper. It remains something purely unique, namely the inclination toward another person for the sake of his value possibilities. Science cannot dispense with conceptual analysis even of what cannot finally be formulated. In accordance with this method we say therefore *that love essentially sees other people (whether one or more) as possible carriers or positers of value, and finds in such comprehension the ultimate value of its own essence.* The aesthetic type we said, in its contemplative attitude, lives only second hand; in the same way, the social type has only an indirect attitude toward life. He does not live immediately through himself but in others. This may be carried to the point where he sees his own value only as it is reflected in other people. But this kind of self-estimation which originates in loving surrender must not be confused with ambition which belongs in the political context.

In perfect love the limits of individuation disappear. The ego feeling and the alter feeling, selfhood and self-sacrifice, liberty and renunciation coincide. The self that loves is a different self

---

[1]) Scheler op. cit. wants to accept this metaphysical meaning of love only in the vital zone of life as a panvitalistic 'Einsfuehlungsethos' but not in the personal zone. Then the feeling of mutual relation of all mental-psychic life would according to our terminology have only an aesthetic i. e. an erotic character. The *Tat twam asi* reaches obviously much deeper. Blood relationship does not only found the vital feeling of oneness but also religious love. In general: Religious love means that we come from God and that if all limits of space and time would disappear it would be essentially the same being full of suffering and happiness which strives out of individuation.

from the desirous and selfish one. It is an over-self which finds itself again, enriched in the ego of another.

One cannot deny that the attitude which honors another life as a possible carrier of value contains a religious factor. For, anyone who conceives another person in this way gives all of life a meaning, namely the direction to value as such. But this religious trait is very pronounced only when everyone is seen in this light. The social type may also appear in a narrower form: a wife may live in her husband, a mother in her children, a servant in his master. Plato, however — starting from the Eros ($\check{\varepsilon}\varrho\omega\varsigma$) which is always colored aesthetically and is thus a love originally due to psycho-physical imaginative empathy — describes this elevation of body to soul, of one to all, of all to the genuine value content and of the value content to God himself. Christian love also may be thought of as a gradual elevation to the all-inclusive. For, it transforms maternal and fraternal love into powers which surround all mankind and all living things. Therefore it does not remain *caritas* in the sense of doing good, but reaches, above everything which may still express itself in individual being and action, from the religious core of one soul to the same depth in the other.

In our description of the social type we must also consider lower levels, the more narrow love directed only to one or a few. But even in these it must appear as the central impulse in life and must be united with the wish for complete union with just these loved ones.

II

The other five value regions may appear as the content of the social type. They then found aims of value which are to be advanced by the aid of love. We cannot, however, discuss them in this sense here, for we wish to isolate love as an essential power in its own right. Our question is: how do they integrate in the social mental act and how far are they formed by the meaning of the social act?

Science seems to the social type to contain too much of the object and too little of the soul. Besides this, knowledge often makes people proud, while love is humble. There is a Christian maxim: 'To love Christ is better than to possess great knowledge.' The objectivity of science is contrary to the spirit of love, especially when man is only dispassionately studied and regarded in his objective reality. Then the observer sees nothing of the dormant possibilities which might be awakened by the first warm breath of love. Mere understanding of man is a purely theoretic attitude. Only if a breath of sympathy, of elevation or surrender and under certain circumstances of forgiveness is added, do we find ourselves in the social region. It is very difficult for love to be also just. For, in justice there is always an element of objective understanding and application of general rules. The prejudiced lover who has no higher culture can hardly be just at all. He sees everything in the circle of the loved ones as good and just, and in those outside, only lack of understanding and evil intentions. Love may be called blind because, according to its nature and measured by the theoretic ideal, it always overemphasizes the positive and disregards the negative. It may however with equal justice be said to have vision insofar as it has an eye for the deeper-lying values. All genuine community strives for a community of convictions, and judges its subjects without sufficient theoretic criticism. And this is why, according to the power of one's own mind, one either tries to win over the loved one to one's own point of view or to subject one's self to his. Only when the onesided tendency to sympathy is overcome can love acknowledge dissenting opinions without becoming weaker. So long as the onesided social attitude predominates, love forces into the background even the will to truth. One would hide an unbearable truth from a person one loved. It is part of the structure of community that truth referred to persons may contain an element of lovelessness. Therefore we have the tragic conflict between truth and justice on the one hand and love on the other.[1]

A similar tension exists between the economic and the social principles. Self-preservation and self-sacrifice have opposite meanings. A person who wants anything for himself cannot live for another. And therefore the caritative destroys the economic principle. The immanent law of economics knows no giving or sacrifice from selfless motives. This is in agreement with the fact that everywhere

---

[1] Romano Guardini, *Gottes Werkleute*, Rothenfels 1925. p. 28. 'That is just the difficulty that one cannot separate truth from love.' That the sharing of theoretic insights may found community and even love does not belong in this context since we do not speak here of forces which develop communities. The stoics assume that the immanent reason of the world founds a συμπάθεια τῶν ὅλων, though be it said only a very rational, bloodless sympathy.

that love is to be the guiding star of life we find the creed of poverty. The monk who is to live in the service of others may not call anything his own. 'For, where your treasure is, there will your heart be also.' The purely social attitude always makes for communism.[1]) It has been remarked that women are not really wholehearted in their economic interests until they have the consciousness that they are earning not for themselves but for those they love. At heart they are thus enriched so that one may speak of a higher balance of happiness in which the gain is after all on their side. Also the gifts of the soul do not make them poorer. Therefore to C. F. Meyer's statement: 'Anyone who loves is always a prodigal', we must add: 'but with infinite goods at his command'.

The relation of the social type to the aesthetic region seems to be less close than that of the previous two realms. And yet there exists here too a somewhat similar tension. Above all we are here concerned of course with the psychically aesthetic. The really social type however, differs from the eroticist because his love is directed not to the charm and beauty of the other, not even to the beauty of his soul, but to the wholly unformed soul because of its value possibilities. The object of his affection is the soul itself as naked life, as a spark of the great mystery of having become human. The more the object of his love is enmeshed in need and evil, in squalor and sickness, the more necessary is his love and the more the other person may flower under its influence. The difference from the eroticist is shown also in the fact that the eroticist in his love always experiences a sort of aesthetic self-enjoyment, while the loving social type wholly forgets itself and regards its narrower personal happiness as a gift of life gladly to be renounced for the sake of loving.[2]) There is thus something formless, something elementary in the highest love which is not merely aesthetic. It does not strive for self-perfection nor cling to the charm of the individuality of self or the other, but is simply light and warmth which shines quite as much upon an object without charm. This distinction between the eroticist and the social type

---

[1]) But not every communism is born out of love. There exists also a communism of desire or of will to power or of theoretic radicalism.

[2]) Jealousy may betray in the eroticist an unconquered remnant of desiring to possess exclusively. This is incompatible with true love.

may best be illustrated in connection with two types of pedagogue. The narrow type enriches himself in contact with the beauty and grace of youth during his time of teaching. The other, embodied in Pestalozzi, turns also to what is wholly undeveloped, even to a child who has been warped by the pressure of life and desires only to be able to elevate and to help him. This is the type of the true teacher. The other always reaches the limits of his ability when he meets with poverty, ugliness or lack of charm. For this reason we classified the eroticist as an aesthetic and not a social type. For, the truly loving nature would like to exclude all sensual elements from his attraction since that would place the deepest meaning of the 'for-another-state-of-mind' upon a transitory foundation. He sees the divine beyond all other forms, and life itself is holy without any aesthetic or biological determination. This is the point of view reached by Tolstoy. With Orientals we find this attitude including even animals and plants, as veneration of the sanctity of life on every level. The aesthete, conversely, is too aristocratic to be capable of true surrender. His love and passing compassion are a little fastidious and he is really living after all only in his own feelings.

Love and power are not mutually exclusive. But the social type desires and knows no influence of power except that of love. And therefore he is really in sympathy only with the patriarchal system. He has no understanding of a legal order which is based on general written laws, since the triumph of this legal order, the impersonality of its functioning and its exclusion of exceptions, is directly opposed to his state of mind. From the point of view of the legal state and formal justice the social mind thus leads unavoidably to anarchism, to an anarchism of love and fraternity as Tolstoy preached it. And he believed that he linked himself up with early Christianity. The world-conquering power of love could, for this reason, be indifferent to the worldly state and render unto Caesar what was Caesar's, because at heart it felt itself superior to all other powers. These two desires are eternally opposed to each other: the belief in a wholly voluntary society born from the power of love, and the will to organisation i. e. the regulation of the influential spheres by laws and if necessary by force. Experience has shown again and again through centuries of human history that only the second form can be really successful. But it is not our problem to judge the question here. We merely wish to define mental types. Dostoievski with tremendous poetical power, has shown these two forces wrestling with each other, in *The Grand Inquisitor*. From another point of view Rudolf Paulsen opposes these great world contrasts in his *Christ and the Wanderer*.[1]) F. W. Foerster has recently tried to construct a political scheme on the basis of the Christian spirit of love and of federalism which is very interesting as a psychological phenomenon but extraordinarily weak as a mental effort.[2])

We must follow this psychology further: love is not a political organizing principle because it is directed more to the possibilities of the soul, one might say more to its essence than to the concrete effects and conditions of life. Purely as love, i. e. as a deep-flowing psychic impulse, it thinks, calculates and controls too little to be a guide in the world of knowledge, economics and political claims. When one says that the love of man thinks of and treats all men as equals, this idea of equality has nothing in common with the radical conception of equality, current in the age of reason of which we spoke in connection with the theoretic type. Love as such demands equality neither before the law, nor in education nor in property; partly because it does not understand these things and partly because it does not regard them as the main sources of happiness. For, the loving person if he asks for any results at all wants only the highest happiness: to be loved. When the demand of social equality appears in the social type we do not have the type before us in its purity but connected with a theoretic or political attitude. Christ was therefore absolutely non-political because he could never look upon political or legal gifts as gifts of love. The pure love which he embodied is so to speak anterior to all these special life interests: '*But seek ye first the kingdom of God,* (that is, the spirit of love) *and his righteousness; and all these things shall be added unto you.*'[3]) Here too is shown the very strong religious core of true love. Scientists, educators, artists,

---

[1]) Leipzig (Haessel) 1924.

[2]) Cf. my discussion in *Vergangenheit und Gegenwart* IX, p. 161 under the title *Staat und Sittengesetz: Eine Auseinandersetzung mit F. W. Foerster*. In the later writing *Jugendseele, Jugendbewegung, Jugendziel*, Zuerich (1923) there is found the characteristic sentence: 'Genuine politics is applied love.' (p. 147).

[3]) *St. Matthew* 6. 33.

economists and politicians with a social bias are far more common types than the purely social for whom the soul of another comes first and all other objects are secondary. Anyone who, in doing good, is conscious of himself and his influence is not a pure social type, still less he who gives only from vanity. And one might even go so far as to say: giving and doing good are already an externalisation of the genuinely social. It is pure only in that reverent love which gives spiritual aid to the other soul.[1])

In no other type is the transition to the religious so easy as in the social. For, since in describing the latter we always had to go back to the soul behind all special expressions of life, we touched thus the totality of life. The soul in this sense is already a religious concept. But we shall see later that ethically this love for the soul in its bare actuality is by no means the highest thing. Indeed in certain circumstances it may even become unmoral. Here we are dealing only with the tendency toward the whole of life which lives in real love even if it is directed only to one or a few persons. If it includes all people then we seem to approach the totality of meaning relation which is characteristic of religion.[2]) And there develops that basic attitude toward existence which sees life itself as sacred.

If we investigate the religious process in regard to its psychological contexts we find that it proceeds along these lines. Reverence for the living soul is the source of love toward all life. The world-meaning is experienced most deeply of all in such love. One objectifies it symbolically in a highest personality, whose greatest power is love. Thirdly, man feels himself so secure in this world-meaning that he finds himself surrounded by the current of highest love. And finally he loves this world-meaning, life as a whole, God, with an intensity such as one can only feel for the highest value. We may formulate the resulting mental context in the religiously founded experience 'God is Love.' The great

---

[1]) *Social work* as a professional function is something wholly different from genuine social work which must always be primarily spiritual aid.

[2]) According to my conviction the extensity of love is less decisive than the intensity. That every human being has only a limited capacity for very deep love relations is as well known as the interest-perspective of pity and love which is also touched upon by Scheler, op. cit. p. 216 ff: Human beings whom we do not know closely may be or suffer what they wish; it moves us very little.

lovers of history as examples, not only embody this interpretation of life but also accumulate for mankind a fund of love into whose ethical enjoyment we are always born anew.

The love of God transcends our reason. We do not understand it but we divine its greatness. Perhaps those people are right who call our love a spark of the infinite power with which God loves himself. This world context, this comprehension of all of fate and the entire world by means of love is commonly represented as an almost tangible anthropomorphically interpreted reality. The highest sociological categories of value are transferred to the relation between God and man. God becomes the Father and men His children. And among themselves they are brothers. Thus there develops a mythology which is founded rather upon sociology than cosmology. It cannot be evaluated as a cognitive achievement but only as the conceptual symbol of the value experiences of the relatedness of all life upon which it is based, of community of soul and the sanctity of all life. Noone understood the origin of this religious mental objectivation as early and as deeply as the man who represents the social type in incomparable purity: Pestalozzi. Family relationships were to him the first and best thing in man, but only because he also found in them the most divine aspect of life. And it seemed to him justifiable to apply these parables to God also. 'God is man's nearest relation.' And for this reason no symbol seemed to him so adequate as that of the paternal relationship. A history of religion founded upon sociology would have to investigate the historical development of this symbolism. Valuable indications are found in Troeltsch and Weber.[1] Guyau's book *L'irreligion de l'avenir* on the other hand presents a onesided exaggeration of the sociological roots of religion. — In the world of Christianity the idea of love is so strongly in the fore-ground of all religious experiences of value, that one may still conceive of Christianity, despite the modern attempts to find theoretic, aesthetic and political elements in it, as the pure type of religion created in the social spirit.

---

[1] Troeltsch *Soziallehren der christlichen Kirchen* for instance p. 549 ff. In Froebel, the pupil of Pestalozzi, this context is also given. But he gives preference to the metaphysical principle of life unity and consciously regards the family relations only as a special case.

III

The values and value dispositions which determine the motives of the social man are complicated insofar as they are, as a rule, interwoven with the other groups of values. It is not therefore always clear which motive is decisive and whether in social behavior the political, the erotic, the motive of consistency or the social motive takes the lead. Purely social motives exist only when the value of the other soul per se (*an sich*) is placed above all other values. Whoever acts thus really lives in the other person. One must not say, however, that the 'well-being' of the other is his highest motive, for well-being, in the accepted sense of the word belongs as a rule to the biological or economic region. Rather, the value character of life itself and the value possibility of the other person outweigh all other motives. The living soul is the highest value for the social type. The expression 'altruism' is however, unsatisfactory for the purest forms of the type, even if one does not only apply it to the economic realm in which it seems to have originated. If one completely understands the way in which the social type experiences, one finds that he feels himself wholly in the other so that the second person almost ceases to be an 'other'.[1]

But our problem is to find whether this value direction necessarily includes the motive of self-depreciation, the *abiectio*. Psychologically this may of course be true. But it would be a narrow interpretation of the spirit of love to regard the furtherance of foreign value life only as personal value sacrifice. The social type on the contrary, not only experiences from the content of the values which he furthers in the other person a reflected value, but he also experiences this social behavior as a personal value enhancement. We find that the act of evaluation directed toward another involves a self-enrichment. Or more simply: every act of psychical surrender is also an enhancement of self, of course a higher self than that of economic egoism. And thus develops the apparent psychological antinomy; that love, surrender and sacrifice alone enrich truly loving natures.

---

[1] That love would by this means become a disguised self-love, or that compassion becomes a merely associated self-suffering, is excluded by the mental height of the sphere in which this tendency to the abolition of individuation is found.

The motivation of the social type is characterized by the fact that its action proceeds from a, so to speak, expanded self, for which the barrier of individuation is broken through in at least one point, namely where it loves. There is a curious contrast between customary purposive action and action 'because of love'. It may be so onesided that social morality would stamp it as immoral. The man, however, whose life-center is love finds sufficient motivation for all action by acting *sub specie alterius*, according to the mind of the other, and in this he enjoys, perhaps wholly unintentionally, his highest blessedness. From one point of view love achieves a greater wealth than anything else, but it is also true that nothing is so self-forgetful as love. On account of this highest value-realization there is here not only a special form of motivation, but also a wholly onesided, closed system of morality.

But social behavior achieves full ethical character only when it becomes the permanent direction of the soul. Momentary compassion is not ethical. To this end is needed the unique voluntary obligation which derives from social behavior its own rational law. This ethical type of mind which directs permanent beneficence to another, we call loyalty. The personal ethics of the social type of motivation is surrendering loyalty. It is a significant fact that loyalty is not classed among the modern virtues. Why is it no longer mentioned? Has it become such a commonplace or has it really become very rare?

IV

The differentiated forms of the social type are very numerous if we include all the basic forms of society in which love and loyalty are the ties. We have, however, no occasion to go into details unless the type itself is altered.

The most important difference originates according as to whether the social behavior is active or passive. By this principle we differentiate the 'loving' natures and those who 'need' love. The latter are mental types only when they have become conscious of their capacity to love. They have the power of love in imagination and the longing to be loved in this way forms their fundamental constitution. Here again we must exclude eroticism as a form of the aesthetic type. The best example of a nature needing love is the Christian in his longing to be loved by God insofar as he longs for this love as a gift from his fellowmen. But it is particularly characteristic of the fundamental constitution of the male principle in the world (which does not always coincide with men) that the need to be loved is stronger than the capacity to love. Because of his onesided development and division of his nature which he resents, his innermost heart longs, so to speak, to be led back to the undivided source of life by a female love. This too brings out the fact that prior to any special values love surrounds the soul.

In considering the conditions under which the social type develops it is only important to distinguish two forms of love; that love which is based on a blood-relation and that in which the relation is purely spiritual. When one remembers that ultimately all of mankind are alike and are related through the species, the sharp contrast disappears. It cannot however be denied that consciously felt blood ties are always more strongly binding than the mere feeling of mankind. Mother-love, the highest earthly form of the social type, is based upon relations of descent. We consider a mother here not only as a creature of instinct but also as a mental type in whom the instinct to love has become the will which organizes the whole personality. This social type seems to reach more deeply than any other into the mystery of life. In 'Mothers'[1] there appears the prime foundation of life. On the other hand, no words suffice to describe the infinite height and greatness to which mother-love may rise as a result of suffering and bliss. Mother Mary is the epitome of this greatest divine mystery of mankind. Fathers, brothers and sisters and other relations, because of their place in life are much less designed to be purely social natures. And yet the mystery is equally great if one being gives up his life for another without the bond of blood-relationship. Woman, even outside of erotic connections, is fundamentally constituted in this way. The deepest friendships are therefore always between people of different sexes at least in regard to mental sex. Woman lives through love. Man naturally cares more for formed work. And in this difference of the typical life-form is also expressed the eternal tragedy of love which lies in the world structure itself and from which nothing can save us — but love. It is possible furthermore that a man should be fundamentally a friend. He then finds the empirical satisfaction of his deepest

---

[1] Goethe's *Faust* Part II.

being in no special mental region but only in that one life relation in which he wholly spends himself as one always ready with spiritual aid. Such natures are more often found in tradition than in history. Perhaps this is because history does not keep the records of such selfless natures, or perhaps such inner greatness is really very rare. And even this human relation seems to send its roots deep into the metaphysical.

The social attitude may, as is already obvious from the above, have a very wide scope without in any way implying value-judgments as to the rank-order of the character in question. Friend, mother and wife, each find their life's meaning in living for one other being. But there are others so organized that they must love all mankind: the Christian, the philanthropist and he who is a cosmopolitan of love.[1]) Naturally intensity often suffers because of extensity. Rousseau's warning is eternally valid: '*Défiez-vous de ces cosmopolites qui vont chercher au loin dans leurs livres des devoirs qu'ils dédaignent de remplir autour d'eux. Tel philosophe aime les Tartares, pour être dispensé d'aimer ses voisins.*' The intermediary types between these two extremes are usually determined subjectively by the power of a definite community in and for which they live. Their whole life structure is then interwoven with this overindividual structure, and in this way a man can love his *gens*, his clan, his nation, his profession and his class. But all these phenomena concern us only when they result from the inner mental structure and not from Fate or external necessity. Often too a certain fate is inborn and constitutional, as the destiny of the slave or the true plebeian. Therefore this pressure develops the men of strongest solidarity and power of love. But as a rule added to this is the political will to power or a religious drive for redemption, so that again the types are not wholly pure.[2])

A final difference between social natures results from the value region which they believe gives the highest furthering power to their will to love. Some apostles believe that they love man most deeply by bringing truth, others want to help him

---

[1]) We have touched above upon the theoretical cosmopolitan. The aesthetic cosmopolitan belongs to the impressionistic natures.

[2]) The deep capacity of certain Jews for love (not to be confused with the aesthetic sympathy of the proletariat) is the inheritance of generations of oppression. The children of usurers or dried-up capitalists often incline with their whole souls to a helping love.

economically and others again would educate and give him a higher sense of beauty. And finally there are those whose love is winged with a religious message: the Messiah who preach only eternal salvation of the soul and are indifferent to all finite and material goods. With all these people it is usually difficult to say whether the desire to help others is the primary thing, or whether they are more deeply moved by the values themselves and only want to make room for them in the souls of other people. And yet anyone who has acquired a keen vision for the structural relations of the mind will be in no doubt. He will find in Pestalozzi for instance the pure nature of love which is only led to all sorts of theoretic speculations by the will to help; while in Fichte the social ideas are more the results of a political will to order and a theoretic joy of discovery than an elementary love of man. One must therefore always ask whether a man brings light in order to guide others, or whether he guides others so that there may be light in the world. The result may ultimately be the same, but the attitude is different in its structure and value, and that is what concerns us here.

V

It seems that one must contrast the loving nature with the hating nature, while the socially indifferent are in between. Many structural reasons may be given to account for a loveless attitude: one may be filled with economic egoism or the individualism of the scholar, one may be an aesthetic self-enjoyer or a religious hermit. But these forms belong to the other types and besides it is not so often the element of hate but rather an indifference to others which is present. Since we explained the mental phenomenon of love as a turning toward value possibilities[1]) of the other soul then two essential determinations of hate may be thought of: it is either a rejection of the value possibilities of another, or the paying attention to that which is contrary to value in him and the will to destroy this element. In the first case hate is directed to man and in the second to that which is contrary to value in him. Just as love is always love for the sake of a value, so hate

---

[1]) I do not mean here by 'value possibilities' that every love has the pedagogical trend to develop the indicated value direction of the other from possibility to reality. But I do mean by this the indicated value of the person as *complicatio* in contrast to *explicatio*.

is also a rejection due to the affirmation of a value. One may hate the other from economic motives, because he harms one; from aesthetic motives, because he is physically or psychically 'ugly'; from theoretic motives, because he is mistaken; or from religious motives, because he is an abject scoundrel and impious. But all these reasons of hate may enter in simply because the other is so constituted in my opinion, because he appears thus to me from a theoretically false judgment, so that I must hate him. And finally it is conceiveable that a complete reversal of values (a pathological perversion of evaluation) has taken place in me when hating, so that I hate what I ought to love. Of the very different forms of this pathology we do not want however to speak here.

The psychology of hate offers peculiar difficulties. Ethical value judgments play an inevitable role. And purely psychologically the hatred of evil, or apparently evil natures is a fact of life. But under the influence of ethical convictions a form of hate develops which merits our special attention because it is possible that it may show the way to the understanding of the negative mental structure of the 'hater.' For, though love is interest in the value possibilities of another, nevertheless in its highest form it does not demand a developed value constitution in the other. Indeed it may even grant him sympathy and encouragement in spite of his evil nature in order to strengthen what is valuable in him. If one conceives love in this highest sense then there could be no hatred. Or more accurately, hate is directed to what is harmful, false, ugly and impious, but not to the person, the human being who is possessed by them.[1]) From a final ethical point of view indeed even the sinner, the liar, the psychically ugly and the criminal deserve an uplifting love. Hate then, should never be directed to the entire being, it ought not to be accompanied by a will to destroy but rather to ennoble. Such an attitude directed to the person is no longer hate but love, because the element of love in it has entirely absorbed the hatred of man. And seen from this ethical height hatred itself is absolute evil because it fails to see value possibility and lets it perish through its own lack of warmth.

But undoubtedly hatred of man does exist as a psychological fact. What if this hatred had no independent origin but were

---

[1]) The ideal Christian for instance hates the sin but not the sinner.

always the perversion or disappointment of a deeper-lying love? Certainly we hate evil. But we only hate the person of such a nature because he disappoints the positive expectations of value which we have placed in him. And the more we have expected of him the more intense is our hatred. Then this hatred of man would only be a perversion-hatred, a disappointed love. But in the attitude of the hater — whether he hates all people, a group or only one man — the social type is always dormant; and that as follows: he loves man as such because love is the greatest need of his life and he hopes from him everything valuable. He hates evil qualities. If now he finds them in man, his expectation is disappointed and hatred only develops because love was frustrated. He blames man for what he should regard as the fault of the structure of the world or the negative side of the realm of values. And if it is true that hate, according to a psychological law increases with hating, he derives the energy for this from a positive ideal which he must in a sense constantly crucify anew. Noone who does not believe in man could hate.

Lastly, the hater tends to make quick theoretical generalisations. He applies to an entire group the disappointment which he has experienced in one case. Thus originate men who hate all women and women who hate all men. Others form thus a hatred for the clergy, for teachers or for all persons with red hair for instance. But deepest of all this reversal of the social type appears in the misanthropist. He is perhaps always born from disappointments, often from those of youthful hopes or imaginary visions. And for this reason the type seldom goes so far as to hurt or destroy mankind. It is instead satisfied to withdraw into itself and painfully to turn away from what is still fundamentally its belief. At most, it is a philosophically hardened scorn of man. The active enemies of mankind are carved out of a wholly different wood. They are extreme forms of the political type or they signify a constitutional degeneracy of the value life which we cannot approach by a psychology of meaning.

5
THE POLITICAL ATTITUDE

I

Only by extreme conceptual isolation can we separate acts of sympathy (i. e. equalising mental acts) from those acts on which social super- and subordination are based. The two are combined in very subtle gradations in every real association of mankind. But an analysis directed to mental structures differentiates the great difference between a helpful interest in the lives of others and the imprinting of one's own will to value upon the inner world and the external behavior of another person. We have chosen the general term 'power' for the mental phenomena which found the relations of domination. And doubtless it is open to being misunderstood and above all open to the danger of being mistaken for force and constraint which are only the ultimate physical consequences of power. But we must emphasize the fact that relations of power and dependency belong to the elementary facts of existence which can be uprooted only with human nature itself. Anyone who wishes to extirpate them would suddenly realize the fact that he needs power to do this, or even that he is already using power.

Power doubtless seems, at first, to be only a social form in which the four other value regions are active. One person can be superior to another through his intelligence and actual knowledge, through the economic and technical means which he commands, through inner wealth and the consequent personality, or finally, through a religious power and value-certainty which others recognize as his being filled with the spirit of God. Power must always 'express' itself in some such form. And yet it is different when a man does not direct himself toward one of these individual value regions but centers instead in the formal quality of having power. Then we have in addition to the quality of the value content the new factor of energy of value life. This energy is primarily subjective, belonging to the individual nature. But it also radiates in social relations insofar as the energy of individual value-life is a condition necessary to direct and to influence others according to one's own evaluations. If we consider power as a social phenomenon, this interest in others is essential. Power is thus the capacity and (usually) the will, to posit one's own value direction in the other, either as a permanent or a transitory motive.

It is characteristic of the phenomenon of love that it turns to the other soul regardless of its actual value constitution purely for the sake of its value possibilities. Somewhat similarly the purely political nature, independent of any specific form of appearance, wishes to feel itself as a power and only fulfills in this way its unique meaning. We said that in every pure love a religious factor is already present, because it has a mysterious relation to the totality of life. Here too is present a total feeling for life in the religious sense: affirmation of one's own being before all individual achievement, vitality and energy. Wherever this appears as an original life urge and not as a rational purpose, we encounter the political attitude.

All of human life is shot through with relations of power and competition. Even in the most modest and narrow circles they play a role. Everyone is somehow a center and an object of power. This side of life is seen most clearly in the organized collective power of the state. Since this represents the highest (sovereign) power in a group and in a region, all individual and subordinated expressions of power are somehow related to it, made possible by it and circumscribed by or directed against it. For this reason, all phenomena of power relations have a certain aspect which one might call, in a broad sense political. We shall therefore occasionally call the man of power the political type even though the attitude exists in circumstances which one could not call political in a narrower sense of the term (cf. page 60 above).

The effect of power upon others always appears in the form of determination. Power posits in him motives, either direct motives by means of the self-experienced power of utility, truth, beauty or sanctity; or indirect motives, by utilizing the actually existing context of motivation (for instance, the mere egoism of self-preservation) as a lever to gain those ends which are valuable to the possessor of power. Indeed finally, it spreads over into the physical region and becomes nothing but mere physical coercion.[1]) Just as war is only the continuation of politics by other means, one may say in general that coercion also is only the continuation by other expedients of motivating determination. Power belongs to mental life only when its means and aims are somehow in the psychical sphere even if it is only the formal aim of personal consciousness and enjoyment of power.

This formal power, however, is also called by another name which expresses negatively its independence of other forces. Freedom may have three meanings: (1) freedom from physical constraint (freedom of action); (2) freedom from the value-positing will of another, of foreign decisive determining of motive (freedom of the will); and (3) the highest: freedom from one's own passions and temptations (inner freedom, self-determination, autonomy of one's higher value-positing). The last form is definitely ethical and indeed regulates the totality of the personal life. From all these appearances, which one might call sociological and moral, we must distinguish that power and freedom which is granted by the positive legal order. The (subjective) law in the sense of a claim (upon acting, possessing or being) is also a form of power and freedom. Here, however, there are present complicated regulations posited by an overindividual collective will. Law is not a simple but a composite mental phenomenon. In the following we must omit these power relations even though they appear as a most perfect system of the regulating of will in the purest historical instance of will to power: Roman imperialism.

II

The purely political type makes all value regions of life serve his will to power. Cognition is for him only a means for control. The maxim: Knowledge is power, which we interpreted for the economic type as technical utilization of knowledge, means here that the achievement of ascendency over man is desired through some social technique. In the positivist sociology this political

---

[1]) Physical coercion is strictly also a determination, which directs itself to the primitive will to self-preservation. Noone should submit to force; he may give up life like the mayor of Cork. 'Noone willing to die need submit to force.' (Fichte, *Ueber den Begriff des wahrhaften Krieges*, Tuebingen 1815. p. 27).

motive has been present from the outset: *voir pour savoir, savoir pour prévoir, prévoir pour régler*. The politician is of course primarily interested in psychology and social science. He always sees man through his own eyes. He is not concerned with a cool systematisation of their species and the objective observation of their behavior (nor in their increased development and purification of motives unless he is a pedagogue) but from the outset he regards them from the point of view of how man, being what he is, can be controlled. He investigates, as it were, the most effective motivations. His knowledge of man is applied and not a purely theoretic formation of concepts. He inclines to ascribe low motives to men, largely because a majority of mankind can thus be influenced. According to him everyone has his price. In this way the classic founder of politics (basing himself to some extent on classic models) looked upon man as a kind of instinctive mechanism which could be guided through fear of punishment and hope for reward.[1] He has warned the practical politician against idealising man. To rule, one must think realistically. Knowledge of man in politics amounts to knowledge of the 'serviceability' of the individual. Human beings are like pawns or dollars and cents. Frederick the Great, Machiavelli's disciple, had the same scornful opinion of men *as they are*. 'Teachers must therefore take great pains to inculcate attachment to religion and bring people to the point where they no longer murder or steal. Thefts will of course occur, for that is part of human nature; all ordinary people are naturally dishonest, and others too especially those who have charge of money or have other opportunities.'[2]

On the other hand, in his dealings with the rabble the man of power takes great pains not to be seen through: 'That is the art, not to let yourself be wholly known and to remain forever a mystery', says Holofernes in Hebbel's *Judith*. Every man of power necessarily cultivates this 'Pathos of distance'.

One must not forget however that the political liberalism has gradually enobled the structure of man in political relations, and

---

[1] Much of what Machiavelli has said seems less strange if we regard it as an isolated political psychology. Galileo investigated the gravity of bodies in a vacuum; Machiavelli the human instinctive mechanism in a society without morals. — Cf. Schmitt-Dorotič, *Die Diktatur*. Muenchen 1921 p. 8f.

[2] Cabinet document to the minister von Zedlitz, September 5th, 1779. Cf. also his treatise: *L'amour propre comme principe de la vertu*.

has made out of mere means and objects of politics, subjects and participants. But it is still true today that the politician must be a realistic student of human nature; that he must take people as they really are, while the pedagogue is inclined to see them as they might be. For politics man is a means to an end, in a favorable case a means to his own good.[1])

Thus truth too may degenerate into a political tool. It still remains a great problem of politics whether it is better to be honest or to make use of apt hypocrisies. The question is always as to the expediency in the isolated political system and never whether it would be moral or would satisfy the law of cognition i. e. of objectivity. And this question must be decided in each case. Anyone who believes truth to be the highest law can never rank power (for instance, the existence of the collective power of the state) as the highest value. But anyone who lives in this onesided sphere of life considers truth and falsehood equal if only they serve the system of power. In our attempts to isolate the region of political values our goal (power) is the highest value and as such is beyond all discussion. Truth is only to be considered as a subordinated (technical) means as long as we remain in the realm of a purely political ethics. One has here the feeling of great immorality. But we are dealing only with psychology and the facts agree with these statements. The maxim: 'The end justifies the means' only lifts the veil from the pure politician's structure of consciousness. In a religio-ethical context this onesided creed of power would not be accepted. To keep back the news of a defeat, from a people whom one knows to be immature, so that they would not rush to their doom would be a sin against the ethics of truth. Under certain circumstances however it would be an ethical service to a life value which unquestionably takes the first place here, since we do not deal with the law of the theoretic region. Truth, in a social application, is not always constructive and is often followed by catastrophies.[2])

---

[1]) This does not exclude the fact that the aim of the politician may be ideal and that he often regards himself as an educator. But that is no longer the pure, isolated political man.

[2]) This however is true also of the system of love. Cf. Romano Guardini, *Gottes Werkleute*, Rothenfels 1925 p. 25. 'One should enunciate truth in such a way that it does not destroy but builds up.'

It is important in this connection to remember that certain social theories are not justifiable and understandable because they truthfully describe objective facts and bring them into logical relations, but because they create a higher will to life and victory. Marxism, for instance, is such a militant doctrine; as is also the conviction (which is really true of all great civilized nations), that they are destined for world-leadership. Political theories, as well as constructions in the philosophy of history are often rooted more in the will to live than in mere historico-social facts and the will to pure objectivity. Alfred Fouillée coined the name *idées-forces* for these ideas which lend energy to the will to life and power. He thus translated the pragmatic doctrine, that truth is a power and not a mirror, and applied it to the political sphere. And thus in the context of political contrasts which strive toward the light arises the question: 'What is truth'? even prior to the question of whether one should follow it.

We hardly appreciate how much this will to exist, this drive for self-assertion, influences our theoretic convictions. We all live with some illusions which make our lives more possible and make us feel that we have a place in the world. Nietzsche reduces this to the point of extreme paradox: 'Truth is that error without which a certain kind of creature cannot exist'.[1] In order to understand the recent political occurrences and their relation to truth, we must remind ourselves that this point of view has never achieved any great importance in Germany, but that in Anglo-Saxon countries pragmatism has become almost the dominant form of the theory of cognition.

For the psychologist of deeper vision there appears finally, the singular phenomenon that at the level of the purely political structure, the organ for objectivity and truth degenerates. Anyone who is always fighting will soon come to feel that what he wills and believes is a sort of 'self-evident' truth and to lose all understanding of an objective justly evaluating[2] attitude. The decisive

---

[1] WW. (Pocket edition) IX. 275. — VIII. 12f; furthermore: 'The criterion of truth lies in the enhancement of the feeling of power.' (Will to Power III. 534). 'Cognition is a tool of power' (III. 307). Cf. A. Riehl *Nietzsche* 6th edition Stuttgart 1920 p. 71f. 128ff. — On the subject Politics and sincerety cf. also Karl Groos, *Bismarck im eigenen Urteil*. Stuttgart 1920, p. 15ff. 44ff.

[2] Righteousness and love of truth originate in the same root.

effect of this constitutional perversion of the sense of truth is found in the fact that rhetoric apparently takes possession of the entire personality. And finally the goal is not to convince but to cajole. Thus rhetoric and not scientific thought is characteristic of the political type. Everywhere in the world where people are interested in politics, the rhetorical ideal of culture was preferred to the philosophical one; by the Greek sophists in both the classic and imperial period, by the Romans since Cicero, by the church politicians of Protestant and Jesuit creed, by the diplomats of the court period, and indeed by all Latin peoples. And the fact that Plato wanted to put his politics on a different foundation from Protagoras and Gorgias, Thrasymachos and Callicles means that he surpassed the onesidedness of the political type through the spirit of truth and moral candor. He ranks the theoretic type above the political. But we must remember that he, too, occasionally applies the noble lie in his state.

In my opinion the proof is valid which recent psycho-pathology has advanced to the effect that natural tendencies to power also play a definite role in hysterical derangements. The will to be 'on the top' and not 'on the bottom' is the point of departure and guiding motive in the delusions with which psychopathic personalities surround themselves and which, under certain conditions, they manufacture into an entire insane plan of life. We can understand these often deeply rooted self-deceptions only from the point of view of the will to power. (I might cite here Alfred Adler who has carried out this theory stimulated by Vaihinger's philosophy of the AS-IF. He did this however in a confused philosophical manner).[1] One may generalize this thought into saying that 'pretension' is fundamentally characteristic of the political type.

The relations of the political type to the economic region are really open only to one interpretation. Wealth is always a political means, not only on account of the freedom which it grants from pressure and the coercion of nature but also because it provides a means of influencing others. For, the assumption that most people belong to the economic type, or at least embody strong traits of it, is in general correct. Nevertheless, we must not confuse the political type with the economic. For the manner in which he

---

[1] Alfred Adler, *Ueber den nervoesen Character* 2nd ed. Wiesbaden 1919 especially p. 148 ff.

acquires goods is usually not purely economic but political. By means of diplomacy and treatises, by conquest or force one can acquire goods without following the immanent law of economics, that of saving and industry.

We must, therefore, carefully observe how many political traits appear in the aims and choice of means of a man who seems to belong to the economic type. The character of the modern entrepreneur for instance, is certainly not purely economic but is also partly based on political relations. And the aim of great enterprises is often less the acquisition of wealth than the developing of power on a big scale, ascendency not only over material goods but over men. Thus the economic seems to be subordinated to the political.

The aesthetic, too, is only a link in the chain of means which are to serve the development of power. The conjunction of aristocratic and aesthetic cultures is structurally founded. The highly cultured and polite personality has about it something 'winning' which pacifies our resentment against the special position which grants this power.[1] In the same way art plays a more ornamental role. Splendor is the symbol of power, of freedom from narrowing necessity. The insignia of power always embody something resplendent, awe-inspiring, suggestive. Art is used only on account of its suggestive power, as for instance, music in the service of the army, rhetorical flourishes to influence a mob, or buildings which have lasted for centuries and are designed to remind us of a great name. Court art still contains something of this trait which is foreign to pure art.

The aesthetic element enters the psychology of power in still another sense. The seeker for power often has, as a tragic constitution, a far-reaching imagination with which he shrouds himself instead of estimating man and circumstances realistically. This type is perhaps on the borderline between the aesthetic and the political. Without a constructive imagination one cannot conceive great designs or world-reforming thoughts. The political nature plays with these thoughts and intoxicates himself with them. A deranged imagination embroils this type in a conflict with the realities of life. And yet we do find, even on lower levels, this experimentation with personal power, a curious kind of play which prepares for reality. Sport is just such a mixture of bodily control,

---

[1] Cf. Karl Borinski, *Baltasar Gracian und die Hofliteratur in Deutschland*, Halle 1894 on the *'homo politicus'* and taste; especially p. 47.

competition and play and we must not depreciate its importance for the training of personal energy. The man schools himself in sport for serious achievements.[1]) A parallel phenomenon is the play of imagination which we find in woman, and in which she grows conscious of the power of her physical charm and psychic attraction. Flirting, originally an expression of aesthetic eroticism, may thus become a pure expression of power if there is nothing behind it but the will to win in competition and to control men.[2]) The 'flirt' is thus the female counterpart of the 'sport', even though in reality the two may be found in either sex. But the man of power does not achieve real perfection of aesthetico-psychic tendencies and inner form. He is too much directed to the factor of external effect. Wilhelm von Humboldt never devoted himself entirely to politics because he deemed it the one thing which does not enrich the inner life of man.[3])

The relation of the political type to a community shows a unique two-sidedness. As a rule there is a sharp contrast between the will to rule men and the desire to help them spiritually for their own sake. In their most extreme forms the two are contrasted to each other as war and love. There does not seem to be room for both of them in one soul. The pure man of power is the man of self-emphasis and self-assertion. He is therefore usually not a warmhearted friend but a misanthrope. Anyone who really wants to rule cannot surrender or sacrifice himself. Anyone who wants to be something is not inclined to live for others. Nietzsche, whose will to power shows a strong aesthetic tinge, was by nature inimical to this loving spirit and social attitude which he stamped as the 'herd morality'. This value judgment reflects only the general contrast of the aristocrat to the masses. The will to power makes one feel superior to others. It demands recognition and honor and strives for freedom, while love always involves us in obligations.

[1]) Cf. Karl Groos (*Die Spiele der Tiere*; *Die Spiele der Menschen* Jena 1896/99) on games of war. — Cf. also loc. cit. on the war instincts of Bismarck.

[2]) The purely female will to power in its most primitive form is directed to the sexual enslaving of man. In the contest between the sexes the man is therefore as a rule most subdued when he thinks to triumph in this sense.

[3]) To Charlotte Diede, May 3rd, 1826 and later.

This pure type of the political man, however, appears very seldom. We always see the highest power as the collective. But this presupposes that men are conscious of a feeling of solidarity and live for one another. Here there is a social bond. Anyone who wants to become the personal representative and executor of this collective power must always assimilate something of the spirit of the community. Here he acts for his fellowmen by dominating them. This synthesis already falls, as we shall see, into the ethical region. The merely individualistic politician is a tyrant, a dictator. He feels that he is the only one who counts and that the others are his property. The possessor of socially founded power, on the other hand, is always a 'leader' too. He wants to make happy and to help the people while he rules. But he too needs recognition (for instance on an ideal or positive legal basis). His power is based on the unity and the community of those whom he leads and he must therefore return something of their social spirit of love. When this relation of power is really based upon love we have the patriarchal system; when it is based on law we have the legal ruler; and we have the demagogue when it is based upon flattery and subjection to the mass instincts ('cheap' popularity).[1] If it is built on mental superiority, on personal energy and the highminded will to serve while ruling, we have genuine leadership which utilizes its power only in the service of the whole and feels an ethical obligation to its followers. But it is clear that this already implies a close interrelation between the social and political motives, and that therefore ethical categories develop which for the time being we have excluded from our psychological consideration. We shall investigate these problems only in parts III. and IV. of this book. Viewed in extreme isolation, the political type is the opposite of the social nature. That is, he aims at the satisfaction of his own vital or mental drive for existence, even at the cost of others.

If the categories of the political region are applied to religious behavior, then the total life appears from the point of view of power relations and deeds. God is preferably regarded as a personal power who, through the mere freedom of his willing, has given the world life out of nothing; in the beginning there was thus the deed. God himself contains the maximum of reality (which is

---

[1] Cf. Plato, *Gorgias*.

logically unthinkable and contains a contradiction in itself) for, the smallest negation would set limits to his power. He is the all-powerful who creates, maintains and rules the universe.[1])

It might seem strange that the political type expresses his religious belief in a symbol which destines him to the greatest dependence. But if one really enters the psychology of political striving one can understand that he whose entire being is directed toward control should feel more keenly than others the limits of his freedom and consequently suffer from dependence more than from anything else. Added to this is the fact (already understood by the individualistic *Stoa* and noticeable again today) that noone becomes so much entangled in dependent relations as the man who enters the conflict in striving to get to the top. — But this is only one side of the situation which plays a role in every form of religiosity. True, the ruler feels himself the servant of God. But for just this reason he also feels himself the agent of God. He regards his power which he has received from the highest world-power, as that of a fief. This 'by the grace of God' is not a questionable construction in the politics of the state, designed to extricate us from the difficulty of the theory of sovereignty of the people, but is rooted in the psychology of this type. Power delegated by the people is a judicial concept which grew out of socio-ethical roots. But psychologically it is absolutely impossible to delegate power: either one has it or not. It is fundamentally an original mental equipment of the soul and furthermore, the product of definitely given sociological conditions. The power, however, which is only given by judicial constructions and paper constitutions is very meager; unfortunately, so many people are inclined to add. Therefore this metaphysical derivation from the grace of God is a happy symbol of the fundamental experience. And if it is understood purely religiously the form of state psychologically

---

[1]) Cf. Dilthey, *Gesammelte Schriften* vol. II. p. 15 on the Roman attitude of will. 'The world is apprehended by means of the following concepts. Its foundation is the mental context as it has been found by the Greeks. This is however filled with the notion of a divine imperator, a world legislation. A single legislation conprehends all living beings, especially mankind. It directs itself to man as a responsible and punishable entity which must therefore be free. Thus the Divine Empirial, the sphere of domination and legal order of the state and the sphere of free will limit one another.'

develops which is known as a theocracy.¹) God appears as the real and true ruler. Holiness and recognition of the existing state coincide. From this we must strictly distinguish the very different mental structure which issues from the political and utilizes current religious ideas as a fit means of acquiring power. This case alone belongs to the pure political type. For, when religion is used to guide people it is no longer pure but is a political instrument. And finally, there is a third relation between politics and religion. When religiosity wholly or partially derives from the roots of the political nature, the relations between God and the soul are constructed in accordance with political and legal categories. God then becomes the ruler of the world, the leader of the army, the ally or enemy. And one concludes mutual agreements with Him which have the character of bargains as soon as an economic factor is added, or become friendly arrangements with the introduction of a social element. The gulf between God and man is easily bridged by a hierarchy of relations of master and servant, so that the entire holy structure is represented in the figure of a divine state. In dealing with mental constructions such as these, one must sharpen one's vision to see how much is due to real veneration and how much originates in the political realities of the corresponding cultural sphere.

The problem of freedom and dependency plays a great role even in a wholly spiritualized religion. The contrast between the religious philosophies of Hegel and Schleiermacher has here its real focal point: the religion of dependency and the religion of freedom differ according to the degree of spontaneity of will which man grants himself. Only where he begins to be politically free can moral freedom be influential in religion and vice versa. The old heroes sat down to table with their gods. Modern man cannot endure a God who sets lower moral standards for the world than the moral man sets for himself. And thus the ethics of freedom becomes one of the essential sources of moral religiosity.

---

¹) Max Weber: (*Grundriß der Sozialoekonomik,* III, 1. p. 124). The carismatic domination (in the widest sense) is based 'upon the unusual affection for the saintliness or the heroic power or the model of a person and the orders created or revealed by it.'

III

The question of the political type's form of motivation leads us into very significant mental contexts. If we regard them primarily in their most abstract and simple form it is obvious that to be superior to everyone else is the constant motive of the political type.[1] If we think of him wholly isolated — so to speak beyond law and community — then his lack of maxims is only the result of his specific will to live, to stay at the top at all costs and to maintain his advantage. In view of this, even material demands take a second place. He must choose, with individual adaptation, the means in every concrete situation. The goal alone remains unchangeable: that he wants to assert himself and have his cause victorious:

> 'Yet if a breach of the law must be made in order to rule,
> It is honorable and beautiful to break the law.'[2]

Politics too (as care for the power of the state) has therefore no place for maxims which precede concrete activity. It is the art of creating and utilizing opportunities. The socalled 'reason' of the state is something wholly different from the *ratio* which was venerated as the source of general validity. It is the art of individual calculation in which there is only one constant factor: the interest of the state.[3]

As long and insofar as human relations are not unequivocally and generally regulated by laws, constellations always appear in

---

[1] Cf. A. Vierkandt, *Machtverhaeltnis und Machtmoral* Berlin 1916, p. 37: 'Besides the recognized morality of love there exists everywhere a political and a business morality of a much more robust sort, according to which one acts without consideration, but of which one does not speak with the same frankness.'

[2] Eteocles in the *Phoenecians* of Euripides (German translation by Wilamowitz, Plato, I, 215).

[3] Frederick the Great demanded in his political testament of 1752 that politics should have the consequentness of a philosophic system. He himself has not acted in accord with this — at least not in foreign politics. — It would be the object of an interesting historical investigation how Newton's system of gravity became the model for internal politics in the political life of the 18th century. One sees that in politics everything is related to everything else and one studies these relations with mathematical objectivity and yet pragmatically i. e. with a view to the application which utilizes the very unique 'constellation.'

which there is opportunity for this sort of behavior. Indeed with the widest extension of the idea of law the absolutely unique fact, the situation which could not be anticipated, can only be controlled in this way by politics. General, previously elaborated maxims would only act as hindrances in the catastrophic episodes of world politics. There is thus a fundamental difference in the whole attitude toward life of a logician like Kant and a politician like Bismarck: 'I could never get all the way through Kant. What he says on morality, especially about the categorical imperative is very beautiful but I prefer to live without the feeling of the imperative. I have never lived by maxims. When I had to act, I never asked myself: By what maxims do you act? but I took hold and did what seemed to me right. I have often been reproached with having no maxims. But if I had to go through life acting on maxims, I should always feel as if I had to traverse a narrow forest lane holding a long pole in my mouth.'[1])

But this is not the last word in the discussion, for even Bismarck did not really mean this. The form of motivation of which we have previously spoken really concerns only the bald technique of power and not its highest meaning. If we designate this by the word freedom, we see at once that freedom cannot consist in doing what one pleases at every moment. The word freedom contains instead an ethical significance. And if we go beyond the merely psychological to the ethical content of freedom, it means finally merely the power to the highest value. In this form of motivation which approaches religion, other factors enter in beside the mere shrewd seizing upon the right moment.

We named above three meanings of freedom: the freedom from physical coercion, from determination by others and from lower impulses. We might also say: freedom of action, of willing and of obeying the ought. Anyone who is not physically coerced may do whatever his motives demand. Anyone who is free from social influences which guide his consciousness in the direction of alien willing, may will in accordance with his own nature. And finally anyone who is not simply driven by his subjective nature may will in accordance with the genuine content and rank order of values. We must presuppose that some directions of value are experienced in consciousness as higher than others. This gradation

---

[1]) Poschinger *Tischgespraeche*, II, 170.

of experience is, as we have seen, not yet identical with the objective rank order of values. And anyone who determines his conduct in accordance with these measures, acts according to his own nature and is free from social value determination. But he is not acting according to that valid law of evaluation which makes from factual values normative or genuine ones. This normative legality too, we simply presuppose here. But we may imagine a condition of conflict in subjective consciousness in which one direction of value is distinguished as normative, while the others only oppose it as instinctively aimed at. This causes a condition of inner strife. And to make the normative value direction dominant necessitates moral energy and self-control. The choice of the genuine and higher value as compared with the allurements of the lower but more intensive values is only possible by means of self-creative willing, a whole-hearted devotion of the entire personality. Energy, in this sense of the word, is therefore an independent, though often overlooked, prime factor of morality. This state of consciousness contains throughout the characteristics of the political region, except that we are dealing here with the same personality which has figuratively become both a ruling and a dependent subject. To will what one should in a moral sense, namely the objectively higher value, one must have a form of freedom which must be called inner or moral freedom. We have just now called it the freedom to do one's duty. Kant, who conceived man as a fundamentally rational being formulated an autonomy of reason. We speak of an autonomy of value positing if it is in accordance with the deepest objective law of value and world-law which lives in us too.

This alone is inner power. Nietzsche who wanted to identify the will to power with biological health and vigor of instincts could not escape from the necessity of designating the instincts themselves as noble or vulgar. He thus arrived at the belief in a rank-order of values. The prime phenomenon of power, in our sense of the term, is found in the energy to follow the highest value which confronts our consciousness as a demand. This kind of self-control is, then, the source of all true external relations of power. For the only real power is that which is based on the genuine content of values.[1]) Everything else only borrows the formal aspect of

---

[1]) This Fichtean thought was certainly active as belief in Bismarck too. 'Unless I believed in a divine order of things which had destined

power. This explains too why anyone who is to be educated as a ruler, must first be schooled to obey a law which he recognizes. The way to leadership lies over the road to obedience and the way to self-control in the development of individual mind, only over the path of obedience to others. And accordingly, from an ethical point of view, moral heteronomy is superior to freedom of mere subjective choice of values, which we have called freedom of the will. Inner freedom, that is, the freedom to obey the 'ought', or autonomy, is reached only by passing through moral heteronomy, a subordination to collective morality, in which as we have seen the genuine ethical values have been partly precipitated.[1]

All these considerations have already led us beyond psychology in the narrower sense. The context becomes clear only when we give a more detailed presentation of our idea of the essence of morality (in part III). But these introductory remarks are nevertheless of a psychological nature insofar as they refer to the psychology of morality. I have treated all this under the head of the political type since I am convinced that in the ethical phenomena, the factor of inner freedom corresponds to the perfect political type. Consistency of behavior, utility, inner harmony and love come from other mental contexts. But this strong will which takes up the cudgel against lower values corresponds to the structure of the political type. Here too is present an aspect of independence and self-assertion. Only it has been lifted to a higher level and limited to the inner theatre of the soul. It is not mere chance that Kant and Fichte, who have brought this ethics of freedom to full philosophic consciousness, lived in the midst of a political movement which made for the expansion of the individual sphere of power. In this conception of freedom we also find a deepening of the political psychology whose meaning has already been pronounced by Plato in his *Gorgias*. We may formulate this insight as follows: *The only man who possesses the qualities to lead others and subject them to the influence of his own value direction is he who through self-control subjects himself to the demands of the highest value in his heart.*

---

the German nation to something great and good, I should have given up diplomacy or never adopted this business.' (28. IX. 1870) Busch, *Tagebuchblaetter* I. 248.

[1] Hebbel's Judith to Holofernes: 'You believe that it (the power) exists in order to oppose the world. How if it were there to control one's self?'

We may, however, advance one step further: if the law to which the ruler subjects himself has significance not only for the concretely given instance but has as its object general modes of behavior, then this will to regularity is also a source of law. But we must add two more factors: (1) the overindividual recognition of this will as one which binds the individual's claims of power; and (2) the content of the hitherto purely formally conceived law, namely a partition of claims to law and duties which originate in a definite grade of social attitude.

But this encroaches on our later discussion. Here we are interested only in the psychology of power. The motivation of the true leader must be based on self-conquest which prescribes, as a rule of conduct for himself and others, an inclusive concept of genuine values. Otherwise we have not leadership but tyranny, not order but chaos. No matter how much mere whim may exhibit a formal will to power (as the pictures of the natures lusting for power shown in Plato's *Republic* and *Gorgias*) it is nevertheless opposed to the immanent psychology of power and can therefore have no influence beyond a momentary success.

IV

The forms in which the political type appears would become infinitely more numerous if we added the representatives of collective power and of legally guaranteed claims. We want, however, to limit ourselves to the pure forms which contain no admixture of social spirit or legal will to regularity. This isolation is all the more justifiable since political natures exist not only in the higher walks of life but also in lesser relations as organizers and fighters, ambitious persons, leaders and tyrants.

In all levels and spheres of society there are rulers and ruled, dependent and independent people. And liberty as well as dependency is distributed among all mankind, though in different proportions. Pre-eminent among them are those to whom power and position are the chief business of life, while others, as mental vassals can live only while leaning on stronger natures. One might speak paradoxically of active and passive political types. The former strive for a position of social eminence and are at their best only as leaders and when surrounded by honor and splendor. They live under the pressure of the temptation (as every type carries within itself the danger of straining its own nature) to sacrifice the content of existence to their ambition. They strive for social eminence, for influence and leadership since they only experience their unique power in this way. The other sort cannot get along without some guidance. They are dependent in their tastes, their judgments, their economic bearing and their whole attitude toward life. This attitude becomes a special type when the need to lean upon others becomes the central point of their existence, and when they wholly spend themselves in the service of another.[1]) This type is much more common among women than men, and is closely connected with the other motives of life, love and loyalty. Modern development, however, everywhere strives against relations of natural dependency. The consequence is the dissolution of all organic relations of domination and their displacement by rational associations of a wholly different structure in which there appears a different type of ruler who has a social tinge.

Thus in the forms of the political type another factor is always present, which is derived from the origin of power and dependency. On one end there is physically born power and on the other, the purely mentally transmitted power.[2]) Mere physical strength, of course, no longer signifies a conclusive apparatus of power in a differentiated total of culture. The biological relations of age and sex, however, are always essential factors. Children are dependent upon the older generation; and women's physical capacity is usually inferior to men's. Fathers and husbands seem therefore to be tempted by nature itself to develop into household tyrants. But even in these relations, the mental factor, the cultural superiority is decisive. Biological dependencies are more and more replaced by mental ones. Between the two, however, there is a power which one could hardly call mental, and which plays an important role in the politico-sociological region: the force of habit.

---

[1]) Also the type of conscious and voluntary servant may have its ethical grandeur. The Prussian officer and official of the old regime express this type. Indeed in a higher moral consideration, serving and ruling may be synonymous. Thus Frederick the Great regarded himself as the chief servant of his state. The heroic sacrifice which Hindenburg is making for the German people and the state arises from the same spirit.

[2]) This is further developed from the point of view of naturalistic and idealistic power morality by A. Vierkandt, *Machtverhaeltnis und Machtmoral*. Berlin 1916.

Max Weber therefore lists, besides the form of domination founded on carismatical relations and on reason, the ascendency which is based on tradition. The influence of habit in forming laws is well known. Custom almost constitutes a legal title, and the binding power of such habit belongs to the characteristic psychological phenomena of the political nature. It often finds, in inherited relations of domination, sufficient proof to continue them even after the value-endowing meaning and power-determining achievements have long disappeared from the relations in question. Besides the physical and mental types of power we must, therefore, also classify the type founded on tradition.

The prestige of the political type seems to increase with the expansion of its sphere of influence. It makes a decided difference whether one appears with a following of two or of a large body of people. Regardless of the energy of the individual, the extent of his influence also depends on the ideal of eminence which he has set for himself. Some people are content to play a leading role in their home-town and experience their big moments in this way. Others feel themselves sufficiently elevated by belonging to some social class. National and racial pride already extend the sphere much further. But in this type too, the intensity as well as the extensity of its relations also come into question. A man may have world renown and yet exercise little influence on the formation of his immediate environment. We find the unique dialectic of striving for power in the fact that with the increase of control the extent of its dependencies also increases. All imperialists who have yearned for expansion have had to experience this. Furthermore, the *Hybris* is the inner danger which is posited with the psychology of striving for power itself. Thus we can understand that the stoic wise man (and still more his cynical predecessor) experienced his highest consciousness of power in the feeling that he was entirely independent and in need of nothing from anyone.

Any person who wants to control large groups finds his own power inadequate and must establish in himself a sort of collective power. He must act in the name of many. We are confronted by the highest type of power; men of imperious natures in whom an overindividual mental power is epitomized, only when a leader knows that a tremendous group is behind him whose cause he has espoused. This growth which follows from the higher purposes themselves contains a mystic factor. Therefore the psychology of power is only complete when we add the theory of overindividual subjects. On this ground then develop the different power types which correspond to the different types of constitution. Plato already delineated these: the aristocrat, the timocrat, the oligarch, the democrat and the tyrant.[1] Montesquieu and Roscher have carried further this theory of types.

Finally the question remains in what region and with what means one wishes to rule. Some individuals search for influence by every means and at any price. Others strive for distinction only in a definite field, nevertheless with marked emphasis of the will to power so that one cannot classify them in the specific regions in question. Anyone who wishes to rule by his knowledge is active as an authority, while he who wants to be noticeable by means of his interesting personality is an aristocrat, either aesthetic or cultural. And whoever seeks renown through wealth is a plutocrat. Finally, anyone who rules through religion approaches the general type of priestly domination and theocracy. Perhaps no expression of the political type is so noticeable as that of the princes of the church, just as no vanity can be stronger than that of the monk. In the methods of domination, however, there is a difference because some really base themselves on the values which they represent, while others seek instead the obscure affective result of these powers and wish to rule by suggestion. Orators and artists dazzle, wealthy and well-born people are 'representative', priests fascinate and stupefy. These symptoms show clearly that it is here less a question of the unique value content of the cause, than of the political technique of utilizing it in order to gain power. And in the sociological texture of power relations, such a tremendous reciprocal interrelation and mixture of dependencies and superiorities appears, that the question: 'Who rules'? often leads us along crooked byways from the throne to some garret.[2] There are also types who are influential without desiring to be so by merely being what they are, while others are constantly forced to adopt artificial means in order to enhance their influence.

---

[1] Plato, *Republic,* book 8 and 9.
[2] Cf. Heinrich Zschokke's novel *Wer regiert denn?*

V

Finally we reach those who reject power and fight it as something opposed to value. If their souls belong to some value region other than the political, nothing of psychological interest appears. Anyone who wholly devotes himself to science, art or religion may decline social influence. Because he wholly lives in his own cause we can understand that he does not also exhibit ambition and thus endanger his powers of concentration.[1]) We have seen that the self-emphasis of the political type is strongly opposed by the deeply and genuinely social natures. But there are some people in whom a painfully disappointed striving for power causes them to denounce it.

If this type of mind appears only in the formation of tactical means then we are confronted by the fanatic of equality. He attacks everything that stands higher than himself and is distinctive, quite regardless of whether it really has or only borrows inner value. He maintains that all people are essentially equal, in order to be able to revolt against all leaders and authority. But it is obvious that this type of democrat only wants to substitute his power for that of the existing authority, and that he would speedily become a dictator if fate permitted him to mount the ladder of influence.[2]) In such a case the dogma of equality is nothing but a battle cry, one of the *idées-forces* by means of which one affirms oneself and suppresses others. With the theoretic type we learned another source of the conception of equality: the radical rationalism which substitutes for the living and working individual, who is interwoven in real relations, the abstract concept of man in order to construct, by the aid of this idea, a rational state. Where both tendencies are united: the disguised will to power and the rational type of mind, the political radical develops whose ultimate aim is often the reverse of what he professes.

---

[1]) To be ambitious and to be at the same time scholar, artist or prophet with all one's soul is mutually exclusive. One must observe in real life which motive really is decisive.

[2]) F. Lasalle at the age of fifteen wrote in his Journal (*Der rote Hahn.* Berlin-Wilmersdorf 1918). 'I would be wholly an aristocrat if I had been born as a prince or a duke. But since I am only of the middle class I shall be a democrat.'

But there is another form of resenting power, which we have already mentioned above, the resigned political type who withdraws into himself and enjoys in this grandiose solitude the intoxicating feeling of his greatness, his being misunderstood and his independence. This type easily combines with the self-enjoyment of an aesthetic imagination. Perhaps Nietzsche's ideal of inner power developed on this level: from a great disappointment in man as such, that is, from an unsatisfied longing for love, an overflow of purely mental power and an aesthetic imagination which created beyond all given conditions intoxicating ideals. Thus the hermit of Sils-Maria proclaimed, to humanity with whom he had broken, the will to power.

THE RELIGIOUS ATTITUDE
Επ' αὐτῷ δὴ εἰμὶ ὃ τῷ μεγίστῳ προσηκάζομεν κύματι.

I

Life is an alternating play of experiences whose content depends upon two factors: Fate, in the broadest sense of the term, and the soul structure of the experiencing subject. These experiences contain values in varying degrees, in other words, the meaning of each experience sounds a value-tone in the mind of the individual. But this does not imply that the value experience is always adequate to express the objective content of the mental context in question. For, it may be relatively isolated, unconnected either by feeling or reflection with the total life. If, on the other hand, an isolated value experience, no matter how subjective, is grasped in its significance for the total meaning of life, it has a religious emphasis. This religiously emphasized value then, which is experienced as the final significance of individual existence is necessarily the highest value which the individual can possibly experience. And vice versa; it is inconceiveable that the highest value experience — even if it were only the experience of a single moment — should not shed its radiance of meaning over the individual's entire mental life. Keeping in mind these facts in relation to value, we can now define *religiosity* as the condition, instinctive or rational, in which a single experience is either positively or negatively related to the total value of life. I call *religious objects* the objective contexts in which these deepest value experiences are created; and *religion* that inclusive concept of objective-mental forms in which these value relations are expressed as dogmas or cults.

We have seen above that among the value experiences and ideas of them which conflict with each other one direction may have a normative character; that is, this particular evaluation may appear in consciousness as a demand. It does not appear as factual but only in the form of an experience of what ought to be. Any objective value may appear with this specific experiential character, but whichever objective value refers normatively to the total life and behavior of the personality is the highest. This personal totality can, of course, only be acquired by the most comprehensive and far-reaching contact with the entire world context. Ethical religiosity is founded in just such a relation of the experience of the norm to the total meaning of individual life. But the typical basic character of religiosity may appear even when the value of life is only measured in regard to actual value experiences. The mere feeling of happiness, or the longing for happiness, is in itself religious, at least from the point of view of a psychology of religion.

We see from these definitions that nothing is outside the realm of religion, although, according to its importance in the total mental life of the person, it may be significant in different degrees.

The highest value experience may be a wholly subjective product of the soul, so to speak its inner pinnacle, or its core. But there is always something which confronts the soul, a 'World' and 'Fate' which influence its experiential context. And indeed, since the actuality of the soul itself and of character may be experienced as Fate, the value of life depends on the meaning of the world insofar as it is susceptible of being personally experienced. The world, as the total of all contexts of being and meaning which act upon the individual soul, is in itself a religious concept. Science tries in vain to grasp the essence of the whole theoretically. Mere cognition of being (in the sense of pure objectivity) does not succeed in reaching the meaning of the world. For, we defined meaning as a relation to value. And religious meaning is the relation to the value totality which culminates in the highest value. The meaning of the world, that is, of the whole, can therefore only be experienced by the religious attitude. In religious terminology, God is that final being who is the meaning of the world, or is created mentally as that which endows it with meaning. Kant's doctrine already emphasized the fact that God is not a purely theoretic concept but is, instead, the objective correlate of the religiously experiencing soul. And without surpassing the limits of psychological study we might formulate this as follows: God is the objective principle which is thought of as the object of the highest personal value experience. And we leave open the question to what degree theoretical insights into the world context help to found religiosity and contribute to the clarification of religious objects. As psychologists we must not attempt to decide whether purely theoretic science can evolve from within itself a concept of God. Even if it could, the theoretic significance would not exhaust its meaning. This meaning is found instead in its relation to us, as Rousseau and A. Ritschl have already taught us, that is, in our highest value experiences, whether the main part of this relation is the result of the influence of the world's structure upon us or whether the soul has actively evolved it. At least the concept of God which serves as the expression of these value experiences, is no longer of purely theoretic origin (not purely constitutive) but its definitions are rooted in the content of experienced final values. Religious value judgments are not, therefore, purely objective reports but likewise statements of emotional conditions (Reischle: *Thymetische Urteile*). A peculiar antinomy appears if the concept which arises thus is subsequently used as a purely theoretical explanation of the world, or even if it is only followed up to its 'immanent logical' consequences. And in this critical analysis the concept collapses. But its achievement consists in that it symbolizes, beyond the mere formulation of the value experiences, the objective meaning contexts from which it caught fire. It is, however, also conceiveable that a religiosity should completely reject these objective symbols or make use of other terms.

The essence of religiosity must, therefore, be seen in the search for the highest value of mental life. The condition of the quest is restlessness and dissatisfaction: *Cor meum irrequietum est, donec requiescat, Domine, in Te*. Anyone who continues to vascillate as to the highest value in his experience is homeless, torn and despairing. But whoever finds the highest value in himself and rests in that, experiences salvation and blessedness. And so the attainment of this religious Good always makes itself felt as salvation. The road to this goal may be experienced as a conversion and insofar as it is reduced to an objective principle which endows the world with meaning and value, is an inner revelation. The meaning of the world is not cognized or proved but comes to us in this unique experience. Its mediations may be purely psychical or may come through extra-psychical regions, as for instance religiously experienced nature or history. But the decisive factor is the 'how' of experience. This unique condition which is favorable to revelation and leads to salvation, results from a characteristic method of soul culture.

We shall now make the very difficult attempt to construct independently of historical epochs the basic types of personality in which the religious experience is the central attitude. A religious man is he whose whole mental structure is permanently directed to the creation of the highest and absolutely satisfying value experience. From our general definition of religiosity, we may conclude that there are three main types of religious man, of which the third, as the intermediary one permits of many differentiations.

This triple classification results from the relation (positive, negative or mixed) of the onesided life values to the total value of life. It is unimportant for psychology whether we are here dealing with genuine life values or only with those subjectively considered so. Apparent values which have come to consciousness as such can never, of course, have a religious emphasis. If all the values of life are experienced in a positive relation to the highest value of life, we have the type of the immanent mystic.[1]) If the relation is negative, we have the transcendental mystic. And if the evaluations are partly positive and partly negative, the divided (dualistic) religious nature develops. We do not mean to imply by this a value judgment. For, we could only be justified in doing so from an ethical viewpoint.

A. Immanent mysticism is an absolute affirmation of life since it finds indications of God in all positive life-values. In trying to raise every region to infinity it reaches the highest total value. Therefore a man of this type is a universalist; like Faust full of infinite longing which finds in every thing a *plus ultra*. He has great vitality, a cosmic enthusiasm, and he finds something divine in every aspect of life. Therefore no aspect should be slighted. Such an immanent mystic tries to complete knowledge

---

[1]) By mysticism I mean any point of view which searches for the absolute unity of the highest values. In general, we oppose the immanent point of view to mysticism because the immanent is identified with the natural. Here, however, we shall start from the value point of view and call whatever affirms the value directions of life 'immanent'. The hidden, mystic element is found in that they are followed up to an infinite highest. The transcendent mystic does not enter positively into these value relations.

in order to approach divine omniscience. But since he relates all knowledge to God, i. e. to a total meaning of the world as a unitary center, he is not an encyclopedist but a metaphysician. He wants to control all of nature technically, to possess all its treasures, in order to master it even if to do so he must devote himself to black magic. He rejoices in the infinite divine beauty of the universe and feels himself like God as a world-reflecting monad. He includes all people in his love and wants to sympathize with all of life. He has the heroic enthusiasms possible only to great leaders, and enjoys a regal freedom.

Giordano Bruno and Shaftesbury are men of this type. Comenius too, resembles them in many respects, but he exhibits also a strong devaluation of the finite. This universal urge to life could only develop, on the ground which the age of Reason had prepared as the basic feeling of modern Protestantism. Goethe was of this type and also gave it poetic form.[1]) And for this reason he gives the modern affirmation of life not only a poetic but also a religious expression. But he has also shown that this life-form must always remain incomplete. His Faust lives through all the fundamental forms of existence one after the other: science, magic, eroticism, power and beauty. He can never grasp them all simultaneously and so ends in the heroic limitations of a task which is both social and economic. To founder in his finity is the usual fate of the immanent mystic. He remains human in spite of his wishes and abandoning the struggle at this point or at some other, he begins a dialectic of religious experience which cuts short his complete affirmation of life. But death may seem to offer an unlimited opportunity for possible transfiguration and purification from the finite physical element.

Immanent mysticism may appear not only in this universal enthusiasm but also in the onesided form of one of the other attitudes, namely whenever these seek to grasp the entire meaning of life with their specific organs of existence. These onesided forms of life-affirming religiosity have already been mentioned in the discussion of each type. In the present investigation, we want

---

[1])   'Willst du ins Unendliche schreiten,
Geh nur im Endlichen nach allen Seiten.'
'If you want to reach infinity,
simply travel through finity in every direction.'

to emphasize not the specific direction of the mind but the fact that in every attitude the entire meaning of the world can be grasped. The theorist only becomes religious when he seeks, through cognition, to fathom the final secret. This type has never been more clearly shown than in Spinoza. Another person finds the final satisfaction and the service of God in the performance of economically useful work. The artist seeks all the highest and richest revelations in the beauty of the world, the soul and art. The social type finds God in infinite love, and the political type in the exhibition of power on a big scale. But they are all searching for salvation in this world and according to their specific mental structure they strive for it in a unique value direction.

These somewhat circumscribed seekers for God, who try to reach infinity by progressing in one direction, naturally experience more strongly than others the inadequacy of their narrow outlook to perceive the meaning of life. Though these onesided people often exhibit a grandiose element, nevertheless they cannot escape the tragedy of a conflict with their limitations which makes them feel a breach in their souls. Thus the theorist may founder at last on his ignorance of the practical world, and the aesthetic type like Euphorion, on the limitations of his imagination. Everywhere the tragic experience that life cannot be completed is forced upon the human mind, and each onesided attitude, because of its own structure, is condemned to failure.

B. Before following the changes (which result from the above) in the attitude toward the individual regions of life, we shall delineate the contrast between the life-affirming and the transcendental mystic. For the latter, no mental organ is sufficient to grasp the ultimate meaning. Therefore he looks for revelation not in mental spheres which have been built in life but in a higher meaning which is found beyond all special relations and is immediately turned toward the divine, grasping it more purely the less it is endangered by an impurity of those immanent values. He thus finds the highest value in utter negation of the world. (We mean by world the inclusive concept of value contexts which are experienced in life as directed toward objects). Accordingly the transcendental mystic finds rest only in a super-world which he has contemplated from the beginning. And it is psychologically unimportant whether this final blessedness is pessimism (i. e. a satisfaction in the belief that everything is meaningless) or whether he builds above the meaningless a higher realm of true meaning. For, one can easily see that the confession of the pessimist has a meaning which satisfies him.

All science is valueless for such a being since it cannot be completed and always leaves the final question unsolved. This confession of ignorance satisfies him for it is a conscious avowal, a *docta ignorantia*. It leads especially to a purely 'negative theology'. His economic vocation loses all religious value for him. For, since the flesh is perishable it is not worth while to try to preserve it. One should mortify it. Asceticism is the road to God, and beauty is merely a sensible phenomenon behind which hide the lures of life which have no attraction for him. And since he does not possess its inner preconditions, the world is not beautiful for him and art is nothing but a meaningless duplication of an original which is in itself valueless. The transcendental mystic rejects all striving for power since power is only affirmation of self. He humbles himself before God. Therefore complete self-devaluation ultimately results. He cannot love human beings because they are as finite and sinful as himself. Nor does he want to chain his heart to anything, even to them. And so liberated from all finite things the transcendental mystic devotes himself only to a formless culture of the soul. He prepares himself for the super-sensible by the complete mortification of all his senses. He cultivates in himself the capacity for ecstasy, that is the mysterious gift of perceiving the imperceptible and communicating with God, the final meaning of the world, in a unique supernatural manner. Though he calls this existence purely spiritual, he nevertheless means by spirit something different from what we do: divine spirit which, before it is formed and made finite, divided and multiplied, cannot be grasped in any individual mental achievement nor translated into any symbol. God is for him the Absolute Complicatio, the undifferentiated unity of subject and object, of the one and the many, of finity and infinity. In short, he comprehends God or the meaning of the world, through absolute contrast with all special meaning forms of the world. He despises science and art. He is a hermit and would be an anarchist in society. He even dreads action because he is afraid of interfering with God's decree. He concentrates all his energy in preparing his soul for inner vision and for the love of God, *fruitio Dei*.

It is not difficult to recognize the limitations of this type too. They consist in the gradual emptying of all content which becomes more noticeable when the type appears in its pure form. The mystic hermit experiences, in his ecstatic visions, nothing which is communicable. He only says that he has experienced something infinitely valuable and he may feel a peculiar enhancement of his soul.[1]) But he cannot completely divorce himself from the pictures and values of this world, for, if he had never lived in this world — he would see nothing in the other. He really only duplicates mental life by trying spiritually to transcend all of its aspects. But he is bound to the language and symbols of this world. If he did not see the contrast, he would not be able to reject one side. Thus it is not merely accidental that these transcendental mystics carry within them the specific coloration of one of the immanent spheres of life. They are either philosophical mystics, who try to transcend finite cognition by means of a higher kind of mystical vision (like Dionysius Areopagita) or aesthetic mystics, whose ecstasy is tinged with eroticism which is however turned toward the divine and original beauty (like Plotinus). They are ascetics who overcome in life the useful and comfortable things of life in order to partake of higher goods and enjoyments; or they love human beings with that spiritual love with which God loves mankind, and so raise the union of souls to a transcendent contact of pure minds with whom, in certain cases, they can communicate even after death. It is conceiveable that a unique feeling of power should be intermingled in the mystics by which they try to force God to descend, and compel human beings to join them.[2]) In all these relations vestiges of the ancient finity are still influential, even though everything is sublimated and surpassed so that finally all these perishable things become a parable of surmised divine forces and relations. One may indeed say that in their final results the two forms of mysticism are not widely separated, but the emphasis is different and must be carefully observed in psychological analysis.

---

[1]) Cf. K. Oesterreich, *Die religioese Erfahrung als philosophisches Problem*. Philosophische Vortraege der Kantgesellschaft. Nr. 9.

[2]) Therefore the possibility of this curious reversal of the center of gravity:
'*Darein ich mich versenke, das wird mit mir zu eins:*
Ich bin, wenn ich ihn denke, wie Gott der Quell des Seins.'

Both types make use of an old world-picture whose outline was sketched by Neo-Platonism: everything is permeated with God, and filled with a higher meaning and nothing exists as valuable per se. Everything finite is a mirror of the infinite. Everything individual is meaningless outside of totality, and time and space are only symbols of pure mind. History shows how, in this new Neo-platonic world-picture, the emphasis may be now on the side of the Logos (cognition), now on the side of Eros (beauty), and now on the side of love (Agape and Sympatheia). If this pantheism approaches the acosmic in its degree of world-negation, it entirely corresponds to transcendental mysticism. It may however be united with a strong belief that God reveals himself in all phenomena and whatever has limited value, indeed that God, so to speak, radiates through everything. As a rule, the conception of a hierarchy indicates the greater or lesser distance of these data from God. But the genuinely religious man never finds ultimate satisfaction in the data themselves.

C. This has already led us to intermediary religious types. For, religiosity seldom appears in such extreme forms as we have pictured. Usually it is a combination of both basic forms. Thus a type develops which confronts both affirmatively and negatively every region of life. And in short the problem of the following analysis is to investigate how behavior in regard to the values of life is transformed if it appears in this specific religious light. From one point of view, these values appear to be genuine but inadequate approaches to God. From the other, they seem to be merely vessels of clay which receive their value only from the Heavenly treasure which they contain.

II

1. The religious type cannot wholly ignore the results of cognition. And scientific achievements are for them, under certain conditions, new and genuine sources of religious experience. But they cannot grant the last word to cognition. For, by means of its fundamental attitude it never states the meaning of these lawful contexts for the deepest experiential center. The intellectual system implies in itself nothing in regard to a total value. This can only be experienced in the focal point of, and of course always in relation to a mental individuality. The entirely new value attitude which appears here is no longer knowledge but, as we usually

say belief, i. e. a trust, supported by the whole value range of the person, in the validity of those values which they experience as the highest. It is however impossible to draw the line between knowledge and belief in such a manner that one can say exactly that where science ends belief begins and vice versa. On the contrary, the same complex of objects (for instance a human tragedy) may be both theoretically grasped and religiously interpreted. Theoretically no miracles exist. But from a religious point of view there are occurrences of such great individual value significance that they transcend the merely theoretically comprehensible causal relation.

To set the limits of these two attitudes is the work of a more detailed critique of a philosophy of religion than we can attempt here. But this much must be emphasized, cognition has only two objective orders which have theoretic significance: the physical and the mental. (The imaginative order is not an object of cognition.) The transcendental world, on the other hand, arises from a religious meaning context. The expression 'transcendental' may have several different meanings. Some people mean by it simply what transcends the finite, that is, infinite objects. With the exception of the concept of limen, the transcending of the finite is also a surpassing of the cognizeable. This first conception of transcendental leads, therefore, to a second, according to which everything that goes beyond the strict forms of cognition and can only be experienced in the religious attitude is transcendental. Finally a third point of view is possible, according to which the transcendental is rooted in the fact that the value-demands of the subject cannot be realized in the actual world order, which is consequently devaluated in contrast with the truly religious meaning.

All three are interwoven in the religious consciousness of transcendence. But this consciousness appears on different levels. As a rule, one ascribes the direction to the transcendental only to the theistic type of pious person who sharply contrasts God to the world. Or in other words: only supernaturalism is thought of as transcendent.[1] And indeed the third factor appears here most strongly: the opposition of value-demanding consciousness (the norms

---

[1] Anyone who uses the term supernaturalism ought of course first to define what he means by 'Nature'. As a rule this term denotes not only the material world but also the reality and finality of culture and history which have become part of it.

which are directed to the world-order) to the actual world context. This transcendence of the given is the most pronounced expression of spiritual freedom. If from here 'another world' is designed in mind, then this other world is really nothing but the reflex of the spontaneity of the will and the absolute moral consciousness. Dilthey called this type of transcendentalism, which is fundamentally religious but always combines a flavor of the political attitude, the 'idealism of freedom'.[1]) This type is frequently met with in minds like Descartes, Kant, Jacobi, Fichte and Jean Paul. But noone has sufficiently analyzed the precise way in which the details of the transcendent world-picture develop from this type of experience.

This (third) factor of contrasting the normative values with the given world order is less pronounced in the pantheistic type. Here, in many cases, nature is viewed as a force which is productive of ideality. And with this naturalistic pantheism there is often found either a logical, or aesthetic or utilitarian factor. [In the first instance logical pantheism (Spinoza) develops, in the second aesthetic (Shaftesbury) and in the third teleological (evolutionary monism; Spencer)]. The more one adds the complex of mental objectivities to the universe as it is and so expands the concept of nature to the mental, the more naturalistic pantheism is elevated to a spiritual pantheism — (Herder, Schleiermacher and Hegel). Even history and society are now apprehended from a pan-religious point of view. Though none of these types maintain a complete transcendence of the values which they affirm, both the first mentioned conditions of transcendental consciousness are present; namely its direction to infinity and its elevation above the purely cognitive point of view. In these relations, even the pantheistic God is transcendent. Or to put it more simply: noone would think of identifying the crude world-order with God. For, the former is experienced even in pantheism by a 'higher consciousness', whose essence it is to observe everywhere in the universe and Fate the total and highest meaning relation.

By means of such an analysis the difference between these two 'worlds' is finally reduced to a difference between experience and mental attitudes. 'Beyond' the level of objects which is determined by cognition lie other contexts which may be religiously

---

[1]) Cf. Kultur der Gegenwart: 'Systematische Philosophie', and Symposium on *Weltanschauung,* Berlin 1911.

experienced and interpreted. The roots of metaphysics too are to be found in these spiritual motives, in spite of its attempt to remain pure cognition. The hopelessness of this aim has already been demonstrated by Kant when he disclosed the development of the *mundus intelligibilis* by moral consciousness, and placed the category of value above the category of being. (*Primat der praktischen Vernunft.*) Something similar may have moved Hamann when he appended to the expression 'things of another world' the note: 'Things of another world are nothing more than certain peculiar views of the present changeable and sensible nature which is all that is given to us.'[1]) Reduced to the final simplest motives, the supernatural world-picture with its creation out of nothing and the God beyond, is a radiation of a central experience of freedom which 'lifts itself above nature'. Pantheism on the other hand, in all its different forms, is a reflex of the experience of dependency which is based on the biological, logical or aesthetic context of life. Finally, it follows from this that such a strong devaluation of the empirical consciousness of reality can be bound up with the theistic viewpoint that the present world degenerates into mere appearance, or at least into a meaningless purely negatively determined matter ($\mu\grave{\eta}$ $\breve{o}\nu$). This sentiment plays as important a part in Plato's dualism as in Kant's and the entire early Christian world lived in this dualism of mind and body. —

But since cognition and its achievements finds in religious consciousness such an opposing force, one must from its point of view, either through reflection or experience, consider the question of the 'limits of cognition'. If we refer to the contrast which thus appears by the naive old phrase 'belief and knowledge' the dualistic religious type has three possibilities of subordinating knowledge to belief. Either science is devaluated by a religiously motivated scepticism; so that there is, so to speak, room for the giving of religious meaning in its constitutive lacks and insufficiencies; or the functional sphere of belief and knowledge is mutually delimited by a sort of double mental book keeping in

---

[1]) In F. H. Jacobi, Works Vol. IV, 2, p. 70. Very characteristic is also the note which Goethe (Maxims and Reflections IV.) adds to this passage in Hamann: For him, as a pronounced immanent mystic, the turning toward another world amounts to watching the blindspot or mental aberration.

regard to its specific spheres of achievement; or finally, above elementary knowledge is developed a higher form of knowledge, which by means of a unique logic, attempts also to satisfy the religious meaning of the world. This third and last type inclines toward the theoretic but is fundamentally different from it in its inner structure.

a) Notice the typical relation between theoretic scepticism and religiosity. The road to the religious interpretation of the world is only opened for certain definitely organized minds by the depreciation of cognitive achievements — because we cannot know we must believe. We seem to find even in Socrates an intimation of this religiously motivated confession of ignorance (*avidya*). And for that reason he has come down to us not only as an unbearable rationalist and 'know-it-all' but also as an awakener of a 'higher assurance' which is a necessary consequence of insight into his ignorance, a sort of '*docta ignorantia*'. This is the way, for instance, in which Count Zinzendorf, Hamann and Kierkegaard have understood him. Hume's scepticism too, was peculiarly useful to the religiously attuned German Romantic philosophers, because he had already given the name *belief* to a certain form of cognitive instinct. The limitation of knowledge to a decidedly external positivism by some representatives of Ritschl's school also shows the same tendency. And fundamentally Kant had already prepared the way for the nineteenth century in this direction by asserting: 'I had to abolish knowledge in order to make room for belief.'

b) The danger of this point of view will be all the more apparent if one is deeply imbued with the honesty of the scientific spirit. Even Kant did not really abolish knowledge but only set limits for it which were founded in its own nature. So we see that the desire for such limitation founds a second type, for, in this case more positive value is granted to the sphere of cognition than by the religious sceptics. This type is nowhere found more clearly than in the mathematician Pascal: 'Nothing is so much in harmony with reason as a denial of reason in questions of belief. And nothing is more contradictory to reason than the denial of the same in questions which are not of belief. Not to admit that there is any such thing as reason, or not to admit anything but reason are two equally dangerous errors.'[1)]

[1)] Pascal, Thoughts. VI. 6. 3. In Jacobi's *David Hume ueber den Glauben* I find this sentence from Pascal as motto: 'La nature confond

In the most modern Protestant theology of Ritschl's type this delimitation between knowledge and belief appears in such a manner that religious reports are no longer viewed as theoretic statements but only as forms of expression (pictorial descriptions) of a pious consciousness which lies behind it and its relation to the world. The dire competition between cognition and piety is thus abolished, and each side is understood in its unique structure. For this point of view it is necessary to show the psychic spiritual generation of every individual religious symbol; that is, to repeat a well-known fact, the origin of God's omnipotence from the consciousness of freedom, his all-lovingness from the social consciousness and his all-wisdom from the theoretic etc. Cosmological definitions of divinity are more difficult to interpret than sociological ones. However the former are generally rooted in the remnants of a mythological way of thinking in which the theoretic, aesthetic and religious motives have not been separated. Physical miracles are expressions of wishes and vestiges of anthropomorphisms. How much in the primitive gods is simply a reflection of an economic system or in general of the impulse for self-preservation! This procedure of analyzing the religious world of ideas was first applied by Hume and Feuerbach. In its execution, however, there is often lacking even today the finer intelligence for the psychic generation of a dogma-complex. The religious way of looking at history must be interpreted as a projection of religious interpretation of life into the development of humanity. In this way the boundary between belief and knowledge is gradually drawn in every instance. And from this fact we might also explain how religious certitude can co-exist with cognitive certainty. The former relies upon value certainties and demands, while the latter recognizes only the certainty of logical and sensible evidence. Religious conviction may be as much higher than the scientific as the inner certainty of value is superior in power to all these forms of evidence.[1]) But psychological dualism remains: the sphere of cognition is saved even though circumscribed, and the sphere of belief may develop

---

les Pyrrhoniens et la raison confond les Dogmatistes. — Nous avons une impuissance à prouver, invincible à tout le Dogmatisme. Nous avons une idée de la vérité, invincible à tout le Pyrrhonisme.'

[1]) This only applies to the psychological inquiry into the facts of mental life. Criticism belongs in a philosophy of religion.

beside it. Modern man, whose conscious structure usually develops along the line of reflection, belongs to this type. He has found a way to partially safeguard the value of cognition and even to regard its results as a new source of religious stimulation.

c) But a third way also is conceiveable in which to look for a balance between theoretic and religious lines of thought. The very fact that all genuine cognition is eternally valid, that is, that it leads from its own nature out of finite limits and founds in consciousness an eternal region is the first step in bringing cognition as close as possible to religion. This experience is most closely related to the ancient concept of the *ratio* which is supposed to be a generally valid and eternal principle. Doubtless this very important concept in the history of the mind contains in itself a religious factor. But the bridge which it throws between finity and infinity is too narrow for specific religious consciousness. Rational knowledge dissects the given world with its exact lines. It satisfies the theorist but for the specifically religious type this rational concept is insufficient. In mysticism we find instead a tendency to found a logic superior to rational logic which, because it is directed to infinity and absolute unity, may be called religious logic.

It finds rational logic inadequate because of the principle of contradiction i. e. if A is posited, Not-A is denied. For finite problems this may be valid. But the infinite (a religious concept) always contains a riddle, namely that it is scattered in a manifoldness of finite entities. The infinite, as illustrated in the concept of God, is filled for rational logic with antinomies which would immediately disappear if one could make up one's mind to abandon the principle of contradiction. These are of course rational reflections which an outsider makes in trying to put himself in the place of the mystical religious type. Mystical consciousness, which is directed to totality and not to the individual, contains from the outset a new intuitive logic which is based on the principle of the *coincidentia oppositorum*, the unity of opposites. This religious logic begins with the infinite. And when it posits a definite and final A it is simultaneously forced to include everything else in the Not-A. The A in itself is absolutely dependent. And only in connection with the Not-A is its relation to the infinite safeguarded. The religious vision which is directed to the infinite finds the resolution of all contradictions in the infinite or in God where they are identical. Whoever posits the thesis is forced to carry out the antithesis unless he wants to make the finite independent, which is of course impossible. For religious logic, both are sections of the infinite, that is, really negations. Until I add to the first negation A[1]) *its* negation Not-A, I do not have a real positive, namely a restoration of the infinite.

This higher logic, which is characteristic of all philosophic mystics and which is known to us in the work of Hegel[2]) — in its most elaborate form which includes the historical process — does not wholly abolish the dualism of knowledge and belief. Rather this dualism reappears here in the form of a lower and religious logic. Cognition of reason and of speculation cannot be completely harmonized. Consequently speculative logic is deemed superior to reflective logic. To translate this into our terminology; the religious thought which is directed to the highest value follows different laws from that of the inferior thought. The cognition of reality is discontinued and a higher logic introduced whose truth is to be understood purely religiously. It has the courage to overcome, by means of a grandiose desire for unity, the painful antinomies which ordinary cognition leaves untouched. One might say that herein is reflected the will to salvation of thought itself. The inadequate, finite element which is an inevitable accompaniment of

---

[1]) Spinoza: '*Omnis determinatio est negatio.*'

[2]) Hegel's tremendous achievement in philosophy is the application of the old emanistic logic of the Neo-platonists which already with them was designed to make comprehensible the course of the world, to the historical consciousness (newly awakened since Herder) and a concrete 'world-history'. Troeltsch has praised this dialectic as the best previous solution of the historical problem. But one must not forget, that even this method debases development to mere appearance behind which there lies an always resting eleatic (Spinozaistic) Absolute. And perhaps religious consciousness demands just this abolition of the developmental process in the eternal. Very different is the basic feeling of the man thinking along positivistic-historic lines and whose central experience is Time and the creation of a new factor which has never been experienced and divined in time. — Moreover even with Spinoza there remains the dualism between the strict *scientia rationalis* and the mystical *scientia intuitiva*, so that it is very difficult to say whether one should class him with the theoretic or the religious type. — I remind the reader furthermore of Froebel's doctrine of the '*Entgegengesetzt-Gleichen*' and of '*umgekehrtem Schließen*'. *Menschenerziehung* (1826). p. 8, 61. et al.

thought, strives toward the condition of highest tranquility, toward unity and identity. Thus after all, religious thought builds a higher world than that of every day. Of course this third type of religious behavior toward cognition shows the tremendous influence of a purely theoretic type which desires to conquer what is ultimate and deepest by means of thought, even if it necessitates the development of a new speculative logic. —

Where the theoretic type does not exercise an influence, liberation in the religious attitude is found in the proper recognition of the limits of achievement of mere theory and the founding of an independent right of a value revelation which reaches beyond the theoretical. In this sense, Schleiermacher maintained the independence of religion from speculation, even though he believed that the two would coincide in their results. There is thus, as we have seen, a more extensive type which finds the religious attitude superior to the two-dimensional theoretic attitude. Then cognition — from religious motives — is reduced to mere positivism which touches neither on infinity nor the question of value, but merely classifies facts and reduces them to legal relations of dependence. — We conclude that a theory of cognition too, finally depends on religious attitudes. The will to value always goes beyond the objectivating mental acts. And the manifold relations of the religious type to the theoretic region are determined by means of the nature of these relations.

2. The tragic incompleteability of life determines the change which takes place in the economic realm viewed from the standpoint of the dualistic religious consciousness. Economic work is considered as religious service, and the goods for the preservation of life are viewed as the gifts of God. But these values are always lower than the highest significance of life. Thus this relation to life also is broken off in the middle. One cannot give oneself wholly either to work or to enjoyment. The religious attitude demands that we should 'possess as if we did not own'. Worldly treasures have no saving power and this state of mind leads to asceticism, that is, the control of the entire physical side of life by a superior meaning. A number of nuances are possible here, differences resulting from historical and geographical conditions, but especially variations depending on which religious system is conceived: from complete renunciation and selflessness

to the collection of goods as proof of divine grace.[1]) One form of economic behavior tries to wrest the useful result from God. Magic is often a pre-scientific attempt or a perversion of economics complicated by religious motives. Sacrifices presuppose a commercial relation with God. In all these phenomena our main effort must be clearly to distinguish between religious and economic motives. The religious influence of the division of labor is especially important since it seems hopelessly to bar the way to the highest meaning of life by making life soulless. Oriental castes emphasize the different levels of religious evaluation of vocations.

3. We have seen that the aesthetic type may have a religion of beauty. Here, however, we must deal with the further question of the part played by aesthetics in purely religious life. If we admit that a work of art is always something sensible-concrete; and that according to its essence it can only represent a section of life, this is in itself a limitation of the religious meaning of art. Strictly isolating both regions one might maintain that it is the triumph of art to reproduce the form of the soul in a finite object, while religious experience only views the individual in relation to the infinite. In his *Reden ueber die Religion*, Schleiermacher regards an experience as religious when its object seems to flow as a limitless unity in infinity. A painting on the other hand has a frame, a symphony a beginning and end, and a poem also its external limits. But it is not impossible that both should influence us together, that is, that the finite work of art should also contain relations to the infinite; or in our phraseology, to the highest and most comprehensive meaning of life. Wherever this is the case, the work of art has value as a world-view, and the aesthetic experience is expanded to a religious one.[2])

A second limitation of art results from the fact that its configurations do not reach immediately into the ultimate meaning-structure of the world. It creates, as we have said, an imaginative objectivity. The religious man cannot, however, long remain in this zone, for he only goes part of the way with art, namely as

---

[1]) Cf. Max Weber, *Die Wirtschaftsethik der Weltreligionen* in the 'Collected Essays to a Sociology of Religion.'

[2]) Cf. my lecture: *Beethoven und die Musik als Weltanschauungsausdruck*. Leipzig, Wiegandt 1909.

far as it is a question of stimulating the soul and making it reverent.[1]) If, however, one asks such a nature to regard the formative and sensible as revelation, then and not till then do we see its complete contrast to the born artist: it feels then the insufficiency of such symbolism and withdraws on the surplus of impulse into itself: 'Only the metaphysical blesses us'. In art there are not sufficient guarantees of truth. According to Plato, art is three steps removed from the real and the eternal. Tolstoy's feeling toward art was of the same kind.

This also applies to nature which is aesthetically experienced. An intensely religious person is unsatisfied by such a relation. He feels that we do not so achieve the central experience of the world, but only a reflection of our own dreams, yearnings and poetizings. Indeed, even in the aesthetic fusion of soul and nature there may be a factor of this religious dissatisfaction. In *Gabriel Schilling's Flight* Lucy says: 'Everything about me has a peculiarly intermittent character. I neither know nor believe that all this, the wind in the trees, the light and the song of the larks is final.' And this is the decisive fact, the isolated experience in itself, especially in mere imaginative enjoyment, always lacks finality. And so even in the deepest appreciation of nature there is always a dissatisfaction and a mystery: the religious longing which strives to go further.[2])

Finally, this different attitude is shown a third time in the contrast of the aesthetic and ethico-religious ways of living. On this level, too, the aesthetic leaves us free. We have an alternative which is unbearable to religious thought. The aesthetic 'either-or' is that of the liberal indeterminateness of life which finally remains, as we have said above, a life at second hand. There is a decisive *'Eins ist not'* in the emphasis with which the aesthetico-religious nature utters the 'either-or'. It knows that sometime the midnight

---

[1]) Cf. Schleiermacher, *System der Sittenlehre* (Schweizer) § 290.

[2]) This is always the moving theme in the letters between F. H. Jacobi and Goethe (Leipzig 1846). Their hearts had found each other in their youthfully rapturous enjoyment of nature and could not free themselves from this truth. But the contrast of types: the aesthetic universalist and the dualistic religious soul burst forth in every new epoch of life and led again and again to tragic conflicts — to Goethe's poem on the Diana of Ephesus and to Jacobi's caustic phrase: 'Nature hides God from me.' Both experienced nature but in different soul structures.

hour will strike when we must all unmask. 'Only the ethical contrast is simple and absolute, and if one does not choose ethically, that is, absolutely, then one only chooses temporarily and may therefore in the next moment choose something else.'[1])

So far we have started with the aesthetic and shown the limits beyond which the religious nature cannot go. One may however, conversely, presuppose the religious in all its uniqueness and ask: what then is the relation of the aesthetic to it as a means and a subordinated act? We know that everything which exercises the function of 'expression' is aesthetic. When a religious mood is expressed in poetry, music, dancing, or any ritual, religious consciousness utilizes aesthetic means to express itself, that is, to objectivate itself and communicate with other souls. The aesthetic here serves the religious. Whole mythologies, such as the Greek for instance, have resulted from a highly aesthetic creativity. If we tried to collect the artistic creations which are designed to express religious experience we should have to include here the greatest works of all time. For, the great artist is filled with highest experience, permeated, as it were, with God.[2])

And yet even here the fate of incompleteability intervenes. No soul has succeeded in fixing all of life's glowing content in a visible, audible or imaginable creation. Still less has anyone succeeded in stamping these finite forms of expression with the highest and purest meaning. We can therefore understand how the deep religious consciousness despaired of the adequacy of these symbols; especially when it was filled with a normative morality. All these symbols have something physical and finite about them. 'God is a spirit: and they that worhip Him must worship Him in spirit and in truth.' A wholly spiritualized religion finally ends in an enmity to art. 'Thou shalt not make unto thee any graven image.' And in this mood is rooted the iconoclasm of all time. The aesthetic symbol, like cognition is unable to seize all of life's meaning.

---

[1]) Kierkegaard, *Entweder-Oder*. Works. Vol. II. Jena 1913 p. 139 et al. It is here that one can see how strongly Kierkegaard himself is caught up in the aesthetic.

[2]) Cf. the psychological treatise of M. Dvorak, *Idealismus und Naturalismus in der gotischen Skulptur und Malerei* in '*Kunstgeschichte als Geistesgeschichte*', Muenchen 1924, on the tension between the sensual and the spiritual of the mediaeval man and the artistic forms of expression which follow from this.

Religion condemns every onesided element of life. God is discovered only in silent meditation.

Neo-platonism which begins with Plotinus, and is the strongest aesthetically formed religion, is based on this experience. It is true that they viewed God as the creator and all essences of the world as ideas or divine thoughts, and even all individuality as a creative idea of God. God himself remains here also unity without multiplicity, the *complicatio* of which the universe may be a symbol, but one which makes for finity. Here too spiritualization is necessary, the negation of all matter and form in order to reach God through ecstasy. The ultimate mystery of religiosity is unformulable even by aesthetics. And consequently the dualistic religious man is finally convinced of the inadequacy of all forms to express the highest content which burns in a soul. Even the aesthetic idea which seems entirely to have mastered matter is always an ideal, that is, a sensible-concrete phenomenon, a reflection but not the ultimate; 'a drama, but alas only a drama.' The 'Mothers',[1] that is, the final metaphysical principle, live beyond time and space in the unformed which cannot be entered: or in other words the Dionysian element can never wholly dissolve itself in the Apollonian. And thus even the salvation which art grants to us is, for the purely religious type, always a temporary and individual one. It is the divination of the truly religious but not religion itself.

4. It seems that love is most closely united with religious value. We have emphasized the fact that there is a religious factor in that form of love which, free from any particular content turns affirmatively to the value possibilities of another person.[2] To feel that all of life is sacred is a total evaluation of existence. Indeed, love contains such a markedly divine factor that one often speaks of the relation between God and man in the figure of this social relationship. The 'intercourse' of Christians with God is said to rest on such a spirit. Love spreads a religious atmosphere and real community of soul always has the character

---

[1] Goethe's *Faust:* Part II.

[2] I do not mean here the erotic love as an aesthetic phenomenon, even though in real life this may be the preliminary stage to this deeper relation of the soul. The same is true of biological love which is rooted in blood relationship.

of religious community. Its meaning can only be sought, if neither intellectual, economic or political purposes take the first place, in that mutual culture of souls which we have mentioned above as religious. We must interpret the early Christian love in this way: the communistic forms of early Christianity are only its consequences and are, moreover, based on very definite historical conditions.

We must admit that in regard to the religious total evaluation, no sphere of life stands higher than the social. Thus even the religions which utterly renounce the world still show that relation to the world which results from the bond of love that unites suffering humanity. Christianity and Buddhism, despite their tendency to devaluate the world, are pronounced religions of love. But it is conceiveable that this bond too may slacken. For, love must repeatedly experience in the realities of existence how little it is capable of building up life unaided. Under these disappointments; that even love cannot completely break down the barriers between mankind; that there always remains a painful individuation, and that one must stifle every bit of personal joy that is still contained in it, the religious man frees himself from this side of life also, and seeks satisfaction only in the love of God. Brand's 'all or nothing' strives to conquer even *Deus caritatis*. He would like to free himself even from that last bond and this is the meaning of a hermit's life, if necessary ready with love but not subordinated to love, rather to be lonely with God. Even he who has not gone so far as these final despairs and blessedness, knows nevertheless that one can only maintain the power of true love if one has periods of solitude and time to collect oneself, otherwise the fountain of love runs dry. This shows too, that religious love in its deepest essence is also religious interest in the soul. It founds a community of those who live religious lives. This feeling is so strong that it is, under certain conditions, carried away to the exaggeration and seeming lovelessness of the expression: 'Let the dead bury their dead'. The peculiar vascillation of the religious man between love of God and love of man and the blessedness of the final refuge rings through Moerike's poem:

> *Kann auch ein Mensch des andern auf der Erde*
> *Ganz, wie er moechte, sein? —*
> *In langer Nacht bedacht' ich mir's und musste sagen: Nein!*

So kann ich niemands heissen auf der Erde,
Und niemand waere mein? —
Aus Finsternissen hell in mir aufzuckt ein Freudenschein:
Sollt' ich mit Gott nicht koennen sein,
So wie ich moechte, mein und dein?
Was hielte mich, dass ichs nicht heute werde?
Ein suesser Schrecken geht durch mein Gebein!
Mich wundert, dass es mir ein Wunder wollte sein,
Gott selbst zu eigen haben auf der Erde!

5. The role which political consciousness (in our wide sense of the word) plays in religiosity must be studied at its source before one considers such derived phenomena as the organisation of the religious community in the church or a religiously founded state. In every religion which does not wholly accept or reject life there is a mixture of self-affirmation and self-denial. The meaning of 'self' in this sense, as we have seen in the first part of the book, is very broad. An ethical religion finds the significance of life in mortifying the lower self for the sake of the higher. But we still omit the ethical point of view and consequently also the different meanings which may be given to the self. Then there remains only the fundamental phenomenon that man, in regard to the highest meaning of existence, feels himself either as wholly receptive or as fighting for the realization of this value. In religious terms: either we are wholly subject to God's grace or we side with Him and try to help the divine to a victory over the world of sin. The pronounced natures of freedom who embody a creative will feel in themselves the divine spark, they are even capable of wrestling with God. They do not submit to the cross but carry it to battle as a standard. This consciousness of freedom may be so enhanced that all other gods are devaluated compared to the God in one's own breast. 'Have not you yourself completed everything, divinely glowing heart?' It is not possible to consider here the wealth of symbols in which one might express this relation of freedom and dependence, for one reason because this would necessitate our considering the ethical question. But this much is certain, every proud elevation of man is finally beaten down by Fate. And thus the heroic inspiration of man cannot be completed. It ends in religious resignation and the eternal litany of humility.[1]

---

[1] Cf. Kierkegaard op. cit. 'The edification in the thought that opposed to God we are always in the wrong'.

'For no man shall strive with gods'.[1]) Indeed, perhaps noone experiences the limits of human capacity more strongly than the man of power who is especially vulnerable at this point.

The will to power and liberty which tries to assert itself against the highest meaning of the world is recognizeable even on primitive levels of religion, in the concepts of a peculiar power of the soul which one seeks to increase by means of magic, cults and prayers. The Daemon in one's own breast feels itself divine. Out of these familiar phenomena there develops, upon a higher level, the conception of a religious aristocracy which is elevated above the average man by means of merit or grace or the combination of both. Predestination, to be the object of God's grace, or to feel oneself as His instrument are only sociological symbols which aim to express this consciousness of inner religious power. But here again we find a unique dualism, namely that in spite of our personal responsibility our power is supposed to be inadequate to do anything; with the feeling of freedom is intermingled a pious feeling of dependence. One might try in vain to illuminate this religious dialectic by logical means which consider all that is conceptually contradictory as irreconcileable.

In like manner, prayer is originally a test of power which is designed to summon God's assistance by means of magic. Later proofs of spirit and force grow out of it. It is not inconceiveable to the religious mind that the belief, the fighting belief, if only it could be absolute, could force miracles even from nature. But this would necessitate a complete unity of the soul; an 'or', that is, a mere doubt that something of this sort might be 'beyond human power', would destroy this power itself. "I believe he died because of this 'or'".[2])

The religious wars of former times, those struggles for the one truth which should conquer the world, are incomprehensible to us moderns, because we have too much of this 'or'. It is wholly false to interpret them as mere political enterprises. Conversely, we have experienced that even today war could only be carried on with God on our side, that is, when *'Dieu le veut'* inspires the fighters to the ultimate sacrifice.[3]) Failure is

---

[1]) Cf. also *'Hyperions Schicksalslied.'*
[2]) Bjoernson, *Ueber die Kraft* I. Final scene.
[3]) Cf. Ferdinand Avenarius. **Baal.**

then all the more disastrous since it signifies not only physical weakness but the much more distressing fact of being forsaken by God who should have given us power.

This paradoxical relation of striving for power and religion finds its expression also in the fact that the state, as the legally organized collective power can never be experienced by the religious man as final and ultimate. Rather this type recognizes a sphere of power which is not susceptible of political organisation. This antinomy may appear in three forms: (1) religious consciousness revolts against the state with higher demands and transforms it. Thus the recognition of individual human rights must finally be reduced to the power of religious motives. (2) The religious consciousness may, however, oppose to the state the organisation of the specific religious community, the church, as a higher value organisation, especially if the church embodies political as well as religious motives. (3) And finally, the religious consciousness may oppose the order of the state because it limits spiritual freedom and seeks to interfere by the mechanical means of legal order with God's grace which is alone effective. If religion is really dealing only with 'souls', the state has no power over them. And when this conception is dominant the political element must give way to the religious forces of the soul. The spirit takes orders from noone.

To summarize: we might express the relation between the religious type and the state as follows; that it moves between two poles (corresponding to the extreme religious types described above): between a religious conception of the state (as it is recently found in Fichte and Hegel) which worships the state as the vessel of the most high, as a physical God; and a religious anarchism which sees in just this will to power, atheism. Between the two there is a third conception which views the church, as an originally purely religiously oriented regulation of life, as the most adequate and highest order of life.

Our problem here presents many antinomies. The constant complication of historical relations obstructs our vision of the fundamental pure structures. The church in the highest sense must always be invisible and unorganized. For, the community in the highest life-meaning, does not admit of any external ties. But it is never possible to isolate this religious meaning from the other spheres of meaning out of which it grows. And for this reason, the church as a visible institution must always take an active part in economic, scientific and social relations; partly from the desire to give religious education, and partly to order and regulate life from its natural and economic basis up to its spiritual heights. The church, however, always finds itself confronted by organized departments of life which have developed from the partial meaning of the individual spheres of existence, as for instance the family or the mundane state. It cannot avoid rivalry with them. The command to 'render unto Caesar the things which are Caesar's and unto God the things which are God's' could only be easily carried out if the two spheres of meaning were entirely separate. In reality, however, they intersect at a thousand points.

The transcendent mystic who wants to be independent of physical things may refuse to acknowledge the state and feel himself at home in a community with the saints. The immanent mystic, in accordance with an ethically purified ideal of humanity will strive to fill the physical conditions of life with the highest moral content. Beyond that, however, he does not need any organized community of belief. For him, life itself is the place of worship — his church. The dualistic religious nature on the other hand is forced continually to renew the borderline between knowledge and belief as well as between state and church. The state for such a type, has only a limited function. He too however knows that it is impossible to regulate real community only by means of final certitude. For him the church is only a social but not an all-inclusive form.

Thus the duality of his inner structure influences sociological relations also. And here again is reflected the unique dialectic of the religious sphere that it cannot be separated from the individual regions of life and yet finds that any single region, just because it is only a single region, rather endangers than completes its meaning.

III

Observation of specifically religious natures should have long ago done away with the prejudice that processes of motivation are alike in all men. Of course religious natures in their decisive activity are determined neither by considerations of utility[1]), general practical maxims, nor moral taste. But one must not say that they are always motivated by the highest value experience. For, it is true in every type that the actually experienced highest value is the decisive factor if there is freedom of choice.[2]) The essential factor is that the motives of religious men are based on the final value context, which not only determines their whole personal life but also the total meaning of the world. In this way they are related to the aesthetic type which has achieved inner form, because they act from their innermost hearts. There is, however, this difference that the religious type places the salvation of the soul higher than its complete and harmonious development. This means that he acts in accordance with the experienced meaning of the world even if he must thereby mortify his fleshly instincts and wholly conquer his lower impulses. We cannot say in general what makes up the highest value for him, since it differs with different people. Even the three basic religious types, which we have distinguished above and shall not take up in greater detail here, are different in this respect: affirmation, negation or dualistic evaluation of life here color the motives. The first is based on the feeling: '*Ein guter Mensch in seinem dunklen Drange ist sich des rechten Weges wohl bewusst*'. The second results from the mistrust of the limited values of life and also from the decided distrust of self: the fundamental motive here is asceticism.[3]) Finally, in the third case there develops the careful inspection of one's own motives to see whether they originate in the higher or lower regions of the soul.

But the formal condition of a man who places his entire existence under the domination of the highest value which surrounds world and soul, may be said in general to be this: that there

---

[1]) For this reason we must not expect the related technical form of motivation for which the purpose is sufficiently legitimized by virtue of its utility and which asks only theoretically for the purposiveness of the means.

[2]) Cf. F. Niebergall, *Wie predigen wir dem modernen Menschen?* Tuebingen 1909 3rd. ed. esp. p. 91 ff. on the motives and quietives of people.

[3]) Joachim Wach, *Der Erloesungsgedanke und seine Deutung*, Leipzig 1922 — p. 30 presents some fine psychological analyses of these types. 'It is clear immediately that the enormous devotion and sacrifice presupposed by all great cultural achievement is not given by the self-affirming individuals but rather born out of the depths of the urge for salvation, out of longing and love.'

is in him a blessed fulness which determines his active or passive behavior. In religious terminology, this presence of the highest world-value in individual consciousness is God's grace. And varying with man's psychological structure and the special situation it may influence him either as the highest intensifying motive which liberates the utmost power up to the point of sacrificing earthly life, or as a quietive which results in patience or aquiescence in an unalterable value determination. Fate can, therefore, be spiritually resisted by a very strong rebellious will, or be patiently endured in the guise of divine Predestination. Thus insofar as Fate in the religious attitude is not grasped theoretically as mere causal connections between circumstances, but as the result of the highest value order of the world and in this way subjectively 'understood' or at least divined as meaningful, Fate is altered for the religious man into Predestination. Upon a primitive level it is made comprehensible through anthropomorphic pictures. On a higher level Predestination is nothing but inner guidance of man to whatever must be truly valuable to his perfection. Similarly with prayer: on the primitive level it is a magic means to influence the way of things in accordance with one's own longing; on a higher mental level it is only a plea for power to value. And since subjective illusion changes nothing in the course of the world, the effect of prayer lies only in the power which it gives to renounce one's own life and accept a given fate, or to maintain, even in spite of this fate, a belief in the highest value. Prayer thus belongs in the context of soul culture. This finding of power is experienced by many people almost catastrophically as an upheaval of deeper life energies; it may however consist in a quiet inner development of the soul. The natures of the first sort, 'twice born men',[1] are then motivated by such experiences of upheaval. The others — acquiescent souls — seem never to reach resolutions or decisions, but instead their activity is a spontaneous overflowing of divine spiritual forces. This form of motivation one might call a 'Daimonion', which need not, as with Socrates, be restricted to warning.[2]

[1] Begbie, H. *Twice Born Men.*
[2] The distinction is elastic insofar as a period of latent religious feeling usually precedes this upheaval, just as quiet growth sometimes urges somewhere to deeds.

People who have once felt what they call 'grace', this suffusion of the entire being with the highest value, strive again and again for its blessedness. They consider their approach to or retreat from this condition as nearness to or distance from God. Usually the ethical experience accompanies it. Then the latter is experienced as consciousness of sin, guilt and discord with God, and the former as a feeling of approbation, reconciliation and salvation of the soul.

Finally in all of this there is a factor which refers not to the subjectivity of the soul but to the harmony or discord of the world with the highest value demands of religious consciousness. These attitudes to the world are on the lower level (where too they are religious) optimism and pessimism. On the higher level they determine the degree of divinity or earthliness, sanctity or impiety of the total world-course. But the unifying function of religious behavior is always the affirmation of the highest total value of existence, whether opposed to the actually experienced course of the world or through a deeper interpretation of it; whether in finding God or conquering the world; whether by surrender to present fate or in inner elevation above its externality and indifference for value. He who has quietly acquiesced, as well as he who passionately resists, may be religious, for, both find in their behavior spiritual salvation and thus power.

The purest examples of these religious motivating forms are found in mysticism and pietism, where religiously interested self-analysis and psychology reach their climax. To elucidate this statement I cite the biography of Jung-Stilling, which offers a wealth of examples for the unique structure of religiously determined decisions of life. With Stilling, its basic form is markedly quiescent. Man is not to act but God in and through him. 'He expected a sign from the Heavenly Father for, since his motive for study was pure belief, he could follow his own will in nothing.' But this distrust of one's own 'sinful' nature is now mixed, in the pietism of the eighteenth century with an almost impersonal interest in one's own impulses, which often enough are charged to God's account. 'It would be terrible if God put impulses and interests in my soul which his predestination forbade me ever to satisfy.' Nowhere does one see more clearly than in Jung-Stilling that this type of motivation may coexist with objective immorality. Stilling continually let God pay his debts.[1]) His marriages were always contracted under the influence of an impulsive emotion, which he blamed on God's causality. Later, when the rationalistic trait in him became stronger, he himself judged these decisions as 'impious', 'for it is the highest duty of a Christian to test under the guidance of predestination every step and especially the choice of a spouse according to the rules of sound reason and propriety, and when this has been done sufficiently, to await God's blessing ... Thus religion and love were combined in his wife's hysterical whims. Neither her parents nor Stilling knew anything of all this. They looked upon it as divine revelation and effect, and followed ...' And even later, Stilling always prided himself on having 'in the main done nothing to determine or decide his fate.'[2])

The same basic type reappears in a much purer form in the Herrnhuter of a higher order, in the *Monologues* of Schleiermacher. But I should have to analyze the entire book to prove that this form of 'introspection', which is directed to the infinite element in one's own soul, leads to very unique consequences in the form of motivation. We are in danger of putting all this on a par with the aesthetic humanity of his contemporaries. But the totality of which Schleiermacher speaks here is wholly different. 'There is no action in me that I can fully contemplate when it is isolated, or which I could call a whole. Every action shows me my whole being; nothing is divided.'[3]) The controlling factor here is the reduction of all action to an inner action, to a total self-determination in the religious sense.

There is an ethics which corresponds to this unique form of motivation. We have already indicated, and shall develop in greater detail in the following part of the book (III), that to every sphere of life there is a corresponding onesided and specific ethics; but that the total norm, morality as a whole, never appears except in a religious meaning-context. Metaphysically speaking, morality is harmony of the individual with the highest world-meaning which he is capable of grasping. In a religious metaphor it is God's joy in man or the being made in the image of God ($\dot{o}\mu o\iota\omega\sigma\iota\varsigma\ \tau\tilde{\wp}\ \vartheta\varepsilon\tilde{\wp}$).

---

[1]) 'Who was it then who awakened the heart of this friend just when it was necessary?'

[2]) Read with this attitude the entire original.

[3]) *Monologen,* originaledition. p. 24.

Just as we have, besides the individual types and their specific religiosity, outlined abstractly the religious type as a special form, it is also possible to designate the unique form in which specifically religiously oriented ethics appears. For, this process in the soul, which is the object of a special methodological culture and aims at salvation, is different from grasping the highest value in the competition of individual values of life. There is a oneness or receptivity for the highest into the soul. We call it purity. When the share of divine grace (beyond the achievement of man himself) is strongly emphasized, there remains as the final meaning of individual soul culture only to keep the vessel pure for both pain and happiness — 'whoever fulfills his destiny is greeted by both.'

IV

Without the mystery of individuation there could be no religion. The most solitary and the all-comprehensive confront each other in religiosity as subject and object. And for this reason the most unique of experiences, indeed perhaps identical with the experience of Fate is: to be wholly alone. We need not therefore make the presupposition that the significance of the world-meaning is multiform. But everyone experiences it in his own way and everyone has his own God. It would be impossible to count the number of types which result from the differentiation of the religious attitude. But several main guiding lines may be drawn. We cannot here classify the historically given religions according to their often very complex motives. In such attempts there is necessarily a reprehensible dilettantism if one starts for instance with the vestiges of earlier religions and their imaginative pictures instead of trying to re-live such life systems from within. Even high-sounding names are not exempt from such reproach. We attempt something more possible: the analysis of the kinds of religious behavior insofar as they are comprehensible from the subject's experiential structure.

As in all previous types we emphasize the distinction between creativity and receptivity. Some people form their own religion and others merely accept it. The highest form of the first type is the religious creative spirit, the savior or prophet who experiences a new revelation of the highest value within himself and if he is also a social nature — tries to inspire others. The 'others' however, if they are purely receptive become the followers of tradition, the orthodox, who believe something to be sacred merely because it always has been believed to be so and who answer each departure from the old values with the cry: 'Crucify him!'. The growth of Protestantism has shown what tremendous cultural crises may develop if free rein is given to the personal religious strivings of everybody.[1] Every orthodox system, however, teaches how, with the passing of original religious experiences, an entire religion may die and leave behind only an empty husk of power, a collection of meaningless symbols.

This distinction is closely approached by another. The followers of historical religion correspond to traditionalists, metaphysicists and mystics, to representatives of a personal religion. Anyone who approaches religion through history, which then is of course the history of salvation, demands an external revelation whether supernatural or thought of as a spiritual superiority. The representation of a religious type, the realization of the 'model' is to him an essential factor in the process of salvation. Thus A. Ritschl puts the religious emphasis on the historical Christ. But anyone who forges his own way to God is inclined to devaluate the historical and to substitute the eternally present valuations: the moral or the rational as bridges to God.[2] Intermediary levels are conceiveable between the two types.

Here a third point of view enters in. All value experience is related to objective contexts, and for this reason depends to a very high degree on theoretic insight. As we have seen, these objects might be due to productive imagination, which, however, must be guided by some mental giving of meaning. Religious behavior is never stimulated merely by the raw material of life, but always presupposes partial value experiences and formations

---

[1] For, the fundamental factor in Protestantism, if one follows its results through 400 years, is the liberation of the individual value system. And this development, and not so much the socalled capitalism, is the cause of the last great cultural crises. For, since this individualization, no truly comprehensive synthesis has followed. All great problems of life must be solved first on the religious plane. And this new synthesis is the task of Protestantism for the future.

[2] Cf. Lessing: 'Accidental historical truths can never become the proof of necessary logical truth' — and Fichte: 'The metaphysical but never the historical is our salvation.' (Works. V. 485).

of meaning which are related by it to a highest and final object. In other words: Before the religious experience appears there must always be given a specific direction of meaning, whether theoretic, economic, aesthetic or all three of them combined and elevated to the social meaning contexts.

If one bears this always in mind one may also classify religious natures according to the region which was the starting point or which fired the interest to the highest value or reverence. Usually listed here — and Max Mueller[1]) has classified religions on this basis — are: Nature, Humanity, and the Individual. Anyone who has followed our discussion must admit the inadequacy of this historical classification from the purely systematic point of view. For, it is left entirely undecided whether nature is meant in its theoretic, economic or aesthetic significance. There is a vast difference between a primitive sun-worshipper and a Spinoza or a Shaftesbury. The first prays above all to the life-preserving power of nature, the second worships its rationality, the third its beauty. The same is true of humanity and the self. A religion may be rooted in love or in expressly political and judicial motives. I cite here the national religions of war. Indeed it may create a world of gods from the ideal of human beauty. If one finds the highest in oneself, then with this mysticism of inner experience there always remains the question of whether it embodies theoretic or aesthetic traits, or those of ethical self-conquest, purification and self-deification. Therefore it seems more accurate to replace the crude object by the mental region in whose formation and meaning it becomes the occasion of religious experience. Thus in an abstract differentiation one must carefully notice whether a religiosity or objective religion is predominantly theoretic, economic, aesthetic, social or political. Indeed even within a historically given religion, which always shows a definite synthesis of these onesided value directions, there are different interpretations of its meaning. The rationalism of the eighteenth century reduced the Christian God of love to a God of truth and law. The Puritans avowed a God of battle, Schiller longed for the gods of Greece and Klinger sought Christ on Olympus. Herr von Rochow, on his side maintains that

---

[1]) Cf. The Gifford lectures on natural, physical, anthropological and psychological religion.

Christ is the most useful idea for mankind that is found on earth, and finally one may do business with the Christian God as formerly people had political dealings with Him.

We have philosophical agnostics and social workers side by side in modern Protestantism with political preachers and aesthetic enthusiasts. Not the idea by itself but the meaning context in which it appears is thus decisive for the classification of religious types.

Further classifications are possible according to the rhythm and method of religious experience. There are some people whose entire lives are accompanied by religion as with a quiet obbligato; Schleiermacher for instance, and others who go through religious excitement and depression like the majority of ecstatic mystics. In some, as we saw, the religious process is continuous, in others it appears catastrophically as a sudden rebirth.[1]) One is suddenly seized by God, another tries to grasp him, that is, he applies a methodical culture to his soul in order to create in himself the experience of God. Some people view everything religiously, even everyday things; others pass through both religious and seemingly indifferent periods. They set apart Sunday as a special day in their lives. With this rhythm of experience there are also partially connected such contrasts as that of supernaturalism and the immanent point of view which we reduced above to the degree of opposition between active value demands and surrender to the higher value context which is offered.

Finally, let us consider the question of how the distinction between the symbol of the highest personal and impersonal world principles is structurally determined. Religious experience as a mental occurrence necessarily takes place in a person. But it is not necessary to reduce its originator to a personal power. One may confront the world reverently without comprehending its meaningful context as the personality of God. The conception of self which is connected with the essence of personality has a limitation which, to some people, seems to make it appear inadequate of the highest. The personality of God is only a symbol of the way in which the spiritual is accessible to man. The religious tendency which tries

---

[1]) Cf. also James's classification into sanguine and melancholic, whose structural principle however is not quite clear. Further typical distinctions are made in my *Psychologie des Jugendalters* especially ch. XIV: Types of the youthful feeling of life.

above all to 'understand' the entire world complex as meaningful from the highest point of view, urges us to assume a person of infinite value-fulness as the world principle, even though the theoretic antinomy between personality and infinity cannot be overlooked. But there is also a 'selflessness' which interprets the course of the world outside of all sociological categories of personal intercourse. One may, finally, love one's fate and honor it as 'destiny' without thinking of it as derived from an anthropomorphic will to value. Just one thing always appears as the heart of personalism, that it is our duty to give necessity a meaning and receive it into the value world of our subjectivity as if it had been expressly formed for our highest destiny. Then God is nothing but the highest personal meaning-giving element in us. — Anyone who says however that the world is meaningless only says so because of a deeply disappointed expectation of meaning. And this too offers a genuine religious type which we shall take up in conclusion.

V

We may imagine a religious attitude in which the highest experience of value arises from the rejection of a supposedly highest value which tries to force itself upon the soul. If inner agreement is denied to the highest value of the experiential context then we have before us a pathology of the value life which we can no longer treat by our psychology of meaning. This phenomenon is called, in religious terminology, 'sin against the Holy Ghost'. It is quite another thing if the transmitted highest meaning of the social environment is attacked from a longing for and divination of something even higher. This is only apparently irreligious. For, in the form of a fight against present religion we find a higher religiosity which, so to speak, would only try to reject the name which has been used in vain. One may be irreligious due to a speculative desire for knowledge, to a materialistic passion for enjoyment, to aesthetic illusionism or to a weak surrender to the practice of human life. Here too we are dealing with disguised religiosities of a simpler level which do not understand themselves. One may, however, be irreligious expressly from religious motives. As a rule this contains a rejection of the traditional religion of a cultural circle:

'What religion do I avow? None of all those
Which thou namest. And why none? Because of religion.'

The positivistic movement with its rejection of transcendental religion has nevertheless created a new sociologically and immanently founded religion of humanity. Thus as early as Comte and later with Guyau in his book *L'Irreligion de L'Avenir,* and with Nietzsche it can be clearly felt that their irreligion only strives toward a higher religion of power and of proud humanity, just as his amorality strives toward a higher morality.

But this inner opposition is rooted still more deeply if it is not stimulated in given forms of religion but is born from the experience that the world, measured against our highest value demands, is meaningless. But this too does not imply a denial of religion itself, but only the completely resigned retreat into silent subjectivity. From what has been said, it follows that atheism need not be irreligious. For, the symbol of God does not necessarily belong to the phenomenal appearance of religion. Atheism is of an independent interest only when it denies not God but the meaning of the world. Even then it has a specifically religious factor namely a silent protest against something which one cannot wholly escape, or a sorrow for something which one has lost with great pain. Jean Paul once held the illogicality of atheism before his soul by playing with the idea that there is no God. His *Rede des toten Christus vom Weltgebaeude herab, dass kein Gott sei*[1]) is for him only an emotional testimony to his unconquerable belief. Thus there is generally some belief, even in genuine atheism, at least a belief in one's own absolute subjective God who has dethroned all other gods.

We are now confronted by the last question of religiosity: what happens when in the innermost heart of a man every value certainty is lacking? In this lies the complete renunciation of the religious attitude. If it is based upon pure suffering and subjective flaccidity then it does not found any type. But even this can finally become the consciously willed philosophy of life: nihilism, even practical relativism (which must not be confounded with the merely theoretic indecision as to how one shall found values intellectually) assert that life has no meaning. But one

---

[1]) Selected works. Berlin 1847. Vol. VIII. p. 336.

must examine this statement more closely. A man of this type may state his conviction in all honesty, though how far it is possible to complete the round of even a single day with such a belief is questionable. And it almost seems as if even this 'confession' contains a sort of deepest blessed certitude. Anyone who can no longer call a God his own gives himself over to the devil. And his essence is not real value indifference but a value reversal. Only if some one could say: 'there exists no genuine value', could irreligion have taken entire possession of him. But no such man exists.

PART III

CONSEQUENCES FOR ETHICS

1
THE ETHICAL PROBLEM

A psychological investigation has neither the right nor the capacity to make ethical value-judgments. It considers the structure of types only in relation to their inner legality, and never from the point of view of their moral value status. And if, in the preceding section, we occasionally touched upon the ethical region it was because morality too has its psychology. There we judged the moral value by popular standards which imply certain value accents in the words and idioms themselves.

But we cannot be satisfied with this if only because some readers have probably missed the specifically moral as a seventh type. For, it is customary, especially among the followers of Kant, to rank the moral with the logical and aesthetic. As early as Plato we find the Ideas: the Good, the True and the Beautiful together, the Good being the highest. Others add as a fourth the religious idea of Holiness. But no matter how differently the relation between the three or four ideas is conceived, it is everywhere assumed that ethics constitutes a specific class of values.

Our conception departs from this traditional one, and its center is that morality does not represent a special sphere of life, but only a form which may or may not be felt in all spheres.[1] To follow this train of thought one must, however, remember that in our investigation we always begin with the most elementary meaning directions. The factor which we have called 'political' does not entirely explain the complicated structure of the state. Similarly, we must not expect that the factor which we designated as the

---

[1] It cannot surprise us that a close relation between morality and religion may appear in the result. (cf. p. 79 ff.) The moral values share with the religious a character of finality and totality. And when we go back from the values which the soul posits to the value of the soul thus achieved in the world order, the moral indeed resides in the religious.

elementary meaning of morality should be identical with any historically given 'system of morals'. Instead we must here create the pre-conditions by which we can finally understand even the most complex phenomena of morality.

To this end we shall proceed again, in accordance with our isolating and idealizing method, to develop the moral element by means of a gradual composition of the meaningful factors which go to make it up.

A few preliminary definitions are necessary. The expression 'value' has many different meanings, the most comprehensive of which includes all of the following three special interpretations. We may designate as 'value': (1) a value essence i. e. a qualitatively determined general species of value, such as the economic, moral or specifically religious. Opposed to these value essences are two forms of actualized values: namely (2) the realization of a value in a material object (or process) which, besides its other qualities may participate in a value essence so that the latter 'appears' in it (the object of value); and (3) the actualization of value in a real psychological subject as an experience of value or an act of evaluation, in which too some value essence may be present. The term 'value direction' may be used to express this latter meaning, i. e. the constant determination of evaluation according to its species.

'Values' of a personality, unless further qualified, mean the unitary phenomenon that a graded complex of value directions has taken root in the constant value disposition of a real subject. Within this meaning one may also speak of the value constitution or the person's total value-direction. Then one means the gradations of values in the constant value dispositions of a being, perhaps we might even include here the single real spheres of objects to which his value-estimation is permanently directed.

One might further distinguish between value determination of character and of behavior. The first consists in the enduring value form which is present in the person's character above all in his 'attitude' which is an essential value set; the second consists of the individual decisions which he makes under the influence of fate and environment. These decisions are subjected, in himself and in the judgments of others, to certain value points of view. The real individual evaluation or the habitual value direction which guides man's self-determination I shall call 'motive'. In this chapter we shall principally confine ourselves to that form of personality evaluation whose criticism is directed to the self-determination of behavior and character, that is, the formation of motives. The unique quality of a motive, in contrast with the feelings previously so beloved in ethics is that it includes the general value essence, the individual act of will and the intended real object of value (or at least the conceived result). Insofar, however, as the decisive factor is not the real object itself but the essentially determining species of value (the first-named factor) ethical judgment, as Max Scheler has decisively proved in opposition to Kant, is freed from the individual purposes of man in the actual world and transferred to the value essences which influence his attitude. For, it is the general value essence which classifies in a definite value region both the decision and the aim. It does not always depend on man and it is at present ethically unimportant whether the intended result (the aim) is really achieved by means of the expedients chosen in accordance with causal laws.[1]) When we say that the moral value character is dependent on the kind and height of the value essence which plays the decisive role in the motivation of a man, we mean that the highest value which can be experienced by a personality is identical with his moral value. Morality, then, is self-determination of personal character and behavior through the highest value. Granting this seemingly simple and obvious theory only two questions remain open: (1) whether man always voluntarily strives toward the objectively[2]) highest value, and (2) whether this form of unopposed striving toward value is the rule.

We shall see that neither the first nor the second is invariably the case. And since it is not always true, it cannot be considered as the decisive criterion of morality. Consequently Kant was right in seeing the specific moral factor of consciousness in the normative one, i. e. the experience of duty.

We approach this conclusion by means of a preliminary train of thought. Assuming that there were a being capable of experiencing only one kind of value, for instance the economic (that

---

[1]) Society moreover considers a certain incapacity for thought, a moral failing; indeed even in law ignorance is considered no excuse. (But for the time being I shall not consider this standard).

[2]) Objective in the critical sense developed on p. 7.

is the value of utility) there would actually be no destiny for him except that of seeking the maximum of utility. 'And if it is his urge it is his duty!' The aim which he strives for is unqualifiedly identical with what he could demand from himself. At most one could only maintain that a kind of specific failure in duty occurs if the person is satisfied with a utility lesser than the highest attainable one. Laziness, wastefulness and indifference are terms of disparagement which one could apply to such a subject; but not lovelessness, for instance, because according to our assumption he is incapable of social value experience. If, on the other hand we picture a being whose value experiences are limited to those which we have called social, and if we assume further that such a being could exist by love alone, he would have no duty except that of love and must be called moral in proportion as he follows this highest command of his nature.

But these are mere constructions. Man is not one of those creatures who live only in one class of values. Different experiences of value meet in his consciousness and there is thus a conflict not only in regard to the rank-order of values of the same class but also in regard to different classes of value. Values which belong to the achievements of cognition may conflict in the development of life with those of politics; the egoistic-economic with the social, and the religious with the aesthetic etc.

Before following this problem further let us construct a human being who comprises all the value directions, and whose attitude and behavior are equally and simultaneously determined by all of them. Such a being would still be a man but, within the limits of humanity, he would be universal — 'would be called Sir Microcosm.' This Faust-like nature would live in the completeness of his value tendencies and wholly fulfill his destiny only when he simultaneously satisfied all his mental urges to the highest degree. One could not speak here of duty, except of duty to universality and superhumanity.

Thus, neither the wholly onesided value personality nor the manysided one offers any problem. The fundamental ethical phenomenon, then, appears only in a being who is both manysided and limited. In man's mental structure there are many value directions. The limitation of his psychic and physical powers does not allow him to live in all of them simultaneously to the highest degree, but, on the contrary, his value tendencies limit each other and perhaps furthermore belong to different levels.

We may express the result of this consideration as follows: specifically ethical experience originates in conflict. Conflicts are not unique phenomena in the context of moral life but they are the pre-conditions of ethical experiences. Two more factors must be added, however. Secondly, as long as only subjective values participate in self-determination, the decision to follow the highest in a conflict would only have subjective value. If there is to be an objective moral standard, then the objective value and not only the chance heredity and environment of the experiencing subject must be decisive. Ethics is always based upon a comparison of objective (valid) values. Thirdly, we have from the outset reduced the objective value, in contrast to the subjective one, to a normative law of evaluation. The objective value is not always seen in the experiential context as an easily affirmed instinctive one, but the characteristic form of its appearance in consciousness is, instead, the experience of duty. This is true of every kind of objective value; but especially of moral values since these may be most purely cognized in conflict. Thus one recognizes the ethical by the normative character with which it stamps the higher or the highest objective value in a conflict of values.

It might be objected to the first point that the values not only conflict with one another but might unite to form value complexes of an ethical character. Thus, for instance, it is characteristic of the values of utility to arrange or subordinate themselves to a higher value species. The social and political value too might unite with the primary classes of value, as we have already shown in the types that the other kinds of value are not wholly excluded but are instead in a subordinated relation within the specific structure. We grant the validity of this objection. But just the last point made shows that in such cases the equality of the values has been abolished and a ranking has taken place in the synthesis. Thus there has preceded a conflict which has been temporarily solved by the specific ethics of the type in question. It is inconceivable however that different value directions should appear in a nature in equal strength or that they should be equally decisive for behavior.[1)]

[1)] If anyone were to cite here Schiller's well-known wavering between 'moral' and aesthetic culture, between the dutiful and the beautiful souls,

Furthermore we maintained that the objective value, by means of its normative character made itself most clearly felt in consciousness. And within every individual class of values we had to distinguish between subjective and objective values. The specifically economic value experience of an individuality, for instance, need not necessarily coincide with the objective economic value. One cannot say once and for all what is the content of the objectively economically valueable, disregarding for the moment the economics of society. One can only say that the objective value is the economic value which is grasped according to the act of evaluating economically and according to norms, that is, all present goods which are valued in accordance with the economic principle. The same is true of the other regions of value. The subjective and objective cognitive values do not coincide; an aesthetic experience need not be, in the fullest and highest sense, aesthetic; and the religion of happiness is not the same as the religion of the Good. Thus within one class of values we find evaluations which are made in accordance with and in opposition to norms.

If now we suppose that in consciousness different value-experiences which are merely subjective coincide and influence both attitude and behavior, the subjective decision will naturally be made in the direction of the value which is experienced as highest. But the genuine objective value can assert itself in the formation of motives only when it is characterized by the impressive experience of duty. Ethical duty in this case designates in the conflict of different values, the highest objective one. Even in these situations of conflict a normative law is active. But we must not define its content by means of the legality which dominates a single class of values, for, it demands a specific synthesis of different and partly conflicting value-directions which are of varying ranks. The normative law which regulates individual consciousness might be called the value law of life itself. Morality is nothing but the world-law effective in our breast which prescribes for us a valuable form of our own subjectivity.

So we agree with Kant that the decisive criterion of morality lies in the experience of duty which distinguishes from other

---

the obvious answer would be that in the very designation there is an implied ranking and that Schiller acknowledged this himself when he ranked highest a kind of duty to the beautiful.

motivating factors the objectively highest value-direction. We do not deny that occasionally a man may voluntarily be in accordance with the 'Good'. But then it is not clear, either to him or to others, whether he would maintain the same direction under stronger temptations. What the overcoming of temptation is for the ethical experiential world, namely the proof of loyalty to what is moral even in a conflict of impulses, becomes for the ethical theory, the criterion of morality. The moral factor is recognized by its normativity. The norm does not create values but regulates their influence in experiencing consciousness.

We shall leave to the fourth and fifth chapters the final difficulty; namely the question whether the moral norm enters into any random and undeveloped consciousness as real experience and whether one might morally demand something which is not even conceived of in the experiential structure of the man in question. Scheler has characterized this problem in the distinction of ideal and normative (i. e. imperative) duty.[1])

Up to this point we have only sketched the general essence of ethics. The most important result for us is that the moral does not represent a content of life which goes beyond the value regions that are known to us, but that it means instead the regulation of these values with a view to that which, if we subject our attitude and behavior to their command of duty, gives the highest value to our personality. *Morality is thus recognizeable as the command of duty which is added to the value-content of life. But in regard to its content it is the personal direction to the highest objective value which completes our being when we intend it.*

This however is only to state the problem. We must ask further whether criteria can be given which justify the normativity of one value direction rather than another.

It was at first doubted whether value-experiences of different classes, as for instance the aesthetic and the economic are commensurable; that it is ridiculous to ask which is greater eight yards of length or six degrees of warmth. We shall not scoff at this objection but must say that the value-directions meet in the same consciousness and can be compared in their significance for the unitary self as a mental center. One cannot express their com-

---

[1]) op. cit. p. 187.

parability in a scale of unities (as Meinong has attempted) but one may assert the 'preference' for one species of value or one value-complex rather than another. Can this preference be reduced to simple principles of choice? In the process of our investigation we must ask first of all whether the attitudes (that is the value classes) can be expressed in a graded rank order, or whether only wholly concrete valuations can be measured with one another or whether — and this is the intermediary possibility — certain value-complexes are always and everywhere preferable to others; and finally whether normative preference is still somehow dependent on the individualized structure of the soul where this moral act of evaluation takes place.

To approach these difficult questions a little more closely it is necessary to ascertain on what principles the present ethical value-systems (in the form of theories as well as actual facts) are founded. Then it will be easier to take up the fundamental principles of evaluation. In the following chapters we shall, therefore, analyze, in accordance with the same procedure which we have applied to the types, the mental factors which are contained in a 'morality'; that is, in a habitual and final system of ethical values which may even have been formed into maxims.

2
THE ONESIDED SYSTEMS OF ETHICS

The ethical problem would be greatly simplified if it were possible to emphasize one class of values as the specifically moral one or even to reduce all other values to it as the finally affirmed one. This attempt has actually been made with every class of value, not only in theory but also in ethical practice. There are therefore as many onesided systems of ethics as there are attitudes, so we need only to summarize what we have said about each attitude in regard to its specific ethics.

1. Corresponding to the economic type is the utilitarian system of ethics.[1] It represents an attempt to reduce all values to those of utility: that is, to make everything fundamentally subserve maintainance of life and adaptation to environmental conditions. The

---

[1] In regard to terminology I mention that I understand by Hedonism the theory which regards the feelings: [i. e. the feelings of pleasant and unpleasant] as the sole criteria of morality, quite regardless of whether pleasure is viewed as the accompaniment of the act or the reflex effect of the result. By Utilitarianism I mean that system of ethics which sees the only motive of purposive behavior in values of utility and thus correlates the moral and the useful. It is secondary whether one refers to one's own use or the benefit of society. (Egoism plus Altruism equals collective utilitarianism). Eudaemonism on the other hand seeks the criterion of morality in the total satisfaction-fulfilling value and meaning which is reflected from the result of activity guided by value to the subject and the formation of his motives. As many levels of Eudaemonism are conceivable as there are levels of human total satisfactions. Energism is a kind of Eudaemonism which finds the moral factor in the act and its value content itself and not necessarily in the actual result. — All these forms of economic ethics confront the ethics of duty; the latter starts from a different point of view but may finally coincide to some extent with the higher forms of Eudaemonism as soon as the thought is added that the ultimate satisfaction of man is found in being and doing what he ought to be and do.

apparently discordant moral evaluation in the historically given systems of morals is harmonized, by a theoretic procedure of translation, with the accepted fundamental principles. And to this end classic models are used. Just as the Epicurean conceived of morality as a kind of balance of happiness, they make here a balance of utility. It has been shown, for instance, that anti-social behavior is injurious to the agent himself just like error and dishonesty. Collective utilitarianism develops if everyone acts in accordance with his own benefit but is also forced to consider the good of others for his own sake. As a rule this is reduced to a biological foundation of impulses and instincts. Conscience is finally represented as an inherited social instinct which contains unconscious purposiveness. Thus there seems to appear a connected, strictly logical system of morals in which, through the whole evolutionary process, utility is always the criterion of genuine evaluation.

And indeed the prevailing system of morals not only condones but demands the striving for one's own good. If anyone neglects his own life, his house, his clothes or his business, society usually blames him. Only in a community of recluses, of beggar monks or of ascetics would the moral judgment be different. Economic egoism may therefore belong among the positive ethical values. There only remains to ask whether it can, alone and to an unlimited extent, be called moral.

The answer must be in the negative. And this because of the simple consideration that utility is not essentially a final but only an intermediary value. The maintainance of life is a *conditio sine qua non* for the actualization of all other values. And consequently economic values are always to a certain degree the most urgent but not the highest.[1] In Plato there is a statement made by Socrates to the effect that doctors cure people without asking whether it is a good thing that they should live. And really it is always a question what is the worth of life, which is preserved by economic means. If life in itself, regardless of how one lives, is an independent value then of course economic values are final. But civilized ethics has progressed beyond this point of view. The man who can in certain circumstances renounce life in order to

---

[1] Gossen's law of final utility which has been evolved out of an isolated economic theory of values, grades within the economic the kinds of needs only in accordance with their urgency.

create a mental value is no longer utilitarian; or better: he is so only to the degree in which he is capable of fulfilling his highest value destiny. The values of utility point then toward an ethical value of its own, and from this only is the ethical character reflected onto the economic region also.

2. Corresponding to the theoretic type is not the ethics of truth (this being instead a branch of the social ethics) but the ethics of general legality. Its essence is the formation of behavior into a closed system, the achievement of inner consequentiality and consistency of personality. Thus the values of objectivity and of legal order are elevated to the highest determining powers of life. To be moral is to live by maxims.

There is no doubt that consistency of behavior is a genuine ethical value regardless of whether we are dealing with a law identical for all beings (as rational creatures) or whether it is a definite law for individuality in its specific structure (as for instance the law of gravity is identical everywhere on earth but the specific gravity of bodies is different). But few will agree with Kant that this consistency, or autonomous normativity in accordance with general laws, solves the whole problem of morality. The proof of general causality in the theory of cognition does not explain all of physics, nor, similarly is the ethical value problem solved by a metaphysic of morals which only gives the form of ethics, that is, its logic. The point is rather to say from which value content one should derive the general maxims of behavior. Our position in regard to Kant's ethics is thus a divided one insofar as we believe that he has (1) correctly designated the criterion of morality in the normative experience (in its character of duty); and (2) that he has developed a onesided form of ethics, namely that of consistency of behavior united with the ethics of freedom which will be mentioned later (cf. above p. 201), but that he has not done justice to the entire scope of the ethical value problem because he has confined himself to the theoretic type. Legality, rationality and identity of personality in the will to value are part of ethics but only part.

3. Not very different is the third onesided form of ethics which corresponds to the aesthetic type; the ethics of inner form. Its essence is the binding of individuality and the universality of experience into a totality, an inner whole in which every impulse of life is correctly measured according to its importance for the personality.

The striving for inner wealth of experience and harmony, for calokagathy, for the μέτρον ἔχον of Plato and for the golden mean of Aristotle, for the aesthetic balance of form and matter, of reason and sensuality is certainly a genuine ethical principle.[1]) But it cannot be carried out without the others, for, if we speak of the proper form and harmony of values the latter must enter into ethical experience. As Shaftesbury has correctly pointed out we must find, for instance, the mean between egoism and altruism. But even between individuality (as a concrete principle of life) and the general validity of ethical maxims, correct balance must be aimed at. According to aesthetic ethics this is entirely a matter of natural taste which judges the proportions of subjectivity. But this is only possible if the individuals themselves and their ethical value content are given to the judging taste. Otherwise we have again the dangerous morality of good instincts and of the heart, whose subjectivity has always been the fate of 'Werther', 'Allwill' and their noble successors. Again only a form has been mentioned, and it almost seems that Kant was right when he asserted that the essential characteristic of ethical consciousness is not only normativity but also formalism.

4. Morality is usually thought of as a product of social life which would immediately disappear if men lived in isolation. That one might have duties toward one's self does not seem to occur to the average man, and consequently solipsism is put on a par with complete immorality; though as a matter of fact if all seeming existence were within myself, the responsibility for the whole world would rest on me and so my conscience would have to be much finer. But the ethical attitude of Christianity, love for one's neighbor[2]) and morality are regarded as practically equal. To do something for another person is equivalent, according to this point of view to moral action. The morality of neighborly love has lifted itself above all other forms of morality. And in the context of this Christian value system self-denial, self-surrender and love are regarded as the main virtues.

---

[1]) For further explanation of this type cf. the introduction to my book *Wilhelm v. Humboldt und die Humanitaetsidee*.

[2]) I remark in passing that I mean by altruism only the attitude toward another which remains on the level of values of utility (cf. above p. 58 f.).

And indeed, to this social type there corresponds the ethics of helpful love and loyalty. And one might formulate its categorical imperative as — live for the other person.

Certainly this embodies a genuine ethical principle. And indeed we have seen that the special emphasis of love in the highest sense is justified by its close connection to the religious. A turning toward the value possibilities of the other soul is based on the sanctity of all life and this belief is genuinely religious. But the principle must be correctly understood and reduced to its meaningful sphere of validity. It has frequently been pointed out that a world where each person always sacrificed himself for someone else would annihilate itself. Love is only a shell in which value should appear. As we have said above, love founds community in value. This cannot, therefore, mean that the lover should sacrifice his own value content.[1]) The duty of love, or if anyone objects to this term, the meaningful impulse to love, only goes so far as that the mutual value belief should be furthered by it and the lover himself subjectively and psychically enriched, that is, made purer. Indeed even the renunciation through love of subordinated value contents of existence is not necessarily moral. For, life and culture would be extirpated if everyone destroyed and wasted himself through love. When love ceases to enrich and further the value-meaning of life it is no longer a creative love but the mortifying love of the transcendental mystic who rejects life and civilization. Thus the ethical principle of love and unselfishness is only one factor of morality. It finds its obvious limitation in the healthy self-affirmation and individual developing of power without which both life and civilization would be finally blotted out.

5. Thus the morality of self-denial is opposed by the morality of self-affirmation, self-appreciation and — insofar as the soul should only affirm the highest — self-control. Every morality which enjoys life and civilisation embodies the conviction that life, even in the individual man, is something positive and deserving of help so that one can joyfully develop all one's powers which subserve the realization of value The highest energy (not in the modern but in the Aristotelian sense) is something moral. Even Aristotle

---

[1]) The error is rooted partly in the fact that altruism as a rule embodies an element of renunciation, but only because economic goods may only be shared if they are divided.

thought of the self-development of man as an evolution from biological to mental make-up. Goethe has further enobled and spiritualized this natural principle into a purified self-realization. And since then the theory of the struggle for existence has brought it into still closer relations with the natural foundations of life. Nietzsche too built upon such an original biological basis in formulating the superman and the 'will to power'. But his creed of power contains a singular feeling of contrast to the herd morality just as if he had not been quite certain of his inner power and had only freed himself in anger from the early Christian table of values. At heart he too knew that the highest subjective power may also be a generous virtue. He only combatted the love which throws itself away, those who wallow in misery, the mystical hallucination that denial and self-annihilation are the highest virtues, and the popular standards of human values.

The will to power is thus a genuine form of ethics, and corresponds to the onesided type of the political man, in our broader sense of the word. We have, however, already seen that all power begins with inner self control. This we might call freedom. It signifies then the freedom to do one's duty, moral liberty in the highest sense, which is also subjection to the highest objective law of value and self-determination. The ethics of freedom, of autonomous avowal of one's duty also belong in this context. To be free from the lower impulses of one's own nature is the true morality of self-control, which originates with Plato and the Stoics, reappears in Christianity as mastery of the flesh by the spirit, and reaches its climax in the philosophies of Kant and Fichte.

But the moralities of love and of freedom share the fact that they are really only formal principles, which must get their content, namely the direction to the highest objective value, from somewhere else. For, in love the question is raised: in the spirit of which value should one love man? And in regard to freedom or power the similar question, which is only too often forgotten in political dissension, arises: freedom for what and in what value order?

Let us summarize the foregoing discussion. All previous ethical principles were in themselves dependent and onesided. The principle of utility referred to a higher value which it served. The legality of behavior likewise, as well as inner form, demanded a value-determining content for law and form respectively. Love and freedom were in themselves only socially founded attitudes whose content had to come from outside. Does the last and highest ethical value then only reside in religion?

6. It cannot surprise us that the content of morality may only be grasped by a religious ethics. For, we have said that the essence of religiosity is the relation of all value experiences to the highest value. Consequently, the essence of morality is the determination of behavior by the highest normative value which connects the person with the objective meaning of the world and by the gradation of the other values according to their contribution to the final value (hierarchy of values).

But we proceed at first as in the former onesided forms of ethics. Corresponding to the religious type is the ethics of blessedness in God, being beloved by Him or made in His image (purity). And by God we mean the revealing principle of the highest value, whether it is perceived in the objective world context or immanently in the depths of the soul. This ethics is differentiated in accordance with the variations of the religious type. The highest value may be derived from the highest affirmation of all positive values of life. It ranks the other values according to the proportion of religious content which each contains; in religious terminology, the nearness or distance of each to God. To be religious then is to devote one's life to the highest of these values. But the highest value may also arise in a rejection of all positive values of life, from their being outbid by a wholly inner, specifically religious value. Thus the ethics of world renunciation, of life rejection, of absolute subjectivity, indeed ultimately of complete depreciation of self is formed in graded order. So we might conceive at first two forms of ethics in the religious sphere: the ethics of the highest expansion of life and that of its greatest limitation.[1]

We have already seen however that those extreme religious types are the two ends of a scale within which the manifold forms of the dualistic religious type may be arranged. And corresponding to this latter type is a dualistic ethics, i. e. an ethics of yes and no, of expansion and limitation of life.

---

[1] 'Life' of course always means here mental life, not mere vitality or egoism.

And indeed every historically given system of ethics which does not actualize one of the extremes clearly contains both directions. We might simply speak of an ethics of 'Thou Shalt' and one of 'Thou Shalt Not' of which commanding and forbidding are the respective meaning directions. 'Creative morality' and 'restrictive morality' always conflict. Life is the material of both and is everywhere endowed with religious meaning so that the content of morality is everywhere and always religious. The separation of religion and morality is only based on the fact that morality guides the character and behavior of the subject in accordance with the value maximum, while ethical religiosity illuminates with the highest normative value the total of life and world and all active objective (overindividual) contexts.

Man would be a God if he could realize unlimited values in his character and behavior. And if he could realize no values whatsoever he would have no moral destiny at all. In each case he would be beyond good and evil but in a different sense. The ethical point of view only originates in the fact of his finity.[1] Because man is finite he feels the demand to broaden himself. But since he cannot do so infinitely he experiences a second demand, to limit himself in a meaning which is in accordance with some objective value. In the conflict of possible values he should follow that which is objectively higher which also means that value which gives him the really moral value. In the first case therefore ethics commands and expands and in the second — at least temporarily — it forbids and restricts, but finally uplifts and purifies.

Let us elucidate this by some examples. (1) The expansive ethics: a man whose character it is to live intensively in just one kind of values should draw the others also into the circle of his world of self-formation. If he turns only to economic values he is confronted by the expanding demands of the regulation of life, form, love and freedom. Assume however that he is directed to the lives of others, then he ought to form himself and give value to his own existence because this is the only way in which love receives true value content. Such an ethics fires Faust: he cannot

---

[1] I utilize this concept only as a heuristic construction and not in the metaphysical sense of the 18th century.

be satisfied with any value of life because he cannot simultaneously live in the other values also. He would like to be a superman, indeed a God. But his destiny teaches him that the moral fate of man has another side which one might call the tragic one.

(2) The restrictive ethics: a man who tries to live in different value directions simultaneously, finds himself in the conflict which arises from the finity of his being. One cannot at the same time search for one's own highest good and sacrifice oneself through love for another. One cannot strive simultaneously for highest truth and beauty, one cannot both will the greatest power and renounce it. If one value-direction, in these situations of conflict which in reality always exhibit a highly unique and complex character, is distinguished from the other by the characteristic of duty, then this value has an objectively higher rank order. The ethical problem which still remains unsolved is: upon what is based the character of this objective superiority of a value direction (not only the mere subjective fact of its being thus experienced)? We seek the reasons for duty in an objective rank order of values. Is such a one valid always and in all situations? And by what criteria can we philosophically develop this objective order which founds the law of duty? No matter how impressive the mere experience of duty may be, it does not contain the philosophical guarantee of its binding power.

We consider the objective rank order of values for the present only as a methodological idea and so may leave it undecided whether there is a gradation between the individual classes of value or whether only the value complexes which are created by concrete life (i. e. the personal value standards in their totality) can be measured with one another. For, as living beings we never confront solely one species of value. Rather, in accordance with our preliminary theory, in every section of life a factor of every value is somehow contained. Our very personality, regarded as an enduring (mental) structure is a hierarchy of values. And this is even more true of historical individual situations where we reach an ethical conclusion: factors of value are here distributed in a way which no science can calculate in advance.

Nevertheless we speak of different ethical ranks and clearly feel them in people of the past or of our own time. And this estimation seems to be based on some objective standard. It is perhaps possible to disclose at least the prime forms of preference and rejection whose complicated application we practise in everyday life. Before we go back to this source we must remember that the minute we enter the mental world we find a collective table of values. From the first day of conscious behavior, finished value judgments of the environment in regard to character and behavior limit us and influence the formation of our motives. As a given authority they oppose our autonomous decisions, indeed they develop their influence before we have achieved autonomy. It certainly is a case here of objective powers insofar as they exist and act independent of the self; but whether they can be called a pure precipitation of objective values in the critical sense will be seen only when we have glanced at their origin and development.

3
COLLECTIVE AND INDIVIDUAL MORALITY

The majority of mankind do not make their decisions immediately from a personal value certainty. Indeed such a degree of inner independence is perhaps confined to the ethical and prophetic genius. There are ready-made decisions for most value conflicts and we usually subject ourselves to them, if not in behavior at least with inner recognition of their obligation.

It is not easy to say who has made these decisions nor in accordance with what principles. They are founded by that anonymous subject which is nevertheless so important that we have created for it the special name 'public opinion'. Public opinion considers it wrong to break one's word, to lie, to have extra-marital relations, to neglect one's parents or to squander one's fortune. Public opinion here means 'society'. But its limits are not definitely determined, for it is by no means all of human society. Instead, the content of moral standards changes with different epochs and continents. Only this much is certain without any further investigation, that human beings who through regular co-operation and mutual activity form a group and have one civilization are always united by a common morality. But within the circle itself the content of this morality differs. The more closely a special group is united, as in a family for instance, the more specialized is the code and the moral value judgments which group opinion has formed in regard to it. And with each region of work or life a specialized morality is always connected. Thus there are specific moralities of trade, of scientific investigation and polemic, of war and even of robbery.

This fact is in itself an indication that the collective value judgments and norms of behavior are not forms of whim, accident or tyranny, but that they are in a meaningful context with the structure of mental social life, especially with its historically unique appearance. Considered from its highest significance the morality of a cultural sphere or a social group is the normative spirit which resides in it, the directive in accordance with value, of this whole, much interrelated objective life. Of course the reality of a social morality falls far short of this ideal.

Who is the anonymous subject, the creator of these value judgments which the individual finds ready-made when he is born or enters into society? Whence comes the unique real power which resides in these opinions without any legal guarantees of power or security by definite organizations?

Society itself has no soul, it cannot value nor judge, it can neither love nor hate. More correctly it can do so only insofar as it lives in the individual and by means of his soul. For the individual alone is certainly not the real carrier of these socio-mental acts, if only because he finds them existing as an objective power when he begins to lead a moral life, and because, under certain circumstances, he may come into conflict with this objective will. He is no more the creator of social morality than he is of that science, art or religion into which he has mentally entered, and to which, in a favorable case he adds a bit of his mind. Naturally, people have tried repeatedly to hypostatize the massivity of overindividual social mental powers as a unique life above all individuals. Indeed this objective mind has been thought to precede the individual one which is only a dependent phenomenon. These statements voice one side of the case correctly, but we must not overlook the other; namely that we grasp the overindividual context only insofar as it lives and acts in the individual. For, that objective life 'in itself' is, taken from the point of view of a theory of cognition, just as transcendental as 'Nature'. It is not correct to begin by mythologically recounting the acts of nature, but even in regard to this overindividual sphere one temporarily depends upon what falls within individual experience and only a complicated process of thought leads from single sense impressions to the building of the lawful whole which we call Nature in the scientific sense. We possess in ourselves the mental laws of construction with which we can rebuild Nature in our consciousness from insignificant data. This is also true of the objective mind, i. e. the historico-social total of mental alternate relations and co-ordination which is comprehensible only through the acts of our individual consciousness in which we fulfill the meaning of this objective form. But when we set ourselves for overindividual meaning, that is, when we follow the objective mental legality which has created it in a long historical process, something overindividual comes to life in our individual souls. We may, therefore, say that science as a mental norm lives in us, of course referred to or appearing in two real temporal forms; namely, the objective position of science and the subjective definiteness of our intelligence and knowledge. In like manner we may say that art lives in us even though we are bound to the real existence of artistic creations and our aesthetic capacity to experience; and thus too with economics and religion.

With the respective overindividual normative sets there is always connected an overindividual collective set. Not only the eternal law of mind lives in us but also mental community. Thus we know ourselves as members of an effectual relation of many experiencing subjects and as typical representatives of some community which works for civilization, from the narrow family circle, beyond class, genus and race, to human community. Finally, the overindividual collective consciousness and the overindividual consciousness of norm fuse in us to form a mental content which is superior to our mere individuality. Whether we confront the meaning of the sociohistorical mental life as individuals, or whether we make ourselves a part of it makes for important mental difference. In the latter case an overindividual mental element is active in us, a collective consciousness, whose facts are either in accordance with or in opposition to norms — for the collective form as well as the individual may either obey or disobey the normative mind.

Thus when I feel myself to be a member of a group with a definite historico-mental content the three following determinations develop in my subjective experiential context. (1) I am carried along by the group mind, coincide with it and feel its greater life in my smaller one, often wholly unreflected so that I might think, for instance that I myself am the brilliant poet and thinker while in reality it is only a developed language which composes and thinks in me. (2) I experience myself as an individual member of socio-mental alternate effectual relations which are always mediated by means of language and mutual psychological interpretation (understanding). (3) I, as an individual sometimes confront, unwilling, resisting, combating the collective mind which wants to be effective in me, in short: I can be either the carrier, receiver or antagonist of the collective mind. This very complex relation is still further complicated by the fact that I may belong to several groups at once which partly dovetail into each other (as the class and the race) or stand relatively indifferently beside one another, or serve antagonistic tendencies. These groups, as total forms, I understand only through personification, that is, by mentally interpreting them in accordance with the model of an individual experience or an act-context. But I must not forget that this shortcut is liable to error from the beginning. For, every group is a complex of mutual effectual relations of individuals in which there may be a mass of antagonistic tendencies and movements which have nothing to do with the central meaning of the collective form.[1])

Let us apply this to the problem of collective morality. In every social group there is created, by means of a continuous reciprocal effectual relation of individuals who work together reasonably in a mutual value sphere, a complex of value judgments on the attitude and behavior of the members. These value judgments are made not in the name of the individual but in that of the group. From life's content and its value determinations (which as historically real forms may also be called purposive contexts) there are differentiated certain points of view, value judgments and meaningful practical reactions in the mutual conviction of all the participants. These must not be considered as part of the unique normativity of any one cultural region, but refer instead to the normativity of the reciprocal effectual relation in which the entire collective mental content is implied. Insofar as we think, value and act in agreement with our community, the community judges through us every member by the specific value standard of whether the respective individual subordinates himself to or opposes the value meaning of the whole. If we designate for a moment a community's pure will to live and its higher will to culture by the short phrase 'social purpose', we have the very simple formula: moral value judgments, norms and practical reactions express what every member, in the name of a community, considers to be harmful or helpful to the community. But this must not be

---

[1]) For instance purely personal sympathies and antipathies in the frame of an objective working community.

interpreted to mean that collective morality reduces everything to economic or utilitarian values. It would be safer to say that it refers to the individual kinds of character and behavior insofar as they are opposed to or in accordance with civilization measured by historically given social culture. If one simply wants to call this 'social purposiveness' one must remember that even society wishes not only to live ($ζῆν$) but also to live respectably ($εὖ\ ζῆν$).

We must here remind the reader that morality (in contrast to law which has the express character of an externally regulative technique) by no means judges only the individual actual kinds of behavior but character as well, the motives of its members. It is really profound while law only delimits the external spheres of power, that is, is specifically rooted only in a single side of culture. Furthermore, morality in general does not excuse a person because he 'cannot help it' or because he is 'made that way' and acts accordingly. It is a limitation of Kantian ethics that it seeks the ethical only on the basis of reflective or rational individual motives. The entirely autonomous morality may only be understood in this way. Collective morality on the other hand, also judges the half instinctive impulses of man, perhaps it pardons an individual deed rather than the entire state of mind which lies behind it. Indeed it will forgive an error but blame stupidity. It judges the whole man with a view to his social cultural value even though he could not be other than he is.

Collective morality, despite its general value judgments and norms applies throughout to the person as a member of society. Only intelligence, as a personal theoretic attribute, and truth, as a virtue, belong to morality and not, for instance, the laws of thought and cognition. In the same way, the psycho-sociological laws of economics do not belong to morality though economic capacity and ability do. Whether a person makes good or bad poems is not a question of morals, but an unharmonious soul and a mean-spirited attitude are blameworthy. It is not the business of collective moral evaluation whether the world as a whole is good or bad, but whether the soul itself is so, and this, its religiously understood total character, falls within the scope of social moral consideration. If it were ever possible to systematize such a collective morality it would resemble a closed theory which ends in value judgments of persons and actions, in norms of character and behavior.

But all this only gives the direction in which the problem is to be found. We have said before and now repeat that ethics by no means originates only in the social life of man but that the individual also, taken by himself could be an object of ethical judgment, and that this takes place with the very formation of motives. What we have just now elaborated is however an important addition, perhaps the most decisive point of social ethics as such. Much is normatively demanded of a human being not in his position as an individual but because he is a member of society. Collective morality emphasizes just this side of man. It regards his value in the light of a social purpose. It would scarcely ask whether an individual were at peace with his God, whether he lived up to his standards in every single action, or whether he has carried his self-development to the highest inner, say aesthetic, completion. The social standard is too crude for this. So long as a person does no injury to general cultural good it is satisfied. Highly developed natures may look deeper into the soul and may make certain special demands of the individual. But the anonymous collective morality is usually satisfied with a very general average standard, because its gift of 'understanding' is not sufficiently particularized. Because of its whole cultural function it cannot be much more than the morality of the average.

If now we regard the matter from the consciousness of the individual we should strictly have to distinguish a dual morality; (1) what he demands of himself, and (2) what the group to which he is morally bound demands of him. The former, personal morality, may be either above or below the average of the second. Thus among artisans there is a certain general standard of good workmanship and reliability. Some fall short of these demands while others expect more of themselves. Similarly with sexual morality, in this respect society sets only very superficial standards. The individual may be even more superficial or more strict but in either case he comes much nearer to the facts psychologically.

Collective morality, however, especially in the first experiences of youth, does not always actually enter into the consciousness of the agent. It must be taught. If it is to maintain itself as an active agency it must, even in daily intercourse, be voiced repeatedly. Otherwise it is possible that an individual in a definite situation should not even know what society thinks. Just how the collective norm acts in individual consciousness is very important. One extreme possibility is that it is experienced as a wholly external demand to which nothing in one's own value consciousness corresponds. In this case it either has no effect whatsoever or is only carried out under the heteronomous pressure of social environment, perhaps mediated by motives which are foreign to the meaning of morality; for instance, that one does not want to be annoyed or anticipates business reverses or even ostracism. But it may also be that the collective norm coincides with one's inner will to value. Then either the individual sees it only as a demand which he would voluntarily obey through his better nature (say for his own sexual purity) or he is imbued with the meaning of social obligation and therefore abandons from social motives what he as an individual would not hesitate to do, (for instance, because he objects to the disintegrating effects of free love on other people and through them upon the community).

But we do not yet understand clearly the origin and growth of collective morality found at a given historical moment as a reality in mass consciousness and as a power over the individual. The ranking of values which has been made by collective morality for typical situations (and only for such) is based on value judgments which must be carried out in some individual consciousness. For, society only judges in its members and through them. Thus collective morality finally refers to individual decisions in questions of value, except that it is not here the individual who decides by himself, but he who thinks, values and acts in the name of society (the normative collective consciousness in the individual). This is in agreement with the fact that every new moral evaluation must once have been fought out personally, and the scene of this battle is the conscience of the individual as a member of society. The situation of conflict which we have regarded as the condition of every ethical decision is thus complicated by the fact that the collective evaluations which are already made also enter consciousness as demands. The individual who avoids this evaluation may do so in a double sense: because of weakness for instance, of sinful disregard of what his comrades' morality demands, or from a higher ethical consciousness which opposes the average morality with a strong moral conviction. But not all higher ethical norms are embodied in the future content of the improved collective morality. It may be that an individual only objects because he is one to whom average standards do not apply. They seem too general, too low or too superficial. Then too he is subjected to the torments of ethical conflict though he himself is the only one who is freed thereby. Only when the teacher of a new morality is a social nature who fights and suffers for others and wants to erect for them a new and higher table of values can the new norms gradually be taken up into collective consciousness and become valid for others.

The origin of collective ethical value judgments and norms is thus, after all, the individual consciousness, whether new standards appear in many people simultaneously or only in one person. In other words: collective morality also originates in personal autonomy, in a personal conscience, of course one of which a meaning relation to the cultural embodiments of the group is part. It is not true that conscience only appears on a high moral developmental level.[1] Instead, at least in leading mature natures, it is morally influential even in simple relations. Special demands are made of the productivity of social consciousness only because a highly differentiated culture always places human beings in new cultural situations; because it leads from country life to money and industrial economics, from rural relations abruptly to city life.[2] But even the oldest and most obvious norm of collective morality has somehow been fought out, and has at some time led to serious conflicts wiht still older customs. It has set son against father and low against high until it was accepted and fell in its turn before the eternally advancing normativity of mind. This normative mind as idea is eternal and we believe that we have completely shown the simple norms in which it is differentiated. But even the synthesis of these partial norms to complex total social norms of behavior changes with every epoch. The factual social relations always create new norm contents which must be studied anew for every cultural sphere and epoch, by means of understanding and des-

---

[1] Perhaps only this could be maintained: that social conscience is older than personal conscience. Every decision on primitive levels is still experienced as a group decision and felt with this sort of responsibility. And only on a differentiated cultural level has the individual really a world for himself.

[2] These claims are often not fulfilled. The power which creates the morals of the new society is often on such an alarming low level that it seems as if it could not master hurried new developments.

cription and, on the basis of this understanding, clarified. For, from the viewpoint of morality, the creative factor is not the actual power of society, but only the normative consciousness which adds to its own personal culture the meaning of social culture.

But if it is really true that all mental life is composed of simple prime motives it should be possible to find certain prime ethical acts, just as in the individual mental regions we have gone back to prime mental acts. For, ethical acts are nothing but normative decisions in value conflicts. Thus we are led back through all this complicated investigation to the simple case in which an individual finds himself asked to decide between two value directions. Which will he experience as objectively higher and normative? Is there always, within the species of values themselves, an objective preference which holds for all situations so that one might say: the social is always higher than the economic? Or can any kind of value be elevated to a preferred value depending on the historical, social or personal situation?

In view of the preceding exposition we must remember that the origin of all moral value positing is ultimately to be sought in autonomy that is, in an individual's conscientious decision. This autonomous choice may have been made from either one of two points of view which can be distinguished only in extreme isolation. Either we are dealing only with the personal ethics as if the value of a human being lay wholly within himself and depended on no social achievement; or we are here dealing also with the value which the individual as a mental being, has for the maintainance and genuine content of a group. Then the dominant collective morality also enters the determining conditions and the ethical decision results from the consideration of what one should be for others, even at the cost of one's own complete value development.

The formulation which we have finally chosen clearly indicates that the basis of all morality which is socially directed lies in social acts, in the manifold gradated union of the soul with the lives of others. A man who lacks this side or has let it atrophy, for instance the pure economic egoist or the eccentric man of power, has from the beginning an anti-social attitude. Society condemns such natures and even self-criticism may see in it a blighting of all life against which the innermost heart opposes the broadening norm: 'love thy neighbor as thyself'. But suppose a man is so indifferent in this respect that he is incapable of experiencing this value and cannot fulfill the demand of his associates? In such souls there may still be high values — they are above all born political natures — yet they remain untouched by the great trait of mutuality, they lack the comprehensive content which only develops in man when he feels himself to be a carrier of a great collective process.

We can thus understand why all group morality so strongly emphasizes social behavior. It is the ground, so to speak the mental direction, in which this morality develops in accordance with its most important destiny. But it would be false and onesided to conclude that morality is everywhere identical with love and surrender. Instead we here only open up the question: what is the content and the constructive (or world-conquering) power of this love? The social mind is only the vehicle of all this, the *conditio sine qua non*. Even an ethics of power would be impossible unless a consciousness of union were somehow at the bottom of it.

Perhaps it will now be possible to outline a chart of moral consciousness containing all factors upon which personal decision of conscience depends. For the time being we simply list them in order to develop these considerations in the next chapter, so far as they can be carried out without regard to definite epochs.

I. *Personal morality which is not yet referred to society* (Duties to one's self.)
    a) The objective rank of the classes of value indicated in the experience of duty.
    b) The actual intensity of value experience.
    c) The content of value experiences in relation to total experience.
    d) The individual soul structure as a variable factor.

II. *Social morality: referred to society* (Duties toward others).
    a) The ready-made collective norm (the judgment of the environment).
    b) The will to community (a social set).
    c) The individual's attitude toward the collective norms as effected under these influences.

Finally we must observe whether there can be an ethics which is ready-made and has an eternal content. We distinguish therefore:

III. *The dependence of morality on temporally real factors.*
    a) From the point of view of society:
        1. The average height of contemporaneous civilization,
        2. the consequently prevailing morality,
        3. its particularization and application to absolutely unique situations.
    b) From the point of view of the individual:
        1. its determination by the contemporaneous culture,
        2. its developed, constant moral inclination (its ethical character and stage of maturity),
        3. its present ethical situation.

It is clear from the beginning that a very general philosophical ethics cannot deal with the historical peculiarities and wholly unique configurations which have been named under the third heading. It must be satisfied to classify them among the factors by which concrete moral decision is influenced in its determination. It is, furthermore, obvious that the factors named under the second heading also belong in the context of a theory of individuality. For, the experience of duty to community receives many different interpretations depending on the ground of the individual soul structure which it strikes.

THE HIERARCHY OF VALUES.

A.

It is a far cry from the simple mental act in which one value is preferred to another, to the complex ethical situation of a man influenced by past civilization, a given collective morality and an entirely unique situation of conflict. But we must begin with the question of whether the value essences as such are already graded so that one is preferable to the other and felt as such in adequate experience. Starting from this question which seems to be wholly objective we enter the realm of conditions which complicate the problem. At first we consider the special objective-subjective experiential situation, then the structurally determined personal capacity for experience and finally the apparently wholly subjective, random value-perspective which can only be interpreted as an error or as pathological. Then however we abandon the isolation of the individual's position in regard to values and study him instead in the context of a historically developed concrete social morality which tries to offer, in the conflict of personal value decisions, many ready-made solutions. Our aim is to decide whether there are scientific criteria which allow us to form an eternal and unequivocal hierarchy of values or of concrete personal value standards.

We must therefore compare the value species or value classes with one another. It is doubtful whether there is a gradation between them, such that, for instance, every economic value is lower than every social value. If one assumes the impossible, namely that the value experiences of every quality can be measured by the same quantity of units, it might be that fifty units of economic value are worth more than one unit of social value, and that sixty units of aesthetic value surpass forty of religious value.

But these measurements must by no means be taken to mean that what seem to be sixty units in one would supercede forty in the same subjective estimation. We ask only for the objective hierarchy of values, that is, for a gradation which is valid for everyone and which is necessarily present in their experience if they all evaluate as they should. All this is only meant as a methodological hypothesis to lead us to the correct formulation of the problem. We disregard for the present all chance data determined by space, time and the individuality of 'value-perspective', and consider only 'adequate experience' of value.[1] Suppose, for instance, that I am not sufficiently mature to appreciate a work of art; everyone will admit that this is my fault and not that of the work of art, even though this does not exactly constitute a moral criticism. Or suppose that a temporary pecuniary difficulty forces me to neglect my friends. This does not mean that my friends are 'worth' less to me than my income. We come up against the same question which Plato[2] put to Protagoras: who sets the standard? And apparently the answer must be: no living man at all but a kind of normal value consciousness which must be constructed above man and every concrete situation.

Besides the attempt to compare value classes as a whole and objective value ranks independently of class on the basis of a quantitative scale which shall be applicable to all of them, there is a third point of view conceiveable; namely, the denial of the possibility of comparing values at all. There is some truth in saying that economic and aesthetic experiences, that is, a satisfaction of need and a contemplative joy, are of such different subjective quality that they are not comparable. Who could express in monetary units how much he values an affection, or state in units of love how much his suit cost him? We have already answered this objection by saying that all values meet in the same soul

---

[1] Adequate experience is only another way of expressing the more than subjective manner of experiencing in which we realize in ourselves according, to norms, the objective content of a value form or value context. The comparison of values absolutely beyond all experience would be meaningless.

[2] *Theaitetos* 161. Compare also in '*Protagoras*' (357) the part on the measureability of goods which is still curiously interpreted by many people as the foundation of hedonism while it is only supposed to lead it to a *reductio ad absurdum* starting with its own presuppositions.

and that they must be influential according to their content in forming character and behavior. We can, therefore, admit in this third case that the different value qualities cannot be expressed in quantitative units and that thus the second possibility is excluded; but maintain the belief that in adequate experience a different judgment of rank in relation to the total of life is united to the perception of quality. And this, and not measurement by units is what we mean here.

Hitherto all investigation has suffered because it treats values like mathematical units which are objectively measureable even though they may appear higher to some people and lower to others than they are in 'reality'. But values do not have any such existence apart from a psychic context. Instead, to our supposition that in the concept of adequate experience is contained the objective rank in which values are to be experienced, we must now add a more subjective point of view; namely, the position of the value experiences as actual processes in life, a position which necessarily changes even if every value is 'adequately preserved in thought'.[1]) Even though we value in accordance with norms we are always in unique situations, and value ranks vary accordingly. They enter into a perspective determined by the real subjective situation, into a form of appearance or experience. The new color which the value experience (previously taken in the absolute sense) receives through its relation to the total life situation of the subject, we call its intensity. We do not yet abandon the fiction of a normal man. But we disregard at present, with all apparent values and value errors, the unique factors of the personal type (its mental structure). But in a normal man, too, values depend on their meeting in consciousness. They receive a different intensity according to the total internal or external position. Thus with the concept of intensity we do not enter another region of avoidable

---

[1]) The addition: 'adequately preserved in thought' is to be interpreted as follows: situations in which mere impulse and blind passion rule arbitrarily are not to be considered, but we assume instead that the subject preserves a dispassionate survey of his life's value content even though the moment makes changing demands. We must for the time being presuppose the tendency to the full content of the participating values even if we observe displacements of intensity in the momentary experiencing because of unique situations.

value errors but remain for the time being in the region of norms and what is demanded by the value law itself. Fundamentally we only mean to indicate that value experiences, in the individual consciousness, are sometimes 'actual', and sometimes not.

For instance, we 'know' by a kind of objective value theory that the *Critique of Pure Reason* merits a very high cognitive value. But this value, which should and would appear to us in adequate value experience may not be present to us; either because we are not thinking of it at the time or because other interests make themselves felt which are so vital as to make this objective value very remote. Then its intensity in experience is strongly depreciated: as for instance, the experiential value of food when we are satiated, or the value of the state, if thanks to its continuous presence we have accepted it as a matter of course.

The stream of life brings first one and then another value context into the foreground of our experience and activity. If 'urgency' were synonymous with the rank of the respective value content one would either have to regard breathing as the permanently highest value or assume that the rank order of values ceaselessly changes. Noone will want to draw either conclusion so we shall try for the present (I) to arrange the kinds of value as constant units in a scale. But we shall see (II) that it is impossible to consider value wholly outside of a total personal life and that we must distinguish, besides the present experiential actual intensity, the content of a value experience in relation to the personal life total.

I

Our first problem then is to investigate the rank order of the classes of economic, theoretic, aesthetic, social, political and religious values under the assumption of adequate comprehension and equal intensity.

At first one might be inclined to say that economic values are the highest. For life must be assured before we can experience the others. We should therefore grant primacy to everything which subserves the maintainance of life, health and vitality. This answer however would be inconsistent with our assumption, for it implies a condition of the value-experiencing subject in which all psychophysical needs are wholly unsatisfied. In this actual special situation economic values naturally appear with incomparably high intensity. A completely loveless, ignorant existence would be physically possible, but the absence of economic satisfaction of needs would threaten life itself.

It follows that in certain special moments economic values are the most urgent. And if one tried to rank values according to their urgency one would arrive at a utilitarian scale of values such as Spencer has given in his introduction to his *Pedagogics*. This, however, gives to economic value an abnormal experiential intensity. One might contrast this case with the equally possible one of a mother who rejects her own urgent needs in favor of her child. Here the social value would have been posited in an enhanced intensity which is only derived from the real situation. For, economic goods are not 'valueless' even to a mother. We wanted, however, to start from the assumption that all classes of value appear in normal intensity — an assumption which is perhaps never really actualized — and then to make general comparisons of the preferences of value classes.

The very definition of values posits two facts: economic values are the lowest and religious the highest. For, economic values are values of utility. They always refer to another value which they serve, and they themselves have as much value as the former reflects back to them. They subserve the preservation of life. Thus they are worth as much as the life which they maintain. Even purely biological life is a genuine value. As soon, however, as economic values become an end in themselves, the meaning of life is reduced to mere enjoyment and comfort. Then material goods (including technique) subserve only the material maintainance of the body and psycho-physical comforts. The religious question of the aim in life remains wholly unanswered in this eternal natural round of acquisition and consumption. Man becomes what Plato says of this kind of desire, a leaky barrel into which one always pours water but which is never filled. How would it be possible to see the highest meaning of life in goods which are essentially consumeable and finite? But religious values, insofar as we think of them as adequately experienced, have been defined from the outset in such a way that there can be no doubt of their highest value. For they are based on the fact that all other values of life are related to its general and total meaning. What is this meaning? It lies as we have seen in moral value, in the normativity of the soul and the fulfillment of its true value destiny. This highest value surmounts space, time and matter: it is blessedness of the entire existence, complete absorption in the world meaning, mental fulfillment of duty. Whether this value experience is expressed in the belief that the highest value-fulness is immanent in space and time, or whether space and time are negated, and eternal infinite transcendance is postulated instead — both mean for the experiencing subject the greatest conceiveable freedom from the restrictions of finity and finality. All ethical religiosity is directed to the mental content of life and thus transcends what appears in space and time to a value context which places the soul in the final meaning.

So there remains only the question of how we should arrange the other values between the extremes of utilitarian and religious values. The character of religious values has already implied a criterion of value rank. It will depend on the degree in which space, time and matter are surpassed. For, the infinite metaphysical longing always goes beyond what is finite and limited to what religious terminology characteristically calls a 'higher world' or an 'other world'. Now we have already seen that the aesthetic attitude translates the material world into an imaginative one, and that the theorist converts it into an ideational one. In each case space, time and matter are surmounted but in a different way. The aesthetic attitude always refers to an imaginative space and time, and through empathic imagination frees the soul from its purely physical limits and transfigures matter. The theoretic attitude refers to an ideational space and time which are both infinite and transforms matter into ideas and essential relations. The first attitude still contains something of the vital soul impulse and its specific uniqueness. In the second there is, so to speak, a timeless consciousness which ideally can grasp what is most distant, though of course only *a priori* and not in concrete but in conceptual contemplation. Apparently neither one can be preferred to the other. They must be ranked equally. The aesthetic attitude is, so to speak, an intensive grasp of the world, a losing of oneself and all one's psychic powers in an individual contemplation. Science grasps the world extensively yet figuratively speaking only its frame-work and not its concreteness or dimension of depth. One cannot have both these attitudes in the same degree but must choose one or the other. And perhaps one might call (if one means by male and female world-principles and not men and women), one the male and the other the female road.[1])

A similar polarity is exhibited by the political and social values. Both the assertion of one's own value and devotion to other souls are necessary to the meaning of. life. But the value of these two attitudes, which we have previously designated as more formal, depends also on the content to which they refer: altruism, love which remains within the limits of utilitarian values is the lowest; and the love which is directed to another soul with all its life possibilities is the highest. Similarly, power which is effective only in the sphere of utilitarian values is lowest and that power which actualizes the religious meaning of life is highest. One might say, further, that the value of a region increases if it is united to a social spirit and decreases if it is only ego-centrically sought for the sake of personal power. For, the love which broadens an individual soul so that it can experience mutual values also frees it from finite limits. But here there appears also the question of how profound both are and it is by no means proved that love is higher in proportion to the number of people to whom it is directed. Finally, the value of collective power, that is, value united to the social spirit, is always higher than a mere individual claim to life. But this fact which is so important for the ethics of power does not belong in our present elementary context.

II

If, in the mental process of life, we have to deal only with the kinds of values as objective constants, the question of the rank order of values would be answered. But we have seen that this is not the case. Values are not rigid essences in the trans-subjective sphere but are always part of a personal mental structure. And it is impossible completely to separate them from this locus of experientiality. We have already seen that their actual intensity depends on their position in the experiential context. Though we have also observed that their changing real appearance cannot set the standard for the genuine valuation of their rank order. This only occurs when the single experience, which develops from the

---

[1]) The vascillation of Plato (in the Eros doctrine) and of Schiller (in for instance the '*Kuenstler*') is characteristic in connection with this value decision.

conjunction of fate and inner growth, receives an importance which fills not only one moment but influences the total meaning of life. Such a function of value experience we call its content.

The content of a value experience depends on more than the species of value. This can be clearly illustrated by a few examples. Even though the cognitive value ranks essentially higher than the economic, to safeguard the foundations of existence is clearly of a higher significance for a personal value total than to learn the Pythagorean theorem. Even though love ranks higher than power, the preservation of a cultural state is more important than the care of one soul and a single life. So even in spheres which might be regarded as essentially equal this point of view brings about differences of rank. A philosophical insight is necessarily nobler than a waltz of Strauss, a poem embodying comprehensive meaning relations deserves preference over some individual conclusion of comparative philology.

Now what is this 'content' of value experience? Obviously, it is its contribution to the value total, in the first place its importance for the totality of the value life, of an individual. Whatever is transitory from this point of view no matter how elevated is the class of value to which it belongs, does not take a high place in the rank order. But anything that is important in this connection, that does exercise a decisive function in mental life is elevated in this scale even if it seems by nature to belong to a lower class.

This reference of a partial value to the mental total of life we have previously called its religious character. Thus we speak of a religious value in a double sense: in the first place as its own species of value which may appear in specific objects and may thus be experienced. We saw, however, that all objects of this kind may already be pre-formed in other species of value; so apparently the second meaning is the more important one: namely, that values from other zones become religious as soon as they are related to the final meaning of life. Thus they receive a religious emphasis over and above their original value accent.

Accordingly the content of a value is equivalent to its religious significance. And though we previously placed the religious value only at the apex of the value pyramid, we must now also locate it on lower levels which thus curve in several places toward the top.

We said that whatever is decisively and constructively related to the total meaning of life has a religious value in the positive sense. We know nothing about this total meaning except what appears in a personal world-view. Thus this contribution amounts, for the present, to the share of a value factor in the totality of a personal moral life. And insofar as this precipitates its total content in a complete view of the meaning of the world which we call personal religion, we can justify our designation of the decisive value content as religious. If religion also assumes the form of a scientifically enlightened world-view we call it metaphysics. And thus we can say in conclusion: the rank of a value experience depends on its metaphysical content.

Not one of the individual spheres of value is wholly without a metaphysical content. By grading values as general essences according to the degree in which they have surmounted space, time and the limitations of energy and matter, in a word, mere finity, we have already ranked them from a metaphysical point of view. But when again we consider these abstract species of value as part of the total mental structure we see that in every partial region metaphysical factors may be contained. Thus, for instance, there is something metaphysical in the very struggle for existence which tries to preserve life in opposition to nature, the urge for liberation from mere material limitations. And again, the more metaphysical content an insight contains, the higher is it ranked in the context of life. The greater value as world-view is embodied in an aesthetic experience, and the less it is characterized as a mere passing mood, the higher it stands in the total order. A religious love (that is, one which is filled with this final content) even if it refers only to one soul, and a will to power imbued with religious meaning rank higher as we have seen than any other love or power. In other words, only the metaphysical is our salvation and value experiences have different contents of revelation. The more they reveal to us of a final world-meaning the higher is their rank in the value order.

The enormous complication of the problem is already apparent from the foregoing discussion. If we regard it from the point of view of a single individual who experiences the ever-changing play of value experience and normative value, we find that he must make the decision of genuine value ranks under consideration of three previously treated conditions: the natural rank, the changing experiential intensity and the content of values which 'he is capable of experiencing'. And even though we begin with the methodological fiction that the rank order of values represents a completely fixed objective system, the grasping of value ranks really takes place as follows: in the moral life process itself, in ceaseless value and norm experiences, conflicts and struggles, the assumed rank order is personally won. It is not a finished product but the final, mature and hard-earned result of moral life.

Then too we have so far simplified the problem by starting with the assumption of a normal human consciousness which is nowhere to be found. We must, therefore, still further treat actual situations and wholly subjective conditions. For, a real man as part of a temporal epoch and a historically determined society is already highly individualized. And he is still further so because, being just the person that he is, he has a wholly unique structure which may shade off into regions where the pathological and incomprehensible begin. This absolute uniqueness cannot be grasped by science which must always refer to typical legal structures.

In this section (A) we disregard the share of historico-social environment in the formation of a value system and consider only the individualizations of the human soul structure which we have described by the name 'Attitudes'. Their importance for the present problem is that in their inner structure a personal value system, either inherited or acquired, is already present. At any rate, the fact that in every individuality certain value directions are psychologically more important than others brings about a special perspective in regard to the assumed sphere of values. Or in other words: granting that an unequivocal eternal rank order of values is valid, the individual nevertheless contains partly acquiescing and partly resisting forces to grasp this situation. This fact can be studied especially well in the 'Attitudes', since they have been developed from their respective predominating value positions.

III

In contrast to the assumption which we made in section I of an adequate value experience we can call the point of view in which the individual onesided soul structures enter our discussion, the 'individual capacity for experience'. We have shown in Part II that the psychic structure prefers some one class of values. The psychological investigation itself showed that by nature some men prefer one species of value and others another. This refers only to the experiences which are subjectively highest and has nothing to do with the assumed objectively valid values. It is clear however that there may be a factor in the respective individual soul structures which either furthers or hinders the carrying out of the normatively demanded value. Each one of these types is predestined to a definite onesided ethics for which it is best adapted. But suppose that the assumed objectively normative value lies in another direction.

There are two possibilities: (1) Either the structure of the soul is so onesided that the objectively higher value does not fall within the personal capacity for experience and can consequently not be influential as an experienced norm. Then there is no ethical conflict for the experiencing agent. Instead the value judgment is made by another person whose nature is richer and broader. And here all formativity too ends. For, what does not exist even as a germ in the soul cannot be implanted from the outside. (2) In the second case the ethical demand is experienced on the periphery of one's own being, for instance in the form of an imagined possibility, which the better self conceives beyond the limited real self. But it lacks power to change this heterogeneous value into a genuine part of the soul, into an effective motive. Then there develops — in contrast to the tragedy of fate — the tragedy of character which has its origin in subjectivity. Such a man breaks down in the struggle between what he ought to and what he can do. Two forms of value confront each other in him: the objectively demanded but unattainable one, and that which is his own but is objectively inadequate. One might also speak of two moralities, one of which is overindividually demanded but for which psychological capacities are lacking and another individual one which is more impulse than duty.[1]) Let us elucidate this by a few examples. The pure economic egoist is hemmed in by the hindering limits of his peculiar kind of energy in regard to the

---

[1]) I remind the reader that we still (Sub A) disregard the validity of a collective morality and that therefore this entire tragedy is intended as a wholly singular experience which results from the inner distribution of forces.

commandment of love even though he is aware of it. The purely aesthetic man who is content in the contemplation of existence fails in any attempts to be economically creative. The purely political type finds his limits in the demands of strict theoretic objectivity. All these natures lack adequate experience for heterogeneous values. And it is not surprising that the respective norm does not achieve any influence over them and that they come to grief in trying to live up to ethical demands for which they lack the psychological pre-conditions.

Two important ethical deductions result from these facts: (1) that inner width and wealth of experiential capacity are essential requisites of morality (as has already been emphasized by Herbart and Th. Lipps) otherwise nothing higher can be evolved. And (2) that in order to grasp the higher and therefore normatively demanded value, an organization of psychic structure is necessary which has not always been recognized in its independent moral significance; namely, the moral energy without which the recognition and assertion of the highest value in the soul is impossible. Conversion, re-awakening, re-birth and self-conquest are the words with which religious and ethical language try to describe this phenomenon, which however as a final mystery, does not seem susceptible of further deduction.

If one considered only the purely factual process of experience without granting to the experience of norm a special emphasized significance, one would have to take everyone as he is and there would be no point in criticizing him ethically. But the theory of types does not allow of this construction. To look for their psychology does not mean to write their apology. The entire question of the rank order of values is meaningful only if it is something which lies above a given individual as an obligation. Otherwise the rank order of values must change not only, as it might appear from the second part of this book, with every value-appreciating subject, but even with every especially emphasized situation in life. And indeed this relativism seems to many to be the final conclusion of wisdom. But this would do away not only with every scientific theory of value but also with every meaning of morality. The man in the street would be the measure of all values.

To anyone who does not want to accept this consequence, there is only one way out, for, the supposition of an entirely adequate experience of value ranks is not substantiated by the facts. Everyone always experiences, in his internal and external situation, unique value perspectives. Everyone is singularly circumscribed in his individuality and destiny, and the content of values varies for everyone. If there is supposed to be an order of values which binds the individual in any particular situation, it is conceiveable only as a normative legality of evaluation. These norms however like the laws of nature — are in each case valid only in relation to concrete constellations, and their content varies in application to these actual conditions of their validity. Everyone lives in a thoroughly individual inner and outer situation of life. But whatever is objectively valuable in it is regulated according to laws of value which, though perhaps never 'understood', are experienced as moral demands on the level of life which one has attained.

And yet there remains the other difficulty. Suppose these norms do not enter as experienced actual demands into individual consciousness? What if they are only a philosophical construction of the supervising thinker who tries to adopt the viewpoint of the normative mind regardless of the fact that real human beings do not divine or feel anything of such demands?

And we must keep in mind yet a further possibility. The attitudes certainly have a lawful and therefore comprehensible structure. It is possible that a normative legality may take root in them applied to their unique kind of soul and moral developmental level. As yet noone has investigated these personal experiences of norm and their legality, just as ethics so far has only moved in very abstract realms above the reality of mankind. It may be, however, that there are processes of value life in the individual soul which are based entirely on value illusions, or even further on perversions of value positing. At this border of the pathological not only our critique but our understanding too finds its limits. Scheler in his essays on the overthrowing of values and elsewhere has illuminated this final subjectivity. But we do not want to follow that line of thought further because it would complicate the problem too much.

The essential result is clear without it: that the actual psychic structure of man can never be the standard of the rank order of values. He is always in a thoroughly subjectively determined perspectival relation to it. This subjectivity can only be overcome if normative laws are recognized, how — under given conditions — one ought to value. And this 'ought' has an entirely different source from that on which psychology depends.

This, however, makes it all the more important to ascertain how the individual finds this 'ought'. For, that it is not offered to him by a finished science is clear to everyone who knows the helpless position of our ethics. The norms which it establishes are usually formal, or at least artificial constructions foreign to life. It was because he saw this that Hegel distrusted the mere theoretic construction of duty. He rightly pointed out that one must study the process of overindividual mind in order to understand the relation of the meaning and content of duty to present mental life, that is, to the distribution of forces on the historical level.

Therefore we now abandon the abstract isolation of the individual man, and the fiction that from the beginning he confronts only value essences. We shall think of him in the context of social morality which has developed in the course of history and in which a form of the overindividually posited 'ought' appears. Finally, we shall touch upon the ideal system of values which reaches beyond this and approaches the meaning of the normative mind itself. Born from the objective mind it always reaches for the stars which though never attained are the final things by which moral will orients itself in the depths of the conscience.

B.

So far our considerations have remained completely in the sphere of personal ethics. We have looked for the gradation of values only in individual consciousness. We started with the assumption of an objective fixed rank order of values and the value forms which appertain to them; and called the meaningful set for the objective values adequate experience, from which we logically deduced the fact that the adequately experienced higher value as compared with a lower one would have to become a norm of behavior in the total development of life. Our next consideration was that values always appear in a total life context which changes the adequate more and more into a perspectival experience and we observed the entire value orientation from the viewpoint of duties toward oneself.

Now, by abolishing the previous isolation we enlarge our view to collective ethics in which not only duties toward oneself but also toward society are considered. Today this social ethics is theoretically referred to all of human society, though in practice it is entirely different. And it cannot be denied that there are certain variations of the content of moral norms in regard to existing cultural situations. They are not necessarily modifications but perhaps only reasonable particularizations of morality. As opposed to personal morality, the value order of collective morality is altered from the outset because a predomiant position is demanded for social values in the consciousness of members of an ethical group. We are now dealing with a social ethics; that is, a value order developed on the basis of social values, and no longer with a personal ethics according to which man faces all values with equal autonomy. The man who is subjectively bound to society is from the outset under the obligation of having to live with others.

I

But there is another reason why man in this moral system no longer confronts pure value rank (A, I.). Society is a historical formation which has developed itself. One can think of it as an overindividual subject which has had many very definite experiences during its existence. There is always not only something typical and normal in these value experiences but also a bit of subjective individuality, and a part of entirely unique total destinies. Let us assume a nation as the carrier of a collective morality; then the definite national character and fate are fused in this morality. Besides this, such a collective morality is capable of change to a certain extent, just as an individual in the course of his life may develop morally or, under certain conditions, morally degenerate. In a word: a collective morality is by no means the pure Good but is the Good in a historical and national form of appearance, partly filled with the spirit of genuine objective norms, partly permeated with rules which originated more from custom, styles or some will to power, and sometimes even ethically perverted.

The unique weighty form of a collective morality results not only from the fact that it expresses itself in objective institutions (for instance marriage, family, community, emergency associations, social forms of the state and religion) but just as much because it lives in the consciousness of almost every member of society by means of its objective value content through transmission, imitation and education. Collective morality becomes effective in the form of value judgments which refer to the behavior of fellow members in certain typical situations and beyond this to their constant attitudes in social relations. We shall not go back to the development of these value judgments. It is enough that in them are stored up the socio-ethical experiences, the opinion and the experience of norm of many generations. In history the influence of Socrates, for instance, clearly illustrates how an unusual personality sometimes transforms the entire transmitted popular ethics. The manner of influence of collective morality is not, however, limited to value judgments which are made either before or after the individual deed. It is expressed in norms which confront the individual member of society as demands, and in practical reactions that follow acts which society judges as moral or immoral. These reactions strengthen or weaken the social spirit in which one meets the individual. A member may be ostracized by society even without any legal measures because of his attitude. But this aspect of collective morality interests us less than the first: its appearance in the form of norms which confront the individual in his social behavior. It is possible to make still finer distinctions in the present socio-psychic reciprocal effects: whether a collective norm lives from the beginning in the consciousness of an individual and plays the role of a hindering or furthering factor in decision; whether it comes to his consciousness as an unlooked for expression of the environment only in the moment when he wills to act; or whether it can only appear to him after the act and then cause repentance or obstinacy. It must suffice for our purpose to investigate the question of how a collective norm enters the complex of actual motives of behavior.

II

It may act, figuratively speaking, either as a foreign or as a native drop of blood in a man's circulation. If the individual clings with all his instincts to the group, if he is with his entire being only a sample of the mass then he will hear in the voice of the collective norm his own voice as a collective being. If, on the other hand, he is already freed from the group as an independent individual then the decisive question is how much he still possesses of the social mind. Only the man who acknowledges society and its estate can recognize socio-ethical demands. If, as an independent personality, he finds in himself the norm which binds him to the lives of others (the social norm) he must take a stand in regard to collective norms as such. Otherwise he is a thoroughly asocial nature who even in a favorable case only acknowledges what contributes to the value of his own personality, but who does not want to go out of his way 'for the sake of others'. One might object to this that such a set is meaningless, inconceiveable and incapable of execution. Everyone is under an obligation to society whether he knows it or not. Everyone is finally and in his better nature a social product. This I do not deny, but we are here dealing not with the question of right and wrong but with a matter of fact. And there is no doubt that there are — at least as far as tendency is concerned — people who reject all social obligation with its collective norms. One finds them most frequently among economic egoists, aesthetic individualists, and affirmers of self (who belong to the political type) especially when they formulate a theory of their own way of life. Humboldt was primarily interested in his own development and social consequences though acceptable were secondary. Nietzsche purposely freed himself from all the standards of a herd morality and acknowledged only his own highest essential norm. The pure 'utilitarians' depend on certain interrelations through their 'interest' but know beyond that no norm of consideration and responsibility (My country, right or wrong). Still others think that they are subjectively freed from the bonds of morality when they have theoretically disclosed the origin of morality from social purposiveness.

We only point out these limiting phenomena in order to reiterate that the basis of social ethics is a fundamentally social set. I must instinctively or in conscious mental acts participate in the lives of others, if I am to emphasize the collective norms at all. The will to community is the *conditio sine qua non* of socio-ethical behavior, just as it is the basis of the will to legal rules whose content is not only the safeguarding of one's own power but which also includes the social mind. But even if this assumption is granted one can take very different stands in regard to the demands of collective norms.

III

The first and most simple case is that of the individual who subjects himself to the collective norm. Perhaps he agrees with it in his innermost heart (this is usual since in objective morality an age-old inherited wisdom is expressed which 'public opinion' usually considers self-evident); or a man is so dependent that he gives in to the 'pressure of social environment (which makes itself felt as a collective influence) just as it is possible to follow every custom and style because of weakness. The collective norm then plays in consciousness the role of the highest and most decisive value for behavior whose intensity no personal norm nor eccentricity can resist.

But it is also conceiveable that a conflict should take place between one's own value direction and the collective norm which enters into consciousness, which may be destructive or constructive. It is destructive if the merely subjective value constitution is victorious over collective morality. Then the will to live and act in accordance with norm is lacking. Social demands are broken in the same way as the personal norms which arise in one's own subjectivity. Only from the psychological point of view is the distinction important whether, in this conflict, the tendency to degeneracy is to be sought in recklessness and weakness, in psychic narrowness, in evil intention or belligerency. But since the collective norm by no means completely coincides with the ideal of pure morality, conflicts may occur because the higher norm lives in the individual consciousness and is asserted against collective expectations (which really only embody an average morality). We have seen above that in this case either the ethical right of one's own entirely unique personality may be decisive without the agent advocating a generalization of this particular behavior, or that a new and purer collective morality may originate in the socially directed individual consciousness. In both cases an eternal responsibility rests on the man who solves this conflict. He who claims for himself a special morality, even if he does so with the genuine religious consciousness of high personal destiny, will never return unscathed from a situation which is too difficult for man. A politician who has to navigate a collective power through uncharted waters where collectively developed general rules are inapplicable or are even undeveloped, experiences the weight of destiny involved in being the personal instrument of the normative mind. But the other sort of person who tries to bring to his companions a new morality and new forms of community assumes the difficult task of breaking old and tried tables of value in order to establish new ones which are vouched for only by his own social conscience and the deeper value longing of humanity which meets him half way. He must be prepared to have people regard this new freedom only as license and not as another obligation. And yet the progress of moral opinion is only possible if people are willing to sacrifice the security of the old to the possibilities of the new.[1])

But these remarks go far beyond what is pertinent to a theory of types. Let us consider only an application related to the psychology of mental individuality and pointing to new ethical factors.

Collective norms too may have a value content which surpasses the experiential capacity of the individual soul structure. We have, however, repeatedly emphasized the fact that all directions of mental life are founded simultaneously in the individual soul though in different proportions. We found the entire social ethics as such insecurely anchored in the soul of the born individualist but its special content as well may go beyond what the subject who is confronted by the norm of his environment is able to perform. Average morality may demand, for instance, that one should be self-supporting and keep one's economic affairs in order. A thoroughly uneconomic man — perhaps a great artist — fails in this respect because it does not strike a sympathetic chord in him as in others. The same system of morals can also establish the norm of conjugal faithfulness. But the individual may be of such aesthetic mobility that he is capable of eroticism but not of true love. Or a man may be asked to defend his rights and assert himself against other people's claims though he may perhaps be such a sensitive, loving nature that he cannot endure conflict, or a thinker who considers every other business more important than the rights of his empirical personality.

Thus before the forum of collective morality character can become guilt, though it is very questionable whether a man would feel

---

[1]) One might say in passing: that only he who has or might have energy enough to keep the 'law' is able to break it.

himself convicted by his own conscience. The more individualities differentiate themselves and develop their own normative world, the more will the two value judgments clash.

We must also add to the fundamental psychic structure the individualizing factor of the general mental and ethical developmental level of the individual. The ruling collective morality may be either too mature or insufficiently so. Applied collective morality usually does not even strive toward final minuteness in this individualization, much less reach it.

Neither moral science nor our present social morality ever approach the wholly unique moral situation. Every collective morality is a function of the objective social culture with its unique historical and geographical conditions, with its ranks of value and the value eccentricities upon which it is based. Despite all historical singularity the normative mind, whose eternal fundamental structure appears here only in a historically unique form, is active in such a collective morality insofar as it has a truly ethical content. The moral attitude of a man (his ethical character) is also very closely related to his individual mental structure. This belongs more or less closely to an eternal type. It is furthermore, because of its historical cultural position, filled with special historical contents. Thus each man has his entire individual ethical law (his Idea.) But this is just as rigid as Kant's categorical imperative and is only the application of eternal norms to a unique mental fact which neither the experiencing agent himself nor another of deep understanding can ever reasonably and completely carry out.

It is difficult to interpret the connection between historical morality and historico-geographic culture in such a way that the collective morality of an epoch clearly appears. One must then still differentiate between what is on the average embodied in society as an insured possession, and what remains unattainable demand, longing and ideal. It is still more difficult however scientifically to illuminate the very specific ethical destiny of a definite type and a special historic kind of mind. They can only be approximated. But both still refer to some structure, that is, to a mental context of achievements which as a whole is constant. The individual ethical special case, however, which is brought about by fate is wholly irreducible. One cannot say what position general morality will and ought to take in regard to it until popular opinion actually has been formed. Only certain directives may be foretold and that out of the ethical social structure which we have previously developed. Correspondingly, one may surmise but not unequivocally deduce how a person whom one knows will behave in a very special situation, that is, in a case which cannot be subsumed under typical moral situations.

In other words, one must not expect from scientific ethics a minutely developed casuistic. We have here (1) outlined the eternal structure of personal and collective morality. (2) We have intimated, that science when historically concrete, may, in the main, structurally grasp the morality of a nation in a definite cultural epoch and the ethics of a clear-cut individual. But (3) as little as we can absolutely predict tomorrow's weather with our advanced natural scientific knowledge, just so little can we understand by means of *geisteswissenschaftliche* categories unexpected occurrences. The ethical decision itself really sets a limit to science for it originates in unexplored religious depths which we are inclined subsequently to project into the characterological picture. Thus for the past and its dead we can only attain a descriptive and understanding moral science.

C.

Our investigation seems to end very negatively. In place of the hoped for objective order of values we have found only subjective factors which determine a value perspective, and always more and more individualizing factors instead of the unequivocal eternal order. From the objective adequate comprehension of general value essences we were led to the actual value experience in its changing intensity, from the supposedly independent values to the experienced value context in which the content of values may be variously embodied. We then added the individual soul structure which may develop as something unique to the point where it is almost incomprehensible. Finally, we also investigated the share of a historically singular social morality whose moral genuineness could by no means be guaranteed in every respect and with which the individual might conflict either destructively or constructively.

Now it is time entirely to abandon this methodological fiction of the eternal sphere of values which would be grasped in 'pure' acts of intentional feeling, preference or rejection. It has accomplished its mission but also shown its inner impossibility. For what is the meaning of this statement that 'values' themselves rest in a sphere of pure essences? Even the supporters of this theory cannot believe that they are always attached to the same object or real objects which are only related by species. But they only appear in the mental process of life which is always divided into a duality of subject and object. They cannot be 'separated' from this process nor 'hypostasized' but always remain meaningful organic members only within this structure.

But if, within the framework of this structure we do not want to do without the judgment, whether genuine or spurious, 'objective or merely subjective', there remains only to assume that a legality of normative character is active in the organically structured process of value experiences and value positings (as we have already worked out in Part I, Ch. V. for the abstractly isolated value regions). But here we are no longer dealing with isolated norms but with the total norm, and also accordingly with gradations of value experiences and value positings which must be expressed partly in structured developments and partly in unsolved conflicts.

Our hypothesis can now only be that a normative legality is active in this totality of mental life just as it is in the particular spheres, which appears in experience as the judgment of inferiority or superiority of values, as the fulfillment of, or failure in duty. And so it seems that we progress no farther than Kant and his school from the assumption of a formal law which regulates the rank of behavior and mind. And the eternal idea of an ideal value system which is nevertheless without content, and which is not merely individually or collectively valid, is based on the idea of such a regulative 'ought'.

And now after all these preparations we may take a step into actuality. We may at least designate the cultural locus where the temporally determined approximations to this ideal value system are carried out. It is certain that they can only succeed in an ethically productive soul which is at the same time broadened by the reception of the most comprehensive contemporary mental content and purified by moral energy. And we are always dealing with the total mental productivity of life which is guided by the normative value law.

Then the cultural work which is based on objective evaluations is represented as a progressive building up, as a creation of value — even though bound by norms and facts — and as a conquest which can only be achieved by productive energy. The attainments of personalities (or groups) are then graded according to their value rank. In all of them, insofar as they value according to norms, there is a struggle and an upward striving, a continual rejection of the lower in favor of the higher value. By such work the moral world or the world of values is gradually built up. There is a rank order of minds as well as of nations, though the criteria of their rank lie finally in the proportion of power which they assert in evaluation, in other words: in their religious value rank and certainty.

This ethical productivity may appear in three typical forms in the cultural context. Greatest and most influential is the religious nature which, from the focal point of its mental individuality, attains a new value point of view for itself and others in defining its position to the collective objective stock of life, and its own kind of experience, which is able to grasp the 'content' of things. Whatever thus rises out of the primal depths of an ethically creative mind becomes, then, an ideal norm system which is elevated to the position of the highest norm even over those who are not yet sufficiently mature for it, not organized or capable of experiencing it. Religious terminology calls this, especially when its result comes from grace rather than one's own deed, revelation.

The second, perhaps less clear-cut form is the artistic creative power which fixes in great plastic pictures the gain of a whole life, which is purified by the moral mind so that it is opened to the contemplation and empathy of those who are capable of surmising the 'content' of the aesthetic elements born in imagination. Homer, Dante, Goethe have not only stimulated mankind aesthetically but also ethically enlightened them by the medium of this symbolism. And they enlighten even those who are not sufficiently mature to understand them. It is in this way that we must interpret the line:

'Und die Sonne Homers, siehe, sie leuchtet auch uns!'[1]

Namely his humanity of eternally noble content has evolved for the world an ideal value system by which the generations of today as well as of yesterday still learn and grow.

---

[1] Schiller: *Der Spaziergang*. 'And lo, Homer's sun shines for us also.'

And finally we must consider philosophy too. Hegel's statement that it, like Minerva's owl, begins its flight only in the twilight is not quite true. Certainly as a science it is bound to the law of objective cognition by means of which it views the manifold materials of life and receives them into the thinking soul: but in the sense of total mental formation of life the philosophic thinker too may be productive. Building on the comprehension of the 'world' and its correctly cognized law, he develops new levels of value life in creative vision. It is his privilege as well as his duty to be always one step in advance of his time. In his problems he must solve the conflicts in which he clashes with contemporary morality and the limitations of his own nature. His intellectual achievements will purify and save others. We still entertain a profound admiration for the mind of Plato which saw amid the chaos of life, with religious, aesthetic and theoretic power of prophecy, the eternal standards which act in our breast and regulate the whole world. And his master Socrates who first saw the pure Good has with him freed us from the deceptive play of apparent values which mislead the soul. He has shown us that we cannot oppose the Spirit without denying and betraying the divine in us. In the train of these two great minds follow the other thinkers who have discovered new stars in the moral firmament.

It follows from the meaning which we have ascribed to religion, namely its essential direction to what is final and total, that the pronounced religious set is the highest among the formations of the ideal mind which are developed by the co-operation of the deepest personal value and norm experiences with the given collective norms of genuine content. We also know, however, that religion always depends on the language of other spheres of meaning. It needs theoretic and aesthetic mental formations to express itself. There is therefore no great religion without myths which combine all three aspects, religious, theoretic and aesthetic. It is for this reason that whenever Plato wants to express anything truly final he is forced to use mythological language. — And yet this fact is also true in another connection: where a religiously intended ideal value system has once historically developed from the depths of the normative mind which constantly renews itself, there it is further formed and elaborated both by high art and great philosophy. There develop these tremendous creative mental productions which we can trace in Christianity from the Church Fathers (St. Augustin) and the agnostics, through the scholastics (Thomas Aquinas) to Leibniz and Kant, Schleiermacher and Hegel; from Dante and the Gothic cathedrals to Michelangelo, Bach and Goethe. Apparently this stream which is fed by the Absolute and announces to the world its measures as Plato did in ancient times, moves apart from the course of history.

If anyone thinks that he can ignore such classic masters because of his own value certainty he makes a great mistake. Anyone who does not stand receptively in the stream of creative mind would have to bring up the same degree of productivity if he wanted to replace this investigating force. And consequently we conclude that the concrete rank order of value is not anything finished but is won step by step in a historico-mental process. It is not grasped by the abstract individual conscience as such but only by what participates in the objective mental life and the realized level of the normative mind. The law of this mind lives in every bosom that has the power to feel it. But its individual norms must be conquered gradually and not everyone is from the outset sufficiently mature and receptive for the higher levels. According to our conclusions too the rank order of values remains a graded order. But one cannot skip a level, every one must be achieved with all the earnestness of personal conscientious decision and formation of life. Anyone who only dimly sees the top is not yet at the summit. And above what we see there are always higher ranges, plastic value positions which arise from the moral battle of life.

The neo-platonic and Leibnitzean thoughts on the gradated realm of the spirit thus become for us stages of moral value content and moral value systems. Above every accomplished level there is a still higher one, even if the absolute proportion to value is denied to the individual and collective value subjects since they value under definite limited historical conditions. The normative mind lives and acts in every one, though it does not absolutely triumph — that would be divinity — and only arrives at a certain historical configuration of the objective mind in which genuine value always struggles with the spurious, the higher with the lower. A being in whom only genuine values rule and in whom the higher values do not partially exclude the lower ones, would be so infinite as to deserve to be called God. God is in us as energy and impulse though we cannot ourselves become God. There is always something above us to which we address our reverence and final longing. When we feel that we approach this highest most closely, we surmise the highest moment. But the highest moment itself never actually comes. Therefore Occidentals who want a culture find salvation not in contemplative devotion to something which already exists and only overcomes us, but in continued striving. Grace only comes to the active man. God only helps to triumph the man who works over himself, and the passive individual receives the visit of God, as it were, unprepared and incomplete. We cannot therefore get away from Fichte's profound thought: 'Think that you in yourself are nothing but through God everything, so that you become noble and strong in this thought. But act as if there were no God to aid you and that you must do everything alone as indeed He will help you in no other way than in having given you to yourself.'[1]

[1] Fichte, Works (Literary remains) III. p. 449.

THE PERSONAL IDEAL

The threads of our investigation converge in a final point: the philosophy of personality. With the preceding exposition we have surpassed the limit which we had to maintain in the abstract representation of the typical attitudes.

There we viewed the individual as a fixed mental structure and saw his inner structural law in the values which were of primary importance for his life. We approached the mystery of personality, for the time being in a purely descriptive way, from the value structure or value constitution. 'Tell me what you value and I will tell you what you are', thus we might paraphrase an old proverb.

Only historical observation and comparison can illuminate in detail how far this personal value structure is pre-formed in the germs of mental individuality, and how much it is changed by the character-forming power of environment and fate. Dilthey distinguishes the acquired structural context (the developed individuality) from inherited structure. William Stern starts his investigation with the principle of convergence; that is, he believes that the developed product grows everywhere both from an inborn factor and from one which is externally influential. Experience testifies to this duality and teaches us above all how strongly social position, vocation and the opinions and customs of his immediate environment determine the individual who is exposed to the combined effects of these forces.

Although natural science may attempt to understand inner form itself as a product of adaptation, *Geisteswissenschaft* would regard this as a deduction of the meaningful from the meaningless. The decisive form for the creation of life lies in man himself. We cannot do without the assumption of a pre-formed structure even though we admit that it can, to a certain extent, be changed by the impressions and experiences of life.

Another question is: when can it be recognized? Only in rare cases is a child's mental direction so strongly emphasized that its future soul form seems to be unequivocally defineable. The working out and establishment of the mental bent usually comes only during puberty which, therefore, besides the first years of life, is the most important time for education. We cannot, however, say whether to a mentally trained vision everything here would appear to be rigid necessity. Many thinkers are inclined to view the attitude of each individual as a sort of timeless idea which in the process of development only unrolls itself temporally before our vision. Aristotle says that everything which appears in the developed condition has been pre-formed in heredity, because he believes that form is both the law and the goal of development. Thus what is valid for the species must also hold true for the differentiated individualities, assuming of course that they signify a constant law of action and reaction in the sense of the first pages of this book. Goethe has purposely emphasized this paradox in the expression: '*Gepraegte Form, die lebend sich entwickelt*', for he experienced himself in this way. And this is all that is meant by the phrase: 'Become what you are' (Pindar), and by the doctrine of intelligible character which continually recurs though in many different forms from the ancient religious contexts (Karma, Atman, Predestination) up to the time of German idealism.

But of course one must remember that life shows innumerable mixed forms and that a wavering between certain limits is all the more possible since we must admit that two souls can live in one breast and struggle with each other (See below IV. 1).[1] In some cases of development the aim seems to be to work out more and more clearly the indicated onesided type; in others to surmount onesidedness. It is a well known fact that in old age there is frequently a transition to the religious attitude. Perhaps then this 'imprinted form' is only the methodological principle of investigation in whose unity we comprehend the manifoldness of an individual

---

[1] Thus we see in Plato the rhythmically alternating psychic currents of the ascetic-orphic and the erotic-enthusiastic motives: the feeling of the cave, the joy of beauty, the desire to die and the necessity of creating. In Schiller we see the continual wavering between the aesthetic drive for unity and the dual experience of unity of thought and wealth of sensible experience.

life process, and also the ethical norm in which the rank of every level is measured, though only from the viewpoint of achieved personal maturity.

We do not labor under the delusion that we have reduced to mental laws the mysteries of development. Here we have a new problem which we do not propose to treat completely but only to indicate a few outlines. And we shall try, purely psychologically for the time being to investigate in methodological specialization personal development, insofar as it is internally determined by its pre-formed attitude. Only later shall we add to this the ethical point of view.

A.

Environment and Fate, as inclusive concepts of external conditions and occurrences which influence an individuality, seem only to play the role of material with which the inner mental personality occupies itself, by which it develops and, under certain circumstances, strengthens itself. I have never heard of a case in which Fate i. e. external influences, radically changed a mature man from one type to another, except for the above-mentioned transition to the religious type which however can actually include all others from the beginning.

Even though we are inclined to regard the individual who develops from within as an instance of meaningful selection expressed in actions and reactions to the external conditions of life, it is nevertheless very important for the result of this developmental process what materials are offered for selection by environment and heredity. The power of education is based on conscious moral regulation of environment and partly of heredity too. It can only offer and cultivate possibilities but not form or implant them at will.

A man who becomes conscious of his own mental development is almost certain to judge it according to the style of his fundamental attitude.[1])

---

[1]) This becoming historical to one's self — in the sense that one feels the inner necessity of personal evolutions and revolutions — is moreover in the secular region something very modern which hardly goes farther back than Goethe. As a religious phenomenon it is much older. — Schiller learned from Koerner, 'that truth too has its seasons with human beings' (to Koerner, 15. IV, 1788).

The theoretic type is inclined to reduce the process of his development to rational, consciously apprehended steps. He believes that every single stage was carried out under intellectual necessity, and that all he has become has been the result of will and choice based on general rules of life.[1]) The autobiographies of rationalists of the eighteenth century (and of the twentieth century too) testify to this conception. The economic man on the other hand, regards his development as a consequence of purposive adaptations in which each time he has mastered a new phase of life. All life is for him a kind of skilfull technique. The aesthetic type, at least of the classic sort, believes that his growth was organic. He has assimilated the impressions of life as material, searched for and made a part of his soul new life conditions and thus became what he is: an organic form endowed with soul. The case is different with the seekers for experience who allow themselves to be determined by new groups of stimuli, and with the expressionists who sometimes see life suddenly 'in a new light' and who regard their existence as a series of subjective changes. Development is reduced to creative love and friendship, to profound mental communities of giving and receiving if the social factor predominates. The political type (in our broader sense of the word) regards himself as self-made, by a deed of freedom. He has conquered the resistance of the dull world by energy of will and created his own sphere of existence. Indeed he interprets his character as the work of a freely willed original deed. The religious man, finally, feels in his development either the grace of God which has tenderly guided all his steps, or the world-conquering power of his own soul which has fought for the divine. Both are sometimes conceived as a quiet continuous activity and sometimes as a sudden conversion or series of conversions in which the highest meaning is revealed. God is active in me, or I in God. Whether calm or tempestuous, the fundamental religious attitude is unmistakeable in all four forms and is easily united to the other onesided forms of self-experience.

Apparently puberty is always the time of life in which mental personality first awakens. Before then it may occasionally show itself in many different ways, but the life of a child is so un-

---

[1]) Wundt was much more than a mere theorist. And yet the wish to experience even death with full consciousness is very characteristic of this great thinker. *Erlebtes und Erkanntes*, Stuttgart 1920. p. 118.

differentiated, subject and object are in him so undivided, that we can scarcely speak of actual mental life or of a participation in the objective historical world. But when the self for the first time confronts the world as something for its own sake, the formations of the mind begin to be active, though not even then in one pronounced direction. Instead, either one of two things is characteristic of puberty: (1) the predominance of the aesthetic attitude in which all other spheres of life may be simultaneously 'experimented with'; or (2) the sudden appearance of certain attitudes. For a time he seeks useful activity, then he is a religious enthusiast; periods of affectionate trust alternate with self-isolation and a wild obstinacy which tries to compel recognition; then again he seizes upon theoretic and technical problems. It almost seems here as if the individual mind stood before a wealth of possibilities. But perhaps it is only apparently so for this quest is not wholly free nor is it a search for purely objective values and obligations but, above all, a quest for one's self. Fundamentally its future is predestined, but the final stamp of this form still depends on the material which life presents and the level of formation which is offered to the searching individuality. With some people this process continues from puberty for ten or fifteen years. The individual form is only gradually disclosed and latest of all with mere aesthetic seekers, like the pure impressionists whose fate it is to have no fixed form but to flutter from flower to flower, sampling each. In others the imagination, which at first surrounded the hidden solid core like a soft shell (but often lets its outlines clearly shine through) gradually falls away. In the place of unlimited possibilities there remains a onesided individuality. The greater opportunity it has had really to be itself in life's activity the more strongly it appears. Very often, however, a forced vocation hides the real essence and thus an inner conflict occurs which eventually saps the best energies.[1])

B.

The mental growth of a human being is not, however, merely a continuous process, not simply development in the narrow sense,

---

[1]) For further detail see my *Psychologie des Jugendalters*. On Goethe's position in regard to this problem which is essentially the same cf. the speech cited above.

but also moral training. Normative powers enter into the instinctive value direction in all possible forms in which moral norms appear: as personal conscience, as collective morality and as an ideal system of value; and are active both as a broadening and a restricting morality. The individual soul participates in these mental powers. They unite themselves to the rest of the environment which, by its mere presence, develops habits and thus a certain form.

The most difficult problem lies in the above-mentioned tension which exists between the duty to experience and the experience of duty.

The duty to experience can only be posited from an over-individual point of view. The author of these commands is either collective morality which demands from the members of the group a definite moral character and behavior; or a still higher ideal system of value which is, of course, also derived from a historical process but seeks to elevate itself to a sphere of absolutely valid standards which transcends time; and strives to avoid obligation to special variable life conditions of a group — either in the name of God, in that of a complete humanity or in the spirit of a genuine idea of culture. Both norms are directed to all individuals who belong to this objective and ideal mind as their superordinated total of culture.

This duty to experience becomes an experience of duty when the overindividual norm is actualized in the individual consciousness and is active there as a real force. It is probably very rare that there is no answering echo. For, with our whole selves we are not only children of nature but also of the historico-social mind to which we belong. Furthermore, because we are human beings we carry the eternal, ideal, fundamental, directions of mind (Ideas) as normative forces in ourselves. But suppose a being is not sufficiently mature for the special content and level of these over-individual norms, or deviates in his instinctive structure from those demands which are permeated by a highly purified meaning content? In the first case we do not even have a strongly conscious experience of conflict because the individual is not yet capable of seeing the overindividual norms. In the second case we have that situation of conflict which is so characteristic of moral life.

Education enters in here as a social measure, and in both cases attempts to obtain a hearing for the authoritative norm. One should never base education merely on collective morality, but always beyond that on an ideal system of values; that is, the final religio-moral meaning of life and a 'classic' educational content. But neither the ideal nor the collective force can be effective from the outside. The aim of all education is to enter into the center of the personally affirming value-positing individual and lay bare that innermost region where the authoritative demand becomes a duty which is acknowledged by the better self and so elevated to the highest personal ideal. Thus there is an autonomous duty too, and this alone, because it is a part of the self, has the power which guarantees progress from the lower value to the demanded higher one. For all personal morality depends on the energy which brings about the sacrifice of the lower life for the higher and the narrower for the broader existence.

We have seen that a morality can arise from these depths which might surpass and purify the given collective morality. Indeed it is the final source in which the ideal value system is always born anew and, under certain circumstances, creatively developed. In the following we shall not speak of this rare climax of moral power, but shall assume that the individual finds himself in a totality of life which is already moral; that is, in an objective mental situation in which the normative (ideal) mind is the guiding power. And we shall further assume that the individual who is filled with the content of this greater mind makes his value decisions in complete freedom and purity of conscience. The norms which he then finds in himself will have one of two effects: they will either broaden him or — for the sake of a higher value — limit him. Both are possible either for the sake of the personal value content or of the social value content, to live for which is an essential moral command. The personal ideal is determined from these four directions and thus also includes the demands of the genuine social will to value.

1. We have previously designated the broadening norm as formative morality. It is primarily rooted in the individuality itself which is conscious of the limits of its personality. From this develops personal striving for culture, and those aspects of man which do not belong to the predominant trend of his nature should be cultivated. It seems to be a personal experience of duty to refine a crude personality into a cultivated one. The man who has a theoretic bent must also develop himself for practical life

in economics, politics and society. The purely aesthetic type must balance his universal receptivity by concrete work. The meaning of self-education is the absorption of an objectively valuable content into the individuality whose central being is not thus extinguished but rather enriched. And when we grasp the world with our theoretic and aesthetic organs, where it is fairly remote, literary culture usually predominates. But it is nowhere limited to this, though in Germany culture is only interpreted as science because we are theoretically constituted. For just this reason however our scientific education often becomes the reverse of culture.[1]

2. Culture is therefore not merely something which one owes to one's self but also a social duty. Our environment demands that we should broaden ourselves subjectively so that we can understandingly and creatively participate in its value content. Society usually prescribes a definite form of such education and this externally imprinted ideal may conflict strongly with subjective ideals. Today even in socialistic circles people fear everything that seems to limit the freedom of a developing man. I consider this a proof that today no virile individuals are born or that they are no longer believed in. For, the human will to spiritual growth only becomes stronger through opposition. A plan of teaching, no matter how stupid, can not immediately extinguish the nature which is there. From the battle of social and personal cultural ideals much stronger formations develop than if the human being had been allowed from the outset to advance only in his personal direction. Just because the individual must take a stand either for or against contemporary culture he must also reckon in his personal ideal with the mental demands of his environment.[2]

---

[1] My pamphlet *Gedanken ueber Lehrerbildung* has been little understood because people could only think of book learning. Whether it is a blessing to make the entire national culture a book culture will I hope be more carefully adjudged by a future time than is being done today.

[2] 'Every moral individuality needs correction by means of the development of the opposite pole of energy; Frederick the Great should take the flute and Napoleon Ossianic poetry. Education may here preach for instance to the heroic character of peace and load the Sigwart-character with a little thunder and lightning. ... Moreover it must remain a law, since every power is sacred, not to weaken anyone, only to awaken its opposite by means of which it harmoniously adds itself to the total.' Jean Paul, *Levana* § 29. In exactly the same sense cf. Schleiermacher in his *Paedagogik*.

3. We have already deduced the restrictive norm from the fact that an individuality cannot be indefinitely expanded and that therefore a lower value must be sacrificed to a higher one. This is necessary even in an isolated soul. One can only be 'something' at the sacrifice of something else, for one cannot be everything. Wholly universal natures are entirely without a center or force. One must learn to sacrifice life in order to find it, not only in affairs of great moment but also in everyday matters. Above all one must victoriously combat the claim completely to give oneself up to sensual impulses. No mental life or creation can be achieved without asceticism. When this is forgotten civilization decays at its roots. The more we conquer the sensual in us, even though it too has a limited right, and the more intensively we experience this 'Die to live' the more mature we shall be. To be mature means to have achieved self-conquests, though such conquests are never possible without some pain. Every conflict leaves behind a tragic suffering because we could not or ought not do what we wanted. But the justification of suffering is that it lifts us to higher levels. People who have not suffered remain shallow and pain gives a depth which is seldom attained in a life of happiness. Onesided attitudes may exhibit a greatness which commands respect, but as mere heredity they are only limits and have no deeper right. As conscious and self-accepted restrictions they receive the firmness which the battle with the inner and outer fate bestows. Frederick the Great, who sacrificed his aesthetic tendencies in order to be a servant of the state, ranks higher than the young Humboldt who wanted only to live his own life. It must not be believed that Goethe made no self-conquests, but such a potent creative power welled up within him that he was able to cover every scar with rosy flesh.

4. The most decisive limitations come to a moral individual as demands of society in which he wants to and must be a subordinated part. From infancy he is surrounded by commandments which all preach: 'Thou shalt not!' It is a well-known fact that collective morality expresses itself far more often in negative than positive commands, even though not all as much as the decalogue. It is always a case of respecting the limits of other lives, indeed actively willing them as one's own limits. If perfect freedom is granted to every person social life is impossible. This is true not only of the

economic sphere with its divisible goods, but also of the formation of one's entire inner life which, beyond its own value must be a value for others. An individuality is complete only when these socially posited values are adopted as its own. For in moral service man becomes richer and not poorer. When the collective consciousness too is ethically alive within him he is filled with a really wide life content. Giving and receiving are so intimately interwoven in human society, especially in a nation, that it is impossible to keep separate the part of every individual. And thus too the limitation demanded by collective morality is a law, even though it does not deserve a pure moral value, which must be fulfilled before it can be abolished. People should greet the liberators of humanity with suspicion if they go to work in any other way, that is without respect; for then there is something in them which is not wholly pure and clean.

When we ask for the exact relation between the broadening and restricting norms we find ourselves at the confines of what can be scientifically determined. The reality of moral life which has developed historically, always shows some interfusion of values which we shall later call forms of mental synthesis. Social Utilitarianism is one of them even though still a primitive fusion of economic and social values. Plato's ethics combines the theoretic with the aesthetic, and in the moral theory of Shaftesbury we find a unique interrelation of egoism, altruism and aesthetic morality. Kant unites theoretic with political elements in forming his ethics and every national ideal of culture contains a graded synthesis of values which is meaningfully related to the level of culture and the historically developed national character.

Any individual who consciously tries to create his own moral life is confronted by the same problem. He must organize his value life. The fact that everything cannot simultaneously come to the fore with the same strength is intimated even in the rank order which he grants in his choice to the individual claims of value. And our description of the onesided attitudes has shown that certain value directions even exclude each other. We must not try to hide this fact. Ethical antinomies are contained in the structure of life itself and are not brought into it by the fault of man. Rather, the unknown forces of life are those which make him guilty. The dialectic of life's laws repeatedly brings about collisions of personal value determinations from which he never escapes completely unscathed. He is imbued with an ideal of unbroken total life development. But how often does economic necessity conflict with the will to love, the will to truth with the will to assert another genuine value, the aesthetic inner harmony with the realism of existence in the state, economics and society. These contrasts cannot be explained away. They are there and in them the tragedy of life begins, for life is, throughout, tragic.

That we return here also to different basic ways in which these different personal value decisions are carried out is only an application of our theory of attitudes. This process is apparently most peaceful in the aesthetic nature which achieves a form of life. Culture for this reason is often thought of preferably as an aesthetic quality of man, for the aesthetic set can include the greatest fulness of life, though only as a contemplative and imaginative possession. And the manysidedness of aesthetic contact with life always contains some danger of shallowness, of having no center in life and of relativity. A practical human being cannot form himself in this way. He must assume the guilt of a limited attitude toward life or he would lack the capacity for action. 'An active man rejoices in partisanship.' And this limitation not only results from his own nature but also from other people's right to live which he includes in his economic, political or social life. Anyone who takes up everything can no longer create. This truth applies also to the defenders of a universal general culture.

Individual standards however, cannot be scientifically deduced. Rather they are only contained in the value constellation which one might call the content of individual conscience. This conscience is not wholly unsupported. For the most part it finds ready-made value decisions of historical society and usually adopts them, and beyond, those highest, timeless, moral guiding stars which we have called ideal systems of value. Every one of them is the result of a moral struggle, so there is no great final world-view whether religious, poetical or philosophical which is not tragic. They are all bloody victories over lower life and one feels in them still the pain of the breach over which they heroically triumphed. No hero is without wounds after the battle. Indeed not even among themselves is there peace: the great religions are in continual conflict with one another. And even within our closed cultural sphere the Christian ideal of love, the Greek-humanistic and the ethico-political ideals of duty signify widely separated world-forces which compete with each other for moral supremacy. The question of what guidance to accept is again wholly a matter of individual conscience when a man has arrived at the point where he no longer merely receives his personal ideal world but builds it from within with free responsibility. And he would really be alone unless the ultimate welled up in him and helped him — his God.

Therefore the norm of the personal ideal can only be pronounced in formal imperatives. As soon as the emphasis is laid in the direction of expansion one might speak of a demand for the compossible maximum of life's value.[1]) Whatever things are 'compossible', that is, can exist side by side in an individual manner of moral life formation, can only (disregarding the general theory of types of individual attitudes) be fought through and decided in every individual case. The aim of personal perfection which lies in the autonomy of a moral man might be expressed in the demand:

Be whatever you can, but be it wholly!

And if one wants to express the negative aspect too, the factor of demanded limitation, this maxim must be replaced by the following one:

Be the highest that you can and ought to be within the limits of the demands of social ethics and your personal value capacity!

Only the value testing voice in one's own breast, which we call conscience, can tell what this highest is concretely, unless it is taken from the ethico-social mind and the ideal value system which is developed above it:

'*Sofort nun wende dich nach innen,
Das Zentrum findest du dadrinnen,
Woran kein Edler zweifeln mag.
Wirst keine Regel da vermissen;
Denn das selbstaendige Gewissen
Ist Sonne deinem Sittentag.*'

---

[1]) I choose this expression in order to indicate a concealed connection with motives of the Leibnizean philosophy. There even God's choice of values is bound to these limits of value agreement.

PART IV
THE UNDERSTANDING OF MENTAL STRUCTURES

1
COMPLEX TYPES

In working out the previous part, we have already abandoned the procedure of isolation and idealization which led to the basic types. For, both personal and collective morality go beyond the onesided mental forms and are based on a synthesis of values turned to normativity which alone corresponds to the complete reality of life.

We have reduced the very complex mental texture to a limited number of basic motives in which we believe that we have grasped independent meaning directions which cannot be further analyzed. Our analysis is not only completely proved by the unique *Gestaltqualitaet* and legality of every motive but is further substantiated by the fact that all phenomena of mental life can be understood as permutations of these simple, partial structures.

It is true that modern philosophy cites, besides the kinds of value which we have called primary, a further supposedly independent class of values of which we have hitherto scarcely spoken; the socalled vital values. Ever since the time of Nietzsche they have played an important part in philosophy, and that such widely divergent thinkers as Bergson, Simmel and Scheler have adopted them in their views of the mind is a fact which must set us thinking. The essence of the vital sphere is, of course, variously defined. If one takes the original meaning of the term literally, one is dealing with those values which are experienced in physical health, energy and purity; that is, in objective terminology, bodily values. Max Scheler, who characterizes these values as 'noble' or 'vulgar' — I should think it would be more correct to say 'noble' and 'ignoble'[1] — maintains that: 'the vital values are a completely independent

---

[1] For only that which follows from an ignoble attitude is vulgar. Physical weakness and sickliness constitute a lack of vitality but are not by any means ignoble.

mode, and can be reduced neither to values of pleasantness and unpleasantness nor to any mental value. I consider that the misunderstanding of this fact is one of the fundamental weaknesses of previous ethical doctrines.'[1])

Vital values, indeed, present the only further class of values whose independence might cause serious discussion. We do not wish to cite as an argument against them the fact that they are rooted in the physical side of life, that is, in the 'life' of the narrow biological interpretation. For, we have had to acknowledge mere dull, lifeless matter, insofar as it could become the foundation of values of utility by means of its purely physical qualities, as the carrier of mentally important values. On the other hand, we have established as the criterion of the independence of a value species, the question of whether it could become the dominating and organizing principle of its own objective mental sphere. And it seems as if in certain stages of civilization, especially at present in sport and all related physical exercises, a special sphere of vital activities is formed. This independence is based on the fact that other phases of cultural development have endangered the aspect of vital energy and health, both in the individual and in the whole. But in any case the process of the differentiation from the eternal total extent of life of a cultural region with a wholly new experiential content and emphasis is a very interesting and remarkable one. Therefore it is a very serious question whether or not we should add, to the previously developed attitudes a seventh; the vital one, as the late development of an eternal and essentially fundamental motive.

We do not want to scoff at this idea. For, even if we could prove that this primal motive is included by the other value directions which are known to us, this would by no means disprove the independence of the primal vital phenomenon. For, we had to show how all the other attitudes affected the rest of the value motives. It could be easily shown that in vital values not only the qualities of pleasantness and unpleasantness (which we regard as feelings rather than as species of value) participate and that they include not only the aspect of physical satisfaction of needs and therefore are related to the values of utilities in the same

---

[1]) *Der Formalismus.* p. 106.

way as the other physically determined instincts and impulses. On the contrary it is indubitable that they enter into higher mental zones. For, in the experience of health and energy of one's own body or that of others there is an aesthetic factor which animates the feeling of self and empathy. There is, furthermore, a deep-rooted still semi-biological feeling of power; and finally, also a factor which is certainly susceptible of ultimate religious meaning: the body too is a divine vessel.

The relation of the two sexes, a fundamental fact of the psycho-physical world, is founded in a zone which is not quite given in any of our former descriptions. The experience of health, race, blood, energy, and physical nobility is a phenomenon by itself even though it may later become, in the more spiritual form, aesthetic empathy for the beauty of an alien soul; in the more mental form, fulness of power which is conscious of its value and in the mystical erotic form, experience of a divine psychic corporality.

Considering all this, and in view of the fact that finally a unique, great and ineradicable zone of life rests upon it in which man may center permanently, or at least in whole developmental epochs, one might think that here is an attitude which deserves a special place. But on the other hand the whole is too much created out of the three fundamental levels of the biological, the erotic-aesthetic and the political, for one not to see that it is only a combination of the well-known primary motives. And furthermore if we regard the sphere of vital life objectively we see that it really does not found a special order of meaning elements in the sense that we speak of logical meaningful units and their laws, of aesthetic forms and their objective structure. Rather, the whole falls into the world which, with its physical, chemical and physiological laws, constitutes the biological zone; though with the notable addition that we have here corporality quickened with soul. And this animation is not merely aesthetic but real.

The question cannot be decided here and needs the most careful investigation. We leave it open and limit ourselves in the following to the syntheses for which we have found sufficient conditions in the six kinds of value. That is, we are dealing only with regions which we can assume are comprehensible as interrelations of those prime motives upon which the attitudes are based.

Among the complex formations which are possible according to rules of combination and permutation some are only important as logical constructions without being very influential in the mental historical world. Others, on the contrary, also appear in objective culture as structures which are so unique and fixed that they deserve special consideration as species of eternal modes.

We can understand them more easily as objective mental forms than in the complexes of acts which are related to them; just as Plato found the essence of justice (a personal virtue) in the objective ideal state. Here belong especially the fusions of the mental region with social forms, that is, communities and dominations. Among the former we must distinguish the kind of community or the form of union from the mutually intended purpose; that is, the economic from the utilitarian community, the artistic community from aesthetically interpreted society, the scientific organisation from union through common beliefs and the religious community from religious neighborly love. Similarly, in regard to forms of domination, which are in themselves a combination of social and political motives, we must distinguish the content of objective political systems from the kind of political acts. In this way there are economic, artistic, scientific and religious (churches) organisations, but also plutocracy, aesthetic aristocracy, scientific authority and theocracy as forms of social influence.[1]

We shall not follow the possible fusions in all their feasible combinations, principally because not only the regularity of the scheme would be decisive in them but because we should have to investigate and individually understand the unique life-function of every region. Let us select at random the point of contact of the imaginative and economic systems. If the utilitarian viewpoint predominates then artistic handicraft develops; that is, the factors of expression-impression and form appear in phenomena which were originally endowed with meaning through the useful purpose for which they were intended and the material necessary to make them. Strictly we should further distinguish here the creative motive (art as a business) and the form of appearance (utilitarian art). If, however, the aspects of expression and imagination predominate while the

---

[1] I still disregard here the difference in all these societies which is due to the degree and nature of statutory regulation.

economic factor is subordinated, then the phenomenon of luxury develops. In common with economics luxury still lies in the material region of what is desireable and consumeable. But it differs in that it contains so much empathic imagination that calculation and thrift are not its principle concern but that the expression of psychic stimulus is the main thing (cf. above p. 135). The fusion of the two regions of meaning should be followed in much greater detail.

Further syntheses of fundamental importance are the conjunction of science and religiosity in metaphysics, of economics and theory in the so-called economy of thought, of the economic and social attitudes in the utilitarian relations (mutualism) upon which all barter and trade are based. In philosophic systems one can always find an aesthetic factor which is connected with rhythm, symmetry and completeness of form, which is not only based on the external materials of representation but which also helps to build up the total. All kinds of social regulations denote a theoretic factor of cognition of law, foresight and general normativity. In science we occasionally speak of '*Methodenpolitik*'. Most of these complex facts, however, have at least been touched upon in the types themselves.

We shall only mention here the three mental directions which in the first section (I. 2) we called objective cultural regions, but which we could not admit in our synthetic constructive procedure as simple. Since we have already given over the previous section to the subject of morality, only technique, law and education remain.

I

Like the other regions, technique as a specific phenomenon of cultural life is visible in its uniqueness only on the level of higher differentiation. The purposive utilisation of bodily organs and every form of tool, especially the skilled activity of the hand and the ingenious inventions of primitive technical processes, belong to the elementary stages of technique. But its own special law only appears clearly when it is separated and observed as a relatively independent activity. Its general essence consists in that, according to both the theoretic principle (strictly objective cognition of law) and the economic principle (least expenditure of energy) it chooses and adapts a system of means which was intended for some other purpose. It thus represents a unique combination of science and economics. In its theoretic foundation technique is the selection of means in regard to the economy of energy; and in its practical application, choice of means on the basis of theoretico-economic selection.

But the most striking characteristic of technique is the fact that it does not by itself found an independent species of value. For this reason we have not accepted it as an independent value region. The mere technician does not ask for the value of an aim for whose sake, on the basis of insight into the legality of occurrences and the most economical expenditure of energy, he combines various means. He presupposes that the value decision itself has been made on a different level or in another region of the soul.

Accordingly technique may serve all other value regions. For, each one can be realized only through activity in the world of space and time, forces and energies; that is, through real purposive activity.

This work is naturally most important in those values which are themselves immediately connected with the zone of actuality. We have seen that primarily economic values are always bound to real matter and energy. The acquisition and consumption of goods which serve the satisfaction of physical needs, and thus the physical preservation of life and its adaptation, embody the meaning of the economic region in the narrow sense, whether it is actualized through individual or social activity. And since the intended value forms and means belong to the same zone, that is the physical one, technique has its greatest and most obvious significance in the service of economic purposes.

Now with increased refinement and spiritualisation of needs, economic goods enter more and more into higher mental value regions. The distinction between what is purely material and what has a tinge of mentality is only the result of an abstract observation. In real life the borderline is not so clear cut. Thus, for instance, the possession of a book or a musical instrument may become a necessity even though life itself does not depend on it, and even though the value of such goods is not purely economic but is instead connected with the imaginative and ideational zones.

On the other hand, we know that these realms too are partly dependent on physical goods and events. And we can therefore understand that the normative law of economic behavior may surpass purely economic production. Consequently there is a technique in the higher realms too, of course only insofar as they are actualized through the zone of legality of real behavior and activity. Anyone who devotes himself to cognition needs a scientific technique, and whoever creates artistically uses an artistic technique. Their methods are then affected by the higher value character of the regions which they serve.

Indeed one can trace the technical basic procedure in the context of psychic activity also. Political technique, or more generally social technique, 'purposively' utilizes the cognized psychic laws of behavior in order to achieve its aims with the least expenditure of energy. But as soon as we deal with the problem of value positing we reach the limit of mere technique. And when it is a question of awaking autonomous value positing in the souls of others, we are in the realm of a wholly different process; namely the developmental or pedagogical.

There is no fixed borderline between these regions. Even the technique of scientific research, of playing the piano and of painting are often separated from the principle of the most economic choice of means and are oriented by a choice of means more in accordance with their own species of value. One sees that here is preserved only the aspect of contact with the legality of real activity, while economic law retreats more and more into the background. And accordingly the term technique may be used either in a literal or a derived sense.

Technique in the literal sense is the combination of matter and energy guided by the theory of causal connection and the economy of energy; that is, the development of a system of suitable means to serve economic ends. Technique in the derived and broader sense is the cognition of the most suitable means for any specific end and the practical choice of means which is based upon it.[1]

---

[1] Zschimmer, in maintaining in his splendid researches on the '*Philosophie der Technik*' that the idea of technique is identical with the idea of freedom from nature, limits the term to mere domination of purely material forces. In this case the concept freedom is either wholly empty or it refers to the capacity of positing values. But the question of what values should be posited, that is, what the economic, social or political aim ought to be can by no means be answered from the technical view-

Economic technique is, so to speak, the increasing of what is immediately useful by means of mediately useful labor-saving devices which are developed by increasingly refined insights and economic methods. Here we may class the acquisition of raw material, the storage and transmission of energy, productive measures, manufacture of tools, methods of conservation, utilisation of waste and all methods of transportation etc. Other measures which approach technique in the broader sense are trade agreements, advertisement, credit and even the politics and law of trade.

Economics always serves either a collective or a personal value system. One might view it in its entirety as a technical system which supplies the 'means' first for the bare preservation of life and then for the superordinated values which life makes possible. Thus natural technique, in the narrow sense, indirectly serves mental life. Tools, the development and transmission of energy, collection and manufacture of raw material are technical as well as economic. There are, however, other techniques which immediately serve the mind, techniques in the broader sense. For, mental achievements too depend on the legal context of psychic and physical means. The writing of this book necessitates continual muscular movements which must be purposely selected and which tire my psycho-physical system just as, in some mysterious manner, does mental effort. Then too the process of thought must be guided in paths which are in accordance with its special ends. Thus there is also a technique of scientific work, that is, on different levels a choice of means based on reflection and in accordance with certain laws: from reading and writing and the external publication of the book, to the economy of literary sources, of division into chapters, the degree of completeness of representation and didactic intention. And correspondingly in the fine arts, there is a technique of composition, a technique of painting and sculpture, indeed even a poetic technique which is especially important in drama. We spoke above of the technique and method of religious experience. Cults always have a technical aspect besides their expressive function and we have called magic a religious preliminary or perversion of technique.

---

point. And even overlooking this methodological objection: freedom from nature is always bought at the price of far-reaching dependence on social organisation, without affirming which great technical achievements are impossible. Thus technique too leads to dependence.

Positivists have developed the concept of social and political technique. Obviously in this case too, the cultural ethical end itself is not the subject of technical consideration but depends on the normative question of whether or not it is valuable, whether it obeys or disobeys duty. But it is a question of actualizing this end under the conditions of space and time, of matter, energy and human nature. To this end an influence over the motives of mankind is necessary which is shrewd technical calculation as long as the positing of motives is thought of purely causally and one does not yet feel that the other person 'ought to do' something in the ethical sense. The latter is no longer technique but education. Though in education itself there is a factor which might be called technical, and which must embody that kind of functional trustworthiness which is only achieved when the choice of means is based on assured causal insights. In a word; technique is always based on the necessity of effective powers but never on duty.

In view of all this one might well speak of a technical attitude. It follows from our last remark that this need not be based on the region of economic activity. And we shall call anyone a technician, in the sense of our isolated basic types who, without consideration of the ethically demanded aim, is solely directed to the economically guided choice of means which is founded upon certainty and scientific exactness.[1] We know very well that the modern engineer mentally represents much more. He is not merely a technician. But if we isolate his technical aspect and construct, according to our isolating procedure the wholly onesided attitude which belongs to it, a special combination of a scientific objectivity and a practical, economic state of mind develops which is part of his whole psychic structure. Even his perception, that is, his sense impressions which are ordered in accordance with space and time, and his ideas have then a 'technical' form. In the material complex he sees the effects and resistances of forces and visualizes even in them the actual or possible purposive relation to which the whole can be subordinated. Similarly many people have 'capable'

---

[1] The modern parliamentary system, for instance, forces the executive official more and more into the role of mere technician. For, the positing of values and the expression of opinion is reserved for the changing ministerial heads. And they too practice to a great extent only the technique of their party.

hands. They have a kind of rational instinct of how to do things. If social technique is combined with such a disposition we have the organiser who knows how to bring an objective purpose and a personal aptitude into the most harmonious relation. The development of a special research, that of psycho-technique, shows how strongly modern life is imbued with such impulses. Many people only view culture from a technical standpoint. And even though a psychologist has no occasion to judge the value of phenomena in life he cannot get away from the impression that here the mill stones are grinding against each other. The great question which appears in the reaction against culture from Rousseau to the present day: just why are all these forces set in motion? is a protest against the technicalisation of life which has replaced real culture.[1]) And indeed almost everything today is technical; that is, devices for specific ends of whose value and right one thinks very little, partly because it has been done so before, partly because one hopes for 'enjoyment' and partly because everything would collapse if the great machine were allowed to stand still even for a moment. This purely technical or 'psycho-technical' spirit has invaded even education and many people, who supposedly wish to bring the greatest freedom, wreak the most dangerous confusion. Technique is a splendid achievement of human intellect, endurance and energy. But as soon as one no longer knows what this wonderful instrument serves it becomes merely another stern natural force which cries out for evaluation. We must know for what end we live before we can say how we ought to live.

There are as many special forms of technician as there are regions of value in which problems await a solution. And insofar as human beings are also subservient parts of this system of means, the technical type gradually merges with that of the organiser. In recent years we have seen splendid achievements in military technique, but it has been shown that the positing and consideration of political aims is even more important. A mere technician, whether only in the sphere of natural forces or also in that of human energies, only takes over the problem without criticizing

---

[1]) (Subjective) culture is not the 'suitability for various ends' but is choice and affirmation of values: it is the direction of personal character to genuine normative values and not till then the capacity to realize them 'technically'.

its value. In this way a dependent relation of technical problems to each other may come about and thus an inner logic of technical research. But the highest point of contact — that is, what ought to be for its own sake — can never be found in this context. And for this reason a technician especially needs a highly developed culture to counterbalance his onesidedness. It is the latter which, in connection with technique, determines the higher responsibility of German engineers.[1])

II

In a certain sense one may regard law too as a social technique, especially when it no longer develops merely from custom but is formed through rational considerations of expediency. For, law is never an end in itself. What has been called 'legal purpose' is not really of a legal nature. It is a socially desired value content which can only be actualized when it is poured into the mould of a partly peaceful and partly belligerent social order. Therefore anyone who wishes to grasp the essence of law must disregard this changing value content and turn his attention to the primary aim of law which is the development of a social order.

And yet not every social order is of a legal nature. Morals and customs assist law and are in part closely interrelated with it. Our problem is thus to find the essential mental factors which constitute the unique aspect of a legal order. It contains a specific interrelation of mental factors which our analysis has previously developed but which now appear in a very specific function. We shall try, therefore, to sum up the main distinct motives which can be cognized when law separates from its original interrelation with morality and custom and actualizes its specific essence in a differentiated form. And we shall start from the positive legal order as objective form with the assumption that all its essential factors are represented by corresponding aspects in the legal con-

---

[1]) For instance, it makes a great difference whether an electric lamp factory only wants to sell as many lamps as possible (economic interest of the producer) or whether it wants to advance the economic utilisation of electricity (economic interest of the consumer); whether it wants to save people's eyes (a socio-ethical viewpoint), or whether its interests are aesthetic (decorative occasions). But in every case the road to achievement is technique.

sciousness of an individual.[1]) The first characteristic which we emphasize will show why it is impossible to start here from individual consciousness.

1. Law, in common with social morality, is rooted in collective consciousness and never in an individual set.[2]) If I wish to experience the meaning of law I must regard myself as a member of society. This is true not only of objective law (in the juristic sense) but also in regard to subjective rights. Otherwise the latter would signify only a will to power and not a will to law. The consciousness of law is therefore only a special form of collective consciousness, and an overindividual consecration lifts it above all merely private affairs. It contains primarily an overindividual will which, as a sociological fact, must at least hypothetically supplement the legal statutes. It also includes a definite consciousness of validity (which will be better defined in sub-section 4). Objectively the 'validity' of positive law corresponds to this. But here we are dealing not with ideal validity which must be granted to the true or the good but with a validity based on legislation; that is, a positive validity. This may somehow be supported by ethically valid norms but it no longer pertains to the immanent characteristic of positive law.

2. Law is distinguished from collective morality which is also based on a consciousness of group and validity because: (a) its regulations only refer to external conditions of power, and (b) it protects these through external collective power. By external power I mean the capacity for a socially important activity which is carried out in a social context. The effects of external power always depend on the physical region in the form of possessing, achieving, inflicting etc. whether these acts are directed to persons or to things which are important to persons. Abstention must be understood here as refraining from external activity. Inner power, on the other hand, entails purely mental forms of superiority over others which are

---

[1]) In this case law, naturally, is isolated from any special content of which it is capable (economic and social situation, the degree of scientific development and culture).

[2]) I remind the reader that I mean by collective consciousness a set which is immanent in individual consciousness but which has an overindividual meaning by means of which an individual knows himself to be a part and a representative of a group and acts as such. Cf. above p. 102.

expressed also by purely mental means. It is clear that law cannot come up to these ways of achieving effects. It cannot bind the freedom of thought, of taste or of conscience. Thus its essence is an external controlling of will and regulation of action and inaction. Within these limits law permits, commands or forbids with a view to the sphere of external freedom and obligation and not to that of opinion and inner freedom. Commanding law regulates the limits and conditions under which I may exercise my individual power. And corresponding to this, expressly or implicitly, there is a forbidding law which limits my personal sphere of power. Both forms of appearance together might be called the binding law in contrast to the permitting law which grants its legal subjects scope either through silence or express guarantee (for instance of so-called natural rights). Binding law becomes a 'forcing' law as Fichte has already shown only in the case of individual resistance and even then only insofar as one is dealing with obligation and not merely legal rules of disposition. This force, however, cannot aim at 'recognition' but only at obedience.

So when people maintain that positive law demands recognition, they only mean that form of recognition which is expressed in external observation of norms, in acts (legality). Positive law does not demand inner recognition unless it be of its total character as factually valid law which must be externally followed. Insofar as it is not freely recognized by a moral consciousness law assures its function through the social power which stands 'behind' law and can compel external obedience in the literal meaning of the letter of the law but which usually achieves subjection by means of its mere presence.[1])

The close connection of law and the sphere of power is expressed in two instances: in its own sphere, insofar as it means delimitation of spheres of freedom and power, of course only with reference to external actions; and in its manner of functioning, insofar as it guarantees this external power to act (or to abstain from action) through an external collective power.

---

[1]) These assertions are not intended to invalidate the theory of recognition. But we must follow the demands of the isolating method. Recognition is moral but not in itself anything legal or legally attainable. We shall see that it may be called a necessary assumption of law. It is characteristic of ideal justice but not of what is legal in the positive sense.

3. A social factor is added to the collective characteristic of validity and the character of power which also seems to be necessarily interrelated with the consciousness of law. Law never guarantees unregulated (purely sociologically developed) actual states of power. It is never merely the right of the stronger but always, in a certain degree, the right of the weaker too. The attitude from which the limitation of one's own sphere of power 'for the sake of others' develops is, however, again not of a legal nature. It may be a source of law but does not belong among its forms of appearance. Rather, the form in which the basic spirit of love exercises itself legally is again only an actual guarantee of alien claims to power and liberty (not the personal ethical value). — W. Metzger[1]) is therefore right in asserting that 'ratification' is the basic form of judicio-social behavior. This does not however exclude the fact that the living source of legal ratification may have been a deeper love of mankind.[2]) This acceptance of another person or group we call the social factor of law.

4. Finally a formal factor appears as almost the most important characteristic of law. It originates not only in an overindividual will which recognizes and guarantees the claims of power with a certain degree of social spirit, but also in the will to law. Another overindividual set which is related to cognition, the will to general regulation, is joined to the collective set. Norms of law never refer to any particular person with a definite mental and moral bias, but always to general (anonymous) exponents of generally formulable rights. For instance, it guarantees private property as such but never the property of an individual specifying a certain object. This becomes obvious as soon as one observes that all individual facts are important for law only when they fall under general legal principles. Even when (*per nefas*) a law is passed for a definite person or a historically unique circumstance, it must be given the general form of a regulation which binds others too. — I call this regularity the theoretic factor of law. From a historical point of view the concept of a law of nature is developed

---

[1]) *Gesellschaft, Recht und Staat in der Ethik des deutschen Idealismus* published by E. Bergmann, Heidelberg 1917, p. 8 ff. 16 ff.

[2]) Thus for example Christian morality was for centuries a source of legal convictions and of laws. But in itself it could not naturally assume the form of law.

only from the experience of these general social laws. Later, the advancing development of laws of nature occasioned the modelling of positive judicial legality more and more after it. Therefore the classic German philosophy of law called it 'second nature'. But this regularity discloses itself historically in yet another connection as a result of theoretic mind. In law which originates primarily from custom and habit experiences of social purposiveness (by which I mean to indicate value agreement in the widest sense and not mere biological utilitarianism) have been precipitated as it were in the form of a collective and objectively general will. These experiences become the foundation for the prediction of subsequent cases and for the normations which are made for them in advance. Laws of nature, as ideal forms, enable us to predict in advance what must happen in definite circumstances which are not in themselves always predicable. And similarly positive legal norms foretell in accordance with general rules what ought to happen in a definite 'legal' situation, itself unforseeable, not however as a moral achievement but only as a regulated use of power by legally constituted society and individual legal members.

Up to this point we have, in accordance with our method, defined law regardless of its ethical value and only in view of its objectively constitutive factors. It demands a valid collective will which delimits spheres of power, which ratifies other people's claims to power also and finally which regulates in advance this distribution of power in the form of generally valid norms. This has reference only to the objective structure of law and not to its historical development.

The functioning of this law has no application to the attitudes but considers only action and external behavior. Positive legal norms are not norms of valuation but of activity, and one must bear this limit strictly in mind.

But the above is again only an idealizing and isolating method. Previously too we looked for the specific form of morality which belongs to every sphere of life. If we attempt the same thing here we are permitted only to cite the specific perfection of positive law. We call this positive justice. Its essence consists in the fact that in the consciousness of an agent who acts 'justly' there is no other motive but the collective will which distributes the claims of power and absolutely obeys all posited general rules. Positive justice does not ask whether the rules themselves are right but it acknowledges them as valid and only looks for the meaningful application which follows from an immanent judicial logic. This is the specifically positive legal morality.

The ethical value of law is entirely different if we ask not only for its specific ethics but consider the latter also in the context of a total ethics. Then we presuppose an ethically intended value system which is referred to the normatively demanded total value constitution in a historically given level of culture. We do not measure ethics with valid law but compare the valid law itself with a superior, not merely formal and positively judicial ethics which includes economic political, social and theoretic values. From this point positive law only appears as a means of asserting justice. We call ideal justice that aspect of total ethics which denotes justice in the moral sense. Thus positive justice is based on the correct inner consequential application of the (*hic et nunc*) valid law. Ideal justice asks for the total value agreement or correctness of the valid law itself. This meta-judicial set acknowledges norms which are directed to personal opinions. The problem of the proper law (formerly natural law) is an ethical one. Only because it refers to a specifically legislative attitude is it emphasized beyond the ethical total problem. Formerly people called this morally founded will to law *volonté générale*. And they meant to indicate more or less clearly, that the so-called proper law must originate from a constructed social will which (1) is not a mere summation of individual wills but the fountain head of ethical validity which holds true for everybody (obligation); (2) should refer in general rules to the general; and (3) should regulate the individual's claims to power in a socio-moral sense. The factor of equality appears here in three forms: (1) as identity of the ethical will in everyone; (2) as formal general validity of rules 'without respect to person' (equality before the law); and (3) as equality of legal claims and duties for all individuals (equality of rights). Ideal, formal and social equality converge at this point.

This conception which is found first of all in Rousseau, reflects a definite historical state of mind. Ideal justice too has a changing content, though as a formal set, namely an ethically determined will to proper law which issues from a total and collectively determined value system, it is constant. Even though different ideas of justice conflict in a given culture, for instance the idea of equality which we have just considered and that of the proportion of social achievement and social claim to law, this is not a proof that the idea itself has no ethical character. We have previously emphasized the fact that conflict is always the source of what is ethical. Here the competing value directions are not present in one soul but only in the same society. And here too, moral attitude signifies only the demand and the will that what is objectively higher, that is the normative value, should be ultimately decisive.

From this point we return to the theory of recognition. True, law is vital only when it is affirmed and supported by the corresponding aspect of the moral consciousness of the members. But this factor pertains not to the immanent structure of law but to its sociological and socio-ethical assumptions. Once the valid positive law has been posited it can neither count on nor wait for this recognition. As law it has instead its unique manner of working. It is, ever in the hands of those who administer it, an absolutely systematic external power. It may, of course, be supported by the power of its inner moral authority, but the immanent morality of law consists in the fact that it ought to be carried out in formal correctness and with no exceptions. For instance, a judge who has been given office by the state must not make decisions according to the Idea of Justice but following positive justice, in the sense of existing law, even though this may be an intolerable, indeed even a sinful thought to expressly unjudicial natures like the social type. The perfection of existing positive law is its inner logic and its reasonable application. Previous to its existence and in the moment of its formation it is subjected to other norms which are ultimately identical with the normative mind that creates genuine culture.[1]

---

[1] An indirect affirmation of this analysis follows from a glance at natural law. Natural law looks upon 'contract' as the original form of justice. This conception is certainly onesided, but it is comprehensible inasmuch as this simple rationally willed legal relation actually contains all the essential constitutive factors of justice. For, the contract implies (1) an overindividual will (a collective will of at least two people) (2) a will which settles claims and achievements and which if need be can be compelled by society; (3) a will based on the relationship of mutuality and granting of validity; (4) an inclusive concept of general rules which in advance unequivocally establish the behavior of the contracting parties, even in the most general sense of the phrase: '*pactis standum*'.

The very difficult distinctions which we have presented here must also be observed when we now propose to construct the onesided legal type which belongs to the sphere of law; that is, we should separate the legal type of the positive legal order (the judicial formalist) from the type of the ideal legal order (the judicial idealist). But in actual life the two are so much interfused that we may be permitted to combine them.

There are two reasons why this type should not be included among the simple types. It is (1) dependent on the objective existence of an overindividual, collective and normative will, and (2) dependent on the presence in the individual of this overindividual, normative and norm-positing will. Above all, one should not confuse the legal type who lives wholly for and in the idea of justice with the type who demands rights for himself. The latter belongs absolutely among the simple types in the category of the political attitude, only that he seeks power under certain given social legal forms, in constitutional ways, but perhaps also by terrorism and breach of law. Similarly, one must not mistake the legal type for the individual who subjects himself to the given legal order and fulfills his duties in this respect. For, this subjection may arise from a very simple obedience (the passive form of the political type) or from a social spirit, namely when one renounces one's own claims. To be a legal type in the pronounced sense one must not simply feel oneself as part of a legal society but also as its exponent and thus as responsible for it. In this case an overindividual spirit is always active in the individual; not only a collective spirit (consciousness of membership and of being a representative) but normative, that is, a spirit determined by norms and which posits norms out of its own nature. It is, for this reason very difficult to rise from a consciousness of being legally wronged to the idea of law. If one has experienced the meaning of law only as a partisan, one does not share its overindividual content. And Michael Kohlhaas[1]) was led, by his feeling of having been unjustly treated, only to an abnormally enhanced will to power but not to the true idea of justice.

Anyone who is controlled by this idea as a real organizing inner life force only demands power for himself in order to help

---

[1]) Cf. Kleist's famous novel.

bring this idea to life. Indeed he would wish that this idea exercised power over individuals and nations only through its ideal strength and would have no need for any other powers to guarantee and administer it. He is by no means a social nature for he holds justice higher than love. And by this he may mean either the eternal idea of justice or the formal justice that a positive legal order which has once been established and characterized by certain forms should be reasonably administered. (In the latter case he is usually conservative because he fears that legal changes will endanger the trustworthiness of its functioning; in the first case he is liberal because he feels that obsolete laws drag on like an inherited disease). He is not thinking of his own advantage nor of the imaginative forms of life but only of what ought to be valid because it is in some way just. Indeed he cannot conceive even God otherwise than as a just judge or a reliable contractor. One may perhaps feel that this type is closely related to those people who form maxims, only that theoretic legality, general validity and logicality are applied here to the interplay of social spheres of power; but the procedure of construction and subsumption of the concepts is related in the two cases. Formalism too is not a mere degeneracy or perversion of law but belongs to the essence of law itself. Morality, especially personal moral value judgments, may individualize. Law, as such, begins to be immoral when it individualizes in a way that cannot be justified by the meaningful application of general rules. One must guarantee a stable order whether it be peaceful or belligerent. The welcome institution of juvenile court procedure, for instance, cannot mean that law shall be re-interpreted according to special circumstances but that, in regard to youth, education (ethical influence) is to be applied beyond mere law. A strict legal nature does not recognize this introduction of an alien viewpoint. It endorses the sentiment: *Fiat justitia, pereat mundus;* which merely means that a valid law should not be applied in accordance with chance purposes but only according to its inner logic and general validity.

III

We select education as a third example of the interfusion of primary cultural motives. Here, however, wholly new relations appear. It is incontrovertible that education is essentially a social activity. Without a spirit of love and a turning to the still undeveloped value-possibilities of the young soul, education would be impossible. But pedagogics is a special form of love.

We have already made the distinction between eroticism and love. By eroticism we meant aesthetic love which is directed to sensible grace or virile appearance and is capable of spiritualisation to the point where it is empathy into the psychic beauty of the other person. Love, in the literal sense, on the other hand, we called that sympathetic turning toward the value content of the other soul and the community of value which is based on this. It appears in its purest form when it has reference not only to some one aspect of an individual but to his entire soul — that is, when it has a religious tinge. On this basis we further differentiated the receptive love which surrenders to the actual value-fulness of the loved one and the out-going love which wants to enrich the other from its own value-fulness. And finally we found the developed value community in which giving and receiving between two value worlds are balanced. Indeed fundamentally, every love which is capable of giving is also receptive, and vice versa. If with this last addition we consider the pedagogical love (in which to be sure there is often an erotic factor also) as part of the out-going love, a still further distinction is necessary.

The caritative love of Christianity, too, belongs among the giving forms of life. But in it the spirit of love itself is the most decisive factor. One person only gives love as the real divine gift of grace to the other; or perhaps he gives religious strength too, whose main source however, in the Christian view of life is also contained in the spirit of love. If he wished to present another person with useful gifts he would be on the level of social work which may possibly originate in love but differs from psychic love. And if he wanted to gladden someone else aesthetically or to teach him theoretically then, in addition to the original motive of psychic love we should have the fact that the value character of the whole inclines towards these value regions.

The following two points of view are primarily characteristic in a negative way of pedagogic love: that it (1) tries not only to influence entirely by love but also (2) does not intend to further any particular value direction in the other person but — positively — seeks to develop by love of the entire soul which is capable of value, all its positive value directions. And this means that genuine pedagogical love and specialisation are mutually exclusive. For instance, anyone who only teaches science without being animated by the belief that in this way he elevates the entire being of his pupil would still, despite his interest in the other, be classed among scientists and not among teachers.

But the most essential point has not been emphasized even when one assumes that one person desires because of love to give another all the cultural goods of which he himself is capable. For, every creative man has this tendency implicitly. One would then have to include every manysided cultured artist, every executive statesman and earnest clergyman among educators. It is true that they all have a pedagogical side, but the passion of teaching has not yet become 'life within their life'. Their love moreover must have vision in a special direction.

The essential difference between immediate cultural creation and education consists in the fact that a culturally creative man, by means of significant mental acts, creates objective value forms from his subject. These then exist for others too and can be understood, enjoyed and developed by them. In such people the cycle of activity moves from subject to object. The educator on the other hand, is filled with a love of the already formed objective mental values even though he himself is not a creator and he endeavors to transform these objective values into subjective psychic life and experience. Above all he wants to awaken them in the attitudes and capacities of developing souls. Therefore with him the cycle is from object to subject. He would like to call values to life and bring them to adequate experience in the developing human being.

Cultural life is carried on by two equally important but objectively different activities: in the creation of culture by which the mental world continually adds new rings of development, and in the transmission of culture by means of which the circulation of fresh sap is maintained in it. This passing on of culture, which is based upon keeping alive in growing minds what has already been achieved, we call education.

But as long as we are dealing only with the transmission of any particular cultural creation we should not use this expression. Otherwise every performance of a drama would be education because it brings the intention of the author nearer to receptive minds. Education penetrates still deeper into people's souls. It tries to make them receptive not only for this or that particular fact but for the total meaning and the total ethical problem of mental life itself. Therefore it is not merely 'transmission' but the creation in another person of a personal value-direction. Thus education is the will, carried by a giving love to the soul of another, subjectively to develop its total value receptivity and value-forming capacity.

This definition implies some very important decisions concerning the essence of education. It maintains: (1) that psychic development can only be influenced by values and not from an objective region as such; (2) that all true education centers in formal development, in the development of energy and not in the transmission of material; (3) that it will always be animated by a religious spirit (in our sense of the term) because it is always directed to the whole soul and its attitude toward all of life.

However, the assertion that education works from the direction of objective value to the subjective value receptivity and value capacity must not be interpreted to mean that its mission is only the passing on of historically given objective cultural possessions from one generation to the next. Certainly it must elevate the young mind to the understanding but not always to the acceptance, of objective historically given culture.[1]) The passage in education through a given culture is instead a means of awakening the genuine will to culture. In the first chapter of this book we distinguished two meanings of objective mind: it may mean the historically given extent of culture with its genuine value content and value perversions which is independent of the individual. But one may also think of the objective mind in a critical sense, as the idea of culture which we have called the normative mind. In education we cannot merely deal with the introduction to the understanding of a given culture. For then it would only be a means of immortalizing existing conditions with all their weaknesses and limited advantages. In true education this is rather practice material meant to give birth in the developing soul to the progressive will to genuine

---

[1]) Many circles of the contemporaneous youth movement seem to entertain the opinion: 'I do not know this culture but I scorn it.'

value. One should not only transmit truths but strengthen and bring to consciousness the will to Truth itself; not practise in existing forms of technique but bring out technical ability and invention; the goal is not mere loyalty to the state but progressive political ethics, the will to the true and just state etc. Or in short: the point is not to transmit a finished meaning of life and culture but to cultivate in a developing soul reverence for the pure and voluntary quest of the highest meaning.

Accordingly, we might re-define education as follows: It is that cultural activity which is directed to personal character formation in developing subjects. It is carried out in the genuine valuable contents of the given objective mind but its final goal is the awakening of autonomous normative thought (a moral ideal will to culture) in the subject. And thus it is obvious that this superiority over given culture can be achieved only in connection with an ideal system of values (Cf. section IV, ch. 4). No education is possible without a classic element. But we are not aiming to develop the philosophical bases of pedagogy but rather at the unique attitude of the educator. It follows from the preceding considerations that in his case we are not dealing with a special synthesis of individual cultural motives but with a special direction in which their meaning becomes productive for his life's structure.

It is clear first of all that he must be regarded as a subdivision of the social type.[1] His love, however, has two directions. It is directed to the growing soul and its still undeveloped value possibilities but is also directed to the ideal meaning and value of life which it would like to develop from these possibilities. He would like to develop the values in which he believes in a purer and richer form in the youthful mind. An erotic element is often contained in this belief in the power and purity of youth. The dual emotion in the innermost heart of the educator is love for ideal values and for the questing soul. But none of this is separated in his mind as we have had to describe it here. Rather he sees in the objective genuine values immediate developmental forces which aid a man to grow, and in the soul he foresees and awakens longing for such values. Youth lacks mature values and these

---

[1] Cf. on this point the beautiful dissertations of Kerschensteiner: *Die Seele des Erziehers und das Problem der Lehrerbildung.* Leipzig 1912.

values in their turn lack youth and vitality. This is the antinomy of needing and possessing which occurs in a pedagogue's soul and from which his unique mental creative process develops. For, the pedagogical process deserves to be compared with creation even more than with development since he who receives must himself finally create.

Just as all the other types which we have developed have at least once been actualized purely in the history of man, so this type, too, has an eternal prototype. In Socrates the pedagogical genius has been realized on earth. And to believe that the center of his being was anything except the love for the growing soul and the divine quality which he surmises in it and helps to bring forth, is to misunderstand him.[1]) This divinity however includes the entire sphere of genuine values which can possibly enter the ethical form of life: Knowledge, Beauty, Justice and thus finally Eudaemonism in the highest sense. Plato has described the development of this value cosmos, how the values rise to that Truth, Beauty and Good which every Eros seeks to approach away from the sensual abundance of the visible world in order to participate in the essence which alone enriches and makes us God-like.

Pedagogical genius too has its manifold forms of appearance which I shall not touch upon here because the subject necessitates an independent and thorough treatment. But we must particularly observe the difference between the erotic and the purely social types. The former, which has been incomparably described by Plato is rooted in the youthfulness of life itself and exhibits the strongest ideal-forming power which exists. But it commonly remains aristocratically individualized and passes by life's hidden, needy and starving forms. Unless in later years it approaches the social type more and more closely its power flags and it becomes a mere mannerism. Even the Socrates of Plato, guided by the prophetess Diotima, did not progress beyond the beauty of all souls. But the true spirit of love was elevated in Pestalozzi to a loving reverence even for what was lowest. — One must further differentiate pedagogues

---

[1]) And the fact that he only initiated an impulse in the youthful soul, just as if he threw a spark into it (the Socratic method) was the important thing for him. Then he left the young man to the creative power of this inner process, and it seems that he did not return to those who proved themselves barren and uncreative.

who try to form man according to their own ideas; that is, who consciously or through their power of suggestion impress their own value world upon the growing individual — and the other type of a more comprehensive understanding who wish only to help everyone to grow in his own way so that finally the latter finds himself, that is, the ideal man in himself. Here too this type seems to me to be nobler because it grasps life more profoundly. Every positive individuality is immediate to God, but only he who carries his own certainty clear and sure in his heart realizes this height.

Hitherto we have spoken only of these interrelations of primary mental motives which, as objective cultural regions, are relatively independent and therefore most noticeable: technique, law and education. But we know that in culture everything is interrelated and that all the cultural spheres are indissolubly bound together in historical reality, just as the significance of civilisation only appears in personal experience as the meaningful interrelation of all of them.

In man too, who experiences and creates culture, there must be such interfusion and he can only participate in the overindividual sphere of meaning because each one of the mental chords somehow re-echoes in him. But he sees this realm only in an individual perspective. He has a specific experiential focus and the personal equation is determined by his experience and act structure which one must bear in mind not only in his relation to the world as a theoretic observer but also when he acts and takes a definite stand. This was the gist of our preceding considerations and nothing more needs to be said.

But we must remind the reader of the opening sentences of this book. Our reduction of the manifoldness of the mental actions and reactions of a subject to an individual mental structure (to be grasped in types) was a theoretic rationalisation. It was an attempt to construct a law which brings connection and meaning into that manifoldness. An individual soul-structure is therefore (for the time being) nothing more than the outline of comprehensibility by which we try to understand phenomena. But anyone who has even the slightest conception of the diversity of living forms knows that the outlines of real men always exceed the simple scheme, that the proportions are greatly varied and indeed that some men seem to have no structure at all. This opinion only mirrors the perplexity of science. Perhaps later when it is more highly developed it will succeed in showing that what is apparently wholly chaotic is only a high degree of complication of simple, meaningful and lucid contexts.

Let us go one step further in this direction. If soul-structure were more than a scheme of comprehensibility it would be very dangerous to maintain that two different structures could be crossed in the same subject but poetical language does not hesitate to speak of 'two souls in one breast'.[1] We regard it as self evident that man, (disregarding the pathological phenomenon of dual personalities in which moreover a third unitary and superordinated observer in the 'self' always confronts the 'dual self')[2] — refers all experiences to one experiential center, but this can only be a general expression for conflicting meaning tendencies which appear in this total of experience. In the first part of this book (I, 6) we separated the different meanings of self, even though a human being can have only one self, and we must observe here that the unity of the self may be variously interpreted, or better, may appear in different degrees. The lowest interpretation would be that which belongs to mere self-perception, to which may be given the contradictory chaotically intermingled experiences. The highest unity of the self on the other hand, would lie in the religious ethical self, the kingly self[3] which refers the content of all its experiences to a highest meaning-endowing and guiding value of existence. There are many intermediary stages. One can imagine that one man finds in his experiences two (or more) predominant value directions which keep him indecisive as to his goal and pull him in two (or more) directions.

We shall omit the ethical problem which is thus opened up and apply the methods of our *geisteswissenschaftliche* psychology to this case assuming, for the sake of simplicity, that only two predominant value directions conflict in the one subject. With the general application of our cognitive scheme we can say that two structures are fused here. We must, however, assume that we

---

[1] Cf. for instance K. Groos, *Bismarck im eigenen Urteil*. Stuttgart 1920.
[2] Cf. K. Oesterreich, *Die Phaenomenologie des Ich*. Leipzig 1910.
[3] Cf. the well-known novel *Der Golem* by Meyrink which is influenced by psycho-analysis and which is more profound than most readers seem to have noticed.

are not dealing with the aesthetic type (the impressionist) who is stimulated by every impression but with clearly expressed value directions which, in the above mentioned way have a structural reflex action on the secondary values too. Such a being lives permanently in the alternation between two circles of self and two objective levels. He comprehends life by means of two different organs. But it is obvious that neither of the two meaning-directions can be fully developed.

For instance, we all know the aesthetic natures over whose shoulder the theoretic analyst looks at every aesthetic enjoyment and whose every naive presentation of harmonious self is destroyed by an interfering act of theoretic introspection. Schiller had in him something of this trait and in his philosophical phase it became dangerously strong. Humboldt called his attention to it: 'The great difference between the truth of reality, of complete individuality, and the truth of the Idea, of simple necessity, this distinction which usually separates poet and philosopher is absent in you. I cannot explain it except that you have such a wealth of mental power which is driven from paucity of essence in reality back to the Idea, and from the poverty of Idea back again to reality.'[1])

We have already touched upon the appearance of the romanticist on the throne who is led astray by the pictures of his imagination, but who would also fail in the sphere of form because he derives objects of aesthetic intoxication from his own sovereignty. Similarly the pure spirit of research can be thwarted by repeatedly arising religious moods without the two being able to achieve a vital synthesis. There are practical natures in whom a dangerous tendency to theorize which destroys more than it clarifies, comes between intention and execution. Women are not the only ones who waver between love and eroticism and consequently get embroiled in the tragic conflict of loyalty and aesthetic impulse. The feminine soul structure in the '*Maid of Orleans*' broke through the martial will which had become her destiny, and that once unconquerable personality was wrecked by this inner conflict. Finally, when the scientist seeks to penetrate the depths of religious certainty a doubt arises in his soul, an 'Or', which rends it asunder.

[1]) Correspondence between Schiller and W. v. Humboldt, published by A. Leitzmann 3rd edition. Stuttgart 1900. p. 66. Cf. my book: *Wilhelm v. Humboldt und die Humanitaetsidee*. p. 394.

All these phenomena have in common, in contrast to what we considered in the beginning of this chapter, the fact that no synthesis results but that there remains instead the tragedy of an unsolved life contradiction. But even such tragedies of character may have an awakening and saving power especially if the temporarily repressed structure catastrophically breaks through the predominant one and thus makes room for itself. This struggle of value contrast lies at the root of Hegel's antithetical dialectic. Not concepts but value determined structures, historical as well as personal, wage their logical war with each other. Whatever has been temporarily suppressed demands its religious right to life. The stream of vital energies cannot endure always to run in the single bed which has once been dug for it. The divine totality of life which is beneath every onesidedness overflows and seeks new paths for itself.

Thus in Rousseau, whose style and aesthetic temperament belonged to the age of reason, the former dreamer of Les Charmettes broke forth, but achieved only a half-awakening whose energy was wasted in literary effort. In Kant the consciousness of personal freedom forces its way through the whole positive structure of cognition, and his systematic art could never succeed in concealing the breaches of this outbreak. Tolstoy never freed himself from the aesthetic world which the awakened religious prophet in him denounced, and similarly with Kierkegaard (see above). How many have at least been able to write their hearts' yearning even though they could not live them. How many have fled from theory in order to accomplish something in their lives! In how many does the aesthetic enthusiasm end in a stoic rational resignation.

But one must not confuse these tragic dual structures with the wholly different phenomena which are based on the fact that a human being with a fixed, principally onesided life-determination creates for himself a second small world into which he retreats in order to regain power for the other principal world. Thus Cicero had, besides the world of great political struggles in which he mingled with a burning ambition, the solace of philosophy to which he could escape when he was forced into inactivity. Others have nature, a garden or a canary bird; others a clandestine love or a secret study in which they devote themselves without ambition to works which will never be completed. It is clear that they do not really live in their second world but only ramble in it and therefore it does not involve tragic conflicts. But for the technique of happiness which our modern time sadly neglects, the founding of such a second world beside the primary great one seems almost the most fruitful advice, for there one finds peace when obstacles appear in the main track of life. Everyone of us needs '*Ausweiche-stellen*',[1]) side tracks or hobbies. They need not be found, as with Rossini, in the culinary art; nor as with Goethe can the deepest organic union with the main stem of personality always be demonstrated. But it is untrue that only the aesthetic region can grant this relaxation. Rather, the strongest contrast to the central destiny seems to be most favorable. And thus even what is apparently inconsistent in our souls is not wholly incomprehensible. For, mankind should be understood not only by relations and agreements but also by contrasts since life is always a flux.

[1]) This fact is also known in psycho-pathology. There is a certain side tracking and avoidance of life in mental aberrations.

2
HISTORICALLY DETERMINED TYPES

It is impossible entirely to exclude the historical problem from our investigations. As soon as we turn to actual people and try to understand them by means of our types we are no longer dealing with the pure theorist for instance, but have before us the rationalist of the eighteenth or the positivist of the nineteenth century; no longer the pure mystic but mediaeval mysticism, Protestant pietism, Schleiermacher's *'Herrnhutertum hoeherer Ordnung'* and the latest aesthetic theosophy. We are dealing no longer with the pure political type but with the old Roman orator, the Renaissance prince, the jesuit, the court diplomat and the modern partisan. Generally speaking we find the eternal type in a historical form whose special color and appearance are determined by the preceding and contemporary mental life. It changes in accordance with its historical developmental level and correspondingly with the historical cultural environment by whose influence it is formed and to which it reacts. But one must not take this to mean that the historically determined form of appearance of a type signifies its developmental level. Despite the fact that the variations are often caused by a cultural region other than the central sphere of the type itself, no concept develops and our types are ultimately general concepts, or better: directions and laws for the mental construction of what is immediate.

For this reason many people incline with Rickert to exclude from historical thought what is generally conceptual and typical; to say that history is entirely unique and could only be grasped by a special 'individualizing' conceptual method. We must reply to this what Rickert himself knew perfectly well and repeatedly emphasized, that not only so-called history but nature too offers to our comprehension thoroughly individual phenomena, and that this uniqueness cannot be understood except by 'composing' general concepts into individual syntheses (which are then called historic concepts). This is precisely our intention in the present chapter; namely to combine the general concepts of our types with other typical formations to form individual concepts which are no longer referred to mental objects in general but to those which have a spatial and temporal coefficient of individuality. For, in the scientific sense individual facts are only accessible to us through general facts and laws. Of course these observations only concern method, the execution is the business of the historian.

Science cannot be supposed to deduce the individuality of phenomena from general concepts. For this would mean that it could cross from the mental sphere into that of reality and no causal bridge leads from the conceptual to the actual. Law and fact — as emphasized by Christian Wolff and Windelband — eternally remain independent forms beside each other. Metaphysics tries in vain to deduce the real world from the conceivable or thought world, just as it is futile to attempt to formulate the laws of mental interrelation from actuality as such. Each always denotes the other but they do not follow from each other.[1])

At most one can make concrete general concepts (and laws) through addition of more and more individual definitions to the extent that they can more easily be applied to the manifoldness of facts in space and time. But one does not approach the full plasticity and immediacy of these facts themselves. The first demand is rather that 'historical' concepts should be much more individualized than those mental prime concepts of man which we have called basic attitudes.

The question of the changing degree of mental equality and differences of man in historical development is quite different from the above because it is entirely historical and factual. It does not coincide with the (timeless) differentiation of general concepts into more and more specialized ones (as Hegel erroneously assumed).

---

[1]) One must strictly distinguish between the metaphysical problem of individuation and the equally metaphysical one of individualisation (making concrete). The first refers to the origin of individual souls from a presupposed world soul or from a basic All-spirit. The second refers to the transition from the all-inclusive concept by ever higher grades of individual determination to the unbridgeable chasm beyond which appears the spatio-temporal and absolutely unique fact.

We are here dealing instead with a temporal process and a historical state, and not till later with the form of concept formation which is adapted to comprehend the essence and the essential relations of these realities.

The science of history and its philosophy must investigate the causes which explain the tendency of both psychic life and society to differentiation. We only make a preliminary construction when we maintain that increasing independence of individual meaning directions proceeds from the closed unity of a religious meaning of life; that human beings who are intermingled in different objective cultural spheres which dominate them become subjectively more and more specialized and thus from a social viewpoint, too, differ more and more from each other. But on the other hand, these 'developmental tendencies' in the consciousness of living individuals are confronted by 'developmental norms' which demand a new synthesis of values, a personal and social summation of achievements to a meaningful unity. In both cases there seems to be a legality of valuation, but in the first case it is psychological and in the second ethical (i. e. normative) which, as a secondary function cannot be wholly excluded from the reproductive consciousness of the historian. Mental developmental processes are based upon this union of the differentiation of values and value syntheses. But we are still far from their formulation into real laws of development. The tension between the tendency of the individual value directions which infinitely posit themselves as normative, and the norm which forms this separative drive into a concrete ethical value system points out two kinds of legality. One is part of the psychology of development, the other of the still unexplored region of the development of valid truths (by which we mean of course only actual social and not purely ideal valid truths). The summation of effects in mental life is a further factor which must be added to the process of differentiation and integration. Social cooperation and the succession of human generations creates, in the course of time, objective value forms which go far beyond the meaning-endowing and meaning-fulfilling energy of the subordinated individual. But by this very fact the individual receives his historic position (in space and time) and his determination by objective mental powers. Historical actual individualisation may be traced from three points of view: (A) in objective cultural regions; (B) from the cultural content which resides in the individual himself; and (C) in regard to the types of development of entire civilisations, insofar as they are open to our historic vision as finished entities.

A. By the objectivations of mind I mean the mental achievements and forms which, in the course of history, have been socially achieved and freed from the individual self, and in their effectual relation confront the individual consciousness as a historical culture.

They are, however, not objective in the sense that they can live and develop independently of all subjective activity. Rather they must be viewed as the product of meaning-endowing acts of innumerable subjects by whose means reality, or the mental zones which are built up above it, is organized in the direction of meaningful (value-determined) formation of life. They usually react in the form of value-determined experiences upon those who are subjected to their influence, and are in the long run only maintained by such actualisation in experience. The construction of total culture can result only in accordance with the standards of individual and collective functions for which, in each case, a specific value direction must be posited as the guiding principle. But all these special achievements and regions of culture must be referred to a unitary context of effects, and their partial meaning to a final and highest meaning. Both total and partial meanings can again only be experienced by an individual mind which has lifted itself, through manysided reflection, to the level of a cultural and historical consciousness.

If it is true that objective culture reflects and objectifies the basic directions of meaning-giving which are contained in the individual subject, the question arises: whence come the striking value conflicts which break out between the ethical value demands of the individual and the given extent of historical culture? I omit here the other question of the causes for the difference between the merely subjective values of an individual and the value extent which is objectivated by culture, and confine myself to those meaning-giving and meaning-fulfilling acts of the subject which are in accordance with the normative law of value. Despite this drastic omission the difference between the value content of a subject and the objective historical culture remains as an incontrovertible fact.[1])

---

[1]) Cf. Simmel, *Der Begriff und die Tragoedie der Kultur.* Logos Vol. II.

To point to the fact that objective culture is always of social origin, while the individual is only responsible for his own life-meaning, is not a sufficient explanation. It is true that culture grows historically: (1) through the summation of countless similar mental acts; and (2) through the alternate effectual relations of these mental acts among countless individuals. The pre-condition for the after effect of such acts in an individual, is memory; in culture, language[1]) and tradition. In some cultural regions co-operation and alternate effectual relations in the same direction heighten the intended objective precipitation — for instance, in science, art and religion —; but in others the maintainance and assertion of life of the real individual play such an important part that the social result is to create both agreement and opposition. This is especially true of the economic and political spheres. A competitive character is so necessary to their structure that in objective economics and politics, countermovements and conflicts must always be created, even though a limited amount of goods and scope of life is more to be blamed for this than the human will. Two objective wills may be directed to the same thing — Charles the Fifth and Francis the First both wanted one thing, Milan — but these two acts embody an opposition; for while one may possess mental goods in common, finite goods and spheres of power can only be owned individually (which is apparently forgotten in some forms of communism). The very competition of economic and political forces which thus develops is a reason for the fact that socio-cultural work not only supports the individual

---

[1]) We have not anywhere mentioned language as a mental phenomenon with a physiological and physical basis. But it seems to me that here too we should be able to find the basic motives of mind. The theoretic and the aesthetic factors have always been observed. And also the point of view of its social purpose (usefulness) in human intercourse, as well as the share of the economic principle is very important in the philosophy of language. The political factor (the sociologically determined necessity of using certain forms of speech and of submitting to enforced group decisions of will which are embodied in language) has been less often considered. Finally there is the religious factor as one which develops language, especially on primitive levels of culture. One should remember that λόγος did not originally refer to reason but to the word of God in man and in the world — a sort of revelation. Cf. Hamann's philosophy of language.

will to value but also, in certain cases, limits it; and furthermore a reason for the change of objective cultural conditions. Kant tried to make this factor — the unsocial sociability, the antagonism of energies — the lever of all history. It is indeed a motivating lever but not by any means the only or the most important one. It must at least be studied in a more comprehensive connotation. For, it would still be conceivable to limit the extravagance of economic and political impulses through social organisation and the shrewdly calculated 'legal order of mutuality'.

As a matter of fact, however, the antagonism in culture reaches far deeper than this seems to indicate. It takes place not only between value-willing individuals but also, as our whole investigation has shown, between the value directions themselves. Even though they are all derived from the unity of life and, at least in the individual soul necessarily strive to the unity of life's meaning, there lives in each a kind of insatiability which would gladly set itself up as absolute and wholly actualize its specific demands. Not only life as a total, but also every side of life which furthers a specific value direction embodies an infinite impulse. The striving for cognition is infinite and so are the yearning for beauty, the thirst for love and the hunger for power and possession.

Our 'attitudes' are nothing but mentally developed structures of individuality which result when one value of individual consciousness is posited as dominant. We have seen how individualities typically differentiate themselves accordingly, resulting sometimes in grandiose extremes but just as often in an incapacity for life, because the salvation which they longed for could not be reached in a limited life direction.

Essentially the same process (on a larger scale and slightly changed) is repeated in objective culture. Each one of its spheres (when it begins to be influential as an objective power in the consciousness of cultural members) has a constantly increasing tendency to achieve independence in such a way that its own highest achievement is attained in a onesided manner. Thus there develops a differentiation of culture into various spheres of activity which recognize only their own onesided values. Science aims to be an end in itself, that is, it wants to be determined only by the law of objective truth. Art tries to be pure art and have no obligations to the other aspects of life (*L'art pour l'art*). Economics has a strong desire to increase its production and gain. The community, if left to itself, would like to include all humanity, while the state too strives for its own exclusive domination. Even religion, under certain circumstances, aims to develop its own law and to free itself from all other mental provinces.[1])

The tendency to differentiation is not equally pronounced in all different historical epochs. And it is the problem of concrete history to investigate the degree in which it is effective. Historical construction is no substitute for it. Here too we are not dealing with 'laws of history' but with mental tendencies which are posited with the value structure of mind itself.

If objective culture were an overindividual formation separate from individual lives and dominated only by the purely objective law of the highest Truth, Beauty and Production, it would be conceivable that the differentiation of cultural spheres could be carried on *ad infinitum*. In that case the human groups which sustain each special region would ultimately be completely separated and in every one would be found the onesided attitude which corresponds to the dominant value of the respective cultural region. A Utopia! For, no matter how much overindividual content culture may have stored up in itself it lives only through the consciousness of the individuals who are its exponents. And these human beings, despite all their imaginable biasses, are nevertheless complete beings in whom no aspect of life could be entirely absent. Every onesided development of energy has here the tendency to awaken to special activity the supplementary and previously degenerate powers either in an individual or in his environment. A wholly onesided attitude is a rarity which flourishes only in the realms of a greatly differentiated culture. But the average man, who has become onesided because of external needs, develops the longing for a balance; and this is still more true in a society whose existence is threatened by such a onesided culture of individuality. Thus insofar as a historically given objective culture reacts upon living individuals and a whole society, there develops above the individual norms the total norm, called by us the ethical norm, which demands new syntheses of what has been differentiated.

---

[1]) Cf. for instance Karl Barth, *Der Christ in der Gesellschaft*, in *Das Wort Gottes und die Theologie,* Munich 1924, especially p. 58 ff.

We do not wish wholly to abolish the result of the differentiation but wish instead to unite it meaningfully with the other value regions to form total achievements.[1]) Hegel would say: it ought be '*aufgehoben*', where the triple interpretation of the word as '*conservation, negation* and *elevation*' is to his advantage. The theatre of such an experience of culture is always the individual soul even if it is bound and determined by society. The demand for a higher synthesis of cultural factors in an attitude which surpasses the former level and is directed toward it from within and without at the same time, always seems to this consciousness to have the character of an ethical demand, a moral total norm of life. Thus we are not dealing here with mere mechanical adaptation to previously existing mental conditions of life, but with a normatively guided creativity. This is in agreement with the fact that in contrast to every natural law which always says unequivocally what must happen, many different sorts of value decisions are conceivable in such a mental situation. Ethical synthesis,[2]) the creation of a new and closed meaning of life and culture, either succeeds or fails. In the former case we have growth, in the second decay. Thus the principle of historical development is not a simple law of occurrence — in this case history would have to progress in constant development — but a law of duty to which, however, justice is not always done.

When the synthesis to a unitary meaning of life and culture (demanded by the given differentiation of civilization) is successful we have periods of great historical development. In epochs of decay, no energy is developed to this end, and such periods remain too greatly differentiated which makes the individual unhappy and therefore powerless, and hinders especially the success of social cultural work in a mutual highest life meaning.

Though these observations suffice for our purpose, we might add that the term 'historical progress' is capable of divers interpretations. Many people think only of temporal advance and, seen from this point of view, what is most recent is of course always newest. Others are interested in progress only in partial achievements: the solution of technical problems, development of economic

---

[1]) Schiller already expressed this normative attitude to history in the sixth letter on aesthetic education.

[2]) Lamprecht following Reinkes biology speaks of 'psychic dominants.'

prosperity, refinement of artistic means of expression etc. This is the feeling of progress in differentiated epochs. But the root of decay usually lies precisely in these partial achievements which can no longer be united to a social total of culture. And this is because every specific impulse, regardless of the others and of the context of life, strives for infinity. This explains why the members of decadent eras are especially liable to have the subjective feeling that they are continually advancing and that they have made wonderful progress.[1]) A conscious feeling of decline is much less dangerous for this also contains a longing for a new synthesis and for an elevation of cultural life which may, under certain circumstances, be a source of energy for rebirth. Eschatology and the feeling that the world is coming to an end have always been signs of a revival. People should, therefore, be less excited about Spengler's book[2]) and instead revise some of their own ideas of progress. The assurance that further advance is possible is embodied only in the ethical and religious synthesis of all cultural energies to a creative total will which also gives each its rank. Otherwise we become poverty-stricken because of the wealth of our mental disintegration.

But we only mention in passing this developmental theory of a philosophy of history which does justice to the ethical factor of mental development instead of measuring history by the standards which we would apply to a natural process. Our real aim is the classification of historically determined types of individuality in the mental objectivations of a definite level which are also of essential importance for the inner structure of the individual.

B. When we speak of historically determined types of individuality we are not necessarily thinking of the onesided attitudes which we have developed purely systematically in part II. On the contrary, we have in mind the representatives of whole historico-mental movements. The mental types of humanist, pietist and rationalist correspond to humanism, pietism and rationalism. But it is interesting to observe that these types too, even though they usually refer to total attitudes, receive their name from a predominant aspect — in this case the literary, the religious and the philosophical. Such titles always refer to the inner structure.

---

[1]) Thus for instance every dubious program of a new sexual ethics is cloaked in the justification: that a 'new type of man' must be created.
[2]) *Der Untergang des Abendlandes.* Munich.

How can we conceive the relation between a typical representative and the objective mental movement? — We understand every individual life by the meaningful cooperation of four factors: disposition, subjective development, natural-mental environment and external fate.[1]) Only in mental isolation can we separate these four factors. In reality they are always interfused to form a total of life from which the share of the individual factors can be freed only with extreme difficulty. Let us now attend specially to the historically individualizing powers which can influence each of the four factors.

1. The mental structure of a man is determined from the outset by the mental milieu of which he is a part, which makes up his daily environment and to which he must adapt all his actions and reactions if he wants to be understood and to cooperate with his fellow men. Just how far such determination goes is the problem of a separate historical investigation. The structure of the objective mind of a certain epoch everywhere enters into the individual structure. It determines its way of thinking, of acting economically, its artistic sense, religion, and above all, the form of community in the state and society. To this extent everyone is a 'child of his time'.

2. Specially to mention the dependency of acquired individual soul structure on the historical fate of the entire generation beside the permanent effects of the milieu, is only a particularisation of this general viewpoint. The passage through decisive temporal occurrences gives something typical to the acquired structure of the individual. The subjective vacillations experienced by different groups during the Reformation, the French Revolution and the World War are not entirely unique and one recognizes in them certain typical curves.

3. and 4. But these external factors are not sufficient to explain the typical structure of people who lived before our time. We must assume the existence of purely subjective laws. Our whole investigation must proceed with the aim of disclosing in man's character the law of life 'according to which he set out'. On the other hand, we have only vaguely touched upon the general

---

[1]) Cf. my article: *Zur Theorie des Verstehens* in the *Festschrift fuer Volkelt*. Munich 1918.

developmental law of the individual (the necessary consequence of the various phases of his life) — III, 5 —. Both disposition and subjective development must now be related to the unique aspects of the historical epoch.

Curiously enough *Geisteswissenschaft* seeks safety at this point in physiological explanation. It refers disposition to heredity, and development to the process of bodily growth, maturity and decay. Noone will deny that there is a relation between the mental and bodily series of phenomena. But nevertheless it cannot be maintained that anything is explained by the reduction to germ plasm and physiological development stages. The problem has merely been transferred into the realm of the material and visible where people are inclined to consider what actually and regularly happens as 'explained' simply because it is so. But there is a great difference between a fact and its causal explanation and a still greater one between causal explanation and understanding through a meaning context.

If one tried to explain the complex of mental dispositions with which the typical man of a historical epoch faces life on the basis of heredity it would remain incomprehensible how anything new could appear in a new generation. For, adaptation to mental environment cannot be considered responsible since this objective mind has a tendency toward conservatism against which youth revolts. One might better seek the cause of the creation of new forms in youth; that is, in the typical psycho-physical level of life than in heredity and adaptation to mental environment. This youth, however, is badly described in the mental sense if we only explain it as physical vigor and glowing vitality.

These problems are not only unsolved but are not even considered by *Geisteswissenschaft*. Is the new ideal of culture with which a generation rises on the historical horizon really only inherited or is the character of sudden breach or upheaval (*Durchbruchcharacter*) which often accompanies these phenomena only an indication of the fact that, except for degenerate nations, the complete abundance of humanity is always born anew and that it is just this complete humanity which conflicts productively with contemporary special and usually onesided culture? Furthermore are the mental levels of development, which we designate by the general terms child, youth (maiden), adult and old man (old woman), nothing more than reflexes of physiological changes, or has this series relations which can also be understood mentally? Finally, is there not something typical in the way in which each reacts to historical objectivities (to milieu and fate)?

> '*Nach ewigen, ehernen,*
> *Grossen Gesetzen*
> *Muessen wir alle*
> *Unseres Daseins*
> *Kreise vollenden.*'

But these laws concern not only organic material growth. They are laws of mental development and in them we find the normative factor which raises them from laws of mere occurrence to ethical and creative laws.

Here I see infinite perspectives. In childhood mental life is undifferentiated and subject and object are scarcely separated. The same unitary life streams through both. In youth the deep chasm opens between subject and object and is temporarily bridged by a manysided facile imagination until the meaningful (value-determined) relations to the world of natural and mental objects are consciously formed, but still without a closed synthesis. In maturity, man confronts the objective world with a fixed, completely developed subjective form. What he is and what he is not has been determined. And in old age he finally dies mentally because of what he is not and never can be.

This is the subjective history of man and an eternal story. But it receives a historically unique tinge through two factors of which the second is the more important and also the more mysterious.

We have already referred to the first. In the process of mental development we may observe formative environmental influences in the nature of mental objectivities by means of which the child, the youth, the adult or the old man participate in objective culture. One could start to write the history of a child in just the same way as people have begun to be interested in the history of youth movements. Besides the eternal general type of child, there is the typical child of the pietistic period (described by Karl Philipp Moritz) or the child of the Romantic period in whom naiveté and genius were thought to be identical. Besides eternal youth there is the Greek youth or the youth of the age of reason, or the young Romanticist. Here the problem is everywhere to combine the formation of types and the writing of history.

In view of all this it seems as if understanding could only deduce in man what results from his being imbedded in special historical mental objectivities. And thus the inner structure of the individual would only be a section of the assumed inherited completeness of dispositions which were emphasized favorably and permitted to grow by precisely this mental environment. Even what developed by contrast and opposition to the present mental life could be understood in this way.

But we have previously maintained (p. 306) an exactly opposite viewpoint namely that the inherited disposition which is not yet recognizeable either by the carrier or the outsider, practises on the present material of life an individual active selection. And indeed we cannot but recognize this further principle of individualisation. We must view the individual as a form which imprints itself from within upon the formation of life. This individual subjective law of action and reaction, of experiencing and creating is the presupposition by means of which we have understood the inner legality of the attitudes. But with our understanding we cannot get any farther than this law according to which man has 'set out' unless we call to our aid the transforming power of environment and fate, that is, an acquired and not an inherited structure. The primary thing for our understanding is entelechy itself. We can reconstruct it only from the active process of life itself as life's formative law. We cannot further deduce from meaning contexts what constitutes the innate individuality of a man, especially of a creative man. For, this is the nucleus, the system of reference by means of which we understand as a unity the individual acts of adaptation and resistance, of acceptance and rejection. We assume that each human being, as opposed to the material of life, — is always an individual form.

The same is also true of the typical mental structure with which the new generation enters historical life. Empirically we grasp only those conditions which the typical mental structure finds ready and in which it expresses itself. But its original essence which is not acquired is again a form beyond which historical understanding cannot go.

Thus the historian must describe the inherited entelechy of a generation and the decisive traits of its determining environment as a total in such a way that the individual and yet — as regards the individual representatives of this generation — typical traits of its mental structure shall clearly appear. The general eternal meaning directions of the mental nature appear here in a special combination with unique stratifications and singular accentuations, and also with a specific content which results from the objective mental extent of its epoch.

Hitherto this problem has been attacked only in relation to a few epochs and only for the mature male structure of consciousness (not even for women). Jakob Burckhardt led the way with his description of the typical renaissance man. Lamprecht followed with ingenious intuitions which embraced all levels of national culture. Especially interesting is his attempt to exclude fate and to some extent the milieu too, as far as possible, and center primarily on the changes of the inner psychic structure of historical types; a work for which the psychology of his time gave him little aid. Dilthey's *Auffassung und Analyse des Menschen im 15. und 16. Jahrhundert* and the following typical description of the man of the age of reason goes more deeply into the total structure of history. Woelfflin transmuted the historical epochs of the renaissance and the baroque into historical types of fine arts. Schmoller's school have constructed constitutional types and their psychic correlatives. Again and again, though with varying degrees of success, people have worked over the Renaissance and Romantic types, while the mediaeval and even the Gothic man have remained only vague constructions. The investigations of Max Weber and Troeltsch are only a beginning in the task of formulating sociologically determined historical types.

Most of the above attempts are based on the desire to comprehend the typical structure of the entire man of an epoch, even though his influence was to be found in one definite direction, for instance in fine arts or religious community. But now it is finally conceivable that we can trace the onesided attitudes which have been evolved in this first systematic treatise through historical epochs: the theoretic man of the seventeenth century differs from the theorist of the nineteenth century, the aesthetic type of the Renaissance (the old humanist) is other than the new humanist and the social character of the Reformation is not the same as the social Christian of today. We shall need refined and profound *geisteswissenschaftliche* categories in order to accomplish this. Today we only feel a general difference which is not brought into sharp relief. Progress may be hoped for only through union of the historical sense with clarified *geisteswissenschaftliche* psychology. The problem which Lamprecht has formulated remains even though we accept none of his solutions.[1])

One danger can hardly be avoided, namely that of judging the typical mental structure of members of a previous historical era by their literary forms of expression. Now most people who seek literary expression are born theorists or aesthetes. But behind them there is a world of active, working and loving individuals whose inner world has not been recorded. Can one believe that literature, precisely the best literature of the day really adequately reflects the people of Nineteen-hundred and twenty? Much is lacking to make the fictitious type of theoretic Marxism and the present day worker coincide, especially since no theory which has determined the actions of man was ever so unpsychological as this theory which only accepts the 'Artifice of productive forces'. The problem in general is to distinguish political and philosophical theories from the life structures which lie behind them. Both series of phenomena however must be reduced to much more delicately worked-out types than those which are at present to be found in the rough limitations of political types such as: socialist, liberal, democrat etc. The political confusions of the moment can be partially traced to the fact that so many people no longer understand themselves because they are influenced by cheap slogans and

---

[1]) Shortly before his death he wrote to me a long basic argument. 'In my opinion the psychological consideration of history and thus also the psychological study of the present is inconceivable without the psychogenetic element. And thus absolute values insofar as they are not given in the evolutionary process of human development, are excluded. You however, no matter what, as a last resort, your theoretical point of view may be, live, with all your practical activity, in a world of absolute concepts which excludes a really psycho-genetic comprehension. You agree in this with Wundt ...' The observations of this chapter show perhaps that I do not overlook the psycho-genetic factor. But Lamprecht overlooked the fact that he too believed, and had to believe, in the eternal laws beyond the change of everything actual, if only for the reason that he explained collective psycho-genesis as a necessary and typically recurring process in all civilisations. Cf. my obituary article *Karl Lamprechts Geschichtsauffassung* Vossische Zeitung, June 6. 1915.

have become blind followers. Thus the union of the historic attitude and the psychological formation of types is important for the understanding of the present too. Only then shall we be able to understand our time correctly which rather hides behind than discloses itself in many borrowed theories and systems of philosophy.

C. In one branch of our present idea of history the instinctively practiced procedure of type formation has attained a far-reaching practical application. Many modern historians believe that entire civilisations develop parallelly in a lawful manner. At least the classic and modern civilisations have been regarded as parallel processes. Others, like Spengler and Lamprecht have drawn upon still other civilisations as comparisons.[1]) Lamprecht is the only one who has attempted on the basis of laws to adduce a consistent proof of these parallel cultural developments. He started with a psycho-genetic theory which, in a deductive manner, was supposed to attest to what was inductively arrived at. Spengler, in unconscious agreement with Schelling, regards civilisations as organisms which are born, which grow and die. Nor did he feel that the assertion of such a law was incompatible with his relativism. The essential part of his achievement consists in what he called the morphology of cultures. And it leads finally back through the decisive principle of 'the soul of culture' to a psychological characterisation that is, to prime types of man. He is far more a psychologist than a historian because he considers these types comparable regardless of the genealogical influence of one culture on another and even points out individual epochs of culture as simultaneities ('*Gleichzeitigkeiten*').

Indeed the danger of all typification is that it fixes the flowing line of history into coexisting forms. Only by rebirth and acts of reception does the course of world history develop from closed civilizations. But Lamprecht has seen quite correctly that in historical renaissance and reception too something typical is present.

It seems as if a culture embodies a mental developmental tendency in the same way as we have maintained of the developmental levels of an individual. And the circle brings us back here to what we have said of the tendency to differentiation in

---

[1]) Cf. my contribution to the symposium *Das Altertum in Vergangenheit und Gegenwart,* 2nd ed. Leipzig 1921: *Vom Neuhumanismus bis zur Gegenwart.*

mental objectivations. A newly appearing civilization begins with the closed religio-mystical unity of all aspects of life, related to the age of childhood. It proceeds through the many steps of differentiations but new syntheses are always attempted. The one and highest in which it is wholly successful is the classic period. It is also the male decision of what it wants to and can be. In the following epochs it always refers back to this ethical act in order to make, after this model, another synthesis of the divergent tendencies. If it possesses a more comprehensive historical consciousness it calls to its aid on every level of its development the mental content of former cultures to which it feels itself related. For, it is possible to find something typical in the structure of entire cultural epochs even if they are greatly separated temporally. And this must always be worked out in greater detail by the history of culture. Today people already compare antiquity, the middle ages and the modern period of Greek culture with the corresponding steps of our civilization. But the relationship seems to lie predominantly in the differentiation of single cultural aspects. In every total culture the synthesis is a thoroughly unique achievement, a decision which chooses from all conceivable possibilities, in accordance with an individual ethical norm, just this form. Civilizations are therefore not only typical processess but also great characteristic total personalities.

Perhaps it is now possible, as has been of late repeatedly attempted in regard to national characters,[1]) to bring these too under the point of view of overindividual attitudes. People have sought to find the aesthetic type in Greek civilization, the political in Roman, the theoretic in the German, the economic in the English and the religio-social in the Russian. But one must not forget that such characterisations are only a lifeless residue, without the vital movement and counter movement. Nations and their cultures are not dominated by one value but are based on historic value syntheses which can be understood only by following their entire history. Anyone who has even glanced at Friedrich Brie's *Imperalistische Stroemungen in der englischen Literatur* (Halle 1916)

---

[1]) Cf. for instance Wundt, *Die Nationen und die Philosophie;* Werner Sombart, *Haendler und Helden;* Heinrich Scholz, *Das Wesen des deutschen Geistes;* Max Scheler, *Die Ursachen des Deutschenhasses;* Mueller-Freienfels, *Psychologie des deutschen Menschen.*

can no longer hope to explain the history of the English mind by one predominating mental motive.

Types are certainly not final ends. For the conception of history they are only means of cognition against which the delineation of individual forms and processes can be more sharply contrasted. In natural science too, laws if they are subsequently placed in the service of vital purposes are means of grasping concrete occurrences and, under certain circumstances, of calculating them in advance. Such prediction, however, has no meaning in history. It could be justified only insofar as a generation gives its life solely to the development of existing mental tendencies. Then one may ask: what must happen? But the healthy-minded question which a generation puts to the future is: what ought to happen? And to this end one needs energy in order to develop the will to a new cultural synthesis even when the social movements which have been left to themselves diverge widely. The future of history depends on ethics and not on fate. Part of this ethics to be sure is also the willingness of a people, under certain circumstances, rather to perish nobly than to live ignobly. Such a will does not however lead to disaster but calls to its aid the strength of the gods. Where this will is lacking the destiny of nature takes its course. But what was said by Fichte is still true: 'The real basis of distinction lies in whether or not one believes in an absolutely primary and original factor in man himself, in liberty, in infinite improvement and infinite progress of our race.' ... 'He, whose life has been claimed by Truth and was immediately born from God is free and believes in freedom within himself and others'.

ON UNDERSTANDING

The word 'understanding' (*Verstehen*) contains shades of meaning from which we must free it for our purpose. In everyday language understanding is not only a form of pure objective cognition but also a sympathizing with the person or object which is understood, a subjective sharing and affirmation of his value direction. To be understood is in itself a joyous preliminary stage to being beloved and misunderstanding is coolness and rejection. We do not here mean understanding in this sense. We refer instead to the — very complex — theoretic act in which we comprehend, in a way which we claim to be objective, the inner meaningful context in character and action, in experience and behavior of a man (or a group) or the meaning of a mental objectivation.[1]

Until the life and expressions of another person are meaningfully connected for me I do not understand him. To explain him by my own subjective life context is insufficient for understanding which comprises more than 'taking the place of another'. It always contains acts of thought and sometimes logical conclusions which are directed to a transsubjective context of experience and in which my own psychic experience really plays the role only of immediate but never of wholly adequate illustration. On the other hand, we must never falsely interpret the objectivity which is thus attained. Anyone who has studied the theory of cognition even a little knows that it never 'copies' an object but always defines it. The concepts and laws by which we define real phenomena do not exhaust them but only draw through the objective world a network of rational lines.

This is also true of understanding. Indeed, as will be made clear from the outset, it is valid here in a very special sense. It

---

[1] Essential supplementary data to this section due to the special viewpoint of developmental psychology, are contained in the first chapter of my *Psychologie des Jugendalters*.

is possible to understand a living human being or a historical character better than he does himself, partly because he has not made himself the object of theoretic reflection but simply lives his life, and partly because he is unaware of all the facts which are necessary to the understanding of oneself.[1]) But with the expansion of life's horizon and with the increasing mental penetration of environment and history, the individual is destined to understand more. For, all understanding presupposes like every mental endowment an original disposition, but is in its higher forms entirely a work of education and culture.[2])

If, now, theoretic understanding cannot simply have its objectivity in copying the inner world of another's experience which is interwoven with the total existence, we are faced with the question: in what sense can it be said that understanding is 'true', that it corresponds to the object and that the judgments which it contains are objectively 'valid'.

Very careful consideration is necessary here. One must not be satisfied with the simple statement that human nature is alike in its fundamental traits and that consequently we can understand each other by superposition. For, every look into daily experience shows that the content of psychic life is not alike even in contemporaries. It would be more correct to say that they are based on similar laws, and thus we gain a first definite point. The mystery of understanding becomes more lucid if we assume that the same basic laws are active in imagination which interprets by cognition, as those which determine the consciousness of the people who are to be understood. Just as, according to Kant, the laws of cognitive consciousness coincide with the basic outline of natural law, so the laws of mental understanding are identical with the law of the mind.

---

[1]) As an example of this I refer to the purposive interpretations of psychic processes, of whose purposiveness for the maintainance of life the subject himself is not reflectively conscious. We must classify here the entire region of experiences which correspond to instinctive actions. The 'interpretation' which Groos for instance gives to the play of man and animals far exceeds a 'description' of the psychic processes themselves.

[2]) Wilhelm v. Humboldt, *Ueber die Aufgabe des Geschichtsschreibers:* 'The more deeply a historical investigator understands humanity and its achievements through genius and study, or the more human he is by nature or circumstances, and the more he gives free rein to his humanity, the more completely does he fulfill the requirements of his mission.'

Whether the basic outline of mental legality has yet been discovered is a wholly different question. We began our investigation with the structure of the individual mind and have reduced it to a limited number of normative laws of valuation (I, 5) which we figuratively called the articulations of individual mental life. We believed that we were able to say of its total structure that, beyond all temporal and spatial differences, cognition is always a value for man; that the economic value always controls him, that aesthetic experience and creation signify a necessary value direction in him and that his relations to society are always guided by the value tendencies of power and love. Above these different value directions we found the ethico-religious value as their normative synthesis. And we maintained, furthermore, that every value region has from the outset its own immanent constructive law and objective organisation which we considered only insofar as they are organized by the dominant value. The cognitive region is dominated by obvious structural conditions of ideal units of meaning which, in their pure form, determine real consciousness only when it subjects itself to the pure cognitive value (the Idea of Truth). The economic region is influenced to a very high degree by physical and chemical natural laws, which however, only interest us here from the superordinated value point of view of utility. The elementary psychological law appears more strongly in the aesthetic region; and so on in the other realms.

The laws of character and process in individual value regions are subordinated to the value positing normative laws insofar as they only receive a mental significance from the passage through the norm- and value- determined consciousness. This difference is very important for understanding. Rules of occurrence are determinant for the choice of means, but norms command or prohibit the positing of a value itself. Accordingly in respect to non-normative laws we must ask, (1) whether and to what extent they are only instinctive, or whether they are so clearly conscious in the mind of the understanding person that a conscious adaptation of the (value-determined) behavior takes place with regard to them. One may think erroneously because one is not yet clear about the structural laws of logic. One may make economic mistakes because one does not know that certain goods are perishable. One may fail aesthetically because one misjudges psychic elementary effects etc. (2) And in regard to normative laws one must ask whether or not the consciousness of the person to be understood is subjected to them. Perhaps someone acts uneconomically, that is, injures the norm of the economic basic law, or disobeys the mandates of truth or love. In all cases of this sort understanding cannot be content with the mere fact that the norm has been violated but must ask further why a valid value did not determine the individual. This brings us to a far-reaching assumption, the real *a priori* factor of understanding. If mental life is to be understood at all, the apparent lapses from meaning (from what is in accordance with objective value) must be susceptible of reduction to deeper special contexts of meaning. If this is impossible, either because the object of understanding is mentally deranged, or because we touch upon a whole within which there are meaningful relations, but which cannot itself be reduced to a more comprehensive total meaning, understanding ceases. This is true even though another level of lawful contexts known to us or not, may 'explain' the case which cannot be understood.

Thus the keynote of understanding lies in the value laws of the mind. To understand means to enter into the special value constellation of a mental context. Secondary factors are attention to the present insight into the laws of character and development of the object of understanding, and the normativity of his behavior in respect to the individual value regions or the total moral region of value. Understanding thus delineates the mental persons or forms against three essential backgrounds: the organization of the value-determined mind as such (value directions and their mutual relations); the ideal of as complete as possible an insight into laws of character and process; and the ideal of normativity in individual spheres or the total moral region. These indications in themselves emphasize the fact that in all understanding there is present a normative factor on the side of the person who understands, as Humboldt already saw in his uncompleted attempts to form a *geisteswissenschaftliche* psychology.[1])

---

[1]) W. v. Humboldt, *Das achtzehnte Jahrhundert.* W. W. II, p. 33—41: 'Beurteilung des gegenwaertigen individuellen Zustandes nach dem idealischen'. — p. 58, 100, 110 f. etc. — Recent references on the theory of understanding are as follows: G. Simmel, *Die Probleme der Geschichtsphilosophie,* Leipzig 1907; W. Dilthey, *Der Aufbau der geschichtlichen Welt in den Geisteswissenschaften,* Berlin 1910; Max Weber, *Roscher und Knies und*

Before we can take up the complications which this simple basic process undergoes through its application to historical individuals or facts we must briefly survey the kinds of understanding themselves. We shall accordingly take up first kinds of understanding in general (A) and then historical understanding (B).

A.

The subjective experiential context of another person is never wholly revealed to us. We can immediately experience only ourselves and our relation with the objective world and understand others solely through their objectivations. All objectivations have two sides, physical and mental. And for mental life the physical and mental objectivity are so closely interrelated that they can only be separated in abstract investigation.

1. Mental meaning shows itself in a number of ways in material objects. Some values adhere directly to matter and these we have called economic values (goods, tools, means of locomotion etc.). In other cases the material (which is sensibly experiential) is only a sign (symbol) or means of eliciting a communicable mental significance. The manifold functions which material may exercise as the carrier of what is mental have never yet been sufficiently investigated. Even the most important means of communication, language, has not yet been viewed in this light. For instance, its function is very different according as to whether it only serves as a means of communicating theoretic sentences or whether, as an aesthetic phenomenon, it is in itself an object of auditory empathy. The fact that human beings have developed a language of sounds was brought about by utilitarian and aesthetic reasons. A language of the eyes would be just as conceivable (though difficult at night) or a language of touch (which, however, would be powerless at a distance). Such languages actually are used in divers ways but they do not speak so clearly and immediately to the soul as the

---

die logischen Probleme der historischen Nationaloekonomie (Schmoller's Jahrbuch Vol. 27, 29, 30 especially vol. 29, p. 1347); Max Weber, *Ueber einige Kategorien der verstehenden Soziologie*, Logos vol. 4; Eduard Spranger, *Zur Theorie des Verstehens und zur geisteswissenschaftlichen Psychologie*, Volkeltfestschrift, Munich 1918. — To this must be added almost all of Theodor Litt's writings, especially *Individuum und Gemeinschaft*, Leipzig 1924. ed. 2.

language of sound. The speech of gesture and pantomime is only part of a more comprehensive symbolism which is posited with the human body as a whole. For every naive observer another person's body is in itself a symbol of soul, and aesthetic empathy takes a large part in the interpretation of this natural symbolism. Erotic relations between human beings develop by means of this immediate aesthetic empathy even before a word has been spoken or the soul has been expressed in any other way. It is therefore no exaggeration to say that we 'see what is psychical'.[1]) But this is a purely aesthetic kind of vision which has doubtful theoretic validity because it cannot be formulated. Physiognomy has unfortunately made no progress since Lavater, but graphology which deals with actual meaning-giving acts, has made some advance. All these indications at least point toward the fact that the concept of a completely mindless matter is a product of scientific abstraction which obtain as little credence from the naive modern man, (and indeed from the scientist himself except when he is engaged in active research), as from the primitive man of the mythological level.

We emphasize here only spoken and written language, so general physical understanding is narrowed to linguistic understanding. Language is no longer, like the body or facial expression, an impulsive symbol but a willed symbol. No matter how its origin and development have come about in detail, once given it is an overindividual physico-mental medium in which meaning passes from soul to soul. But it is further developed in every one of these actualisations and carries, beside its generally identical content, very delicate nuances of the individualities who express and understand it. And an aesthetic factor is always present too. If we disregard the aesthetic process of empathy and the whole plastic situation of speaking in which human beings take up a position toward each other, there remains as the essence of language the communication of a theoretic content of meaning which must be grasped by the other in just one theoretic sense. And to this end it is only necessary that one should 'understand this language', that is, possess the coordination of hearing and consciousness of meaning in one's experience. The interpretation of a mental meaning

---

[1]) Cf. Simmel, *Vom Wesen des historischen Verstehens*, Berlin 1918, p. 8 and his *Rembrandt*. — Oscar Wilde, *'Dorian Gray'*.

by physical signs applies to this linguistic understanding, though it has been mistakenly elevated to the essence of understanding itself.[1]) Therefore it is the most important special case of 'ideo-physical' understanding.

But further acts of understanding lie behind this linguistic one and these principally concern us here. They are not based merely on physical signs. I can understand what someone says but beyond that is raised the question: (1) do I understand the speaker or writer, of whom the report is only an infinitesimal section as a total being? It may be that he makes a mistake or that he wants to lie, that he lives under special conditions which I fail to understand, or that he is my intellectual superior to such an extent that I am incapable of understanding him. Christ's words: 'Blessed are they that hunger and thirst after righteousness for they shall be filled' are comprehensible to me since I speak the language. But do I understand him? — And (2) do I really understand the whole significance of these words? Certainly I understand them as words which have been combined to form a grammatical sentence. But it is quite a different matter whether or not I understand their religio-ethical meaning. In both cases the physical objectivation of the mental factor into words is only a preliminary aid.

Or take a simpler example. A historian pictures the cultural struggle of the seventies, and if I can speak the language I am able to understand his words. But in order to have a complete intellectual understanding I must know the viewpoint from which he writes and the real meaning and relation of the facts about which he writes. In short: we must go beyond linguistic understanding to personal and objective understanding. But here the

---

[1]) The process is to be more accurately thought of as follows: Simultaneously with hearing there occurrs in the hearer a silent verbal repetition (that might in some way be proved experimentally). In this 'soliloquy' (s) the personal consciousness of meaning (c. o. m.) is united on the basis of mental tradition and culture with the complex of sound. If one also considers the intonation (i) of the other person there takes place in consciousness an abbreviated process comparable to a logical analogy. — (m. o. o.) equals meaning of the other.

$$(m. o. o.) — (that is x) : (i) = (c. o. m.) : (s)$$

Indeed the above is superfluous. (c. o. m.) is immediately connected with (m. o. o.) and (s). But in exact thought this is attributed to the other as his opinion.

guide of physical objectivation deserts us, and we have only mental objectivations which consist in the fact that they are part of greater objective contexts of meaning. We cannot understand Socrates by means of his facial expression and bodily gestures, nor through his (unwritten) writings, nor by his words and deeds; but through his inner character, his cultural environment and his contemporaneous and posthumous influence on culture. We do not understand the World War through forced marches, exchanges of telegrams and territorial changes, but through historico-sociological causes, the 'mentality' of the warring nations and persons, economic conditions and constellations of power. Here understanding does not necessarily proceed from the physical to the mental but it develops a connection between mental factors; it is based upon the legality of mind itself.

2. Let us first consider personal understanding in the above-mentioned sense. Its basic form is found in the fact that the meaningful context of a person's acts and experiences is found in the unity and totality of his mental character. We understand the individual expression of life by means of the unity of the person. Two things are necessary to this end: a) that we take the total structure of the individual mind as the standard, that is, presuppose in him the entire differentiated act and experience complex from which the mental individual is made up, just as it is given in us as the mental basic structure. Without this *a priori* assumption (which however refers only to the legality and not to the concrete content of the mental structure) the other person would be incomprehensible to us. b) We must re-create the meaning of the individual mental act which empirical observation of his behavior directly or indirectly gives to us, and understand it from his position to the whole. Inasmuch as the first (the total structure) and the second (the individual act or experience) always appear in a unique form which does not wholly coincide with our equally unique kind, all understanding even of immediate environment has something of the character of historical understanding of which we shall speak later. Furthermore, insofar as the object of understanding is always wholly sensible and concrete and must be entered empathically in order to be grasped as an individuality, all understanding embodies an aesthetic factor. And insofar as it always refers to the whole human being and really finds its complete

realization only in the totality of the world order all understanding has a religious aspect.[1]) In view of what has been said above we shall not be misunderstood when we say: *we understand each other in God.* In order wholly to understand the character and development of an individual one would have to include the entire mental life and its highest meaning from which he has been carved. Finally, personal understanding differs according as to whether it goes back to the inner development of a human being or comes to rest in his permanent nucleus (his hypostatised character). Development however, as we have already seen, is inconceivable unless we posit a constant carrier which maintains itself according to an inner law through all changes. Thus after all we base ourselves upon the entelechy or individual idea of a man in our incompleteable endeavors wholly to understand him.[2])

3. Objective understanding seems to be more difficult to analyze. It is incontrovertible that we understand mental objectivities according to their objective content even when they have been entirely separated from their subject, though this understanding is not so vivid as that which derives from the depths of the total personality.

I can understand the meaning, not merely the words, of an old script even if I know nothing about its author. I can understand Beethoven's music without going back to his life history. I can understand Roman law as a logical system without knowing, in every case, the 'motives' of the legislators. In certain circumstances, I understand the modern economic system as a total even though I know nothing of the infinite number of individuals who support it with their economic will to value. All these examples necessarily contain a historic factor and refer to historically unique facts. We shall simplify our problem by asking: how is it that we understand science, economics, the state, religion etc. as objective cultural systems without in any case starting from the living exponents who are influenced by them and who create them with their meaning-endowing acts?

---

[1]) Cf. Simmel, *Das Problem der historischen Zeit. Vortraege der Kantgesellschaft* Nr. 12.

[2]) Then we understand the context in him; we understand also his determination through the objective-mental context, of which he is a part; but the original law 'according to which he set out' remains an ultimate fact beyond which understanding does not guide us.

It is obviously not true that we can grasp these objects without any relation to a subject. For, in their complete separation from all 'possibility of experience' they are transcendent for us. But we actualize them by basing them on our own mental structure as the meaning-giving and meaning-fulfilling subject.[1]) Thus, within certain limits, we understand science through the meaning-giving theoretic acts which create science in us. We understand the economic system from our economic needs, and the state as a general phenomenon comes to life in us insofar as we have within us a politically and judicially determined collective consciousness. If it is a question of contemporaneous cultural systems, the specific mental law conforms in us to the developmental levels of those objectivities. But if we mean cultural systems of former times, we have to put ourselves in a historical frame of mind. Some old astistic products are so eternally true that we hardly need to adjust our mental attitude, of which we shall speak in B. The creations of Homer and Sophocles, Shakespeare and Beethoven are still immediately related to us. But to achieve even an approximate understanding of Ovid and Racine, Klopstock and Jean Paul, a historical viewpoint is necessary. Such affinities, moreover, alter very rapidly with the passage of time; at any rate, unless in their creations they somehow follow an eternal mental law they would be wholly inaccessible to us. The distinction is gradual, and perhaps we may say: the more human the mind which created an objective work, the more decisive and clear-cut the lines which united it to objective values, the more easily do we understand him without entering into the subjective ardor of the creator. The more subjectivity and historical uniqueness has entered into the work, the more necessary it is to find, or at least to re-construct the mind of the creator or the creative epoch. There are even scientific systems which today we can only understand historically, though in objective science the demand of general validity ought to determine the whole process. Structural deviation from theoretic validity is a sure indication that in the development of such scientific systems (for instance, the speculative natural philosophy of the nineteenth century) heterogeneous motives like the aesthetic

---

[1]) This mental structure of ours is not meant here as our special individuality but as the firm nucleus of eternal laws of meaning which in us too unifies all experience.

and the religious played a decisive part. And there again the understanding person has an impulse to go back to the entire constitution of consciousness which has given rise to these mental creations.

B.

Thus we abandon the artificial abstraction in which so far we have disregarded the historical individuality of objects of understanding. Only in relation to a structural difference does understanding become a complete problem and very fruitful for the comprehending mind.

We who try to understand are not identical with the eternal abstract structure of the individual mind. We are immersed in objective cultural contexts which result from a long socio-historical process. They are based on an entangled mass of summations and reciprocal effects, of differentiations and integrations. The simple outline of objective culture — the articulation in value regions and their teleological relations to each other — is not only very particularized but also interwoven and confused. And the inner structure of man who, in all his experiencing and acting is surrounded as with the atmosphere by these historical objectivities, this structure too is greatly individualized.

But just because of this, every individual participates in the most particularized cultural contents and groups. Because his own experiences and achievements are interwoven with so many cultural contexts, the scope and mobility of his understanding is enormously increased. He also has the capacity of understanding simpler levels of culture from his later point of view, while the reverse is wholly inconceivable; namely that a member of a primitive culture should understand a more differentiated and higher one. For this reason, the immediately preceding generation usually fails to understand youth, at least to the extent in which a new life-direction has appeared which would not previously have been possible. And it is unimportant whether this younger generation is, from a cultural ethical point of view, on the declining plane or whether it develops a new productivity. And conversely: youth, with its naive conscious structure, does not understand the more complicated mentality of old age which is based on a stratification of experienced levels.

In understanding a highly differentiated culture one strives to penetrate into the past with an ever increasing range of vision. But it does not follow that the whole historic process and all aspects of contemporary culture are equally accessible to the understanding of its highly developed members. Only a section of the total culture is always actual and consciously penetrated thus, and inasmuch as this section is identical for a mentally prominent group, one can call it the historically expanded mutual intellectual medium in which this particular group lives. The intellectual world of an epoch is made up of everything which is accessible to its understanding. It does not coincide with the entire historical process or the whole objective mind. These are made conscious only in scientific activity and the learned results only partially penetrate the common life.

How ought we to conceive the understanding of deviating structures?

Anyone who tries to understand starts naively from his conscious structure and as much of his contemporary culture as he is in contact with. In other words: every naive man thinks unhistorically and is inclined to posit himself and those who resemble him as generally valid. But the very experiences of present life bring about such a subjective change that one sees the world from the consciousness of others. This 'taking the place of another' is a mysterious capacity. It jumps from a few factual data to the total picture of the alien life. In imagination we have ready a manifoldness of situations on which we model our future behavior. This stock of individual life situations helps us to enter into the other person with our interpretive imaginative powers. The bases of this capacity are artistic and may be developed to the point of genius. The finer development of the total picture in its individual aspects and traits, in its characteristic differences from us and its individual lawful structure is the problem of scientific reflection which must work with increasingly refined concepts.

This process of theoretico-scientific interpretation is always based upon three or four factors, as the case may be, which can be separated only in abstraction. The first is the observation or collection of individual data which are to be found in historical traditions, linguistic expressions, actions and events etc. Then the interpretive imagination forms from them an intuitive total picture of the past individual in which character, total milieu and the main events of his time are at least indicated. Next, by means of this imagined total situation, the comprehending person finally judges the concrete behavior of the historically unique individual. He does this by substituting the general outline of mental structural laws with those variations called for by the intuitive picture, and meanwhile subjectively works out the meaning-determined acts and experiences which result from this unique position (or individual character). There may be a fourth stage also. If the interpretation of such acts and experiences does not result in a meaningful context, or if the character and behavior of the personality are not adequately comprehended, the intuitive starting point which was made the basis of this process in a preliminary, more aesthetic intuition, is corrected.

When we try to find an example suitable to elucidate these four factors, we notice, in all interpretations which go back to historical transmission, that even the most primitive chronicle attempts to give a complete result of understanding. There is perhaps a certain misconstruction in all true writing of history, even if the historian has an exceptional mind, in that he never finds pure facts, even if unrelated, but always 'theories'; and that these are necessarily seen from a limited historical perspective. Even in relation to our contemporaries the case is not very different. With an utter stranger too, we immediately establish a total picture in which the available data (for instance his physiognomy, his vocation, his dialect, a sentence which he has uttered and a movement which he has made) are combined to form a total impression. This process, no matter how much of an obstacle it may be for objective and meticulous understanding, is characteristic of the fact that we only understand from the total and not by the mere summation of much disparate evidence. Individual traits always derive their meaning from their relation to the whole. The historian goes to such lengths that he would exclude as spurious a generally accepted trait if it contradicted the whole which, in every other respect, is comprehensible and substantiated.

With historic figures such as Socrates and Christ one has the impression that these great men were far from being understood by their contemporaries. The Gospels give much unrelated matter which may be united to form an immediate picture but which remains incomprehensible in many respects or is susceptible of various interpretations. Plato's picture of Socrates gives us a deeper insight (while Xenophon only saw what was on his own level) but therefore something is added to his interpretation. Let us take the point of view of an investigator who wants to understand the 'historical' Socrates.[1]) According to our survey he will go through several abstractly differentiated stages.

1. He reads in Xenophon and Plato a number of incidents from the life of Socrates. He tries, as far as possible, to avoid the interpretation of either writer in order to test the raw material and let it speak for itself (insofar as he may assume it to be genuine after a critical test of the process of transmission). But he can by no means prevent that during the assimilation of these data, (2) they form a total picture which he has before him in a historical intuition. This total picture naturally combines the essential reports on the life, teaching and death of Socrates, on several important expressions of his belief and his influence etc. But we assume that there remain (as has so far actually been the case) psychological contradictions, and that it has been impossible really to understand Socrates subjectively as a meaningful whole. The picture of a philosopher who seeks to grasp the essence of virtue by means of logical analogies and definitions but never achieves a tangible result; who continually teaches his pupils the expediency ($\tau\grave{o}$ $\sigma v\mu\varphi\acute{\epsilon}\rho o v$) of virtue but himself dies because of it, and would rather suffer injustice than commit it; who appears to one person as a sophist and a revolutionary and to another as an enemy of democracy and a traditionalist (who eulogises the old $\mathring{\alpha}\rho\epsilon\tau\acute{\eta}$) such a picture is indeed without connection or meaning. The historian has intuitively grasped all the unique data but he has not yet reached the vital center of the individual whom he wants to understand. And it is at this point that there takes place a change which is of interest for the theory of scientific understanding.

3. Nothing that he so far knows about Socrates could have been divined *a priori*. He had to derive it from other sources.

---

[1]) I choose this example in memory of Heinrich Maiers' original work on Socrates which combines faithfulness in detail with a great sweep of understanding and the sense of productive understanding in an exemplary manner.

(We omit the consideration of the mystery of how, despite this, he could achieve a historically concrete total picture).[1]) But now he draws, within the picture, lines which live within him *a priori* with the legal structure of his own mind which is likewise historically determined. He applies this structural legality to the given unique historical situation of Socrates and his epoch. But now he organizes the material through a network of categories which are 'neutral' inasmuch as they apply both to the comprehending individual and to him who is understood. Both are now — and this is the immanent assumption in every historical act of understanding after the unique position has been worked out — essentially on the same plane, or in other words, they are in the context of the same timeless complex of meaning which only expresses itself in historical phenomena and gradually evolves. Let us assume that the historian's primary aim is to find the central aspect of Socrates. He seeks in his essence, his character, that fixed point of unity by means of which the manifoldness of Socrates' life expression may be understood, disregarding, of course, the purely external aspect of fate which cannot be deduced from character but nevertheless elicits his specific reaction. Positing one after another the mental acts as central in Socrates and subjectively working these out at the same time from the point of view of the total situation, the investigator may perhaps think of Socrates as a theoretic systematiser and logician. He finds (again while carrying out the total act structure with its historically unique deviation) that he cannot from this point of view understand the total life and its individual facts. He therefore tests all the essential traits of Socrates in the same manner as a utilitarian type. He finds that this structural hypothesis too is impossible, even though as in the first case he cannot deny that there is some degree of justification for making it. He applies the standard of the Christian nature of love and finds that something which he cannot formulate is lacking. He finds — perhaps after further trials which we shall omit here — that the pedagogical factor is the central one in Socrates with an addition of purely philosophical scientific temper and a religio-ethical tendency of a very decided tinge in which

---

[1]) Undoubtedly the acts of the third stage participated in this but without entering into reflective consciousness.

there lies the individual essence of the historical Socrates which exceeds the pedagogical basic type. In all this we must not forget that in the attempt to understand there is always a consciousness of what Socrates (as being the man he was and at his time) should be in the ethical sense. Through this relation to the normative aspect of understanding there develops an awareness of the rank order, in this case of the personality of Socrates. And finally the difference between the historically determined mentality of Socrates (who for instance did not find at hand a ready-made scientific system of ethics) and the historically differentiated consciousness of the person who seeks to understand, shows itself in this process. And we find that despite his ethical nobility Socrates was in all other respects a child of his time.

4. But we have not yet reached the end of the entire process. If now the previously found intuitive picture is lawfully organized and changed to a meaningful comprehensible context, by means of this recreative application of the total structure and the partial structures of the mind this result affects the former levels too. (a) The mysterious aesthetic capacity of grasping individual data in a total picture (which of course is always aided by previously existing tradition) is at any rate always based on the fact that in every conception of humanity the general structural laws of mind are effective, although, without necessarily bringing the single participating acts individually into consciousness. Thus it comes about that we never cherish single feelings, volitions or ideas which are reported to us but always immediately create from them meaning contexts. In like manner we almost never apprehend single facts, deeds and events but organize them at once by a teleological point of view to a mental complex. But this pre-scientific intuition is in turn enlightened and corrected by the higher conscious endeavor of scientific understanding. We do not retain the first momentary picture but draw within its rapidly sketched outlines more and more accurate lines which are based upon structural reflection and, in certain cases, even necessitate a correction of the outline. Thus, for instance, Xenophon's picture of Socrates gives way, for subjective reasons, more and more to that of the *Apologia* and the *Critias*. — And this brings us to the last fact: (b) even the raw material of tradition can be carefully and critically sifted from the point of view of the complete context of understanding. At least in connection

with individual traits which are wholly inconsistent the deductively developed question of their genuineness is brought up, and in certain cases this contains a wholly new formulation of the problem applied to the existing source material.

By returning to our starting point we have completed the circle which in its individual stages only becomes conscious in methodological introspection. Most historians work out everything at once in a total mental process which is nevertheless influenced by and changed in accordance with the existing philosophical and *geisteswissenschaftlichen* concepts. The characterology of the nineteenth century especially, may be traced through three main stages: the first based on the Kant-Schiller-Humboldt conception of the duality of independent activity and receptivity of man, and the second on the renewed speculative theory of ideas, and the third on the Ethology of positivism (Mill, Taine). Recently a synthesis has taken place between the positivistic and idealistic currents which can already be recognized in Dilthey and in which this investigation must also be classified.

We have now described historical understanding. But we have not yet criticized it nor have we answered the question: to what extent and in what sense may we speak of the objectivity of understanding? This last problem will illuminate understanding in a wholly new light, but we must be content here with a few indications.

It is not difficult to prove that the capacity to enter into a unique state of mind different from our own by means of the analogous variation of our own structure, is the vital part of understanding, but also a dangerous source of error. For, this historic 'empathy' is originally an aesthetic function. Its significance for the practical ends of human intercourse has grown enormously with the increasing development of individuality and the differentiation of culture. But the demands of modern *Geisteswissenschaft* on the inner capacity for transformation and re-creation far exceeds what practical intercourse demands of the aesthetic function of empathy and the psychically re-creative procedure. One cannot say that the appreciation of this problem has been developed as much as it ought to be by our historians and investigators of culture. Spengler's book was very influential because in his poetic style he offered a new perspective to those who longed to see in this way.

But until a conceptual illumination of these vital comprehensive functions has taken place one must always fear that a merely subjective-poetical imagination is substituted, and results in the misinterpretation of human beings of previous epochs. And in spite of its strong historical sensorium this is what Romanticism has done with the Middle Ages, and we have not yet freed ourselves from the after-effects of this poetical transformation. But history should not be fiction. It must instead originate, with faithful adherence to transmitted facts in a feeling for those laws in whose network the facts appear as individual lines. A fact is fixed and affirmed in the conception of history by passing through a legal context which gives the decisive direction to the understanding and selection of facts. We cannot here substantiate this any further since it is an essential part of the philosophy of history.

But does the scientifically refined understanding really attain the full objective context to which it is directed?

The affirmation of this question is unlikely from the outset because we never carry in us the pure and absolute structure of the mind, but always a historically determined and individual mentality which is also influenced by historical mental objectivations. True, in it too the eternal legality of mental structural contexts is influential, but applied to and embodied in a historically unique level and a specific individuality. We have seen, however, that we must substitute not our actual content of consciousness — but the legality of our psychological imagination as the foundation of past phenomena in order to draw them (against us as a background), and that we must at the same time transport ourselves into the alien total position in order to grasp the different character of people of former times. This applies as well to the level of the intuitive total picture as to the re-creation of the structurally determined mental acts both individually and in their totality. Our whole description has implied that neither the pure object nor the pure subject make their appearance but that — always presupposing the genuine will to objectivity — there is created a resultant, a phenomenon of contact (*Beruehrungsphaenomen*), a superior third element.

This is true not only when an obvious relation between the understanding person and the former epoch or person is found, but also in the case of an extensive difference between the subject and the object of understanding.

In the first case the deviation of the objectivity aimed at is found in the fact that we over-emphasize in the former mental structure the similarities to ourselves. We then assimilate these aspects so intimately into our world that the structural differences which are also present do not come out strongly enough. Our own very concrete manner of experiencing, which should only serve as an intuitive constructive aid for the processes of critical transformation, is seen immediately into the object and considered equivalent to its character. This has repeatedly been the fate of 'the' socalled antiquity which has really always been present in the occidental mind, (since the appearance of the newer peoples in history) from renaissance to renaissance and had each time to cloak itself in the dress of the contemporaneous epoch. In this linking up of past and present there is doubtless a teleological factor of mental life. But measured by the pure ideal of cognition, there seems to be here a limitation of understanding. Such relations of life have their total ethical right. From a scientific standpoint they are painful reminders of the fact that we had repeatedly to take a fresh aim at the pure object but could never hit our mark. And thus we finally unearth the mystery that the mind of epochs is little more than the widely embracing mind of the historian who follows history and, despite his will to objectivity, attracts just that homogeneous material which he can understand, because of the limits of his consciousness of which he is unaware. All other aspects of history, and perhaps the most instructive, sink below the threshold of observation. History becomes, as it were, the backward extension of the present man, and a union of past and present.

The position of the second case seems to be still more unfavorable. The foreign aspect of a historical mental structure is felt so strongly that the intuitive living total picture cannot be evolved. Consider for instance the understanding of a primitive religion even through sufficient external traditions; or of a human being whose total mental structure differs from our own to such an extent that we search in vain for a connecting link or a familiar element. In this case understanding only skims over the surface of this foreign aspect. It draws its uniqueness against our own and is satisfied with the contrast of this subjectively unattainable goal with what is familiar.

History really leads us daily to such limits.[1]) Every historian, for instance must notice that former epochs had a background of a wholly different consciousness of reality. They believed in miracles and magic, in spiritual motivating forces and demons. They were willing to be motivated by a vision of God or base their action on the position of the stars. (Observe the motivations in the Old and New Testaments or in Otto von Freising). Who would assert that we can wholly enter these conscious structures? We cannot see beyond our own world and that is probably not the ultimate one. How seldom does a great historian succeed in achieving any degree of intimacy with his subject or give even a vivid reflection of past life. And even if he does, we feel as if one of our contemporaries was parading in a costume of bygone days.

In both of the cases just discussed; the assimilation and the contrast by means of understanding, the same final conclusion is reached. Understanding does not succeed in grasping the unique mental character of the object, despite all serious will to objectivity. If, as historians, we are not to despair in the face of this fact we must attempt to justify this limited conception of history, for these incomplete data must accomplish something. In the beginning of the chapter we emphasized reasons for the fact that understanding is not imitation but mental formation. Nothing remains (since it neither attains full objectivity nor may, in accordance with its nature rest in mere subjectivity), but to assume that all understanding has its significance in the creation of a third element, something higher than the subject or the object. This third element which, despite the strictest will to objectivity is the final thing that understanding can achieve, attracts our interest in the highest degree. What is it that is finally born from the will to understand?

We remind the reader once again that the psychological power of imagination (which is stimulated by the transmitted data of the

---

[1]) 'It needed the entire effort of a nineteenth century philosophy of religion, history of art and critical sociology, not to teach us to understand at last the dramatic work of Aeschylus, the teachings of Plato, Apollo and Dionysius, the Athenian state and Caesar's imperialism — for we are still far from having achieved this — but to make us feel how subjectively distant and strange this all is, more foreign perhaps than the Gods of Mexico and Indian architecture'. Spengler, *Untergang des Abendlandes*. Vol. I. p. 37.

past while mentally we change ourselves in a legal manner in accordance with the phenomena of history) is permeated with a curious totality of life and is historically determined. In it mind appears on a definite historical level of consciousness. Even though we must assume that the same teleological and normative laws are valid in individual and collective mental life from the outset, it makes a great difference in mental questions how far these laws and the developmental process of mind determined by them have been assimilated in consciousness. For, a law brought to consciousness means, for mind, self-determination and thus growing freedom. This is the profound and long forgotten meaning of the doctrine of the permeation of nature by reason in Schelling, Fichte, Schleiermacher and Hegel's doctrine of the self-realization of the mind. While the mind which lives in man gradually perceives its own laws, it grows in understanding and liberates itself. But these laws, as we have made clear from the beginning are not laws of events but normative laws of value realization.

They may be followed in three directions.

1. The differentiation in the total mental structure (which takes place in individuals as well as in mental objectivations although in a different rhythm, — cf. IV. 2 —) is elevated to consciousness. This process resembles the expansion of the consciousness of culture according to its different value tendencies and objective achievements. It finds its scientific precipitation in the system of cultural sciences and cultural psychology which is achieved by a historical epoch.

2. The temporal process of development of mind which leads to this epoch as its preliminary result, is followed through the preceding eras and its inner teleological context is revealed. The separate levels of the differentiation of individual consciousness and objective cultural systems enter the light of present day reflection. But the objective and subjective mental structure of the present guides us through the different stages and to this extent the entire process subserves the self-understanding in the present. It is identical with the development of historical consciousness and finds its scientific expression in the history of culture or of mind. — But it never appears in the guise of an inevitable mechanical necessity. Instead, on every level there develops for the re-creative understanding too a new concrete norm, a new complex normative

mind whose demands the generations living at that time may or may not have fulfilled. This normative attitude in understanding justifies our making value judgments on history. If history were a process which obeyed causal laws there would be no point in making value judgments as to the height of specific eras. But in this way every act of understanding is also oriented from a cultural-ethical point of view. It embodies (as a kind of secondary function) the questions of what a man, an epoch and a culture might have been and thus ought to have been in the value-determined sense, on their level and despite their handicap. As a result therefore:

3. The normativity of mind is elevated to consciousness. It receives a broader basis through the reflection of culture and history. Every epoch should be judged by its own nature (immanent value judgment). But since we necessarily lend to each epoch something of our own mind and thus raise it above its isolation, value judgments also embody a relation to us and to our degree of culture and consciousness.

The fact of understanding is thus complicated to the highest degree. And yet only at this point do we free ourselves from the far-reaching abstractions with which we had to begin our investigation, which has been entirely carried out from the breadth, the time and the height of our level of consciousness. But when we immeasureably widen our horizon by cultural psychological, historical and normative value reflection, there develops a mental medium of tremendous overindividual importance. In this triple determination of understanding the mind realizes itself. We leave the narrowness of the determined individual conscious structure — not to the extent that we become wholly an object to ourselves — but only insofar that from our historical level we mentally organize the whole 'developmental process'. '*Aus dem Kelche dieses Geisterreiches schaeumt uns die Unendlichkeit*', not yet as something given but as a problem which lies before and above us to be understood in its own meaning.

To summarize this again: the self-realization of mind has reference to three closely interrelated factors which are contained in it:

1. To the differentiated structure which was present in it from the beginning and which has gradually developed itself more clearly, even though with partial regression, until it also comes to the consciousness of the individual carrier of mind;

2. To the manifoldly changed or obstructed historical process in which the present concrete form of mental life (culture) has been developed through differentiations and ethical value syntheses;

3. To the ethical rank which has been attained at any given time in the historical process, and finally to the one special rank which in the present stage of the world development as we understand it, is its destiny.

Thus this comprehensive understanding of culture contains three factors: the consciousness of self-differentiation, of self-development and of the total ethical self-determination of the mind. And it is clear that at any given time one can only understand the simpler from the more differentiated level, the earlier from the later epoch and the lower from the ethically higher. We know these three directions of understanding as systematic analysis of culture, as cultural history and as the historical value judgments which reach a climax in a normative philosophy of history, a final meaning-endowing of it. For, it is not true that we have no right to form value judgments, but only that they must not be made from an accidental subjectivity, and that a mature personality who has reached a height of value must be the judge, a personality in which mind itself is epitomized. 'Do not believe history', says Nietzsche, ,unless it originates in the minds of the rarest spirits. People who have not had greater and higher experiences than others will not be able to interpret anything great and noble in the past.'[1])

Considering the fact that we are dealing in historical understanding with the self-realization of mind, two further contexts are comprehensible which we shall only touch upon in passing.

In all understanding there is a simultaneous selection from given data and transmitted facts. Understanding is not imitation but a forming process which is guided by the objective demands themselves. Thus not the entire infinity of past and present happenings can become part of the conception of culture, but only what is important in the three directions which we have mentioned; that is, the structurally significant, the genetic and the ethical or normatively significant. The tendency toward understanding may limit itself to the smallest corner of some local history or the

---

[1]) W. W. I. (Grosse Ausgabe) p. 337.

details of a personal story. But these too are not exhaustively treated and instead only illuminated from a structural, genetic and value critical point of view.[1])

And finally, in all historical understanding the past and the present fuse with the future, though never in the sense that the future may be causally predicted from the past, as people today often erroneously assume. Historical consciousness and the consciousness of cultural organization are the only bases upon which, for the investigator of mind there develops the experience of the total norm by which he measures the ethical problem of the future. If this vital power of what ought to develop is lacking, understanding too embodies something which is dead and sterile. We may therefore continue the above quotation from Nietzsche: 'The message of the past is always an oracle and you will understand it only as knowers of the present and as builders of the future.' This embodies the final recompense for the fact that our striving for objectivity of understanding is eternally incompleteable. The third realm, which is developed above mere subjectivity and the strictest objectivity is the overindividual realm of meaning in which we comprehend past, present and future by the same mental effort. The 'content' of history is for us this super-historical fact which we have achieved in understanding and which will grow through our ethical labors. Theodor Litt, in his brilliant investigations, arrives at the same conclusion: 'Not only is the present historically understood from the past, but also the past from the present. Indeed, what is to be understood is really neither the one nor the other, but the subjective factor which develops in both phenomena.' But further: 'Historical understanding of the present is not only a synthesis of past and present but an anticipatory interpretation of the future.'[2]) This conclusion surmounts what might appear too individualistic and unhistorical in the methodological starting point of our investigation which was

---

[1]) I thus return to the point of view which, from a deep feeling for the influential elements of history, I have at least divined in what seems to me today a very inadequate dissertation: *Die Grundlagen der Geschichtswissenschaft.* Berlin 1905.

[2]) *Geschichte und Leben,* 1st ed. Leipzig 1918 p. 9 and p. 11. In the 2nd ed. of 1925 the ideas have been re-formulated but the essential meaning has been retained.

directed primarily to the mental structure of the individuality. In the result we approach the conception that mind as a great mutual medium includes the individual and the objectivations which grew out of the summation, reciprocal effects and stratification of innumerable individuals. And if we understand ourselves or other people, the past or the meaning of the future, we might say from the other point of view in agreement with Hegel: it is mind itself which thus in its individuations and actualisations understands itself.

4
THE RHYTHM OF LIFE

The difference between classic and expressionistic music lies essentially in the proportion of their use of melody and motif. A melody is a formed total in which articulate parts are recognizeable. Its possibility of change lies in its transposition into other keys, changing harmonization and 'variations' whose general *Gestaltqualitaet* in the whole tonality remains the same in spite of extensive changes of rhythm and harmony. In every melody there is a motif or a number of motifs which have been interwoven to a form. It must not therefore be called an element of musical meaning.

A motif, on the other hand is a characteristic rhythmical sequence of intervals. There is a corresponding definite *Gestaltqualitaet* in psychic experience which has a mental significance (a content of feelings of significance), however, which, with that great variety of possible interpretations, is characteristic of this world of sound. A motif is capable of infinitely greater change and definiteness than a melody. It may be spun out over an entire phrase. It may be freely treated in rhythm, harmony and indeed in all the details of tonality, and it may interrelate with other motifs to make one form. Finally, it may be developed into a melody and beyond that to a whole formed or free-flowing phrase.[1]

The philosophical factor in music lies in the treatment of the leitmotifs. These give to musical composition its fundamental spiritual significance whose essence remains the same during the whole course of the composition while also capable of that degree of transformability which is commensurate with the inner affective impulse and its

---

[1] As an example I cite the opening theme in the first movement of Beethoven's fifth symphony. Here preference is given to the motif. It appears subsequently as melody but does not dominate in this form but on the other hand influences the movement in its original independent form.

frequently evanescent indeterminateness. In the treatment of the musical motif we achieve the closest approximation to the moving trends of inner life (*Bewegungslinien des Innern*) and their laws of tension, ramification, enhancement and relief, which is at all possible in the realm of objective-sensible symbols.

One might hope to 'exhaust' life musically, but philosophically its depths cannot be plumbed. Modern life no longer moves in closed and formed melodies nor in rational counterpoint — it has been resolved into a number of leitmotifs, now clear cut and now more veiled. And yet again the motifs are interwoven and contrasted, sometimes enhancing their content to the highest intensity of life's meaning, at others gradually echoing away after softly vibrating in the accompaniment. —

Our entire study might be regarded as an endeavor to discover the leitmotifs of life and to examine their repetitions and infinite variations, their harmonies and contrapuntal movements. We are conscious of the limits of what has hitherto been achieved. We do not yet possess all the data necessary to read the whole score. But in this book, which is devoted only to the philosophy of personality, it is not our intention to exceed our previous outline. We shall only indicate in a few words what roads must be followed in order to approach more closely the essence of reality.

The first two necessities still come within the scope of individuality. We ought to take up scientific method and artistic formation in biography. But people have not yet clearly grasped this problem. It is not sufficient to relate the life of a human being, one must understand him and enter into the law of his inner structure, for in relation to this alone, experiences derive a meaning. Accordingly every biographical investigation must be finally directed to the focal point of the personality in question, to its law of development and culture. This has not been often accomplished. As a comparatively unknown example which has this penetrating characteristic, I cite Wilhelm v. Humboldt's *Rezension von Goethes zweitem roemischen Aufenthalt*. In the unpublished works of Dilthey (for the new edition of the first volume of his biography of Schleiermacher) is a fragment which reveals with inimitable artistry of historical analysis the hidden continuity of Schleiermacher's religious consciousness from the *Bruedergemeinde* through the rationalistic sermons to the socalled pantheism of the

Reden ueber die Religion.[1]) This development of decisive structural relations was a conscious aim in Simmel's *Goethe*. There the empirical Goethe with his experiences and unique traits disappears behind the metaphysical essence of character which Simmel calls 'the idea of Goethe'. We do not want to debate here the categories by which he strives to grasp the law of this personality. In the conception and interpretation of a man whose life lies completed before us there is always an active element of the forming power of the understanding individual. But empirical material must not, on this account take a second place. Both must be constantly related to each other to such an extent that the selection of individual traits is always determined by the structural context which can only be pronounced after careful utilisation of historical facts. For, the structure itself is not 'visible', rather it is only the law which (as a unifying bond) we think into the divergent wealth of individual experiences and acts. Therefore for understanding there is a unique reciprocal relation which, purely logically might almost be called a vicious circle. We understand all character only by means of the life's history, but the history of a life only becomes a comprehensive context when we possess at least a few fixed points of character. This method of reciprocal illumination is only a new proof of the conception (developed above) that from the beginning of understanding there develops organically in us an intuitive total picture which we only gradually clarify structurally by means of the addition of new single traits and deductive preliminary experiments.

One can understand a mind like W. v. Humboldt's only when one bases the conception on the classical idea of aesthetic humanity as the law of his experiencing and behavior which is active anterior to all reflection. Pestalozzi's sympathetic world of confused feeling is clear only from the point of view of the spirit of love which in him amounted to genius and influenced and ennobled all his uncultivated powers.[2]) But frequently the real structural context is much more hidden. It may perhaps express itself in wholly erroneous self-interpretations; for, between the possession of an

---

[1]) It is now added to the 2nd edition published by H. Mulert, Berlin 1922, p. 588 ff.

[2]) A further illustrative example — Rousseau's mental individuality — may be found in my speech *Der gegenwaertige Stand der Geisteswissenschaften und die Schule*. Leipzig 1925 2nd ed. p. 22.

attitude and the understanding of self there is a great difference. The biographer and student of character must go beyond expression to the real context of life.

They understand this life's context by means of their own totality of mind which does not always exist in them as a developed possession but as an inclusive concept of lawful determinations which controls even their re-creative imagination. This is the reason for the deductive factor which is certainly a part of understanding. And this too accounts for the possibility of predicting (*a priori*) what was and what was not mentally possible in an era; what things are compatible and what incompatible in one soul. The definite character really appears only as a determination of numerous possibilities, of which 'humanity' as structure and as idea is capable, and which are actualized as concrete forms of humanity in history.

We must not be misled by the theories which people sometimes evolve in regard to their own characters or for the development of their world. A Jesuit is less a follower of Christ than an exponent of humanistic ecclesiastical politics. Hobbes seems to be a strict theorist but the system which he developed is not held together by the logic of his thought but by a will to power which appears both in the bases and the application in the law of natural right. Rousseau believed that he embraced mankind with the ardent love of a will to help and yet every one of his activities only catered to the self-enjoyment of his imagination. Many people seek religion in the form of science, others look for science under the illusion that they only develop religion.

Thus it is always a question of the function which is exercised by a character trait and a special achievement in the total structure of the mind. All the elementary psychic capacities which are disclosed by the psychographic procedure of differential psychology must also be drawn into this context.[1] This entire study would be blind, a mere random collection of unrelated facts without such reflection on structure. Real correlations of psychic achievements can only be revealed when one approaches the object by way of thought. All dependent relations which are merely numerically discovered need structural interpretation, just as in natural science every functional equation must first be physically interpreted. This

---

[1] Cf. W. Stern op. cit.

is true also of the much discussed region of intelligence testing. For the word intelligence itself denotes a structure, namely a context of dispositions and achievements which belong to thought and cognition. These however are classed in very different partial contexts of the process of life and may be liberated from them only with certain limitations. There is no general intelligence, but only for one's normal milieu and its nearest offshoots.

The psychic difference of structure between the sexes is a second problem which lies in the sphere of *geisteswissenschaftliche* psychology of individuality. We have already decided, in the whole arrangement of our study, that this difference is not based on the elementary meaning directions as such. All the mental acts and achievements which appear in man appear in woman too, but their structural relations, that is, their interweaving to form an individual total mind, differ enormously. It seems as if even the modern woman is less capable than man of devotion to differentiated achievements of a strictly objective nature. By 'objective' I mean all those achievements whose value and content arise from the fact that they must carry on their existence apart from the individual soul. Usually a woman can only achieve this if she can herself create them in the experience of '*Seele fuer Seele*' (soul for soul). It must however be added that the highest productivity of man is impossible without psychic union with a female spirit. Intellectual achievements usually arise from the union of both sexes. But the function exercised by the two psychic principles in either sex is characteristically different and in this lies the mystery which characterology must solve.

If one goes back to the natural destiny of woman one crosses the border from the psychological to the metaphysical, not only because we must consider here the relation of physical and psychic life but also because we can no longer avoid the question of the ultimate meaning and value of physico-mental life. There is no doubt that a woman's happiness is different from a man's. This fact also contains the limitation of purely male evaluation of culture which only expresses half of life's destiny. Thus Faust embodies two solutions of which Goethe (as a man) really only carried out one. In creative work he enjoyed the anticipation of the highest moment, but by its side is the pregnant sentence: '*Das Ewig-Weibliche zieht uns hinan*'. And above both is spread the whole heavenly vault of beatifications that is, of truly final meaning relations.

The inner rhythm of life is attuned to the finest vibrations by the contrast and supplementation of the sexes. One would inadequately comprehend the leitmotif of the mental world if one were incapable of hearing this tremendous chord of individualisation which resounds even in the depths of the physical world as the eternal alternation of sharps and flats. At any rate all this is still within the limits of a pure psychology of individuality. But in the formulation of two further problems we intentionally exceed these limits and consider the rhythm of life which has an overindividual character. The interrelation of the cultural world cannot be comprehended solely from a consideration of the individual. The sociological and historical study of culture is also necessary.

We included the two basic forms of the bonds by which man may be united to his fellows in the political and social factors. The political and social types, with their countless variations, are the purest ideal basic types which correspond to these leitmotifs. They may be understood as the formations of individuality of a simpler law. But it is impossible to deduce from one isolated individual all the overindividual social forms which, in historical development, have grown above the individuals and then reacted upon them. To this end we need to form new concepts. When one makes a cross-section of a historical epoch one arrives at a social structure which is a formation of overindividual significance. It is a context of effects which forms the participating individuals and subjectively organizes them. The context itself can only be comprehended through collective types of a higher order; such as a genteel constitution, professionalism, class, aristocracy, officialdom, parties, union, the fictitious personality before the law etc. Naturally, one must add to all these overindividual subjects the mental reflections in individual consciousness. But the special colors into which the rays here divide are not to be understood from the point of view of an individual but only by historical collective forms which existed before them and are superior to them.

In a new set of investigations one must study the unique manner in which the collective consciousness of a group is active in the unique consciousness and decisively influences the individual who belongs to it. Here too there are many stages to be developed between the most general type and that which has been most historically individualized. The degree in which the individual devotes himself to the Total, living in him, always calls forth a collective moral value judgment which is derived from the specific group.

In order to elucidate the many possibilities of collective sets, I select as an example the phenomenon which, in the vague language of modern social theory, is called 'socialism'. Unless one goes as far as Spengler (for whom socialism seems to mean all union in the will to power on a later cultural level), in transforming this expression, its only remaining general characteristic is that of an approximate equalisation of the members. In this sense there is first a socialism which begins wholly with the individual and which only views social community (voluntary, organized or legal) as an arrangement whose ultimate and entire aim is the individual. Such a socialism, then, is really only a special form of individualism which here uses a system of social means to gain its end. It may be union in economic endeavor (socialism of solidarity); it may aim at political tendencies and seek to further the collective power of the weaker classes (political socialism which is often to be recognized through its tendency to class dictatorship). It may be pure socialism of people who are and think alike and who therefore easily formulate a common theory — for instance through the construction of a rational equality of all social elements — (constructive socialism); and finally, as characterized above, it may be an aesthetic movement for the general beautiful sympathy of hearts (artistic socialism). In actuality these factors appear in a mixed form. And obviously despite this individualistic starting point the resultant in each participant is a collective consciousness which contains, on the basis of a feeling of comradeship, a kind of higher meaning and of enhanced power.

Genuine socialism differs from all these forms because it posits from the outset the social whole (community, fraternity, legal union, the state) as the real value; and acknowledges the individuals who in other respects are regarded as essentially alike, only with reference to this total of value, that is, insofar as they are ethical exponents of it. Here again two important varieties are possible: the whole, as well as the relation of individuals, may be based either on love or on organized power. In the first case a great current of love holds the total together and surges through the individual. Here the question is less of a mutual and equal participation of all external goods and occupations (for instance the right to vote) than of the deep essentially psychic relations by means of which, in a higher sense, we live and move and have our being. To this extent every family, despite its apex of authority is constituted in the socialistic spirit. But the highest example is the idea of a Kingdom of God in the sense of a realm — not as in Kant of free and lawfully acting 'reasonable' people — but of souls who love in the sense of the divine meaning of life. The other case is the socialism of (conscious and willed) organization, in which individual claims to power are limited from an over-individual point of view by a legislative collective power. The mere principle of solidarity which is based on brotherhood does not disclose the whole spirit of this socialism, for even the maxim: 'One for all and all for one' might be based on an accidental harmony of individual interests. Rather the two parts of this maxim must be united by a third supplementary one: 'The whole in all and over all.' And to this end there is the assumption that the total as such itself contains a definite ethical spirit which may demand something for itself and which subjects the individual to its ends. And this can only have been developed on the basis of a historical creation.

Thus in order to understand this overindividual mental structural context of which we living individuals are a part, and to comprehend its unique vital rhythm of life we need a further overindividual set in addition to the sociological one; historical consciousness which genetically understands the unique element in the culture of each contemporary period and structurally illuminates it as a collective formation with a superior value content. The individual only understands himself, with all his mental roots and branches by this expansion of the historical and social horizon. 'History alone tells man what he is' (Dilthey). Mere analysis of what is contained in the immediate consciousness of the present in the individual never leads to complete understanding. Here are contained rather the most serious illusions concerning the justification and scope of a movement in life, its possibilities and its final hidden meaning. Anyone who tries to understand Russian Bolshevism by its theoretic self-justification, Marxism interpreted from the point of view of the Paris Commune, overlooks its most important bases, namely the agrarian problem and the character of the Russian. In brief: mental movements do not originate in an abstract individual intelligence but in the vast ocean of mind which has already become history and in which an individual is only a single wave.

The present can only understand itself when it is reflected in history. Frequently a selection takes place in this way and an evaluation which is wholly determined by the passionate onesided will of the present. History becomes the instrument of the will to life or the political will to power. If it is to serve the highest ethical mission, the conception of history must start with the purest will to objectivity and an ethical consciousness founded thereon. So in this ingenuous surrender to the objectivity of the mental and in this objectively founded will to value, an unconscious and involuntary relation to the present mental structure is contained. For, all will to objectivity and normativity cannot separate us from the mental breadth and level which we have reached and which determines our field of vision of the past and future. And thus, in understanding, the life of the present is linked up with the mentally formed content of the past to create the meaning of the future. So we could only interpret the entire rhythm of life on the background of a philosophy of history. But such an analysis of modern mind exceeds the bounds which we have set ourselves.[1] We still remain within the limits of the individual who is always fundamentally isolated, and only search for that eternal law in which the individual with his little span of life classifies himself in or opposes himself to the sweeping rhythm of life.

And this brings us back to the beginning of our investigation. We said that the totality of the mind exists in every mental act; that is, every endowment of meaning contains the other fundamental directions of meaning-endowment subordinated and changed according to its dominant content. And this embodies the divinity of all life, that not one of the meaning contexts, be it never so insignificant, can be separated form the total meaning of the individual life and that the latter is inseparable from the overindividual mental context. Thus everything has a religious significance and is only a segment of the infinite meaning texture of the whole.

---

[1] Cf. the cross-section of the time at about 1900 which Troeltsch has published in Preussische Jahrbuecher Vol. 128 (1907) under the title *Das Wesen des modernen Geistes*.

But precisely for this reason, because every individual and determined element by being just what it is cannot at the same time be the infinite other, for this very reason every individual form of life is fragmentary and unsatisfactory. It lacks finality, 'fulfillment'. An infinite urge acts upon every soul which comes unspoiled from the sources of life, an unquenchable longing for value, and this yearning is the nucleus of life itself and its motivating force. In everyone there is a surplus over and above the real development of life. In every soul there is a spur, in the Faustian sense, of unlived life. There is no final form in which the demanding will to value could satisfy itself; the waves of this metaphysical agitation re-echo even in resignation.

In the heart of youth this experience is most tempestuous. It always finds a ready-formed life when it begins independently to participate in the mental world. But it accepts this historical level of mind as a matter of course without a thought of gratitude. With full ardor it feels only the dissatisfied aspects of its value-demanding subjectivity and thus it opposes to the present picture of culture another new picture which receives its light and color entirely from the contrast to what has been achieved. It always carries out its affirmations in the form of the rejecting No. It was on account of this phenomenon that Hegel believed that history moves in logical contrasts. But here not concepts but value positings and onesided attitudes war with each other. History does not progress in the threefold beat of dialectics but in an antithesis of value.

And therefore every first step of youth has the character of a further differentiation of culture. This divergence is already determined by the sociological rift between the older and the younger generations. But once matured this generation also will have to do its part in the creative synthesis between the ageing form of life and the new value direction. And not till then has the new been taken up in the existant historic growth. This explains the 'spiral tendency' of human development, for mental life always returns again and again in former directions but always on a different level.

The creating of value by humanity may therefore be compared to a stream which never completely fills its bed but always flows where the channel is deepest: humanity at each period lives in that for which it has the greatest longing. There we must find its belief, its most intense value and its metaphysical rhythm.

In some periods the affirmation of earthly values is relieved by a decisive No. All the energy of life then turns inward and there builds the destroyed world up again much more beautiful and resplendent than it was before. Such ascetic periods are like the temptation in the wilderness: great forces collect to stream suddenly free over the earth again and take possession of it in a new sense.

This is the drama of the great world. Where is its final answer? We must not look for it in a mental world which is completely beyond, which has its own purposes, independent of individual souls and which slyly stakes the happiness and despair of human beings in order to free and complete itself. For, this overindividual factor in history and society has its life only in the focal points of the individual souls who fill all this with meaning and subsequently take it back again into the solitude of the divine centre. Only in this earthly vessel do we have the divine treasure. Ranke has formulated the epigram: 'Every epoch is immediate to God' as opposed to the superficial belief that the highest reveals itself only at the millenium. He would have been more justified in saying: 'Every man is immediate to God'. In his subjectivity the heavenly ladder rises and it is granted to him to ascend it. But this very ascent is a struggle with God, and everyone must wrestle with his Lord.

It is characteristic of the present day to have great respect for the word 'community'. Youth meets in this ideal, but it is still a question in what spirit one seeks community. Mere coexistence does not constitute a striving for higher regions. But I think I can guess what makes up the content of this spirit of community. It is the unbroken totality of life which in youth is always born anew and which is most conscious of itself where a given one-sidedness or narrowness of life is boldly rejected. This is the outstanding characteristic of the emancipation of youth. But it is part of the essence of youth to carry within itself, for the time being as a stimulating imaginative ideal, the normative picture of the future or what ought to be. Youth's attitude is aesthetic and its ideal pictures are centered in the imaginative zone. If they are to form reality and touch the earth they must penetrate beyond the realism of work and the idealism of thought to the metaphysical zone which is the final and most genuine sphere beyond the three reflecting worlds and unites them. If this metamorphosis is successful the 'No' of youthful emancipation becomes the 'Yes' of earnest life formation. Whether this can still be the business of youth is an irrelevant question, and it is sufficient to remark that we must all go through this stage. This crisis does not come without reverence of great understanding, without the broadness of saving love and the belief in world-conquering power. But if it does come, God is near.

We have not pursued our way through the labyrinth of mental formations in order to lose ourselves in the wealth of possibilities. Our vision must be trained also on the hierarchy of types, on their degree of genuine value content and divinity in which every one participates. The simple basic motifs of life are developed into hymns in which the primal powers are developed to pure rhythm and forms. Transfigured longing is the stamp which mind has imprinted on every genuine successful creation.

Even Plato's intuitive mind only dared to express the final essence in great myths, in which the reverent poet in him won the ultimate victory over the philosopher. There is a point beyond which even the wings of thought cannot carry us and where only an allegory can intimate justice to the immortal essence. And if we should ring out the rhythm of life in such a mighty final psalm, there would well up from the struggling motifs which interrelate and conflict with each other in the labyrinth of the human breast, and which heroically rise from the darkness of suffering into the light of calm and tranquil mentality the symbolic chorus:

Freude, schoener Goetterfunken,
Tochter aus Elysium . . .

But the German soul has most deeply experienced the hell of despair, and therefore in it alone can the victory of this 'Nevertheless' (in spite of it) be most genuine.